Literary English Since Shakespeare

Edited by
GEORGE WATSON
St. John's College, Cambridge

1970
OXFORD UNIVERSITY PRESS
London Oxford New York

Preface

This collection links more than twenty essays, five of them new (those by Watson, Davies, Rogers, Ingham, and Donoghue), on the literary uses of English since the sixteenth century. There are two sections. The first treats such wide issues as the state of linguistics at the present time, style, the literal and the figurative, and the statistical analysis of literary English. The second is devoted to individual writers or schools of writers from Shakespeare to the Moderns.

Such a book plainly needs no justifying, since the linguistic study of English literature is now widely felt to be among the most inviting prospects of English studies. There is no denying, however, that the subject is in an early and highly unequal state of development. No book by a single hand exists, or perhaps could exist, which attempts as much as this; and it is remarkable how little even of essay-length is so far available, how tentative even the best attempts often are, and how many major English authors are still unapproached in these terms.

Considered attempts to reconcile modern linguistics with the study of English literature did not become common until the 1960s. Earlier ventures in the study of literary language are not usually concerned with English, or not mainly with English, or not with those aspects of English which are fully characteristic of its genius as a language.

Early examples include Gustaf Stern, *Meaning and Change of Meaning* (Gothenburg, 1932), which attempted to put semantics to the service of literary studies; and G. Udny Yule, *The Statistical Study of Literary Vocabulary* (Cambridge, 1944), a mathematician's approach to the problems of word-frequency. Attempts to bridge the gap from the literary side have more often had a French application than an English. Albert Thibaudet's chapter "Le Style de Flaubert" in his study of Flaubert (Paris, 1922) is a notable forerunner; and Leo Spitzer's *Linguistics and Literary History* (Princeton, 1948), P. Guiraud's *La Stylistique* (Paris, 1954), and Stephen Ullmann's studies, especially his *Language and Style* (Oxford, 1964), continue an active tradition in Romance studies. But in the English-speaking world the enquiry has remained awkwardly interdisciplinary and hard to isolate. Literary language has been the concern now of the practical critic, such as William Empson in his *Seven Types of Ambiguity* (London, 1930), now of the linguistic philosopher on one of his rare excursions into literary language, and now of the professional linguist. I have already discussed the prospects and problems of reconciliation in a chapter on linguistics in *The Study of Literature* (London, 1969). Three departments of knowledge are involved here, in principle and in practice. I hope the book will serve to stimulate enquiry as well as to satisfy a need. It seems inconceivable, whatever the immediate difficulties, that the three disciplines should not some day learn to exchange what they know.

GEORGE WATSON

St. John's College
Cambridge, England
November 1969

The claims of our own language it is hardly necessary to recapitulate. It stands pre-eminent even among the languages of the west. It abounds with works of imagination not inferior to the noblest which Greece has bequeathed to us; with models of every species of eloquence; with historical compositions which, considered merely as narratives, have seldom been surpassed, and which, considered as vehicles of ethical and political instruction, have never been equalled; with just and lively representations of human life and human nature; with the most profound speculations on metaphysics, morals, government, jurisprudence, and trade; with full and correct information respecting every experimental science which tends to preserve the health, to increase the comfort, or to expand the intellect of man. Whoever knows that language has ready access to all the vast intellectual wealth which all the wisest nations of the earth have created and hoarded in the course of ninety generations. It may safely be said that the literature now extant in that language is of far greater value than all the literature which three hundred years ago was extant in all the languages of the world together.

Macaulay, *Indian Education*
(Minute of 2 February 1835)

Contents

Language and Literature

From Shakespeare to Modernism

⍦

Language and Literature

NOAM CHOMSKY

ɤ

The Current Scene in Linguistics

The title of this paper may suggest something more than can be provided. It would be foolhardy to attempt to forecast the development of linguistics or any other field, even in general terms and in the short run. There is no way to anticipate ideas and insights that may, at any time, direct research in new directions or reopen traditional problems that had been too difficult or too unclear to provide a fruitful challenge. The most that one can hope to do is to arrive at a clear appraisal of the present situation in linguistic research, and an accurate understanding of historical tendencies. It would not be realistic to attempt to project such tendencies into the future.

Two major traditions can be distinguished in modern linguistic theory: one is the tradition of "universal" or "philosophical grammar," which flourished in the seventeenth and eighteenth centuries; the second is the tradition of structural or descriptive linguistics, which reached the high point of its development perhaps fifteen or twenty years ago. I think that a synthesis of these two major traditions is possible, and that it is, to some extent, being achieved in current work. Before approaching the problem of synthesis, I would like to sketch briefly—and, necessarily, with some oversimplification

From *College English*, XXVII (1966), pp. 587-95. Reprinted by permission of the publisher and author.

—what seem to me to be the most significant features in these two traditions.

As the name indicates, universal grammar was concerned with general features of language structure rather than with particular idiosyncrasies. Particularly in France, universal grammar developed in part in reaction to an earlier descriptivist tradition which held that the only proper task for the grammarian was to present data, to give a kind of "natural history" of language (specifically, of the "cultivated usage" of the court and the best writers). In contrast, universal grammarians urged that the study of language should be elevated from the level of "natural history" to that of "natural philosophy"; hence the term "philosophical grammar," "philosophical" being used, of course, in essentially the sense of our term "scientific." Grammar should not be merely a record of the data of usage but, rather, should offer an explanation for such data. It should establish general principles, applicable to all languages and based ultimately on intrinsic properties of the mind, which would explain how language is used and why it has the particular properties to which the descriptive grammarian chooses, irrationally, to restrict his attention.

Universal grammarians did not content themselves with merely stating this goal. In fact, many generations of scholars proceeded to develop a rich and far-reaching account of the general principles of language structure, supported by whatever detailed evidence they could find from the linguistic materials available to them. On the basis of these principles, they attempted to explain many particular facts, and to develop a psychological theory dealing with certain aspects of language use, with the production and comprehension of sentences.

The tradition of universal grammar came to an abrupt end in the nineteenth century, for reasons that I will discuss directly. Furthermore, its achievements were very rapidly forgotten, and an interesting mythology developed concerning its limitations and excesses. It has now become something of a cliché among linguists that universal grammar suffered from the following defects: (1) it was not concerned with the sounds of speech, but only with writing; (2) it was based primarily on a Latin model, and was, in some sense "prescriptive"; (3) its assumptions about language structure have been refuted by modern "anthropological linguistics." In addition, many linguists, though not all, would hold that universal grammar was misguided in principle in its attempt to provide explanations rather than mere description of usage, the latter being all that can be contemplated by the "sober scientist."

The first two criticisms are quite easy to refute; the third and fourth are more interesting. Even a cursory glance at the texts will show that phonetics was a major concern of universal grammarians, and that their phonetic theories were not very different from our own. Nor have I been able to discover any confusion of speech and writing. The belief that universal grammar was based on a Latin model is rather curious. In fact, the earliest studies of universal grammar, in France, were a part of the movement to raise the status of the vernacular, and are concerned with details of French that often do not even have a Latin analogue.

As to the belief that modern "anthropological linguistics" has refuted the assumptions of universal grammar, this is not only untrue but, for a rather important reason, could not be true. The reason is that universal grammar made a sharp distinction between what we may call "deep structure" and "surface structure." The deep structure of a sentence is the abstract underlying form which determines the meaning of the sentence; it is present in the mind but not necessarily represented directly in the physical signal. The surface structure of a sentence is the actual organization of the physical signal into phrases of varying size, into words of various categories, with certain particles, inflections, arrangement, and so on. The fundamental assumption of the universal grammarians was that languages scarcely differ at the level of deep structure—which reflects the basic properties of thought and conception—but that they may vary widely at the much less interesting level of surface structure. But modern anthropological linguistics does not attempt to deal with deep structure and its relations to surface structure. Rather, its attention is limited to surface structure—to the phonetic form of an utterance and its organization into units of varying size. Consequently, the information that it provides has no direct bearing on the hypotheses concerning deep structure postulated by the universal grammarians. And, in fact, it seems to me that what information is now available to us suggests not that they went too far in assuming universality of underlying structure, but that they may have been much too cautious and restrained in what they proposed.

The fourth criticism of universal grammar—namely, that it was misguided in seeking explanations in the first place—I will not discuss at length. It seems to me that this criticism is based on a misunderstanding of the nature of all rational inquiry. There is particular irony in the fact that this criticism should be advanced with the avowed intention of making linguistics "scientific." It is hardly open to question that the natural sciences are concerned precisely with the problem of explaining phenomena, and have little use for accurate description that is unrelated to problems of explanation.

We have much to learn from a careful study of what was achieved by the universal grammarians of the seventeenth and eighteenth centuries. Contemporary linguistics would do well to take their concept of language as a point of departure for current work. Not only do they make a fairly clear and well-founded distinction between deep and surface structure, but they also go on to study the nature of deep structure and to provide valuable hints and insights concerning the rules that relate the abstract underlying mental structures to surface form, the rules that we would now call "grammatical transformations." What is more, universal grammar developed as part of a general philosophical tradition that provided deep and important insights, also largely forgotten, into the use and acquisition of language, and, furthermore, into problems of perception and acquisition of knowledge in general. These insights can be exploited and developed. The idea that the study of language should proceed within the framework of what we might nowadays call "cognitive psychology" is sound. There is much truth in the traditional view that language provides the most effective means for studying the nature and mechanisms of the human mind, and that only within this context can we perceive the larger issues that determine the directions in which the study of language should develop.

The tradition of universal grammar came to an end more than a century ago. Several factors combined to lead to its decline. For one thing, the problems posed were beyond the scope of the technique and understanding then available. The problem of formulating the rules that determine deep structures and relate them to surface structures, and the deeper problem of determining the general abstract characteristics of these rules, could not be studied with any precision, and discussion therefore remained at the level of hints, examples, and vaguely formulated intentions. In particular, the problem of rule-governed creativity in language simply could not be formulated with sufficient precision to permit research to proceed very far. A second reason for the decline of traditional linguistic theory lies in the remarkable successes of Indo-European comparative linguistics in the nineteenth century. These achievements appeared to dwarf the accomplishments of universal grammar, and led many linguists to scoff at the "metaphysical" and "airy pronouncements" of those who were attempting to deal with a much wider range of problems —and who at that stage of the development of linguistic theory were discussing these topics in a highly inconclusive fashion. Looking back now, we can see quite clearly that the concept of language employed by the Indo-European comparativists was an extremely primitive one. It was, however, well suited to the tasks at hand. It is, therefore, not surprising that this concept of language, which was then extended and developed by the structural and descriptive linguists of the twentieth century, became almost completely dominant, and that the older tradition of linguistic theory was largely swept aside and forgotten. This is hardly a unique instance in intellectual history.

Structural linguistics is a direct outgrowth of the concepts that emerged in Indo-European comparative study, which was primarily concerned with language as a system of phonological units that undergo systematic modification in phonetically determined contexts. Structural linguistics reinterpreted this concept for a fixed state of a language, investigated the relations among such units and the patterns they form, and attempted, with varying success, to extend the same kind of analysis to "higher levels" of linguistic structure. Its fundamental assumption is that procedures of segmentation and classification, applied to data in a systematic way, can isolate and identify all types of elements that function in a particular language along with the constraints that they obey. A catalogue of these elements, their relations, and their restrictions of "distribution," would, in most structuralist views, constitute a full grammar of the language.

Structural linguistics has very real accomplishments to its credit. To me, it seems that its major achievement is to have provided a factual and a methodological basis that makes it possible to return to the problems that occupied the traditional universal grammarians with some hope of extending and deepening their theory of language structure and language use. Modern descriptive linguistics has enormously enriched the range of factual material available, and has provided entirely new standards of clarity and objectivity. Given this advance in precision and objectivity, it becomes possible to return, with new hope for success, to the problem of constructing the theory of a particular language—its grammar—and to the still more ambitious study of the general theory of language. On the other hand, the substantive contributions to the theory of language structure are few, and, to a large extent, the concepts of modern linguistics constitute a retrogression as compared with universal grammar. One real advance has been in universal phonetics—I refer here particularly to the work of Jakobson. Other new and important insights might also be cited. But in general, the major contributions of structural linguistics seem to me to be methodological rather than substantive. These methodological contributions are not limited to a raising of the standards of precision. In a more subtle way, the idea that language can be studied as a formal system, a notion which is developed with force and effectiveness in the work of Harris and Hockett, is of particular significance. It is, in fact, this general insight and the techniques that emerged as it developed that have made it possible, in the last few years, to approach the traditional problems once again. Specifically, it is now possible to study the problem of rule-governed creativity in natural language, the problem of constructing grammars that explicitly generate deep and surface structures and express the relations between them, and the deeper problem of determining the universal conditions that limit the form and organization of rules in the grammar of a human language. When these problems are clearly formulated and studied, we are led to a conception of language not unlike that suggested in universal grammar. Furthermore, I think that we are led to conclusions regarding mental processes of very much the sort that were developed, with care and insight, in the rationalist philosophy of mind that provided the intellectual background for universal grammar. It is in this sense that we can look forward to a productive synthesis of the two major traditions of linguistic research.

If this point of view is correct in essentials, we can proceed to outline the problems facing the linguist in the following way. He is, first of all, concerned to report data accurately. What is less obvious, but nonetheless correct, is that the data will not be of particular interest to him in itself, but rather only insofar as it sheds light on the grammar of the language from which it is drawn, where by the "grammar of a language" I mean the theory that deals with the mechanisms of sentence construction, which establish a sound-meaning relation in this language. At the next level of study, the linguist is concerned to give a factually accurate formulation of this grammar, that is, a correct formulation of the rules that generate deep and surface structures and interrelate them, and the rules that give a phonetic interpretation of surface structures and a semantic interpretation of deep structures. But, once again, this correct statement of the grammatical principles of a language is not primarily of interest in itself, but only insofar as it sheds light on the more general question of the nature of language; that is, the nature of universal grammar. The primary interest of a correct grammar is that it provides the basis for substantiating or refuting a general theory of linguistic structure which establishes general principles concerning the form of grammar.

Continuing one step higher in level of abstraction, a universal grammar—a general theory of linguistic structure that determines the form of grammar—is primarily of interest for the information it provides concerning innate intellectual structure. Specifically, a general theory of this sort itself must provide a hypothesis concerning innate intellectual structure of sufficient richness to account for the fact that the child acquires a given grammar on the basis of the data available to him. More generally, both a grammar of a particular language and a general theory of language are of interest primarily because of the insight they provide concerning the nature of mental processes, the mechanisms of perception and production and the mechanisms by which knowledge is acquired. There can be little doubt that both specific theories of particular languages and the general theory of linguistic structure provide evidence for anyone concerned with these matters; it is within this general framework that linguistic research finds its intellectual justification.

At every level of abstraction, the linguist is concerned with explanation, not merely with stating facts in one form or another. He tries to construct a grammar which explains particular data on the basis of general principles that govern the language in question. He is interested in explaining these general principles themselves, by showing how they are derived from still more general and abstract postulates drawn from universal grammar. And he would ultimately have to find a way to account for universal grammar on the basis of still more general principles of human mental structure. Finally, although this goal is too remote to be seriously considered, he might envisage the prospect that the kind of evidence he can provide may lead to a physiological explanation for this entire range of phenomena.

I should stress that what I have sketched is a logical, not a temporal order of tasks of increasing abstractness. For example, it is not necessary to delay the study of general linguistic theory until particular grammars are available for many languages. Quite the contrary. The study of particular grammars will be fruitful only insofar as it is based on a precisely articulated theory of linguistic structure, just as the study of particular facts is worth undertaking only when it is guided by some general assumptions about the grammar of the language from which these observations are drawn.

All of this is rather abstract. Let me try to bring the discussion down to earth by mentioning a few particular problems, in the grammar of English, that point to the need for explanatory hypotheses of the sort I have been discussing.

Consider the comparative construction in English; in particular, such sentences as:

(1) I have never seen a man taller than John.

(2) I have never seen a taller man than John.

Sentences (1) and (2), along with innumerable others, suggest that there should be a rule of English that permits a sentence containing a Noun followed by a Comparative Adjective to be transformed into the corresponding sentence containing the sequence: Comparative Adjective-Noun. This rule would then appear as a special case of the very general rule that forms such Adjective-Noun constructions as "the tall man" from the underlying form "the man who is tall," and so on.

But now consider the sentence:

(3) I have never seen a man taller than Mary.

This is perfectly analogous to (1); but we cannot use the rule just mentioned to form

(4) I have never seen a taller man than Mary.

In fact, sentence (4) is certainly not synonymous with (3), although (2) appears to be synonymous with (1). Sentence (4) implies that Mary is a man, although (3) does not. Clearly either the proposed analysis is incorrect, despite the very considerable support one can find for it, or there is some specific condition in English grammar that explains why the rule in question can be used to form (2) but not (4). In either case, a serious explanation is lacking; there is some principle of English grammar, now unknown, for which we must search to explain these facts. The facts are quite clear. They are of no particular interest in themselves, but if they can bring to light some general principle of English grammar, they will be of real significance.

Furthermore, we must ask how every speaker of English comes to acquire this still unknown principle of English grammar. We must, in other words, try to determine what general concept of linguistic structure he employs that leads him to the conclusion that the grammar of English treats (1) and (2) as paraphrases but not the superficially similar pair (3) and (4). This still unknown principle of English grammar may lead us to discover the relevant abstract principle of linguistic structure. It is this hope, of course, that motivates the search for the relevant principle of English grammar.

Innumerable examples can be given of this sort. I will mention just one more. Consider the synonymous sentences (5) and (6):

(5) It would be difficult for him to understand *this*.

(6) For him to understand *this* would be difficult.

Corresponding to (5), we can form relative clauses and questions such as (7):

(7) (i) something which it would be difficult for him to understand
(ii) what would it be difficult for him to understand?

But there is some principle that prevents the formation of the corresponding constructions of (8), formed in the analogous way from (6):

(8) (i) something which for him to understand would be difficult
(ii) what would for him to understand be difficult?

The nonsentences of (8) are formed from (6) by exactly the same process that forms the correct sentences of (7) from (5); namely, pronominalization in the position occupied by "this," and a reordering operation. But in the case of (6), something blocks the operation of the rules for forming relative clauses and interrogatives. Again, the facts are interesting because they indicate that some general principle of English grammar must be functioning, unconsciously; and, at the next level of abstraction, they raise the question what general concept of linguistic structure is used by the person learning the language to enable him to acquire the particular principle that explains the difference between (7) and (8).

Notice that there is nothing particularly esoteric about these examples. The processes that form comparative, relative, and interrogative constructions are among the simplest and most obvious in English grammar. Every normal speaker has mastered these processes at an early age. But when we take a really careful look, we find much that is mysterious in these very elementary processes of grammar.

Whatever aspect of a language one studies, problems of this sort abound. There are few well-supported answers, either at the level of particular or universal grammar. The linguist who is content merely to record and organize phenomena, and to devise appropriate terminologies, will never come face to face with these problems. They only arise when he attempts to construct a precise system of rules that generate deep structures and relate them to corresponding surface structures. But this is just another way of saying that "pure descriptivism" is not fruitful, that progress in linguistics, as in any other field of inquiry, requires that at every stage of our knowledge and understanding we pursue the search for a deeper explanatory theory.

I would like to conclude with just a few remarks about two problems that are of direct concern to teachers of English. The first is the problem of which grammar to teach; the second, the problem why grammar should be taught at all.

If one thinks of a grammar of English as a theory of English structure, then the question which grammar to teach is no different in principle from the problem facing the biologist who has to decide which of several competing theories to teach. The answer, in either case, is that he should teach the one which appears to be true, given the evidence presently available. Where the evidence does not justify a clear decision, this should be brought to the student's attention and he should be presented with the case for the various alternatives. But in the case of teaching grammar, the issue is often confused by a pseudo-problem which deserves further discussion.

To facilitate this discussion, let me introduce some terminology. I will use the term "generative grammar" to refer to a theory of language in the sense described above; that is, a system of rules that determine the deep and surface structures of the language in question, the relation between them, the semantic interpretation of the deep structures and the phonetic interpretation of the surface structures. The generative grammar of a language, then, is the system of rules which establishes the relation between sound and meaning in this language. Suppose that the teacher is faced with the question: which generative grammar of English shall I teach? The answer is straightforward in principle, however difficult the problem may be to settle in practice. The answer is, simply: teach the one that is correct.

But generally the problem is posed in rather different terms. There has been a great deal of discussion of the choice not between competing generative grammars, but between a generative grammar and a "descriptive grammar." A "descriptive grammar" is not a theory of the language in the sense described above; it is not, in other words, a system of rules that establishes the sound-meaning correspondence in the language, insofar as this can be precisely expressed. Rather, it is an inventory of elements of various kinds that play a role in the language. For example, a descriptive grammar of English might contain an inventory of phonetic units, of phonemes, of morphemes, of words, of lexical categories, and of phrases or phrase types. Of course the inventory of phrases or phrase types cannot be completed since it is infinite, but let us put aside this difficulty.

It is clear, however, that the choice between a generative grammar and a descriptive grammar is not a genuine one. Actually, a descriptive grammar can be immediately derived from a generative grammar, but not conversely. Given a generative grammar, we can derive the inventories of elements that appear at various levels. The descriptive grammar, in the sense just outlined, is simply one aspect of the full generative grammar. It is an epiphenomenon, derivable from the full system of rules and principles that constitutes the generative grammar. The choice, then, is not between two competing grammars, but between a grammar and one particular aspect of this grammar. It seems obvious how this choice should be resolved, since the particular aspect that is isolated in the descriptive grammar seems to be of little independent importance. Surely the principles that determine the inventory, and much else, are more important than the inventory itself. In any event, the nature of the choice is clear; it is not a choice between competing systems, but rather a choice between the whole and a part.

Although what I have just said is literally correct, it is still somewhat misleading. I have characterized a descriptive grammar as one particular aspect of a full generative grammar, but actually the concept "descriptive grammar" arose in modern linguistics in a rather different way. A descriptive grammar was itself regarded as a full account of the language. It was, in other words, assumed that the inventory of elements exhausts the grammatical description of the language. Once we have listed the phones, phonemes, and the rest, we have given a full description of grammatical structure. The grammar is simply the collection of these various inventories.

This observation suggests a way of formulating the difference between generative and descriptive grammars in terms of a factual assumption about the nature of language. Let us suppose that a theory of language will consist of a definition of the notion "grammar" as well as definitions of various kinds of units (e.g. phonological units, morphological units etc.). When we apply such a general theory to data, we use the definitions to find a particular grammar and a particular collection of units. Consider now two theories of this sort that differ in the following way. In one, the units of various kinds are defined independently of the notion "grammar"; the grammar, then, is simply the collection of the various kinds of unit. For example, we define "phoneme," "morpheme," and the like in terms of certain analytic procedures, and define the "grammar" as a collection of units derived by applying these procedures. In the other theory, the situation is reversed. The notion "grammar" is defined independently of the various kinds of unit; the grammar is a system of such-and-such a kind. The units of various kinds are defined in terms of the logically prior concept "grammar." They are whatever appears in the grammar at such-and-such a level of functioning.

The difference between these two kinds of theory is an important one. It is the difference of factual assumption. The intuition that lies behind descriptive grammar is that the units are logically prior to the grammar, which is merely a collection of units. The intuition that lies behind the development of generative grammar is the opposite: it is that the grammar is logically prior to the units, which are merely the elements that appear at a particular stage in the functioning of grammatical processes. We can interpret this controversy in terms of its implications as to the nature of language acquisition. One who accepts the point of view of descriptive grammar will expect language acquisition to be a process of accretion, marked by gradual growth in the size of inventories, the elements of the inventories being developed by some sort of analytic or inductive procedures. One who accepts the underlying point of view of generative grammar will expect, rather, that the process of language acquisition must be more like that of selecting a particular hypothesis from a restricted class of possible hypotheses, on the basis of limited data. The selected hypothesis is the grammar; once accepted, it determines a system of relations among elements and inventories of various sorts. There will, of course, be growth of inventory, but it will be a rather peripheral and "external" matter. Once the child has selected a certain grammar, he will "know" whatever is predicted by this selected hypothesis. He will, in other words, know a great deal about sentences to which he has never been exposed. This is, of course, the characteristic fact about human language.

I have outlined the difference between two theories of grammar in rather vague terms. It can be made precise, and the question of choice between them becomes a matter of fact, not decision. My own view is that no descriptivist theory can be reconciled with the known facts about the nature and use of language. This, however, is a matter that goes beyond the scope of this discussion.

To summarize: as the problem is usually put, the choice between generative and descriptive grammars is not a genuine one. It is a choice between a system of principles and one rather marginal selection of consequences of these principles. But there is a deeper and ultimately factual question, to be resolved not by decision but by sharpening the assumptions and confronting them with facts.

Finally, a word about the matter of the teaching of grammar in the schools. My impression is that grammar is generally taught as an essentially closed and finished system, and in a rather mechanical way. What is taught is a system of terminology, a set of techniques for diagramming sentences, and so on. I do not doubt that this has its function, that the student must have a way of talking about language and its properties. But it seems to me that a great opportunity is lost when the teaching of grammar is limited in this way. It is important for students to realize how little we know about the rules that determine the relation of sound and meaning in English, about the general properties of human language, about the matter of how the incredibly complex system of rules that constitutes a grammar is acquired or put to use. Few students are aware of the fact that in their normal, everyday life they are constantly creating new linguistic structures that are immediately understood, despite their novelty, by those to whom they speak or write. They are never brought to the realization of how amazing an accomplishment this is, and of how limited is our comprehension of what makes it possible. Nor do they acquire any insight into the remarkable intricacy of the grammar that they use unconsciously, even insofar as this system is understood and can be explicitly presented. Consequently, they miss both the challenge and the accomplishments of the study of language. This seems to me a pity, because both are very real.

Perhaps as the study of language gradually returns to the full scope and scale of its rich tradition, some way will be found to introduce students to the tantalizing problems that language has always posed for those who are puzzled and intrigued by the mysteries of human intelligence.

ERICH AUERBACH

Realism and the Three Styles

The interpretation of reality through literary representation or "imitation" has occupied me for a long time. My original starting point was Plato's discussion in book 10 of the *Republic*—mimesis ranking third after truth—in conjunction with Dante's assertion that in the *Commedia* he presented true reality. As I studied the various methods of interpreting human events in the literature of Europe, I found my interest becoming more precise and focused. Some guiding ideas began to crystallize, and these I sought to pursue.

The first of these ideas concerns the doctrine of the ancients regarding the several levels of literary representation—a doctrine which was taken up again by every later classicistic movement. I came to understand that modern realism in the form it reached in France in the early nineteenth century is, as an aesthetic phenomenon, characterized by complete emancipation from that doctrine. This emancipation is more complete, and more significant for later literary forms of the imitation of life, than the mixture of *le sublime* with *le grotesque* proclaimed by the contemporary romanticists. When Stendhal and Balzac took random individuals from daily life in their dependence upon current historical circumstances and made them the subjects of serious, problematic, and even tragic representation,

From *Mimesis* (Francke, 1946), translated from the German by Willard Trask (Princeton University Press, 1953), epilogue, pp. 554–57. Reprinted by permission of the publishers.

17

they broke with the classical rule of distinct levels of style; for according to this rule, everyday practical reality could find a place in literature only within the frame of a low or intermediate kind of style, that is to say, as either grotesquely comic or pleasant, light, colorful, and elegant entertainment. They thus completed a development which had long been in preparation (since the time of the novel of manners and the *comédie larmoyante* of the eighteen century, and more pronouncedly since the *Sturm und Drang* and early romanticism). And they opened the way for modern realism, which has ever since developed in increasingly rich forms, in keeping with the constantly changing and expanding reality of modern life.

Looking at the problem in this fashion, I came to realize that the revolution early in the nineteenth century against the classical doctrine of levels of style could not possibly have been the first of its kind. The barriers which the romanticists and the contemporary realists tore down had been erected only toward the end of the sixteenth century and during the seventeenth by the advocates of a rigorous imitation of antique literature. Before that time, both during the Middle Ages and on through the Renaissance, a serious realism had existed. It had been possible in literature as well as in the visual arts to represent the most everyday phenomena of reality in a serious and significant context. The doctrine of the levels of style had no absolute validity. However different medieval and modern realism may be, they are at one in this basic attitude. And it had long been clear to me how this medieval conception of art had evolved, and when and how the first break with the classical theory had come about. It was the story of Christ, with its ruthless mixture of everyday reality and the highest and most sublime tragedy, which had conquered the classical rule of styles.

But if one compares the two breaks with the doctrine of stylistic levels, one cannot but see at once that they came about under completely different conditions and yielded completely different results. The view of reality expressed in the Christian works of late antiquity and the Middle Ages differs completely from that of modern realism. It is very difficult to formulate the specific character of the older Christian view in such a way that the essential points are brought out and all of the pertinent phenomena are included. A solution which struck me as on the whole satisfactory resulted from an investigation of the semantic history of the word *figura*. For this reason I use the term *figural* to identify the conception of reality in late antiquity and the Christian Middle Ages. What I mean by it is repeatedly explained in this book; a detailed presentation is to be found in my essay on *figura* (which has been reprinted in my *Neue Dante-Studien, Instanbuler Schriften* No. 5, İstanbul 1944, now Berne). In this conception, an occurrence on earth signifies not only itself but at the same time another, which it predicts or confirms, without prejudice to the power of its concrete reality here and now. The connection between occurrences is not regarded as primarily a chronological or causal development but as a oneness within the divine plan, of which all occurrences are parts and reflections. Their direct earthly connection is of secondary importance, and often their interpretation can altogether dispense with any knowledge of it.

These three closely related ideas, which gave the original problem form, though at the same time they narrowed its scope, are the base upon which the entire study is built. Naturally it involves a variety of other motifs and problems inherent in the abundance of historical phenomena which had to be treated. But most of these are in some way related to the ideas mentioned, and at any rate those ideas form the constant point of reference.

A systematic and complete history of realism would not only have been impossible, it would not have served my purpose. For the guiding ideas had delimited the subject matter in a very specific way. I was no longer concerned with realism in general; the question was to what degree and in what manner realistic subjects were treated seriously, problematically, or tragically. As a result, merely comic works, works which indubitably remained within the realm of the low style, were excluded. They could at most be referred to occasionally as contrasting illustrations, in the same sense in which completely unrealistic works in the elevated style were to be mentioned from time to time. The category of "realistic works of serious style and character" has never been treated or even conceived as such. I have not seen fit to analyze it theoretically and to describe it systematically. To do that would have necessitated an arduous and, from the reader's point of view, a tiresome search for definitions at the very beginning of my study. (Not even the term "realistic" is unambiguous.) And it is most probable that I could not have managed without an unusual and clumsy terminology. The procedure I have employed—that of citing for every epoch a number of texts and using these as test cases for my ideas—takes the reader directly into the subject and makes him sense what is at issue long before he is expected to cope with anything theoretical.

The method of textual interpretation gives the interpreter a certain leeway. He can choose and emphasize as he pleases. It must naturally be possible to find what he claims in the text. My interpretations are no doubt guided by a specific purpose. Yet this purpose assumed form only as I went along, playing as it were with my texts, and for long stretches of my way I have been guided only by the texts themselves. Furthermore, the great majority of the texts were chosen at random, on the basis of accidental acquaintance and personal preference rather than in view of a definite purpose. Studies of this kind do not deal with laws but with trends and tendencies, which cross and complement one another in the most varied ways. I was by no means interested merely in presenting what would serve my purpose in the narrowest sense; on the contrary, it was my endeavor to accommodate multiplex data and to make my formulations correspondingly elastic.

The individual chapters treat individual epochs, in some cases comparatively short ones, as little as half a century, in others much longer. There are frequent gaps—that is to say, periods which have not been treated at all: antiquity, for example, which I use only by way of introduction, or the early Middle Ages, from which but too little has been preserved. Additional chapters could have been inserted later to deal with English, German, and Spanish texts. I should have liked to treat the *siglo de oro* more extensively; I should especially have liked to add a special chapter on German realism of the seventeenth century. But the difficulties were too great. As it was, I had to deal with texts ranging over three thousand years, and I was often obliged to go beyond the confines of my own field, that of the romance literatures. I may also mention that the book was written during the war and at Istanbul, where the libraries are not well equipped for European studies. International communications were impeded; I had to dispense with almost all periodicals, with almost all the more recent investigations, and in some cases with reliable critical editions of my texts. Hence it is possible and even probable that I overlooked things which I ought to have considered and that I occasionally assert something which modern research has disproved or modified. I trust that these probable errors include none which affect the core of my argument. The lack of technical literature and periodicals may also serve to explain why my book has no notes.

Aside from the texts, I quote comparatively little, and that little it was easy to include in the body of the book. On the other hand it is quite possible that the book owes its existence to just this lack of a rich and specialized library. If it had been possible for me to acquaint myself with all the work that has been done on so many subjects, I might never have reached the point of writing.

With this I have said all that I thought the reader would wish me to explain. Nothing now remains but to find him—to find the reader, that is. I hope that my study will reach its readers—both my friends of former years, if they are still alive, as well as all the others for whom it was intended. And may it contribute to bringing together again those whose love for our western history has serenely persevered.

OWEN BARFIELD

✍

The Meaning of "Literal"

We call a sentence "literal" when it means what it affirms on the face of it, and nothing else. If some sentences are not literal, that is because it is possible, by recognized linguistic usage, to affirm or express one thing and to mean another thing, either instead of or as well as the first. An extreme case of meaning another thing instead (which I will call "substituted meaning") is the prearranged code. In P. G. Wodehouse's *Leave it to Psmith,* a young man outside an Underground Station goes up to a number of complete strangers in turn and tells them to their surprise (and sometimes annoyance) that "There will be rain in Northumberland tomorrow." But what he really means is: "Are you the person who advertised in the Personal Column and later wrote asking me to meet you here?" Perhaps the code is hardly a *linguistic* device; but it will serve as a kind of marker for the terminal point of "substitution"; and we may profitably compare with it the *cliché,* or completely *fossilized metaphor.* If, for example, I tell anyone to "leave no stone unturned," there is hardly more of "stone" in my meaning than there was of "rain" in Psmith's. All that is left is the substituted meaning: "Try every way you can think of!"

When we turn from "instead of" to "as well as," that is, to sen-

From *Metaphor and Symbol,* edited by L. C. Knights and B. Cottle (Butterworths, 1960), pp. 48–57. Reprinted by permission of the publisher, the author, and the Colston Research Society.

tences which convey a secondary meaning, while still in some measure retaining the primary, or literal, one (I will call this "concomitant
meaning"), we have already crossed the frontier between prose and
poetry. At least I think our examples would practically all have to
be taken from among sentences which are characteristically—though
not necessarily successfully—poetic. They would range from allegory
at one end of the scale, where the two meanings continue alongside,
on more or less parallel lines, to what I suppose is best called "symbolism" at the other—loaded sentences like:

> E il naufragar m'è dolce in questo mare,

or:

> The cat looked long and softly at the king.

I have distinguished concomitant meaning from substituted meaning, but no doubt in all cases, where it makes any sense at all to
distinguish the literal meaning from some other or others, a possibility is implied of transference or substitution. For if there are at
least two concomitant meanings, and these are distinguishable from
one another, we must be able to attend to either one to the exclusion of the other; and if we attend only to the non-literal meaning,
we are substituting it for the literal. Thus, the ordinary word for
the converse of "literal" is "metaphorical," from μεταφέρειν—meaning
"to carry across" or "transfer"; and the problems of the relation between the literal meaning and any other confront us nowhere more
strikingly than in the metaphors of poets.

As an example of such problems, you might expect that the element of concomitance (retention of the literal meaning alongside
the substituted one) would bear some relation to the verisimilitude
of the literal meaning. But that is not in practice the case. The
literal meaning of

> The moon is my eye,
> Smiling only at night . . .

or

> There is a garden in her face . . .

is a pretty tall story; whereas Psmith's remark about the rain was all too likely to be true. Yet it is in the first two cases that the literal meaning continues to command our attention, while in the last it drops out altogether. I only mention this in passing and am not proposing to pursue it.

So far, I should imagine, everyone is with me. But at this point opinions begin to differ. It was Dr. I. A. Richards in *The Philosophy of Rhetoric* (1936) who introduced two terms which are very useful to people who try to deal with this kind of subject, when he referred to the literal or surface meaning of an expression as the *vehicle* and any other meaning which it also properly conveys as the *tenor*. These two terms I propose, with grateful acknowledgements, to adopt.

Now there is a school of thought which holds that the tenor of a meaningful metaphor could always, if it were thought fit, be expressed literally. The passenger in the vehicle could, if he chose, get out and walk. If it were not so, these thinkers hold, the tenor would not deserve the name of "meaning" at all; it would amount to no more than an emotional overtone. A meaningful expression, as distinct from an emotive one, imparts information; and there is no information (they insist) which is not communicable by discursive and literal statement. It is not, by the way, only those who are insensitive to the working of imagination who take this view. Apart from Dr. Richards, Susanne Langer, in her book *Problems of Art* (1957), in the course of making an acute and valuable distinction between art as symbol and the use of symbols *in* art, commits herself to the general statement that "there is a literal meaning (sometimes more than one) connoted by the symbol that occurs in art." And again, genuine symbols "have meanings, *and the meanings may be stated.*"

The other school of thought holds that the tenor of a meaningful metaphor or symbol *cannot* always be expressed literally. However it may be with codes and allegories, there are also "creative," or "seminal," or anyway some sort of metaphors and symbols, whose tenor cannot be communicated in any other way than through the symbol, and yet whose tenor is not purely emotive. Whether what is so communicated is information will depend on how we choose to limit the word "information"; but it is certainly meaning. The adherents of this school might well object to my use of the word "concomitant" and prefer some such term as "manifold" or "multiple," but I will continue to use the word "concomitant" without implying any particular relation between vehicle and tenor, or that the one is always clearly distinguishable from the other.

The meaning we attach to the word "literal" in many of the contexts in which it is commonly used (and these are of course not limited to the realms of poetry and art) will be found, I believe, to depend a good deal on the issue between these two contrasted views. At the moment, however, I shall content myself with having stated them, while I move on into another field and try approaching the subject from a different direction.

Hitherto we have been considering only sentences, but it is not only sentences that possess this quality of being a vehicle with a tenor. That is also very frequently the case with individual words. Since I shall be saying a good deal about "meaning," I had better mention that I am aware that there is a sense of the word "meaning" in which an individual word outside a sentence has no meaning. But this limiting sense of the term "meaning" is really based on the premiss that all meaningful language is discursive and therefore that the only meaningful symbols are the discursive symbols of logic. In other words it presupposes that the first of the two schools of thought which I have mentioned is right and the second is wrong. I shall be suggesting later that there are difficulties in the way of such a supposition. Meanwhile it is enough that, when I talk about the meanings of individual words, I shall be talking about whatever it is that lexicographers and etymologists do talk about. For reasons which I hope will appear, I do not think it is possible to form any reliable ideas on this subject without taking full account of the historical approach, and it is so that I approach it.

Consider the four words, *outsider, noble, gentle* and *scruple*. If we approach them etymologically, we find a sort of graduated scale in the relation between vehicle and tenor which they exemplify. When we meet the word *outsider,* we are normally still aware, even without reflection, of its vehicular connotation of spatial externality, even though our main concern is with its tenorial significance— which will be caddishness, or original genius, according to the context. *Noble* is still used occasionally to signify social rank, irrespective of high character (which is of course its tenor). *Gentle,* a word with a similar history, has already ceased to be used with a class or social import except in the obsolescent compounds *gentleman* and *gentlewoman.* In the case of *scruple,* it takes a little erudition to be aware that once upon a time it, too, was a vehicle with a distinguishable tenor; for we have to go to another language (Latin), from which it is derived, in order to ascertain that *scrupulus* originally meant a small, sharp stone—the kind that gets into your shoe and worries you.

In all these four cases the vehicle is a reference to something in the outside world, while the tenor conveys a moral quality or a feeling not accessible to sense-observation. (I am going to call it something in the "inside" world. There will not be much danger, during this paper, of anyone forgetting that we talk in metaphors.) And of course, as soon as we start exploring the history of language in this way, the deluge of available examples makes us feel like the sorcerer's apprentice. The shortest way I can think of to get our minds straight into the middle of all that line of country is to quote a few sentences from the section on *Language* in Emerson's longer essay on Nature:

> Every word which is used to express a moral or intellectual fact, if traced to its root, is found to be borrowed from material appearance. *Right* means *straight; wrong* means *twisted. Spirit* primarily means *wind; transgression,* the *crossing of a line; supercilious,* the *raising of the eyebrows.* We say the *heart* to express emotion, the *head* to denote thought, and *thought* and *emotion* are words borrowed from sensible things, and now appropriated to spiritual nature. Most of the process by which this transformation is made is hidden from us in the remote time when language was formed . . .

I have chosen Emerson, but the observation is one with which, it seems, everyone agrees. For instance, it was summed up as follows by Jeremy Bentham:

> Throughout the whole field of language, parallel to the line of what may be termed the material language, and expressed by the same words, runs a line of what may be termed the immaterial language. Not that to every word that has a material import there belongs also an immaterial one; but that to every word that has an immaterial import, there belongs, or at least did belong, a material one.
>
> Essay on Language, Section IV

It is fairly obvious that, if we are to consider the meaning of the word "literal" in any general sense—that is, not simply as a technical term in the art of rhetoric—all this is very relevant indeed and requires further examination. For instance, it is clear that the words of this "immaterial" language, of which Bentham speaks, are, or were at one time, what we have been calling *vehicles,* with an immediately physical reference, but having as their *tenor* the "immaterial" language. Or, avoiding the technical terms, it is clear that they were used *figuratively.* Are we equally justified in saying that they are, or were, used *metaphorically?* Was the figurative import always created by a definite mental act of substitution? In some cases it certainly was. The word *scrupulus* is a good example of these cases—I am not even sure that there isn't a passage in Cicero somewhere, where he introduces the metaphor with a rhetorical flourish. But the facility with which, from a few such cases, the general inference has been drawn that *all* immaterial language came about in this way is remarkable. Bentham, Herbert Spencer, Max Müller all take this long jump in their stride and, though other voices have been raised in this century—for instance, Ernst Cassirer, Bruno Snell and R. B. Onians—it is still the general view. Dr. A. S. Diamond, in his book *The History and Origin of Language* (1959), simply takes it for granted.

If this inference were correct, it would follow that all nouns which today have an immaterial import and no other (*transgression, supercilious, emotion* and so forth), have behind them a history in which we can distinguish the following four stages: a first stage, in which they had an exclusively literal meaning and referred to a material object; a second stage, in which they had concomitant meanings; a third stage, in which they had a substituted meaning, though the original one had not quite vanished; and a fourth and final stage, in which their meaning has again become (though much altered) exclusively *literal.* The Greek word πνεῦμα and Latin *spiritus* and *anima* are commonly given as the typical examples of stage 2. We think of the third chapter of St. John's Gospel where the same Greek word πνεῦμα has to be translated *spirit* in one sentence and *wind* in the next sentence of the same verse. I have already given *outsider* as an example of stage 3 (for the *quality* it denotes is immaterial) and the modern English word *spirit* will do very well once more for our example of stage 4.

Under examination, however, this presumed historical progress gives rise to a number of questions, two of which were briefly considered many years ago by Professor C. S. Lewis in a paper entitled "Bluspels and Flalansferes," which was printed in his *Rehabilitations* (1939). He distinguished between the *magistral* and the *pupillary* metaphor: "The first is freely chosen; it does not at all hinder, and only very slightly helps, the thought of its maker. The second is not chosen at all; it is the unique expression of a meaning that we cannot have on any other terms" (pp. 140–41). The two questions he raised are: *When* and *What*. When exactly, at what point in its history, did the stage 3 meaning of the word *spiritus* (during which it still connoted something to do with *wind* or *breath*) turn into stage 4—the present-day meaning of our word *spirit*? And (much more difficult semantically) *what* happened, when it ceased to be a vehicle with a tenor, and became a mere literal word? Now the fact that we cannot say exactly *when* a change has taken place does not of course mean that it did not take place; and we perhaps need not worry unduly about the first question—though in point of fact it is a good deal easier to presume a gradual transition in such a case than actually to imagine the process in detail. Just as it is easy to talk of an emendation "creeping" into a text, but very difficult to form a concrete picture of any halfway point in that mysterious journey.

The problem of *what* happened is a much more prickly one; for it raises the whole question of what a literal word of immaterial import *does* mean. What does it refer to? Anatole France had a very simple answer for this question. He said these words really still have only their original, material import—and for that reason we need not worry too much about philosophy. The metaphysician constructs his system by putting together noises which are no more than the perfected cries of dogs and monkeys, cries to which we have gradually attached a significance which we believe to be abstract, when they are in fact only loose or vague. Obviously this will not do. Nobody except an *esprit fort* seriously thinks that the word *spirit* means "wind" today; but what *does* it mean? Nor is it only words like *spirit, soul, mind* which are puzzling. To what, precisely, does each one of them refer—the tens of thousands of abstract nouns which daily fill the columns of our newspapers, the debating chambers of our legislatures, the consulting rooms of our psychiatrists? *Progress, tendency, culture, democracy, liberality, inhibition, motivation, re-*

sponsibility—there was a time when each one of them, either itself or its progenitor in another tongue, was a vehicle referring to the concrete world of sensuous experience with a tenor of some sort peeping, or breathing or bursting through. But now they are just "literal" words—the sort of words we have to use, when we are admonished *not* to speak in metaphors. What do we mean when we say that?

It is here that the blessed word "entity" generally rears its head. An abstract noun, used literally, means—or is thought to mean—an entity of some sort, a real entity, if you are a Hegelian idealist; a fictitious entity, if you are a positivist. Bentham tells us that:

> With every name employed an entity stands associated in the
> minds of the hearers, as well as speakers; and that entity,
> though in one half of the whole number of instances, no other
> than a fictitious one, is, in all of them, apt to be taken for a
> real one.

And he goes on to emphasize the misconceptions, errors and ambiguities that have arisen as the result. I do not know that the Logical Positivists have added much to this way of putting it. What I want to question is the validity of this whole approach to the problem, this whole way of thinking about it.

Why have people fallen into the habit of talking and thinking on the footing that nouns refer, or at all events are expected to refer, to entities? You will remember that the presumed history of these literal words of immaterial import has gone through four stages, in the first and last of which their meanings were exclusively literal, while in the two intermediate stages they functioned as vehicles having a tenor. We may call the first stage—at which they are presumed to have referred solely to material objects—the "born" literal, and the last stage—at which they are presumed to refer to immaterial entities, real or fictitious—the "achieved" literal. Now I believe it will be found that our whole way of thinking about the achieved literal is based on a tacitly assumed analogy with the born literal. We assume that it is not the natural, simple nature of a noun to be a vehicle with a tenor, because nouns did not begin that way. They began life as plain labels for plain objects and that is their true nature. It was only later, as a result of the operation of human fancy in metaphor-making, that they came to be used for a time as vehicles with a tenor; and when that stage is over and they have once more achieved literalness, we feel that they have reverted to their pristine innocence and become once more labels for objects, even if we are firmly convinced that the new objects do not exist. Better a fictitious entity than none at all—for a noun to be the name of!

If I am right about this, and there is a confusion between our notion of achieved literalness and our notion of born literalness, it is clearly important to be sure that at least our notion of born literalness is roughly correct. And that is what I now propose to examine.

At the beginning of this paper we found that there were two schools of thought about the relation between vehicle and tenor; one holding that they are always detachable, and that the tenor could also be expressed literally; the other holding that that is not always the case. Let us therefore consider the concept of born literalness from each of these contrasted points of view in turn.

The concept of born literalness assumes that all words of immaterial import began with an exclusively material reference and subsequently acquired an immaterial tenor as a result of the metaphor-making activity of human minds. Now adherents of the first, or detachable, school of thought—which I will call the *explicationist* theory of metaphor—are bound to assume that the immaterial tenor, upon its first appearance among our primitive ancestors, could in the alternative have been expressed literally. But in order to achieve this, those ancestors must already have possessed other words with an immaterial reference. But how did *those* words acquire their immaterial reference? Not by metaphorical activity—unless there had already been still other words available; and so on *ad infinitum*. It follows that, *if* you believe that whatever can be expressed metaphorically can also be expressed literally, you cannot at the same time believe that man's first words had a purely material reference and that an immaterial tenor was subsequently added by way of metaphor.

The second—or *implicationist*—theory of metaphor, which holds that the tenor cannot necessarily be taken apart from its vehicle and expressed literally, escapes this difficulty. But it still has to assume that the immaterial content, which afterwards became the tenor, was *conceived* separately and without the help of any verbal vehicle. Somehow or other our ancestors had acquired a bit of self-knowledge (knowledge of the "inner" world) without the help of the instrument of speech and then they chose a word with which to clothe that bit of knowledge metaphorically. I am a primitive man, who has just become aware of a sort of immaterial something within me, but I have no word for it. In my experience up to now, it is not even the sort of thing for which there *are* words. What I *have* got available is a bunch of strictly literal labels for things like *sun, moon, cloud, rock, river, wind,* etc. None of these words has any immaterial overtone at all. That is an essential condition; for otherwise they would not be literal (as born literals are assumed to be literal); they would already be vehicles with a tenor. The word for *wind,* for example, means to me simply what we today call *air* or *oxygen,* the physical stuff that keeps on coming into and going out of me. I now take the step of substituting my word for, and with it my thought of, *wind* for my wordless thought of the sort of something. That is the picture.

And of course it is an impossible one. It is not impossible that new meanings should make their first appearance as metaphor. On the contrary in our time it is the common way. Discovery, consciousness itself, and symbolization go hand-in-hand. But we must remember that metaphors and symbols today are created by minds already acquainted with figurative language as a normal mode of expression. What we are trying to imagine now is the first metaphor in a wholly literal world. And that does imply precisely this primitive and verbally unsupported notion of the "sort of something" which I have tried to depict. But it is impossible to believe that things happened in this way.

It is impossible to believe, because consciousness and symbolization are simultaneous and correlative. We can believe that a growing awareness of the sort of something which we today mean by *spirit* was inextricably linked with a new use of the word for *wind.* What it is impossible to believe is, that up to that moment the word for *wind* had been as semantically aloof from the sort of something as Psmith's remark about rain in Northumberland was semantically aloof from the information he intended to convey to Freddie Threepwood.

If there was no prior, no "given" affinity between the concept "wind" and the other immaterial concept of "spirit," the latter concept must have been originally framed without the aid of any symbol. It must moreover, as tenor, have been separable from its vehicle when it acquired one. The first of these two consequences is, in my view, epistemologically untenable on several grounds; but it is enough that the second is pointedly inconsistent with just that "implicational" type of metaphor which is the only one we are any longer concerned with, since the explicational type has already been shown to be incompatible with born literalness. If, on the other hand, there *was* any prior affinity between the concept of *wind* and the other (immaterial) concept, then the word must already, from the moment of its birth, have been a vehicle with a tenor.

I think we are bound to conclude that this was in fact the case. We have escorted the concept of "born literalness" to the frontier and there is really nothing left to do but to hand it over to the consular representatives of the land of Not-being, or perhaps better say the land of dream. It occupies a clear and conspicuous place in so many minds that I hardly know what to call it. "Chimera" suggests fancifulness and vagueness, but the historical fallacy of born literalness is neither vague nor fanciful. Perhaps *spectre* is the best word. Literalness is a quality which some words have achieved in the course of their history; it is not a quality with which the first words were born. And let us be clear about the consequences. The born literalness which we have rejected is a literalness of the material, not of the immaterial language. We mean by a "literal" word or meaning one which is not a vehicle with a tenor or one which is a vehicle without a tenor. But the vast majority of the words by which we today denote the objects of the outer world have at some stage in their history been vehicles with a tenor, and, if that is so, it follows (except in places where a tenor was added by late and deliberate metaphorical construction) that they *began* life as vehicles with a tenor. They too can only have *achieved* a literalness with which they were not born. Just as our immaterial language has acquired its literal meanings by dropping the vehicular reference, so our material language has acquired its literalness by dropping the tenorial reference. That which the physiologist takes to be the literal meaning of the word *heart,* for example, is no less "achieved" than that which the theologian takes to be the literal meaning of the word *spirit.* Whatever else the word "literal" means, then, it normally means something which is the end-product of a long historical process.

Abandoning the spectre of born literalness, we shall also abandon the whole dream of fixed entities with which literal meanings must somehow correspond. What then are we left with? What solid ground have we to stand on? The Linguistic Analysts have already suggested that there is none. According to them, the meaning of a word is the way it is used in sentences, and it may be that there is not much to quarrel with in this doctrine, if it stops there. They do not however appear to stop there, for they seem to infer from this a sort of lowest common measure and to equate the meaning of any word with (to quote Mr. Gellner) "the way it is used by an unimaginative man about the middle of the morning." On the other hand, when it is a question, not of inference or assumption, but of any further development of the doctrine, they *do* stop there. For they do not appear to be interested in any sort of historical enquiry. Whereas, if the meaning of a word in the twentieth century is the way it is used in the twentieth century, I would have thought that that makes it all the more interesting and important to enquire into the way it was used from time to time in previous centuries

Although I have been dealing with words, it cannot be said that my conclusions affect words only. If the word on its very first appearance was already a vehicle with a tenor, then the given affinity which I suggested between the concept of *wind* and the concept of *spirit* must have been "given" in the nature of things and not by some kind of friction in the machinery of language. I think it will be found that to assume otherwise is merely to smuggle back into our thinking the spectre of born literalness, or at all events of the sort of world, the sort of relation between nature and the mind of man which must have given rise to born literalness and could not therefore (as we saw when we laid the spectre) have given rise to an immaterial import. Bruno Snell put it neatly in his book *The Discovery of Mind* (1946, translated 1953), when, in dealing with one of Homer's metaphors, he maintained that man could never have come to experience a rock anthropomorphically if he had not also experienced himself "petromorphically."

It follows that neither nature nor man will ever be understood, though certainly physical nature—and perhaps physical man, too —may in the meantime be very skilfully *manipulated*, until we accept that nature is the reflected image of man's conscious and unconscious self. We must remember that the human body is itself a part of nature. As long as the historical fallacy of born literalness holds sway, Freud's half-truth that many images have a bodily significance will be swallowed, without leading, as it should, to the reflection that this is only possible because the body itself has an imaginal significance. I think it also follows that the mind of man is not, as Coleridge put it, "a lazy onlooker" on an external world but itself a structural component of the world it contemplates.

I conclude that the second of the two schools of thought mentioned at the start—the Implicationist school—has hold of the truth. The other, the Explicationist, view is founded on the assumption that all meaningful language is discursive; this assumption is itself based on the premiss that literalness of meaning is some kind of unclouded correpondence with a mindless external reality which was given from the start; and this premiss in its turn requires the spectre of born literalness to keep it in countenance.

As to the meaning of the word "literal," there is no difficulty about it, and everyone knows what it means as a technical term in the art of rhetoric. In any wider sense, bearing on the general relation between material and immaterial language, what we call literalness is a late stage in a long-drawn-out historical process.

There is of course a sense in which words must be said to mean what they are believed, and therefore intended, to mean; but nouns of the so-called material language do not in fact correspond with real and wholly material entities. The belief that they do so is responsible for the fuss about entities, real or fictitious, upon which to found the meanings of nouns of the so-called immaterial language. In this factual sense there is indeed no such thing as literalness. The most we can safely say, therefore, is that the literal and discursive use of language is the way in which it is used by a speaker, who is either unaware of, or is deliberately ignoring, that real and figurative relation between man and his environment, out of which the words he is using were born and without which they could never have been born.

G. UDNY YULE

✍

On Sentence-Length

Section I. Introductory

One element of style which seems to be characteristic of an author, in so far as can be judged from general impressions, is the length of his sentences. *This* author develops his thought in long, complex and wandering periods: *that* finds sufficient for his purpose a sequence of sentences that are brief, clear and perspicuous. Since the length of a sentence can be readily measured, for practical purposes, by the number of words, it occurred to me that it would be of interest to subject this impression to statistical investigation.

In carrying out the investigation, I met with more difficulties than I had foreseen. There are two terms used above: (1) Sentence, (2) Word. What is a sentence? What is a word, or what for present purposes is to be regarded as a word? *Sentence.* Let me cite the *New English Dictionary:*

> SENTENCE. *sb.* 6. A series of words in connected speech or writing, forming the grammatically complete expression of a single thought; in popular use often (= Period *sb.* 10) such a portion of a composition or utterance as extends from one full stop to another. In *Grammar,* the verbal expression of a proposition, question, command, or request, containing normally a

From *Biometrika,* XXX (1938), pp. 363–87. Reprinted by permission of the publisher.

35

subject and a predicate (though either of these may be omitted by ellipsis). In grammatical use, though not in popular language, a sentence may consist of a single word. . . . English grammarians usually recognise three classes: simple sentences, complex sentences (which contain one or more subordinate clauses), and compound sentences (which have more than one subject or predicate).

From these definitions I conclude, I hope rightly, that we may drop the term "period" and use the term "sentence" to cover *any* sentence (or as I should have been inclined to write, "period"), however complex and however compound in the senses defined. It is convenient to be able to avoid a term which to a statistician would generally suggest a different meaning. Now, not being a grammarian but just one of the populace, I confess that I started with the popular notion of a "sentence" in this general sense: "such a portion of a composition as extends from one full stop to another," and thought I would have nothing to do but tot up the words from full stop to full stop. The first definition, however, reads: "the grammatically complete expression of a single thought." I feel some doubts as to the "*single* thought." (Is not "I am tired and hungry" a sentence, and does it not convey two thoughts, the thought of being tired and the thought of being hungry?) But the "grammatically complete expression" surely is essential to make a word-series a sentence; the word-series must be what Webster calls a "sense unit," and the trouble is that, especially in older works, "a portion of a composition" which "extends from one full stop to another" is often *not* the grammatically complete expression of anything. When the author or compositor has used punctuation in this fashion, it is no longer possible simply to add up words from one full stop to the next, paying little or no attention to sense: it is necessary for the reader frequently to pull up and ask himself if the words just read do or do not form a sentence; and if they do not, what are in fact the limits of the sentence within which they must be assumed to lie. I need hardly point out how much this increases labour, and even, if the sentences are very long and complicated, brings in largely the element of personal judgement. Two readers, at least unskilled readers like myself, may well differ as to where a given sentence terminates.

Here is quite a simple illustration of the difficulty from a modern essay on *The Politics of Burns*:

There are several points here all at once calling for notice, and seldom getting it from friends of the poet:
The extraordinary talent for history shown by Robert Burns.
His attention to British History in preference to Scottish.
The originality of his views.

In this passage there are four word-series, the first divided from the second only by a colon (though the second begins with a capital letter), the second divided from the third, and the third from the fourth, by full stops. But neither the second, nor the third, nor the fourth words-series is a grammatically complete expression. The whole passage must be taken together, as it seems to me, as one single sentence. I am of course simply illustrating my difficulty, not criticizing the punctuation.

On the other hand, where an author has written a very long and meandering sentence, a question may well arise between two different readers as to whether a halt should not be called in the middle, and a full stop entered where author or compositor has placed only a colon.

I say author *or* compositor, for it must not be assumed that one is necessarily laying sacrilegious hands on the deliberate construction of the author himself. "So far as punctuation is concerned," says McKerrow, "there seems very little evidence that many authors exercised any care about it whatever. After all, even at present, few authors trouble to punctuate their MSS. with any care or consistency. Such punctuation as is to be found in ordinary MSS. of the sixteenth and seventeenth centuries is indeed most erratic and seldom goes beyond full stops at the end of most of the sentences and some indication of the caesura in lines of verse." I had, before I started the present work, expected that this comment would apply much more to intermediate punctuation than to full stops, trusting that authors would at least insert "full stops at the end of *most* of their sentences." But it applies to both. If punctuation, even as regards full stops, is largely the work of the compositor, there need be no hesitation in overriding them if necessary: indeed, the use of personal judgement seems unavoidable.

Let me add that at first I by no means realized the full extent of this difficulty, and when I did often felt myself horribly incompetent to deal with it. I am sure my final decisions could often be contested, and were not infrequently inconsistent with one another.

But after all, difficult cases are but a small proportion of all sentences in most writers and, if only as an exploratory piece of work, I hope the investigation may still retain interest and value.

Word. Compared with the difficulties as to the sentence, the difficulties concerning words are really of a minor kind. One large class is indicated by the lines of Calverley:

> Forever; 'tis a single word!
> Our rude forefathers deemed it two:
> Can you imagine so absurd
> A view?

Our rude forefathers also wrote *it self, any where, every where* and so forth, where their rude descendants write *itself, anywhere, everywhere.* How shall we reckon such expressions? It is best, I think, to follow modern usage and I generally endeavoured to do so; but in rapid counting it is very easy to make a slip. Hyphened words present the same sort of difficulty. *Law-courts, china-manufacturer, news-journal, well-earned,* I would count as two words each; *out-of-the-way* as four: but *co-acervation, contra-distinguish, tri-syllabic, pre-disposed, re-produce,* as one each. A *something-nothing-everything* (Coleridge) presents a special problem: I think it should be three words. But how many words is *matter-of-factness?* Coleridge calls it *a* word, "an uncouth and new coined word."

Then there are abbreviations such as *viz., i.e., etc.* or *&c.* The first there is no reason to reckon as anything but one word. The second, third and fourth, in spite of their meaning, I also reckoned as one each: eye and mind grasp them as wholes.

Finally, what are we to do with figures? Dates may occur even in literary or historical essays: any year stated in figures (1825 or 1798) I reckoned as a word. Whether days of the month ever occurred I do not recall: but I would reckon the day of the month stated in figures, as in January 10th, as a word for the month and a word for the number of the day. Any actual number if stated in figures would be reckoned as one word whatever the number.

In all such instances as the above I really do not think it is of very much practical consequence what rule is adopted: nor even of much practical consequence if the treatment is not always self-consistent. Sentences vary too much in length for what are after all minor errors of measurement to be of much consequence.

Quotations. I may mention in conclusion one other difficulty. What is to be done with quotations? Two cases seem clear. If the author makes a brief quotation forming grammatically part of his own sentence, he is only substituting someone else's words for his own and they must be counted in: as in Lamb's

> But I am none of those who—
> *Welcome the coming, speed the parting guest.*

If, on the other hand, the author simply quotes a complete sentence from somebody else, *that* is not the author's writing and must be omitted: as for example when the same author writes

> A *gag-eater* in our time was equivalent to a *goul,* and held
> in equal detestation.—suffered under the imputation.
> —*'Twas said*
> *He ate strange flesh.*

The quotation must be dropped. But no rule can be applied strictly to living literature. Thomas à Kempis, for example, quotes the words of scripture so freely that if one cut out scriptural quotations one would eliminate a considerable proportion of his work. He has made scripture his own, and what he has written must stand as his.

A serious difficulty arises only when, say, an essayist is discussing a poet and makes a long and purely illustrative quotation. This may be of any length, and it may be so made as virtually to form part of the sentence of the critic himself, or may follow almost indifferently a colon or a full stop at the end of the critic's sentence. Quotations made in the first way, and even those made in the second way after a colon, I tended at first to include. But, on coming across *very* long quotations, it became obvious that this was unsatisfactory, and I then adopted the easier method of simply cutting out all pages on which this source of trouble was serious. This is, I think, the best course.

Section II. Illustrations from Bacon, Coleridge, Lamb and Macaulay

This section is in part purely illustrative, showing what sort of distributions of sentence-length we may expect, but in part is concerned with the fundamental question how far sentence-length is really a *characteristic* of an author's style. If, that is to say, we take two lengthy passages, each containing a few hundred sentences, from a given fairly homogeneous work, will they present us with proportional numbers of sentences of each particular length in reasonably close agreement with one another? If they do not; if, although dealing with the same sort of material in the same sort of way, the author is liable capriciously to vary in the length of his sentences, sentence-length is not a *characteristic* of his style in any proper sense of the term, and one's impression to the contrary will be proved mistaken. If, however, there is reasonably close agreement, we can accept sentence-length as a characteristic. It is necessary, I think, to insert the condition that the author shall be dealing with the same sort of material in the same sort of way, since (again judging from general impressions) it seems clear that sentence-length may be affected by the author's matter as well as by his individuality: argumentative passages, for example, may well tend to longer sentences than matter purely descriptive.[1]

The four authors chosen as illustrations are Bacon, Coleridge, Lamb and Macaulay; and their works, Bacon's *Essays,* Coleridge's *Biographia Literaria,* Lamb's *Elia* and *Last Essays of Elia,* and Macaulay's *Essays.*

The fundamental tables, all in the same form and showing the numbers of sentences with 1 to 5, 6 to 10, 11 to 15 words, and so on, are given in the Appendix.

Table A gives the data derived from Bacon's *Essays.* Here, when I had got to the end of Essay XXVI, "Of Seeming Wise," I judged myself to be about half-way, and called this batch of 462 sentences sample A: I then proceeded to the end of Essay LI, "Of Faction," and as this had given me 474 sentences, or approximately the same number, I called it sample B. The total number of essays being 58, the two samples together cover almost 90% of the essays. Table A shows, in addition to the distributions for the two samples A and B, the total distribution for the two together. From inspection it will be clear that the two samples are very concordant, though figures are inevitably slightly irregular and fluctuating. In both the frequencies increase rather abruptly in the interval 11–15; in both they reach a maximum in the interval 31–35, and then tail away very slowly indeed, so that there is a considerable number of sen-

tences of 101–200 words in length and a few over 200. The record
is a sentence of 311 words, as punctuated, i.e., from full stop to
full stop. The reader will find it in the penultimate paragraph of
Essay XXVII, "Of Friendship." It might well be broken up: but
I do not think at this early stage I had attempted any revision of
punctuation, hardly having realized the difficulty mentioned in the
preceding section.

Table B gives the data from Coleridge's *Biographia Literaria*.
I began at the beginning and continued to about the middle of
chapter IX, when I had a batch of just over 600 (actually 601)
sentences, which I judged sufficient: this is sample A. For sample
B I meant to take a similar batch from near the end and began
with chapter XX in vol. II, not noticing that a great part of the remainder of this volume consisted of "Satyrane's Letters." The result
was that chapter XX to the end gave me only about half the number
of sentences wanted, and to complete the sample I went back to the
beginning of the volume (chapter XIV) and worked on from that
point to about the middle of chapter XVIII. This gave me sample
B of 606 sentences. Again, inspection of the table shows that the
distributions for samples A and B are closely alike and somewhat
different from those of Table A. The actual maximum frequency
occurs earlier, at 26–30 for sample A, and 21–25 both for sample
B and for the two samples together; and the distribution is less
scattered, there being a smaller proportion of the very long sentences
of over 100 words in length. With *Biographia Literaria* the quotation difficulty became at times acute: a page or two, or a shorter
passage, was omitted here and there to evade it.

The data derived from Lamb's essays are given in Table C. Sample A was taken from *Elia* (1st edition, 1823), from the beginning
to some two-thirds of the way through "Mrs. Battle's Opinions on
Whist." Sample B was drawn from the middle of the *Last Essays
of Elia* (1st edition, 1833), starting with the essay "Detached
Thoughts on Books" and continuing to the end of "Barbara S—."
Once more, the general consistence of the two samples looks quite
satisfactory. Short sentences are much more frequent than with
Coleridge, and the greatest frequencies occur in the intervals 6–10
and 10–15, which are almost equally frequent.

Finally, in Table D we have the data from Macaulay's *Essays*.
Sample A was taken from the beginning of the essay entitled "Lord

Bacon" (1837): sample B from the beginning of the essay on the
Earl of Chatham (1844). In this instance the two samples do not
agree quite so well as in previous tables. The first three frequencies
are quite concordant and agree in placing the maximum frequency
at sentences of 11–15 words. But thereafter the frequencies of sample
B exceed those of sample A right up to the interval 46–50, after
which the position is reversed, so that the second sample is less
scattered than the first. But the difference is not great.

So far we have dealt only with the similarities and differences
suggested by brief inspection of the tables, but it is desirable to
summarize in terms of statistical measures. Distributions of this
kind, with long tails, in which rather wild outliers may occur, might,
it seemed to me, be best dealt with by the method of percentiles.
While therefore I have calculated the arithmetic means as the most
familiar form of average, I have also given the median, and for the
rest have contented myself with the lower and upper quartiles Q_1
and Q_3, the interquartile range Q_3-Q_1 as a measure of dispersion,
and the ninth decile D_9 as an index to the extension of the tail
of the distribution. These percentiles are calculated on the usual
convention that the intervals may be regarded as 0.5–5.5, 5.5–10.5,
10.5–15.5, etc., and the distribution treated as continuous.[2]

These constants, for Tables A–D, are given in Table I. The table

Table I

Constants for the distributions of sentence-length in samples from
Bacon, Coleridge, Lamb and Macaulay (Tables A, B, C and D of
Appendix). Q_1 = Lower Quartile, Q_3 = Upper Quartile, D_9 = Ninth
Decile)

Constant	Bacon			Coleridge		
	A	B	TOTAL	A	B	TOTAL
Mean	48.4	48.5	48.5	41.2	39.5	40.3
Median	39.4	39.4	39.4	35.7	34.2	34.9
Q_1	27.2	26.4	26.8	22.9	21.8	22.3
Q_3	61.7	60.2	60.9	53.2	49.9	51.3
Q_3-Q_1	34.5	33.8	34.1	30.3	28.1	29.0
D_9	89.5	91.9	91.0	74.5	70.3	73.1

Table I (*continued*)

Constant	Lamb			Macaulay		
	A	B	TOTAL	A	B	TOTAL
Mean	26.2	26.3	26.2	22.8	21.4	22.1
Median	18.3	19.6	19.1	18.2	18.9	18.6
Q_1	10.5	11.5	11.0	11.5	12.0	11.7
Q_3	33.3	34.0	33.7	28.2	27.5	27.8
$Q_3–Q_1$	22.8	22.5	22.7	16.7	15.5	16.1
D_9	57.5	53.9	54.9	44.2	39.1	40.6

brings out very well the degree of consistence of each author with himself, and his differences from the others. For samples A and B of Bacon, mean, median, lower quartile, and interquartile range agree within less than a unit, upper quartiles differ by 1.5 units and ninth deciles by 2.4, no very great differences from the practical standpoint especially in the constants most affected by fluctuations of sampling. For Coleridge, the two samples differ by between 1 and 2 units in the case of mean, median, and lower quartile; the upper quartiles differ by 3.3, the interquartile ranges by 2.1, and the ninth deciles by 4.2. For Lamb the differences are less than a unit in the case of mean, upper quartile, and interquartile range, the difference is exactly a unit for the two lower quartiles, 1.3 units for the medians, and 3.6 units for the ninth deciles. For Macaulay the constants seem almost more self-consistent than inspection of the table would lead one to expect. The differences are, for means 1.4, medians 0.7, lower quartiles 0.5, upper quartiles 0.7, interquartile ranges 1.2, ninth deciles 5.1: the lessening of the scatter has affected mainly the ninth decile. For Coleridge all the constants given are lower than the corresponding constants for Bacon, the differences being most conspicuous for the upper quartile and the ninth decile. Comparing Lamb and Macaulay, medians and lower quartiles are the same, but Macaulay's mean, upper quartile, interquartile range and ninth decile are appreciably lower than the corresponding figures for Lamb.

We may conclude accordingly that sentence-length *is* a characteristic of an author's style. There is no discrepancy between the results of our statistical investigation and the judgement made from general impressions. Given similar material and mode of treatment, an author's frequency distribution of sentence-lengths does remain constant within fairly narrow limits. At the same time, it must be admitted, the limits cannot be precisely defined. In case of dispute as to whether two works are or are not by the same author, a judgement based on frequency distributions of sentence-lengths for the two must in the end be a personal one, and founded on such differences as are observed between samples from works known to be by the same author. Hence the importance of the illustrations that have been given.

The test is numerical, but not exact. For there can be no question of applying the ordinary tests based on the theory of simple sampling. The "samples" we have taken are in no sense random samples: they are continuous passages, or collections of continuous passages, and if (as was my practice) the lengths of sentences are written down in order as they occur it is very clear that the resulting numerical series is not a random series but a "clumped" series. Short sentences tend to occur together. The tendency is much clearer for some authors than for others and for Macaulay is a characteristic trick of style, a point being emphasized by a series of hammer-blows from sentences of very few words: for example,

> These are the old friends who are never seen with new faces, who are the same in wealth and in poverty, in glory and in obscurity. With the dead there is no rivalry. In the dead there is no change. Plato is never sullen. Cervantes is never petulant. Demosthenes never comes unseasonably. Dante never stays too long.

Or again,

> The two sections of ambitious men who were struggling for power differed from each other on no important public question. Both belonged to the Established Church. Both professed boundless loyalty to the Queen. Both approved the war with Spain.

It is obvious that a series formed from the lengths of such sentences is not a random one and that consequently differences between samples taken as we have taken them may greatly exceed the limits of *simple sampling* without, for practical purposes, being of any real significance. The differences between the upper quartiles and between the ninth deciles of the two samples from Coleridge, for example, are 10 or 11 times the standard errors, but cannot be regarded as very material.

Appendix of Tables

These tables are all in the same form, showing the numbers of sentences having the length (in words) stated in the left-hand column, in a sample or samples from the source stated in the heading and more fully in the preceding text. Thus, in a sample taken from the first portion of Bacon's *Essays,* column A shows that there was only one sentence (out of 462) of a length between 1 and 5 words, 8 with a length between 6 and 10 words, 24 with a length between 11 and 15 words, and so on. Blank lines have been omitted in the tails of the tables to save space.

Table A

Bacon's *Essays* (1597–1625)
A, first half to end of XXVI. B, second half to end of LI

No. of words	Sentences			No. of words	Sentences		
	A	B	TOTAL		A	B	TOTAL
1– 5	1	2	3	121–125	3	4	7
6– 10	8	8	16	126–130	2	3	5
11– 15	24	25	49	131–135	2	1	3
16– 20	22	23	45	136–140	1	2	3
21– 25	46	53	99	141–145	3	2	5
26– 30	43	42	85	146–150	–	1	1
31– 35	57	55	112	151–155	1	2	3
36– 40	38	37	75	–	–	–	–
41– 45	24	38	62	166–170	–	1	1
46– 50	31	25	56	–	–	–	–
51– 55	23	28	51	186–190	1	–	1
56– 60	25	21	46	191–195	–	–	–
61– 65	19	17	36	196–200	1	–	1
66– 70	12	13	25	–	–	–	–
71– 75	19	8	27	211–215	1	–	1
76– 80	7	11	18	–	–	–	–
81– 85	12	11	23	226–230	–	1	1
86– 90	6	7	13	231–235	–	1	1

Table A (*continued*)

No. of Words	Sentences			No. of Words	Sentences		
	A	B	TOTAL		A	B	TOTAL
91– 95	6	9	15	–	–	–	–
96–100	2	11	13	311–315	–	1	1
101–105	7	3	10				
106–110	9	3	12				
111–115	4	1	5				
116–120	2	4	6	TOTAL	462	474	936

Table B

Coleridge, *Biographia Literaria* (1817)
A, vol. I to p. 134. B, vol. II, pp. 1–66 and 104–end (p. 182)

No. of words	Sentences			No. of words	Sentences		
	A	B	TOTAL		A	B	TOTAL
1– 5	9	2	11	101–105	4	6	10
6– 10	21	37	58	106–110	2	2	4
11– 15	46	44	90	111–115	1	1	2
16– 20	46	49	95	116–120	5	1	6
21– 25	58	73	131	121–125	2	3	5
26– 30	64	56	120	126–130	1	1	2
31– 35	55	57	112	131–135	1	1	2
36– 40	51	52	103	136–140	–	–	–
41– 45	49	52	101	141–145	–	2	2
46– 50	39	37	76	146–150	1	2	3
51– 55	24	29	53	151–155	–	1	1
56– 60	22	23	45	156–160	–	1	1
61– 65	21	18	39	161–165	1	–	1
66– 70	20	17	37	171–175	–	1	1
71– 75	20	9	29	166–170	–	–	–
76– 80	10	6	16	–	–	–	–
81– 85	6	9	15	196–200	1	–	1
86– 90	7	7	14				
91– 95	9	4	13				
96–100	5	3	8	TOTAL	601	606	1207

Table C

Charles Lamb, *Elia* (1823) and *Last Essays of Elia* (1833)
A, *Elia*: from beginning to middle of "Mrs. Battle's Opinions on Whist." B, *Last Essays*: "Detached Thoughts on Books" to "Barbara S—" inclusive

No. of words	Sentences			No. of words	Sentences		
	A	B	TOTAL		A	B	TOTAL
1– 5	29	30	59	81– 85	7	6	13
6–10	115	100	215	86– 90	3	—	3
11–15	111	100	211	91– 95	5	2	7
16–20	61	85	146	96–100	2	1	3
21–25	62	56	118	101–105	3	1	4
26–30	36	46	82	106–110	1	—	1
31–35	36	46	82	111–115	1	1	2
36–40	21	29	50	116–120	1	—	1
41–45	16	19	35	121–125	1	1	2
46–50	19	16	35	126–130	1	2	3
51–55	13	18	31	131–135	1	—	1
56–60	5	6	11	136–140	2	1	3
61–65	15	11	26	—	—	—	—
66–70	2	5	7	171–175	—	1	1
71–75	7	8	15				
76–80	3	8	11	TOTAL	579	599	1178

Table D

Macaulay's *Essays*
A, from first portion of essay on "Lord Bacon" (1837). B, from first portion of essay on "The Earl of Chatham" (1844)

No. of words	Sentences			No. of words	Sentences		
	A	B	TOTAL		A	B	TOTAL
1– 5	26	20	46	71– 75	4	—	4
6–10	100	104	204	76– 80	4	4	8
11–15	126	126	252	81– 85	2	—	2
16–20	89	111	200	86– 90	2	—	2

Table D (*continued*)

No. of Words	Sentences			No. of Words	Sentences		
	A	B	TOTAL		A	B	TOTAL
21–25	82	104	186	91– 95	—	1	1
26–30	51	57	108	96–100	1	1	2
31–35	26	35	61	101–105	1	—	1
36–40	29	39	68	106–110	—	—	—
41–45	16	22	38	111–115	1	—	1
46–50	10	14	24	116–120	—	—	—
51–55	12	8	20	121–125	1	—	1
56–60	9	3	12				
61–65	7	1	8				
66–70	2	—	2	TOTAL	601	650	1251

NOTES

1. Compare, for example, in Hazlitt's *Lectures on the English Comic Writers,* the style of the first essay "On Wit and Humour" with that of the subsequent lectures on definite groups of writers.

2. As offprints at least of this paper may fall into the hands of some who are not statisticians, I may be forgiven for a note of explanation. The arithmetic mean is the common form of average, the sum of the quantities to be averaged divided by their number. Given a frequency distribution, it is calculated on the assumption that all observations falling into any one interval have the mid-value of that interval, e.g. that all sentences in the interval 6–10 are eight words long: this gives quite a close approximation. The lower quartile is the sentence-length such that one quarter of all sentences are shorter and three quarters longer. But sentence-lengths are discontinuous: sentences of 25 words or less might be less than a quarter of the whole, sentences of 26 words or less more than a quarter; hence some convention is necessary if a precise value is to be stated. The convention is that given in text above, and we proceed by simple interpolation. Thus in the total distribution of Table A the total number of sentences is 936, one quarter of which is 234. The first four frequencies up to and including sentences of 25 words, or up to the conventional limit 25.5, give a total of 212, and accordingly we require 22 more. There are 85 in the next interval, which is an

interval of five words, and the lower quartile is therefore approximately

$$25.5 + \frac{22}{85} \times 5 = 26.8.$$

The upper quartile, the value exceeded by only one-quarter of the observations, and the ninth decile, the value exceeded by only one-tenth, are similarly determined.

A. C. BRADLEY

Monosyllabic Lines and Words

The origin of this paper was as follows. One day, when I had no book by me, I was amusing myself by recalling passages in Shakespeare; and one of these was Hamlet's farewell to Horatio:

> If thou didst ever hold me in thy heart,
> Absent thee from felicity awhile,
> And in this harsh world draw thy breath in pain,
> To tell my story.

I was struck by the difference between the second and the third of these lines; one of them having five words, and the other ten, while the former has two "Latin" words, and the latter none.[1] And then I noticed that all the words of the latter are of one syllable.

Thereupon I amused myself by recalling such monosyllabic lines in other plays; and when I had a Shakespeare by me I found invariably a considerable number of them, and in some plays as many as two hundred. An examination of dramas by writers contemporary with Shakespeare, and later, gave, in various degrees, the same result.

Meanwhile, however, I naturally asked myself whether such lines occur in non-English dramas, and, if so, to what extent. The Greek, Latin, and Italian plays examined showed none. Some by

From *A Miscellany* (Macmillan, 1929), pp. 245–67. Reprinted by permission of the publisher.

Corneille, Racine, and Molière yielded but a few (never more, I think, than ten); and this could not be fully explained by the fact that the lines here have six accents, while those counted in the English plays are of five. But in German dramas of five-accent lines the case is altered. In Goethe's *Tasso* I counted thirty-six; in Schiller's *Don Carlos* twenty-one; and in Lessing's *Nathan* almost seventy (but the percentage is only about two).

The main conclusion to be drawn from the examination of plays was that English drama is markedly peculiar in the prevalence of monosyllabic lines.

Turning next to non-dramatic verse, and confining my study to English, I made a record of such lines in poems of five-accent lines, from Shakespeare to Bridges. Then I made a special study of Shakespeare's plays; and, finally, I dealt with prose. First, I compared short passages by foreign atuhors with English translations of them, my object here being two-fold: (1) to find the proportions of monosyllabic words and of other words in the foreign original and in the translation; (2) to find in each the *number* of words, monosyllabic and other, this number proving to be much the higher in the English translation. Afterwards, I compared English authors with one another as regards the prevalence of monosyllabic words.

Poems

The following list, referred to in this paper as the *Main List*, shows the percentage of monosyllabic lines in poems (or parts of poems) of lines of five accents. When a poem contains lines of more, or less, than five accents, these lines are ignored.

		Total lines.	Mono. lines.	Percentage.
SHAKESPEARE	*Venus and Adonis,* stanzas			
	1–50	300	30	10
	Sonnets, 1–50	700	63	9
SPENSER	*Fairy Queen,* I. v. stanzas 1–23	184	6	3.2
	Astrophel	216	14	6.4
MILTON	*Paradise Lost,* I. ll. 1–270	270	11	4.07
	Lycidas	178	6	3.3
DRYDEN	*Absalom and Achitophel,* ll.			
	1–229	229	6	2.6

		Total lines.	Mono. lines.	Percentage.
	Macflecknoe	217	8	3.6
POPE	Essay on Man, 1.	294	10	3.4
	Epistle to Arbuthnot, ll. 1–214	214	19	8.8
GRAY	Elegy written in a Country Churchyard	128	3	2.3
COWPER	Receipt of my Mother's Picture	121	9	7.4
CRABBE	The Frank Courtship, ll. 1–210	210	5	2.3
WORDSWORTH	Tintern Abbey	160	7	4.3
	Michael, ll. 1–159	159	10	6.2
COLERIDGE	Destiny of Nations, ll. 1–269	269	7	2.5
	Lines on an Autumnal Evening	106	2	1.8
SCOTT	Harold the Dauntless, VI. i.–vi.	108	5	4.5
BYRON	Corsair, ll. 1–192	192	11	5.7
	Vision of Judgment, i.–xx.	160	15	9.3
SHELLEY	Epipsychidion, ll. 1–146	146	11	7.5
	Triumph of Life, ll. 1–258	258	16	6.2
KEATS	Isabella, ll. 1–120	120	8	6.6
	Hyperion, ll. 1–134	134	6	4.4
TENNYSON	Passing of Arthur, ll. 1–153	153	24	15
	Gardener's Daughter, ll. 1–140	140	16	11.4
BROWNING	Pauline, ll. 1–140	140	28	20
	Ring and Book : The Pope, ll. 1–197	197	10	5.07
ARNOLD	Sohrab and Rustum, ll. 1–153	153	22	14.3
	Thyrsis	216	16	7.4
SWINBURNE	Laus Veneris, ll. 1–120	120	28	23.3
	Tiresias, ll. 1–120	120	18	15
MORRIS	The man who never laughed again, ll. 1–140	140	23	16.4
	Defence of Guenevere, ll. 1–129	129	19	14.7
BRIDGES	Eros and Psyche, August	217	26	11.9
	Growth of Love, Sonnets 1–9	126	16	12.6

NOTES ON THE MAIN LIST

It may naturally be objected to this list that, owing to the shortness of the passages used, one cannot be sure that they represent fairly the practice of the authors. This is true; but I may say that at first I used much longer passages, and that the percentage results were almost identical with those of the present record.

The reader, again, may ask why the list begins with Spenser and Shakespeare, and not with Chaucer. The main reason is that, for the purpose of the list, the poets from Spenser and Shakespeare onwards are fairly on a level, since almost any word which is monosyllabic in these poets is so in Pope or Tennyson. But a host of words which are always monosyllabic in these poets are not so in Chaucer. For instance, there are three such words in a single line of the Prologue to the *Canterbury Tales:*

The tendre croppes and the yonge sonne.[2]

It may be asked, lastly, why the record ignores the long interval between Chaucer and Spenser. The reason is that I wished the Main List to be short, and to deal only with authors with whom the reader would certainly be familiar. This could hardly be said even of the leading Scottish poets of this interval; but some of these poets, with others of less note, are recorded in an Additional List.

I will now add some notes on the Main List, beginning with two salient points, before coming to particular authors. (1) It will be seen that the Shakespeare percentages are not reached or nearly approached again till we come to Byron. As to this I can only suggest, as possible, that Shakespeare's vocabulary was less influenced by literary study, especially of Latin poetry, than that of the later poets, and that it was also influenced by the dramas of his predecessors and by his own concern with the theatre; for the dialogue of persons in a play usually yields a larger number of monosyllabic lines than does the narrative of a poet. (2) Perhaps the most salient fact in the list is the very marked superiority of the percentages beginning wtih Tennyson and Browning to those of the poets immediately preceding them. I cannot suggest any explanation of this fact.

The following are notes on the records for some of the authors. Milton: *Paradise Regained* has the percentage 4.1; *Comus,* 2.9; the Sonnets, 7.5. Dryden: the percentages in everything examined are low. Pope: *Rape of the Lock,* about 3, but *Eloisa to Abelard,* 7.6. Crabbe: in all tales examined less than 3. Wordsworth: the percentages in the *Prelude* and *Excursion,* so far as examined, are much lower than those in the list. Coleridge: the percentages in all poems examined are low. Byron: in *Cain*, Act I., the percentage about 12. Shelley: in *The Cenci*, Act v., almost 10. Keats: *Isabella*, the *whole* poem, 3.3; *Lamia*, 5.3. Tennyson: *Dora*, about 21. Browning: *A death in the desert*, 13.3; *Lippo Lippi*, 17.3.

The following list shows the percentage of monosyllabic lines in passages by some poets not included in the Main List:

LYNDSAY	*Testament of the Papyngo*, 150–345	2.5
DUNBAR	*Merle and Nichtingale*	5.8
MARLOWE	*Hero and Leander*, Sestiad I.	3.9
DRAYTON	*Legend of Matilda*, 1–175	4.6
JONSON	*Elegy on Lady V. Digby*	10.1
DONNE	*Elegies*, I.–IV.	12.2
SOUTHEY	*Joan of Arc*, Book IX.	3
BROWNING, E. B.	*Aurora Leigh*, 1–214	4.2
ROSSETTI, D. G.	*A Last Confession*, 1–141	19.8
MEREDITH, G.	*Modern Love*, I.–X.	11.2
SWINBURNE	*Ave atque Vale*	13.4

The following are examples of very low percentages (alexandrines ignored):

AKENSIDE	*Pleasures of Imagination*, Book I.	1.1
COWPER	*The Task*, Book I.	1.5
THOMSON	*The Seasons*, Spring	0.8
	Autumn	0.5
JOHNSON	*Vanity of Human Wishes*	1.3
GOLDSMITH	*Traveller*	1.5
BURNS	*Cotter's Saturday Night*	1.1
SCOTT	*Vision of Don Roderick*	1.7
LANDOR	*Gebir*, Books III.–V.	0.8
CAMPBELL	*Pleasures of Hope*, Part I.	1.7
COLERIDGE	*Religious Musings*	1.4

NOTE ON NARRATIVE POEMS

In a drama the dramatist makes the persons or characters speak, but does not himself speak. In a narrative poem the poet himself may be said to be speaking when he describes scenes or persons, or narrates events or actions. But, in addition, he may make the persons or characters speak. In that case, it will be found, the percentage of monosyllabic lines is almost always (perhaps always) higher in these speeches than in the passages where the poet is speaking.

The following are some examples:

		Narrative.	Speeches.
SHAKESPEARE	*Venus and Adonis*, 1–300	6.7	14.4
SPENSER	*Fairy Queen*, III. ii.	3	6.6
MILTON	*Paradise Lost*, I.	1.8	5
POPE	*Rape of the Lock*	2.8	3.4
WORDSWORTH	*Hartleap Well*	4	8.4
BYRON	*Vision of Judgment*	5.9	11
SHELLEY	*Rovolt of Islam*, XI.	4	12.5
KEATS	*Isabella*	2	11.4
TENNYSON	*Morte d'Arthur*, 1–272	6.6	13.1
MORRIS	*Man who never laughed again*	5.7	25.7
BRIDGES	*Eros and Psyche*, June	5.3	14.1

Shakespeare

In these records, to economize space, I have referred to the plays by the capital letters of their titles; *e.g.* "T" for *The Tempest*.

The following are examples of monosyllabic lines. The plays used are in the order of the Folio and of most of the current editions:

T.	This is as strange a maze as e'er men trod.
MM.	Ay, but to die, and go we know not where.
MND.	Love looks not with the eyes, but with the mind.
MV.	In sooth, I know not why I am so sad.
AY.	As I do live by food, I met a fool.
AW.	It is not so with Him that all things knows
	As 'tis with us that square our guess by shows.
TN.	Oh, it came o'er my ear like the sweet south.
WT.	We were as twinn'd lambs that did frisk i' the sun.
KJ.	How oft the sight of means to do ill deeds
	Makes ill deeds done! Hads't not thou been by,
2 *H* 4.	O God! that one might read the book of fate.
H 5.	God's will! I pray thee, wish not one man more.
Cor.	These eyes are not the same I wore in Rome.
JC.	My heart doth joy that yet in all my life
	I found no man but he was true to me.

AC.	Fall not a tear, I say; one of them rates
	All that is won and lost: give me a kiss.
KL.	You do me wrong, to take me out o' the grave.
	Thou art a soul in bliss; but I am bound
Cym.	False to his bed! What is it, to be false?
	To lie in watch there, and to think on him?
M.	What hands are here? Ha! they pluck out mine eyes.
H.	I do not set my life at a pin's fee;
	And, for my soul, what can it do to that?
RJ.	O then, I see, Queen Mab hath been with you.
O.	Keep up your bright swords, for the dew will rust them.

The following are examples of passages consisting mainly of monosyllabic lines:

I

King.	This ring, you say, was yours?
Dian.	Ay, my good lord.
King.	Where did you buy it, or who gave it you?
Dian.	It was not given me, nor I did not buy it.
King.	Who lent it you?
Dian.	It was not lent me neither.
King.	Where did you find it, then?
Dian.	I found it not.
King.	If it were yours by none of all these ways,
	How could you give it him?
Dian.	I never gave it him.
King.	This ring was mine: I gave it his first wife.
Dian.	It might be yours, or hers, for aught I know.

All's well that ends well, v. iii. 271.

II

Oliv.	I prithee, tell me what thou think'st of me.
Vio.	That you do think you are not what you are.
Oliv.	If I think so, I think the same of you.
Vio.	Then think you right: I am not what I am.
Oliv.	I would you were as I would have you be!
Vio.	Would it be better, madam, than I am?

I wish it might, for now I am your fool.

Twelfth Night, III. i. 150.

III

Nurse.   Fie, how my bones ache! what a jaunt have I had!
Jul.   I would thou hadst my bones, and I thy news.
         Nay, come, I pray thee, speak: good, good nurse, speak.
Nurse.   Jesu, what haste? can you not stay awhile?
         Do you not see that I am out of breath?
Jul.   How art thou out of breath, when thou hast breath
         To say to me that thou art out of breath?

Romeo and Juliet, II. v. 26.

RECORD OF PLAYS

In this record I have ignored some of the plays, in order to confine the inquiry to what may be called the unmitigated Shakespeare. In dealing with the remaining plays I have given the number of mono-syllabic lines of five accents, both those in blank verse and those in rhyme. And I have recorded also the percentage of these lines in the total of blank-verse lines of five accents in each play, this total being that given by Fleay as revised by him in Ingleby's *Shakespeare, the Man and his Book.*[3] In counting the monosyllabic lines I used the "Universal" edition of Shakespeare (Warne & Co.), as its print is somewhat larger than that of the "Globe."

I have not attempted to deal fully with the rhymed lines; but an experiment with three plays (*MV, TN, MM*) showed that the per-centage of monosyllabic lines in Fleay's total of rhymed lines in these plays is 10.6, and that they often occur in a couplet ending a scene.

	Number of Monosyllabic blank-verse lines.	Percentage.	Monosyllabic Rhymed lines.
T.	114	8.2	5
TGV.	97	6.8	2
MM.	95	6.4	5
CE.	90	7.7	26
MA.	56	9.06	2
LLL.	36	5.8	96
MND.	61	8.3	67

	Number of Monosyllabic blank-verse lines.	Percentage.	Monosyllabic Rhymed lines.
MV.	145	7.7	10
AY.	82	9.4	4
AW.	83	7.05	42
TN.	55	7.59	11
WT.	152	7.8	3
KJ.	189	7.8	24
R 2.	141	6.4	71
1 H 4.	119	7.6	4
2 H 4.	120	8.4	5
H 5.	72	3.7	8
R 3.	223	6.8	9
TC.	98	4.7	28
Cor.	172	7.1	6
RJ.	202	9.8	56
JC.	166	7.6	5
M.	136	8.5	18
H.	195	8.2	11
KL.	180	8.6	5
O.	233	9.7	8
AC.	201	7.7	2
Cym.	215	8.4	17

The following shows the order of the plays in regard to the prevalence of monosyllabic blank-verse lines:

RJ.	9.8	MV.	7.7
O.	9.7	AC.	7.7
AY.	9.4	1 H 4.	7.6
MA.	9.06	JC.	7.6
KL.	8.6	TN.	7.59
M.	8.5	Cor.	7.1
2 H 4.	8.4	AW.	7.05
Cym.	8.4	R 3.	6.8
MND.	8.3	TG.	6.8
T.	8.2	R 2.	6.4
H.	8.2	MM.	6.4
KJ.	7.8	LLL.	5.8
WT.	7.8	TC.	4.7
CE.	7.7	H 5.	3.7

NOTES

The Histories, on the whole, have lower percentages than the Comedies and Tragedies. Five of the eight Tragedies have high percentages. The following plays are near one another both in date and in percentages: *AY* and *MA*; *KL* and *M*; *T* and *WT*; *TGV*, *R* 3, *R* 2.

We may now ask: In what kind of passage, and in what kind of speech, is the monosyllabic line frequent or rare?

The main answer is that it tends to be frequent in animated dialogue, whether serious, commonplace, or comic, and perhaps specially frequent when the speeches are short; and that it is, on the whole, infrequent in more or less long speeches (whether soliloquies or not), and perhaps specially infrequent when they convey information to the audience concerning a "situation" or a character. But when a long speech is animated by the movement of thought or imagination or passion, the monosyllabic line may be frequent.

The rarity of these lines in passages mainly conveying information may be illustrated from the opening scenes in some of the plays. I took at random *CE, MM, R* 2, 1 *H* 4, *H* 5, *R* 3. The first scenes in these plays have 36 monosyllabic lines in a total of 814 lines; *i.e.* a percentage of only 4.4.

Instances of the frequency of monosyllabic lines in long speeches of a certain kind may be found in *Hamlet* and *Othello*. Hamlet's soliloquy, "How all occasions do inform against me," has six in thirty-five complete lines; and the soliloquy, "O what a rogue and peasant slave am I," has seven in fifty-four. Othello's soliloquy, "It is the cause," has five in twenty-one; and again the speech, "Behold, I have a weapon," has three in twenty-one. But there is much animation or passion in all these speeches.

It may be worth while to record here the result of an earlier experiment, made to test a vague impression that decidedly long speeches have exceptionally few monosyllabic lines. For this purpose I took a "long" speech to be one of thirty-five, or more, lines. I then ascertained the total of the lines contained in the whole of these "long" speeches in the plays dealt with, and also the number and percentage of monosyllabic lines in this total. The percentage proved to be five.

That this percentage is very low the reader will see if he refers to the list of the plays,[4] where he will find that only two of them have a percentage so low, while four of them have one of nine, seven one of eight, ten one of seven, and four one of six. The remainder are *Love's Labour's Lost* (5.8), *Troilus and Cressida* (4.7), and *Henry V* (3.7).

APPENDIX

The following list records the percentage of monosyllabic lines in plays, or parts of plays, of the time of Shakespeare and later. Where, as too often, the edition of a play has not numbered lines the percentage is only approximate.

MARLOWE	*Edward II.*	7.4
GREENE	*James IV.*	7.2
BEAUMONT and		
FLETCHER	*Philaster,* v.	10
JONSON	*Sejanus,* I.	6.2
WEBSTER	*White Devil,* I. ii.	7.3
MASSINGER	*Duke of Milan,* III. i.	3.3
FORD	*'Tis pity she's a whore,* II. iii. v.	7.3
DRYDEN	*All for Love,* I.	7
CONGREVE	*Mourning Bride,* I.	6.6
COLERIDGE	*Remorse,* I.	7
SHELLEY	*The Cenci,* I.	8.6
BYRON	*Cain,* I.	12
TENNYSON	*Becket,* v.	14.1
BROWNING	*Strafford,* v. ii.	13.4
SWINBURNE	*Mary Stuart,* I. i.	19
BRIDGES	*Achilles in Scyros,* 1–195, and 616–787	13.1
YEATS	*The Countess Cathleen,* I. and II.	13.6

It will be seen that, as with the record of Poems, the highest percentages are to be found in works of the nineteenth and twentieth centuries.

Prose

ENGLISH AND OTHER LANGUAGES

The object of this record is two-fold: (1) to ascertain the proportion of monosyllabic and of other words in passages of Englsh and of some foreign languages; (2) to ascertain the *number* of words, monosyllabic and other, in these passages.

The method is to compare a passage in a foreign language with an English translation of it.

It is obvious that a short passage cannot safely be taken as adequately representing the characteristics of a language or an author; but it may be of use for the particular purpose of this inquiry, and I may add that, in all cases, the passage has been chosen after a comparison with several others. The English translations are not my own.

	Mono. words.	The rest.	Total words.	Percentage Mono.	Percentage rest.
THUCYDIDES	37	53			
GREEK TESTAMENT	19	63			
	56	116	172	32.5	67.4
English Translation	104	52			
	89	25			
	193	77	270	71.1	28.5
TACITUS	12	50			
VULGATE	30	73			
	42	123	165	25.4	74.4
English Translation	79	32			
	122	32			
	201	64	265	75.8	24.1
DANTE	42	87			
BOCCACCIO	33	74			
	75	161	236	31.7	68.2
English Translation	118	40			
	98	26			
	216	66	282	76.5	23.4
MONTAIGNE	68	32			
PASCAL	53	32			
	121	64	185	65.4	34.5
English Translation	84	32			
	75	32			
	159	64	223	71.3	28.6

	Mono. words.	The rest.	Total words.	Percentage Mono.	Percentage rest.
GOETHE	51	47			
LESSING	51	37			
	102	84	186	54.8	45.1
English Translation	64	38			
	74	25			
	138	63	201	68.6	31.3

NOTES

(1) The percentage of monosyllabic words in the total of foreign words in this record is 41.9; their percentage in the total of English words 72.8.

As regards this percentage the order of the languages, from highest to lowest, is English, French, German, Greek, Italian, Latin. The Greek and Italian are very near one another; the French and German not so.

It will be seen that the very low percentage of Latin is due to the passage of Tacitus. I therefore examined four other passages in his *Histories,* and found the percentage in them, taken together, to be 16.4. The percentage in some passages of Cicero was 21.1, which is still decidedly lower than those of the other languages. A passage of Livy gave a percentage of 17.1.

(2) *Number* of words. It appears at once from the record that, in general, the number of words is much larger in the English translations than in the foreign originals. The following are the details:

	Total.	Foreign.	Percentage.	English.	Percentage.
Greek-English	442	172	38.9	270	61.08
Latin-English	430	165	38.3	265	61.6
Italian-English	518	236	45.5	282	54.4
French-English	408	185	45.3	223	54.6
German-English	387	186	48.06	201	51.9
	2185	944	43.2	1241	56.7

It will be seen that, as regards the total of words in the passages used, the English superiority in number of words is almost the same in relation to Greek and to Latin, and again in relation to Italian and to French; that this superiority is decidedly largest in relation to Greek and Latin, and smallest in relation to German; and that, in this matter, there is only a minute difference between Greek and Latin, and between Italian and French.

Postscript. When I had brought this work to an end, it struck me that it might be worth while to see if I could with ease write a few lines in which there was no word of more than one syllable; and the lines that I write now seem to show that I could have done this with ease if I could have thought of a word of one syllable which meant the same as the word "syllable."

This paragraph, which *was* written "with ease," contains seventy-seven words, all of which, except "syllable," are of one syllable.

ENGLISH AUTHORS

The following is a record of the monosyllabic and non-monosyllabic words in passages taken from the works of authors of the seventeenth and following centuries.

In preparing this record I naturally chose such passages as I thought characteristic of the authors; and, if the result in any degree surprised me, I examined other passages. But my main interest was not with the particular authors, but with the *total* result.

	Mono. words.	Other words.		Mono. words.	Other words.
HOOKER	70	27	BURKE	68	30
BACON	77	30	AUSTEN	67	27
CLARENDON	73	29	SCOTT	69	37
MILTON	78	30	LANDOR	66	28
BUNYAN	78	25	LAMB	75	32
DEFOE	96	11	CARLYLE	84	33
ADDISON	79	24	RUSKIN	70	18
STEELE	73	33	MACAULAY	71	36
RICHARDSON	74	32	THACKERAY	68	22
FIELDING	71	27	ARNOLD, M.	70	29
STERNE	73	18			
GIBBON	60	41	Total	1756	681
JOHNSON	66	43	Percentage	72.05	27.9
GOLDSMITH	80	19			

It will be seen that the percentage of monosyllabic words in this record is almost identical with the 72.8 of the English words in the record for English and foreign languages.

In the present list the higher and the lower percentages would be found, on the whole, where we should expect them. Defoe has the highest, and next come Sterne, Goldsmith, Addison, and Bunyan. On the other hand the passages from Gibbon and Johnson have percentages of only 60; and some, taken later, from Hume, Bentham, and Butler, fall short of 70.

In experimenting with Burke I found great differences in different passages, the number of monosyllabic words being sometimes high. I owe to a friend a short extract containing 42 in a total of 46. But this, unlike the passage used in my record, occurs in a speech.

The comparatively low percentage, about 65, in the passage from Scott surprised me; but I found it fairly constant, and that even in passages of rapid dialogue. I may add that, in dealing with novelists, I avoided such passages, as they naturally tend (as in drama) to a free use of small words.

After completing this record I looked at some authors earlier than Hooker, with this result: More, 53 and 25; Latimer, 72 and 19; Ascham, 74 and 16; Knox, 70 and 13; Foxe, 75 and 26. The percentage of monosyllabic words in the total is a little more than 77, higher than that in the main list.

The following are figures for passages in authors of the nineteenth century not dealt with in the list: Dickens, 84 and 20; George Eliot, 76 and 31; Newman, 92 and 23; Emerson, 81 and 18; Stevenson, 82 and 24. The percentage of monosyllabic words in the total is about 78.

NOTES

1. The word "pain" comes *ultimately* from Latin.
2. In four long passages in various poems by Chaucer I found the following percentages: 1.5, 1.3, 1.06, 2.7.
3. The reader interested in this matter should ignore the figures given in Fleay's *Shakespeare Manual*, 1876, p. 135.
4. It should be observed that this list deals only with blank-verse lines, while the "long" speeches dealt with in the "experiment" may contain rhymed lines as well as blank. But I have no reason to think that this difference is important.

☙

From Shakespeare to Modernism

OTTO JESPERSEN

≮

Shakespeare and the Language of Poetry

In this chapter I shall endeavour to characterize the language of the greatest master of English poetry and make some observations in regard to his influence on the English language as well as in regard to poetic and archaic language generally. But it must be distinctly understood that I shall concern myself with *language* and not with literary *style*. It is true that the two things cannot be completely kept apart, but as far as possible I shall deal only with what are really philological as opposed to literary problems.

Shakespeare's vocabulary is often stated to be the richest ever employed by any single man. It has been calculated to comprise 21,000 words ("rough calculation, found in Mrs. Clark's Concordance . . . without counting inflected forms as distinct words," Craik), or, according to others, 24,000 or 15,000. In order to appreciate what that means we must look a little at the various statements that have been given of the number of words used by other authors and by ordinary beings, educated and not educated. Unfortunately these statements are in many cases given and repeated without any indication of the manner in which they have been arrived at. Milton's vocabulary is said to comprise 7,000 or 8,000 words, that of the Iliad and Odyssey taken together 9,000, that of the Old Testament 5,642, and that

From *Growth and Structure of the English Language,* first published in Leipzig in 1905, from the last revised edition (Blackwell's, 1948), pp. 199–221. Reprinted by permission of the publisher.

of the New Testament 4,800; A. S. Cook (in *The Nation,* Sept. 12, 1912) computes the vocabulary of the English Authorized Version at 6,568 words, or at 9,884, if inflected forms of nouns, pronouns, or verbs are included.

Max Müller says that a farm-labourer uses only 300 words, and Wood that "the average man uses about five hundred words" (adding "it is appalling to think how pitiably we have degenerated from the copiousness of our ancestors"), and the same statements are found in writings by Abel, Sütterlin and other philologists. But both figures are obviously wrong. One two-year-old girl had 489 and another 1,121 words, while Mrs. Winfield S. Hall's boy used in his seventeenth month 232 different words and, when six years old, 2,688 words, at least, for it is probable that the mother and her assistants, who noted down every word they heard the child use, even so did not get hold of its whole vocabulary. Now, are we really to believe that the linguistic range of a grown-up man, however humble, is considerably smaller than that of a two-year-old child of educated parents or is only one-seventh of that of a six-year-old boy! Any one going through the lists given by Mrs. Hall will feel quite certain that no labourer contents himself with so scanty a vocabulary. School-books for teaching foreign languages often include some 700 words in the first year's course; yet on how few subjects of everyday occurrence are our pupils able to converse after one year's teaching. Sweet also contradicts the statement about 300 words, saying "When we find a missionary in Tierra del Fuego compiling a dictionary of 30,000 words in the Yaagan language—that is, a hundred times as many—we cannot give any credence to this statement, especially if we consider the number of names of different parts of a waggon or a plough, and all the words required in connexion even with a single agricultural operation, together with names of birds, plants, and other natural objects." Smedberg, who has investigated the vocabulary of Swedish peasants and who emphasizes its richness in technical terms, arrives at the result that 26,000 is probably too small a figure, and the Danish and French dialectologists Kristensen and Duraffour completely endorse this view. Professor E. S. Holden tested himself by a reference to all the words in Webster's Dictionary, and found that his own vocabulary comprised 33,456 words. And E. H. Babbitt writes: "I tried to get at the vocabulary of adults and made experiments, chiefly with my students, to see how many English words each knew. . . . My plan was to take a considerable number of pages from the dictionary at random, count the number of words on those pages which the subject of the experiment could define without any context, and work out a proportion to get an approximation of the entire number of words in the dictionary known. The results were surprising for two reasons. In the size of the vocabulary of such students the outside variations were less than 20 per cent, and their vocabulary was much larger than I had expected to find. The majority reported a little below 60,000 words." People who had never been to college, but, with an ordinary common school education, were regular readers of books and periodicals, according to the same writer reported generally from 25,000 to 35,000 words, though some went higher, even to 50,000.

These statements are easily reconciled with the ascription of 20,000 words to Shakespeare. For it must be remembered that in the case of each of us there is a great difference between the words *known* (especially those of which he has a reading knowledge) and the words actually *used* in conversation. And then, there must always be a great many words which a man will use readily in conversation, but which will never occur in his writings, simply because the subjects on which a man addresses the public are generally much less varied than those he has to talk about every day.[1] How many authors have occasion to use in their books even the most familiar names of garden tools or common dishes or kitchen implements? If Milton as a poet uses only 8,000 against Shakespeare's 20,000 words, this is a natural consequence of the narrower range of his subjects, and it is easy to prove that his vocabulary really contained many more than the 8,000 words found in a Concordance to his poetical works. We have only to take any page of his prose writings, and we shall meet with a great many words not in the Concordance.[2]

The greatness of Shakespeare's mind is therefore not shown by the fact that he was acquainted with 20,000 words, but by the fact that he wrote about so great a variety of subjects and touched upon so many human facts and relations that he needed this number of words in his writings.[3] His remarkable familiarity with technical expressions in many different spheres has often been noticed, but there are other facts with regard to his use of words that have not been remarked or not sufficiently remarked. His reticence about religious matters, which has given rise to the most divergent theories of his religious belief, is shown strikingly in the fact that such words as *Bible, Holy Ghost* and *Trinity* do not occur at all in his writings, while *Jesus* (Jesu), *Christ* and *Christmas* are found only in some of his earliest plays; *Saviour* occurs only once (in *Hamlet*), and *Creator* only in two of the dubious plays (3 *Henry VI* and *Troilus*).[4]

Of far greater importance is his use of language to individualize the characters in his plays. In this he shows a much finer and subtler art than some modern novelists, who make the same person continually use the same stock phrase or phrases. Even where he resorts to the same tricks as other authors he varies them more; Mrs. Quickly and Dogberry do not misapply words from the classical languages in the same way. The everyday speech of the artisans in *A Midsummer Night's Dream* is comic in a different manner from the diction they use in their play within the play, which serves Shakespeare to ridicule some linguistic artifices employed in good faith by many of his contemporaries (alliteration, bombast). Shakespeare is not entirely exempt from the fashionable affectation of his days known as Euphuism, but it must be noticed that he is superior to its worst aberrations and he satirizes them, not only in *Love's Labour's Lost*, but also in many other places. Euphuistic expressions are generally put in the mouth of some subordinate character who has nothing to do except to announce some trifling incident, relate a little of the circumstances that lead up to the action of the play, deliver a message from a king, etc. It is not improbable that the company possessed some actor who knew how to make small parts funny by imitating fashionable affectation, and we can imagine that it was he who acted Osric in *Hamlet*, and by his vocabulary and appearance exposed himself to the scoffs of the Danish prince, and the nameless gentleman in *Lear*, III, sc. 1, and IV, sc. 3. But the messenger from Antony in *Julius Cæsar* (III, 1, 122) speaks in a totally different strain and gives us a sort of foretaste of Antony's eloquence. And how different again—I am speaking here of subordinate parts only—are the gardeners in *Richard the Second* (III, sc. 4) with their characteristic application of botanical similes to politics and vice versa. And thus one might go on, for no author has shown greater skill in adapting language to character.

A modern reader, however, is sure to miss many of the *nuances* that were felt instinctively by the poet's contemporaries. A great many words have now another value than they had then; in some cases it is only a slightly different colouring, but in others the diversity is greater, and only a close study of Elizabethan usage can bring out the exact value of each word. A *bonnet* then meant a man's cap or hat; Lear walks unbonneted. To *charm* always implied magic power, to make invulnerable by witchcraft, to call forth by spells, etc.; "charming words" were magic words and not simply delightful words as in our days. *Notorious* might be used in a good sense as "well-known"; *censure,* too, was a colourless word ("And your name is great In mouthes of wisest censure" (*Othello* II, 3, 193). The same is true of *succeed* and *success,* which now imply what Shakespeare several times calls "good success," whereas he also knows "bad success"; cf. "the effects he writes of succeede unhappily," *Lear,* I, 2, 157. *Companion* was often used in a bad sense, like *fellow* now, and inversely *sheer,* which is now used with such words as "folly, nonsense," had kept the original meaning of "pure," as in "thou sheere, immaculate, and silver fountaine" (*Richard II,* V, 3, 61). *Politician* seems always to imply intriguing or scheming, and *remorse* generally means pity or sympathy. *Accommodate* evidently did not belong to ordinary language, but was considered affected; *occupy* and *activity* were at least half-vulgar, while on the other hand *wag* (vb.) was then free from its present trivial or ludicrous associations ("Untill my eielids will no longer wag," *Hamlet* V, 1, 290, see Dowden's note to this passage). *Assassination* (only *Macbeth* I, 7, 2) would then call up the memory of the "Assasines, a company of most desperat and dangerous men among the Mahometans" (Knolles, *Hist. Turks,* 1603) or "That bloudy sect of Sarazens, called Assassini, who, without feare of torments, undertake . . . the murther of any eminent Prince, impugning their irreligion" (Speed, 1611, quoted *NED*).

Even adverbs might then have another colouring than their present signification. *Now-a-days* was a vulgar word; it is used by no one in Shakespeare except Bottom, the grave-digger in *Hamlet,* and a fisherman in *Pericles.* The adverb *eke,* in the nineteenth century a poetic word, seems to have been a comic expression; it occurs only three times in Shakespeare (twice in the *Merry Wives,* used by Pistol and the Host, once by Flute in *Midsummer Night's Dream*); Milton and Pope avoid the word. The synonym *also* is worth noticing. Shakespeare uses it only 22 times, and nearly always puts it in the mouth of vulgar or affected persons (Dogberry twice in *Much Ado,* the Clown once in *Winter's Tale,* the Second Lord in *As You Like It* II, sc. 2, the Second Lord in *Timon* III, sc. 6, the affected Captain in *Twelfth Night* I, sc. 2; the knight in *Lear*

I, 4, 66, may belong here too; further Pistol twice in grandiloquent speeches, 2 *Henry IV* II, 4, 171 and V, 3, 145, and two of Shakespeare's Welshmen, Evans three times, and Fluellen twice). It is used twice in solemn and official speeches (*Henry V* I, 2, 77, where Canterbury expounds lex Salica, and IV, 6, 10), and it is, therefore, highly characteristic that Falstaff uses the word twice in his Euphuistic impersonation of the king (*1 Henry IV* II, 4, 440 and 459) and twice in similar speeches in the *Merry Wives* (V, 1, 24, and V, 5, 7).

Shylock is one of Shakespeare's most interesting creations, even from the point of view of language. Although Sir Sidney Lee has shown that there were Jews in England in those times and that, consequently, Shakespeare need not have gone outside his own country in order to see models for Shylock, the number of Jews cannot have been sufficient for his hearers to be very familiar with the Jewish type, and no Anglo-Jewish dialect or mode of speech had developed which Shakespeare could put into Shylock's mouth and so make him at once recognizable for what he was. I have not, indeed, been able to discover a single trait in Shylock's language that can be called distinctly Jewish. And yet Shakespeare has succeeded in creating for Shylock a language different from that of anybody else. Shylock has his Old Testament at his fingers' ends, he defends his own way of making money breed by a reference to Jacob's thrift in breeding parti-coloured lambs, he swears by Jacob's staff and by our holy sabbath, and he calls Lancelot "that foole of Hagars off-spring." [5] We have an interesting bit of Jewish figurative language in "my houses eares, I meane my casements" (II, 5, 34). Shylock uses some biblical words which do not occur elsewhere in Shakespeare: *synagogue, Nazarite* and *publican; pilled* in "The skilful shepheard pil'd me certain wands" is a reminiscence from Genesis XXX, 37. But more often Shylock is characterized by being made to use words or constructions a little different from the accepted use of Shakespeare's time.[6] He dislikes the word *interest* and prefers calling it *advantage* or *thrift* ("my well-worne thrift, which he cals interrest," I, 3, 52), and instead of *usury* he says *usance*. Furness quotes *Wylson on Usurye,* 1572, p. 32, "usurie and double usurie, the merchants termyng it *usance* and double usance, by a more clenlie name"—this word thus ranks in the same category as *dashed* or *d–d* for *damned*: instead of pronouncing an objectionable word in full one begins as if one were about to pronounce it and then shunts off on another track. Shylock uses the plural *moneys,* which is very rare in Shakespeare, he says an *equal* pound for "exact," *rheum* (rume) for "saliva," *estimable* for "valuable," *fulsome* for "rank" (the only instance of that signification discovered by the editors of the *NED*); he alone uses the words *eaneling* and *misbeliever* and the rare verb *to bane.* His syntax is peculiar: we *trifle* time; *rend out*, where Shakespeare has elsewhere only *rend*; I have no mind *of* feasting forth to-night (always *mind to*); *and so following*, where *and so forth* is the regular Shakespearian phrase. I have counted some forty such deviations from Shakespeare's ordinary language and cannot dismiss the thought that Shakespeare made Shylock's language peculiar on purpose, just as he makes Caliban, and the witches in *Macbeth*, use certain words and expressions used by none other of his characters in order to stamp them as beings out of the common sort.

Shakespeare's vocabulary was not the same in all periods of his life. I have counted between two and three hundred words which he used in his youth, but not later, while the number of words peculiar to his last period is much smaller. Sarrazin [7] mentions as characteristic of his first period a predilection for picturesque adjectives that appeal immediately to the outward senses (*bright, brittle, fragrant, pitchy, snow-white*), while his later plays are said to contain more adjectives of psychological importance. But even apart from the fact that some of the adjectives instanced are really found in later plays, this statement would account for only a small part of the divergencies. Probably no single explanation can account for them all, not even that of the natural buoyancy of youth and the comparative austerity of a later age. It is noteworthy that in some instances he ridicules in later plays words used quite seriously in earlier ones. Thus *beautify*, which is found in *Lucrece, 2 Henry VI, Titus Andronicus, Two Gentlemen*, and *Romeo*, is severely criticized by Polonius when he hears it in Hamlet's letter: "That's an ill phrase, a vilde [i.e. vile] phrase, beautified is a vilde phrase." Similarly *cranny*, which Shakespeare used in *Lucrece* (twice) and in the *Comedy of Errors*, is not found in any play written later than *Midsummer Night's Dream*, where Shakespeare takes leave of the word by turning it to ridicule in the mouth of Bottom and in the artisans' comedy. The fate of *foeman, aggravate* and *homicide* is nearly the same. Perhaps some of the words avoided in later life were provincialisms (thus possibly *pebblestone, shore*, in the sense of "bank of a river," *wood* "mad," *forefather* "ancestor," the pronunciation of *marriage* and of *Henry* in three syllables). In the first period Shakespeare used *perverse* with the unusual signification "cold, unfriendly, averse to love"; later he avoids the word altogether. In such instances he may have been criticized by his contemporaries (we know from the *Poetaster* how severe Ben Jonson was in these matters), and that may have made him avoid the objectionable words altogether.

One of the most characteristic features of Shakespeare's use of the English language is his boldness. His boldness of metaphor has often been pointed out in books of literary criticism, and the boldness of his sentence structure, especially in his last period, is so obvious that no instances need be adduced here. He does not always care for grammatical parallelism, witness such a sentence as "A thought which, quarter'd, hath but one part *wisdom* And ever three parts *coward*" (*Hamlet* IV, 4, 42). He does not always place the words where they would seem properly to belong, as in "we send, To know what *willing* ransome he will give" for "what ransom he will willingly give" (*Henry V* III, 5, 63), "dismiss me Thus with his *speechlesse* hand" (*Coriolanus* V, 1, 68), "the *whole* eare of Denmarke Is by a forged processe of my death Rankly abus'd" (the ear of all Denmark, *Hamlet* I, 5, 36), "lovers *absent* howres" (the hours when lovers are absent, *Othello* III, 4, 174), etc. He is not afraid of writing "wanted lesse impudence" for "had less impudence" or "wanted impudence more" (*Winter's Tale* III, 2, 57) and "a beggar without lesse quality" (*Cymbeline* I, 4, 23), nor of mixing his negatives as he does in many other passages.[8] Alex. Schmidt, who collects many instances of such negligence, rightly remarks: "Had he taken the pains of revising and preparing his plays for the press, he would perhaps have corrected all the quoted passages. But he did not write them to be read and dwelt on by the eye, but to be heard by a sympathetic audience. And much that would blemish the language of a logician, may well become a dramatic poet or an orator."[9] There is an excellent paper by C. Alphonso Smith in the *Englische Studien,* vol. XXX, on "The Chief Difference between the First and Second Folios of Shakespeare," in which he shows that "the supreme syntactic value of Shakespeare's work as represented in the First Folio is that it shows us the English language unfettered by bookish impositions. Shakespeare's syntax was that of the speaker, not that of the essayist; for the drama represents the unstudied utterance of people under all kinds and degrees of emotion, ennui, pain, and passion. Its syntax, to be truly representative, must be familiar, conversational, spontaneous; not studied and formal." But the Second Folio is of unique service and significance in its attempts to render more "correct" and bookish the unfettered syntax of the First. The First Folio is to the Second as spoken language is to written language. The "bad grammar" of the First Folio (1623) may not *always* be due to Shakespeare himself, but at any rate we have in that edition more of his own language than in the "correctness" of the Second Folio (1632).

Shakespeare's boldness with regard to language is less conspicuous, though no less real, in the instances I shall now mention. In turning over the pages of the *New English Dictionary,* where every pains has been taken to ascertain the earliest occurrence of each word and of each signification, one is struck by the frequency with which Shakespeare's name is found affixed to the earliest quotation for words or meanings. In many cases this is no doubt due to the fact that Shakespeare's vocabulary has been registered with greater care in Concordances and in Al. Schmidt's invaluable *Shakespeare-Lexicon* than that of any other author, so that his words cannot escape notice, while the same words may occur unnoticed in the pages of many an earlier author. But anyhow, Shakespeare uses a great many words which were new in his times, whether absolutely new or new only to the written language, while living colloquially on the lips of the people. My list [10] includes the following words: *aslant* as a preposition, *assassination, barefaced,* the plural *brothers* (found also in Layamon's *Brut,* but seemingly not between that and Shakespeare's youth: Gosson, Lyly, Sidney, Marlowe), *call* "to pay a short visit," *courtship, dwindle, enthrone* (also in Lyly, earlier enthronize), *eventful, excellent* in the current sense "extremely good," *fount* "spring" (also in Kyd, Drayton), *fretful, get* intransitive with an adjective, "become" (only in "get clear"), *I have got* for "I have," *gust, hint, hurry* (also in Kyd), *indistinguishable, laughable, leap-frog, loggerhead* and *loggerheaded, lonely* (but Sidney has *loneliness* some years before Shakespeare began to write), *lower* verb, *perusal, primy.* Further the following verbs (formed from nouns that are found before Shakespeare's time): *bound, hand, jade,* and nouns (formed from already existing verbs): *control, dawn, dress, hatch, import, indent.* Among other words which were certainly or probably new when Shakespeare used them, may be mentioned *acceptance, gull* "dupe," *rely,* and *summit.* I shall give below a list of words and expressions the existence of which in the English language is due

to Shakespeare. The words here given would probably have found
their way into the language even had Shakespeare never written
a line, though he may have accelerated the date of their acceptance.
But at any rate they show that he was exempt from that narrowness
which often makes authors shy of using new or colloquial words in
the higher literary style. Let me add another remark apropos of a
list of hard words needing an explanation which is found in Cock-
eram's *Dictionarie* (1623). Dr. Murray writes: [11] "We are surprised
to find among these hard words *abandon, abhorre, abrupt, absurd,
action, activitie* and *actresse*, explained as 'a woman doer,' for the
stage actress had not yet appeared." Now, with the exception of the
last one, all these words are found in Shakespeare's plays.

Closely connected with this trait in Shakespeare's language is the
proximity of his poetical diction to his ordinary prose. He uses very
few "poetical" words or forms. He does not rely for his highest flights
on the use of words and grammatical forms not used elsewhere, but
knows how to achieve the finest effects of imagination without
stepping outside his ordinary vocabulary and grammar. It must be
remembered that when he uses *thou* and *thee*, *'tis, e'en, ne'er, how-
e'er, mine eyes,* etc., or when he construes negative and interrogative
verbs without *do,* all these things, which are now parts of the conventional language of poetry, were everyday colloquialisms in the
Elizabethan period. It is true that there are certain words and forms
which he never uses except in poetry, but their number is extremely
small. I do not know of any besides *host* "army," *vale, sire,* and
morn. As for the synonym *morrow,* apart from its use in the sense
of "next day" and in the salutation *good morrow,* which was then
colloquial, it occurs only four times, and only in rime. There are
some verb forms which occur in rime only, but the number of occasions on which Shakespeare was thus led to deviate from his
usual grammar is very small: *begun* (past tense) eight times, *flee*
once (the usual present is *fly*), *gat* once (in the probably spurious
Pericles), *sain* for *said* once, *sang* once, *shore* participle once, *strown*
once (the usual form is *strewed*), *swore* participle once—fifteen
instances in all, to which must be added eleven instances of the
plural *eyen.* Rhythmical reasons seem to make *do* more frequent in
Shakespeare's verse than in his prose,[12] and rhythm and rime sometimes make him place a preposition after instead of before the noun
(e.g. go the fools among).[13] All these things are rare enough to

justify the statement that a peculiar poetical diction is practically non-existent in Shakespeare.

In the Old English period the language of poetry differed very considerably from the language of ordinary prose. The old poetical language was completely forgotten a few centuries after the Norman Conquest, and a new one did not develop in the Middle English period, though there were certain conventional tricks used by many poets, such as those ridiculed in Chaucer's *Sir Thopas*. Chaucer himself had not two distinct forms of language, one for verse and the other for prose, apart from those unavoidable smaller changes which rhythm and rime are always apt to bring about. We have now seen that the same is true of Shakespeare; but in the nineteenth century we find a great many words and forms of words which are scarcely ever used outside of poetry. This, then, is not a survival of an old state of things, but a comparatively recent phenomenon, whose causes are well worth investigating. At first it might be thought that the regard for sonority and beauty of sound would be the chief or one of the chief agents in the creation of a special poetical dialect. But very often poetical forms are, on the contrary, less euphonious than everyday forms; compare, for example, *break'st thou* with *do you break*. Those who imagine that *gat* sounds better than *got* will scarcely admit that *spat* or *gnat* sounds better than *spot* or *not*: non-phonetic associations are often more powerful than the mere sounds.

More frequently it is the desire to leave the beaten track that leads to the preference of certain words in poetry. Words that are too well known and too often used do not call up such vivid images as words less familiar. This is one of the reasons that impel poets to use archaic words; they are "new" just on account of their being old, and yet they are not so utterly unknown as to be unintelligible. Besides they will often call up the memory of some old or venerable work in which the reader has met with them before, and thus they at once secure the reader's sympathy. If, then, the poetical language of the nineteenth century contains a great many archaisms, the question naturally presents itself, from what author or authors do most of them proceed? And many people who know the pre-eminent position of Shakespeare in English literature will probably be surprised to hear that his is not the greatest influence on English poetic diction.

Among words and phrases due to reminiscences of Shakespeare may be mentioned the following: *antre* (Keats, Meredith), *atomy* in the sense "atom, tiny being," *beetle* ("the dreadfull summit of the cliffe, That beetles o'er his base into the sea"), it *beggars all description*, *broad-blown*, *charactery* (Keats, Browning), *coign of vantage* (*coign* is another spelling of *coin* "corner"), *cudgel one's brain(s)*, *daff* the world aside, *eager* "cold" ("a nipping and an eager ayre"), *eld* (superstitious eld), nine *farrow*, *fitful* ("Life's fitfull fever"), *forcible feeble*, a *foregone conclusion*, *forgetive* (Falstaff: "of uncertain formation and meaning." Commonly taken as a derivation of *forge* v., and hence used by writers of the nineteenth century for: apt at forging, inventive, creative," *NED*), a *forthright* (rare), *gaingiving* (Coleridge), *gouts* of blood, *gravel-blind*, *head and front* ("A Shakesperian phrase, orig. app. denoting "summit, height, highest extent or pitch'; sometimes used by modern writers in other senses," *NED*), *hoist with his own petard*, *lush* (in the sense "luxuriant in growth"), in my *mind's eye*, the *pink* (of perfection, in Shakespeare only, "I am the very pinck of curtesie"; George Eliot has "Her kitchen always looked the pink of cleanliness," and Stevenson "he had been the pink of good behaviour"), *silken dalliance*, *single blessedness*, *that way madness lies* ("Too kind! Insipidity lay that way," Mrs. Humphry Ward), *weird*. The last word is interesting; originally it is a noun and means "destiny, fate"; the three *weird sisters* means the fate sisters or Norns. Shakespeare found this expression in Holinshed and used it in speaking of the witches in *Macbeth*, and only there. From that play it entered into the ordinary language, but without being properly understood. It is now used as an adjective and generally taken to mean "mystic, mysterious, unearthly." Another word that is often misunderstood is *bourne* from *Hamlet* ("The undiscovered country, from whose borne No traveller returnes"); it means "limit," but Keats and others use it in the sense "realm, domain" ("In water, fiery realm, and airy bourne"; quoted *NED*). There are two things worth noting in this list. First, that it includes so many words of vague or indefinite meaning, which perhaps were not even clearly understood by the author himself. This explains the fact that some of them have apparently been used in modern times in a different sense from that intended by Shakespeare. Second, that the re-employment of these words nearly always dates from the nineteenth century and that the present currency of some of them is due just as much to Sir Walter Scott or Keats as to the original author. *To cudgel one's brains* is now more of a literary phrase than when Shakespeare put it in the mouth of the gravedigger (*Hamlet* V, 1, 63), evidently meaning it to be a rude or vulgar expression. Inversely, *single blessedness* is now generally used with an ironical or humorous tinge which it certainly had not in Shakespeare (*Dream* I, 1, 78).

It must be noted also that none of the words thus traceable to Shakespeare belong now to what might be called the technical language of poetry. Modern archaizing poetry owes its vocabulary more to Edmund Spenser than to any other poet. Pope and his contemporaries made a very sparing use of archaisms, but when poets in the middle of the eighteenth century turned from his rationalistic and matter-of-fact poetry and were eager to take their romantic flight away from everyday realities, Spenser became the poet of their heart, and they adopted a great many of his words which had long been forgotten. Their success was so great that many words which they had to explain to their readers are now perfectly familiar to every educated man and woman. Gilbert West, in his work *On the Abuse of Travelling, in imitation of Spenser* (1739), had to explain in footnotes such words as *sooth, guise, hardiment, Elfin, prowess, wend, hight, dight, paramount, behests, caitiffs.* William Thompson, in his *Hymn to May* (1740?), explains *certes* surely, certainly, *ne* nor, *erst* formerly, long ago, *undaz'd* undazzled, *sheen* brightness, shining, *been* are, *dispredden* spread, *meed* prize, *ne recks* nor is concerned, *affray* affright, *featly* nimbly, *defftly* finely, *glenne* a country borough (the real meaning is "valley"; the wrong sense here given to it is due to E.K.'s notes to Spenser's *Shepherd's Calendar*), *eld* old age, *lusty-head* vigour, *algate* ever, *harrow* destroy, *carl* clown, *perdie* an old word for asserting anything, *livelood* liveliness, *albe* altho', *scant* scarcely, *bedight* adorned.

In later times, Coleridge, Scott, Keats, Tennyson, William Morris and Swinburne must be mentioned as those poets who have contributed most to the revival of old words. Coleridge in the first edition of the *Ancient Mariner* used so many archaisms in spelling, etc., that he had afterwards to reduce the number in order to make his poem more palatable to the reading public. Sometimes *pseudo-antique* formations have been introduced; *anigh,* for instance, which is frequent in Morris, is not an old word, and *idlesse* is a false formation after the legitimate old *noblesse* and *humblesse* (OFr. noblesse, humblesse). But on the whole, many good words have been recovered from oblivion, and some of them will doubtless find their way into the language of ordinary conversation, while others will continue their life in the regions of higher poetry and eloquence. On the other hand, many pages in the works of Shakespeare, of Shelley, and of Tennyson show us that it is possible for a poet to reach the highest flights of eloquent poetry without resorting to many of the conventionally poetical terms.

As for the technical *grammar* of modern poetry, the influence of Shakespeare is not very strong, in fact not so strong as that of the Authorized Version of the Bible. The revival of *th* in the third person singular was due to the Bible.[14] *Gat* is more frequent than *got* in the Bible, while Shakespeare's ordinary form is *got;* the solitary instance of *gat* only serves to confirm the rule.[15] The past tense of *cleave* "to sever" in Shakespeare is *clove* or *cleft; clave* does not occur in his writings at all, but is the only biblical past of this verb. *Brake* is the only preterit of *break* found in the Bible; in Shakespeare *brake* is rarer than *broke;* Milton and Pope have only *broke;* Tennyson, Morris, and Swinburne prefer *brake.*

On the whole, however, modern poets do not take their grammar from any one old author or book, but are apt to use any deviation from the ordinary grammar they can lay hold of anywhere. And thus it has come to pass in the nineteenth century that while the languages of other civilized nations have the same grammar for poetry as for prose, although retaining here and there a few archaic forms of verbs, etc., in English a wide gulf separates the grammar of poetry from that of ordinary life. The pronoun for the second person is in prose *you* for both cases in both numbers, while in many works of poetry it is *thou* and *thee* for the singular, *ye* for the plural (with here and there a rare *you*); the poetical possessives *thy* and *thine* never occur in everyday speech. The usual distinction between *my* and *mine* does not always obtain in poetry, where it is thought refined to write *mine ears,* etc. For *they sat down* the poetical form is *they sate them down;* for *it's* poets write *'tis,* and for *whatever* either *whatso* or *whatsoever* (or *whate'er*), for *does not mend* they often write *mends not,* etc. Sometimes they gain the advantage of having at will one syllable more or less than common people: *taketh* for *takes, thou takest* for *you take, movèd* for *moved, o'er* for *over,* etc.; compare also *morn* for morning. But in other cases the only thing gained is the impression, produced by uncommon forms, that we are in a sphere different from or raised above ordinary realities.

As a matter of course, this impression is weakened in proportion as the deviations become the common property of any rimer, when a reaction will prob̲a̲b̲l̲y̲ .... ̲ favour of more natural forms. The hist......... .... forms is rather curious: howe'er, e'er, ... iliar forms, used in daily talk. Then .... in the abbreviated fashion whenever .... onounce them in that way, while .... t the pronunciation given to their .... spelling. The next step was that .... vulgar by schoolmasters with so .... eared from ordinary conversation .... etry. And now they are distinctly .... f common mortals.

.... language, some can be traced .... those already mentioned I shall .... meant to overflow (Fr. sur-onder, ... Skeat, both the modern significa- .... ference to round, and the cur- .... , The soft impeachment is .... Sheridan's Rivals, act V, ... generally known by Scott, and to croon .... Burke originated the expression the Great Unwashed. A certain number of proper names in works of literature have been popular enough to pass into ordinary language as appellatives,[16] as for instance pander or pandar from Chaucer's Troilus and Criseyde, Abigail "a servant-girl" from Beaumont and Fletcher's Scornful Lady, Mrs. Grundy as a personification of middle-class ideas of propriety from Morton's Speed the Plough, Paul Pry "a meddlesome busybody" from Poole's comedy of that name, Sarah Gamp "sick nurse of the old-fashioned type" and "big umbrella" from Dickens's Martin Chuzzlewit, Pecksniff "hypocrite" from the same novel, Sherlock Holmes "acute detective" from Conan Doyle's stories.

Ordinary language sometimes makes use of the same instruments as poetry. Here I shall give some instances of riming locutions: highways and byways, town and gown, it will neither make nor break me (cf. the alliterative make . . . mar), fairly and squarely, toiling and moiling, as snug as a bug in a rug (Kipling), rough and gruff, "I mean to take that girl—snatch or catch" (Meredith), moans and groans.[17] Compare also such popular words as handy-dandy, hanky-panky, namby-pamby, hurly-burly, hurdy-gurdy, hugger-mugger, *hocus pocus, hoity toity* or *highty tighty, higgledy-piggledy, hickery-pickery. Hotchpot* (from French *hocher* "shake together" and *pot*) was made *hotch-potch* for the sake of the rime; then the final *tch* was changed into *dge* (cf. *knowledge* from *knowleche*): *hotchpodge,* and the rime was reestablished: *hodge-podge.*

Rhythm undoubtedly plays a great part in ordinary language, apart from poetry and artistic (or artificial) prose. It may not always be easy to demonstrate this; but in combinations of a monosyllable and a disyllable by means of *and* the short word is in many set phrases placed first in order to make the rhythm into the regular 'aa 'aa instead of 'aaa 'a (' before the *a* denotes the strongly stressed syllable). Thus we say "bread and butter," not "butter and bread"; further: bread and water, milk and water, cup and saucer, wind and weather, head and shoulders, by fits and snatches, from top to bottom, rough and ready, rough and tumble, free and easy, dark and dreary, high and mighty, up and doing.[18] It is probable that rhythm has also played a great part in determining the order of words in other fixed groups of greater complexity.

NOTES

1. Inversely, many authors will use some (learned or abstract) words in writing which they do not use in conversation; their number, however, is rarely great.

2. Thus, on p. 30 of *Areopagitica,* I find the following 21 words, which are not in Bradshaw's Concordance: Churchman, competency, utterly, mercenary, pretender, ingenuous, evidently, tutor, examiner, scism, ferular, fescu, imprimatur, grammar, pedagogue, cursory, temporize, extemporize, licencer, commonwealth, foreiner. And p. 50 adds 18 more words to the list: writing, commons, valorous, rarify, enfranchise, founder, formall, slavish, oppressive, reinforce, abrogate, mercilesse, noble (n.), Danegelt, immunity, newness, unsutableness, customary.

3. I have amused myself with making up the following sentences of words not used by Shakespeare though found in the language of that time: In Shakespeare we find no *blunders,* although *decency* and *delicacy* had *disappeared; energy* and *enthusiasm* are not in *existence,* and we see no *elegant expressions* nor any *gleams* of *genius,* etc.

4. The act against profane language on the stage is not sufficient to explain this reticence.

5. Contrast with this trait the fondness for classical allusions found in Marlowe's *Barrabas.*

6. He says *Abram,* but *Abraham* is the only form found in the rest of Shakespeare's works.

7. *Shakespeare-Jahrbuch,* XXXIII, 122.

8. Besides using such double negatives as were regular in all the older periods of the language (*nor, never,* etc.)

9. *Shakespeare-Lexicon,* p. 1420.

10. See now also G. Gordon, *Shakespeare's English* (Soc. for Pure English XXIV, 1928) and G. H. McKnight, *Modern English in the Making* (New York, 1928), ch. X.

11. *The Evolution of English Lexicography,* Romanes Lecture (Oxford and London, 1900), p. 29.

12. W. Franz, *Shakespeare-Grammatik,* 2nd ed., 478, and *Nachtrag,* p. 590.

13. Franz, p. 427.

14. When modern clergymen in reading the Bible pronounce *lovèd, dancèd,* etc., they are reproducing a language about two hundred years earlier than the Authorized Version.

15. *Gat* is the only form of this verb admitted by some modern poets, who avoid *get* and *got* altogether. Shakespeare uses the verb hundreds of times. In the Authorized Version *get* is pretty frequent, but *got* is avoided in the New Testament while it is found seven times in the Old Testament (in five of these places the revisers of 1881 substituted other words: gathered, bought, come); *gat* is used 20 times, all of them in the O.T. (three of these were changed in 1881); *gotten* is found 23 times in the O.T., and twice in the N.T. (five of these, among them both the instances in the N.T., were changed in 1881). Milton makes a very sparing use of the verb (which he inflects *get, got, got,* never *gat* in the past or *gotten* in the participle); all the forms of the verb only occur 19 times in his poetical works; while, for instance, *give* occurs 168 times and *receive* 73 times. The verb is rare in Pope too. Why is this verb tabooed in this way?

16. Aronstein, *Englische Studien,* XXV, p. 245 ff., Josef Reinius, *On Transferred Appellations of Human Beings* (Göteborg, 1903), p. 44 ff.

17. As Old English has *mœnan* "moan," the modern verb may have derived its vowel from the frequent collocation with *groan,* OE. *granian. Square* may owe one of its significations to the collocation with *fair.*

18. Compare also such titles of books as Songs and Poems, Men and Women, Past and Present, French and English, Night and Morning. In some instances, rhythm is obviously not the only reason for the order, but in all I think it has been at least a concurrent cause.

MORRIS W. CROLL

The Baroque Style in Prose

I. Introduction

In the latter years of the sixteenth century a change declared itself
in the purposes and forms of the arts of Western Europe for which
it is hard to find a satisfactory name. One would like to describe
it, because of some interesting parallels with a later movement, as
the first modern manifestation of the Romantic Spirit; and it did,
in fact, arise out of a revolt against the classicism of the high Renaissance. But the terms "romantic" and "classical" are both perplexing
and unphilosophical; and their use should not be extended. It would
be much clearer and more exact to describe the change in question
as a radical effort to adapt traditional modes and forms of expression
to the uses of a self-conscious modernism; and the style that it produced was actually called in several of the arts—notably in architecture and prose-writing—the "modern" or "new" style. But the term
that most conveniently describes it is "baroque." This term, which
was at first used only in architecture, has lately been extended to
cover the facts that present themselves at the same time in sculpture
and in painting; and it may now properly be used to describe, or

From *Studies in English Philology: a Miscellany in Honor of Frederick
Klaeber,* edited by Kemp Malone and Martin B. Ruud (University of Minne-
sota Press, copyright 1929), pp. 427-56. Reprinted by permission of the
publisher.

at least to name, the characteristic modes of expression in all the arts during a certain period—the period, that is, between the high Renaissance and the eighteenth century; a period that begins in the last quarter of the sixteenth century, reaches a culmination at about 1630, and thenceforward gradually modifies its character under new influences.

Expressiveness rather than formal beauty was the pretension of the new movement, as it is of every movement that calls itself modern. It disdained complacency, suavity, copiousness, emptiness, ease, and in avoiding these qualities sometimes obtained effects of contortion or obscurity, which it was not always willing to regard as faults. It preferred the forms that express the energy and labor of minds seeking the truth, not without dust and heat, to the forms that express a contented sense of the enjoyment and possession of it. In a single word, the motions of souls, not their states of rest, had become the themes of art.

The meaning of these antitheses may be easily illustrated in the history of Venetian painting, which passes, in a period not longer than one generation, from the self-contained and relatively symmetrical designs of Titian, through the swirls of Tintoretto, to the contorted and aspiring lines that make the paintings of El Greco so restless and exciting. Poetry moves in the same way at about the same time; and we could metaphorically apply the terms by which we distinguish El Greco from Titian to the contrast between the rhythms of Spenser and the Petrarchans, on one hand, and the rhythms of Donne, on the other, between the style of Ariosto and the style of Tasso. In the sculptures of Bernini (in his portrait busts as well as in his more famous and theatrical compositions) we may again observe how ideas of motion take the place of ideas of rest; and the operation of this principle is constantly to be observed also in the school of architecture associated with the same artist's name. In the façade of a Baroque church, says Geoffrey Scott, "a movement, which in the midst of a Bramantesque design would be destructive and repugnant, is turned to account and made the basis of a more dramatic, but not less satisfying treatment, the motive of which is not peace, but energy." [1]

And finally the change that takes place in the prose style of the same period—the change, that is, from Ciceronian to Anti-Ciceronian forms and ideas—is exactly parallel with those that were occurring in the other arts, and is perhaps more useful to the student of the baroque impulse than any of the others, because it was more self-conscious, more definitely theorized by its leaders, and more clearly described by its friends and foes. In some previous studies I have considered the triumph of the Anti-Ciceronian movement at considerable length; but I have been concerned chiefly with the theory of the new style; and my critics have complained, justly, that I have been too difficult, or even abstract. In the present study I hope to correct this defect. Its purpose is to describe the *form* of Anti-Ciceronian, or baroque, prose.

There are of course several elements of prose technique: diction, or the choice of words; the choice of figures; the principle of balance or rhythm; the form of the period, or sentence; and in a full description of baroque prose all of these elements would have to be considered. The last-mentioned of them—the form of the period—is, however, the most important and the determinant of the others; and this alone is to be the subject of discussion in the following pages.

The Anti-Ciceronian period was sometimes described in the seventeenth century as an "exploded" period; and this metaphor is very apt if it is taken as describing solely its outward appearance, the mere fact of its form. For example, here is a period from Sir Henry Wotton, a typical expression of the political craft of the age:

> Men must beware of running down steep hills with weighty bodies; they once in motion, *suo feruntur pondere;* steps are not then voluntary.[2]

The members of this period stand farther apart one from another than they would in a Ciceronian sentence; there are no syntactic connectives between them whatever; and semicolons or colons are necessary to its proper punctuation. In fact, it has the appearance of having been disrupted by an explosion within.

The metaphor would be false, however, if it should be taken as describing the manner in which this form has been arrived at. For it would mean that the writer first shaped a round and complete oratorical period in his mind and then partly undid his work. And this, of course, does not happen. Wotton gave this passage its form, not by demolishing a Ciceronian period, but by omitting several of the steps by which roundness and smoothness of composition might have been attained. He has deliberately avoided the processes of mental revision in order to express his idea when it is nearer the point of its origin in his mind.

We must stop for a moment on the word *deliberately*. The negligence of the Anti-Ciceronian masters, their disdain of revision, their dependence upon casual and emergent devices of construction, might sometimes be mistaken for mere indifference to art or contempt of form; and it is, in fact, true that Montaigne and Burton, even Pascal and Browne, are sometimes led by a dislike of formality into too licentious a freedom. Yet even their extravagances are purposive, and express a creed that is at the same time philosophical and artistic. Their purpose was to portray, not a thought, but a mind thinking, or, in Pascal's words, *la peinture de la pensée*. They knew that an idea separated from the act of experiencing it is not the idea that was experienced. The ardor of its conception in the mind is a necessary part of its truth; and unless it can be conveyed to another mind in something of the form of its occurrence, either it has changed into some other idea or it has ceased to be an idea, to have any existence whatever except a verbal one. It was the latter fate that happened to it, they believed, in the Ciceronian periods of sixteenth-century Latin rhetoricians. The successive processes of revision to which these periods had been submitted had removed them from reality by just so many steps. For themselves, they preferred to present the truth of experience in a less concocted form, and deliberately chose as the moment of expression that in which the idea first clearly objectifies itself in the mind, in which, therefore, each of its parts still preserves its own peculiar emphasis and an independent vigor of its own—in brief, the moment in which truth is still *imagined*.

The form of a prose period conceived in such a theory of style will differ in every feature from that of the conventional period of an oratorical, or Ciceronian, style; but its most conspicuous difference will appear in the way it connects its members or clauses one with another. In the period quoted above from Wotton the members are syntactically wholly free; there are no ligatures whatever between one and another. But there is another type of Anti-Ciceronian period, in which the ordinary marks of logical succession—conjunctions, pronouns, etc.—are usually present, but are of such a kind or are used in such a way as to bind the members together in a characteristically loose and casual manner. The difference between the two types thus described may seem somewhat unimportant; and it is true that they run into each other and cannot always be sharply distinguished. The most representative Anti-Ciceronians, like Montaigne and Browne, use them both and intermingle them. But at their extremes they are not only distinguishable; they serve to distinguish different types, or schools, of seventeenth-century style. They derive from different models, belong to different traditions, and sometimes define the philosophical affiliations of the authors who prefer them.

They will be considered here separately; the first we will call, by a well-known seventeenth-century name, the *période coupée,* or, in an English equivalent, the "curt period" (so also the *stile coupé,* or the "curt style"); the other by the name of the "loose period" (and the "loose style"); though several other appropriate titles suggest themselves in each case.[3]

II. *Stile Coupé*

(A)

One example of the *période coupée* has already been given. Here are others:

> Pour moy, qui ne demande qu'à devenir plus sage, non plus sçavant ou eloquent, ces ordonnances logiciennes et aristoteliques ne sont pas à propos; je veulx qu'on commence par le dernier poinct: i'entends assez que c'est que Mort et Volupté; qu'on ne s'amuse pas à les anatomizer. (Montaigne)

> 'Tis not worth the reading, I yield it, I desire thee not to lose time in perusing so vain a subject, I should be peradventure loth myself to read him or thee so writing, 'tis not *operae pretium.* (Burton)

> No armor can *defend* a fearful heart. It will kill itself, within. (Felltham)

> Oui; mais il faut parier; cela n'est pas volontaire, vous êtes embarqués. (Pascal)

> L'éloquence continue ennuie.
> Les princes et les rois jouent quelquefois; ils ne sont pas

toujours sur leurs trônes, ils s'y ennuient: la grandeur a besoin
d'être quittée pour être sentie. (Pascal)

The world that I regard is myself; it is the microcosm of
my own frame that I cast mine eye on: for the other, I use it
but like my globe, and turn it round sometimes for my recreation. (Browne)

Il y a des hommes qui attendent à être dévots et religieux
que tout le monde se déclare impie et libertin: ce sera alors le
parti du vulgaire, ils sauront s'en dégager. (La Bruyère) [4]

In all of these passages, as in the period quoted from Wotton,
there are no two main members that are syntactically connected.
But it is apparent also that the characteristic style that they have
in common contains several other features besides this.

In the first place, each member is as short as the most alert intelligence would have it. The period consists, as some of its admirers
were wont to say, of the nerves and muscles of speech alone; it is
as hard-bitten, as free of soft or superfluous flesh, as "one of Caesar's
soldiers." [5]

Second, there is a characteristic order, or mode of progression,
in a curt period that may be regarded either as a necessary consequence of its omission of connectives or as the causes and explanation
of this. We may describe it best by observing that the first member
is likely to be a self-contained and complete statement of the whole
idea of the period. It is so because writers in this style like to avoid
prearrangements and preparations; they begin, as Montaigne puts
it, at *le dernier poinct,* the point aimed at. The first member therefore exhausts the mere fact of the idea; logically there is nothing
more to say. But it does not exhaust its imaginative truth or the
energy of its conception. It is followed, therefore, by other members,
each with a new tone or emphasis, each expressing a new apprehension of the truth expressed in the first. We may describe the progress
of a curt period, therefore, as a series of imaginative moments occurring in a logical pause or suspension. Or—to be less obscure—we
may compare it with successive flashes of a jewel or prism as it
turned about on its axis and takes the light in different ways.

It is true, of course, that in a series of propositions there will
always be some logical process; the truth stated will undergo some

development or change. For example, in the sentence from Montaigne at the beginning of this section, the later members add something to the idea; and in the quotation from Pascal's *Pensées sur l'Éloquence,* given below it, the thought suddenly enlarges in the final member. Yet the method of advance is not logical; the form does not express it. Each member, in its main intention, is a separate act of imaginative realization.

In the third place, one of the characteristics of the curt style is deliberate asymmetry of the members of a period; and it is this trait that especially betrays the modernistic character of the style. The chief mark of a conventional, or "classical," art, like that of the sixteenth century, is an approximation to evenness in the size and form of the balanced parts of a design; the mark of a modernistic art, like that of the seventeenth, and the nineteenth and twentieth, centuries, is the desire to achieve an effect of balance or rhythm among parts that are obviously not alike—the love of "some strangeness in the proportions."

In a prose style asymmetry may be produced by varying the length of the members within a period. For example, part of the effect of a sentence from Bishop Hall is due to a variation in this respect among members which nevertheless produce the effect of balance or rhythmic design.

> What if they [crosses and adversities] be unpleasant? They are physic: it is enough, if they be wholesome.[6]

But the desired effect is more characteristically produced by conspicuous differences of form, either with or without differences of length. For instance, a characteristic method of the seventeenth century was to begin a succession of members with different kinds of subject words. In the sentence quoted from Wotton the first two members have personal subjects, the third the impersonal "steps"; in the quotation from Pascal the opposite change is made.

> Mais il faut parier; cela n'est pas volontaire, vous êtes embarqués.

In both of these periods, moreover, each of the three members has a distinct and individual turn of phrase, meant to be different from the others. Again, in the period of La Bruyère quoted at the beginning of this section, each new member involves a shift of the mind to a new subject. (Observe also the asymmetry of the members in point of length.)

Sometimes, again, asymmetry is produced by a change from literal to metaphoric statement, or by the reverse, or by a change from one metaphor to another, as in the last example quoted from Pascal, where the metaphor of one embarked upon a ship abruptly takes the place of that of a man engaged in a bet. Or there may be a leap from the concrete to the abstract form; and this is an eminently characteristic feature of the *stile coupé* because this style is always tending toward the aphorism, or *pensée,* as its ideal form. The second passage quoted from Pascal illustrates this in a striking way. It is evident that in the first three members—all concrete, about kings and princes—the author's mind is turning toward a general truth, which emerges complete and abstract in the last member: *la grandeur a besoin d'être quittée pour être sentie.*

The curt style, then, is not characterized only by the trait from which it takes its name, its omission of connectives. It has the four marks that have been described: first, studied brevity of members; second, the hovering, imaginative order; third, asymmetry; and fourth, the omission of the ordinary syntactic ligatures. None of these should, of course, be thought of separately from the others. Each of them is related to the rest and more or less involves them; and when they are all taken together they constitute a definite rhetoric, which was employed during the period from 1575 to 1675 with as clear a knowledge of its tradition and its proper models as the sixteenth-century Ciceronians had of the history of the rhetoric that they preferred.

In brief, it is a Senecan style; and, although the imitation of Seneca never quite shook off the imputation of literary heresy that had been put upon it by the Augustan purism of the preceding age, and certain amusing cautions and reservations were therefore felt to be necessary, yet nearly all of the theorists of the new style succeeded in expressing their devotion to their real master in one way or another. Moreover, they were well aware that the characteristic traits of Seneca's style were not his alone, but had been elaborated before him in the Stoic schools of the Hellenistic period; and all the earlier practitioners of the *stile coupé,* Montaigne (in his first phase),

Lipsius, Hall, Charron, etc., write not only as literary Senecans, but
rather more as philosophical Stoics.

Senecanism and Stoicism are, then, the primary implications of
stile coupé. It must be observed, however, that a style once established in general use may cast away the associations in which it
originated; and this is what happened in the history of the curt style.
Montaigne, for instance, confessed that he had so thoroughly learned
Seneca's way of writing that he could not wholly change it even
when his ideas and tastes had changed and he had come to prefer
other masters. And the same thing is to be observed in many writers
of the latter part of the century: St. Évremond, Halifax, and La
Bruyère, for instance. Though these writers are all definitely anti-
Stoic and anti-Senecan, all of them show that they had learned the
curt style too well ever to unlearn it or to avoid its characteristic
forms; and there was no great exaggeration in Shaftesbury's complaint, at the very end of the century, that no other movement of
style than Seneca's—what he calls the "Senecan amble"—had been
heard in prose for a hundred years past.

(B)

The curt or serried style depends for its full effect upon the union
of the several formal traits that have been described in the preceding
section. We have assumed hitherto that these traits are as rigorous
and unalterable as if they were prescribed by a rule; and in the
examples cited there have been no significant departures from any
of them. But of course slight variations are common even in passages that produce the effect of *stile coupé*; and some searching is
necessary to discover examples as pure as those that have been cited.
This is so evidently true that it would need no illustration except
for the fact that certain kinds of period eminently characteristic of
seventeenth-century prose arise from a partial violation of the "rules"
laid down. Two of these may be briefly described.

(A) In a number of writers (Browne, Felltham, and South, for
example) we often find a period of two members connected by *and,*
or, or *nor,* which evidently has the character of *stile coupé* because
the conjunction has no logical *plus* force whatever. It merely connects two efforts of imagination to realize the same idea; two
as-it-were synchronous statements of it. The following from Browne
will be recognized as characteristic of him:

> 'Tis true, there is an edge in all firm belief, and with an easy
> metaphor we may say, the sword of faith.

Again:

> Therefore I perceive a man may be twice a child, before the
> days of dotage; and stand in need of Æson's bath before three-
> score.[7]

Often, too, in a period consisting of a larger number of members
the last two are connected by an *and* or the like. But this case can
be illustrated in connection with the one that immediately follows.

(B) The rule that the successive members of a *période coupée*
are of different and often opposed forms, are asymmetrical instead
of symmetrical, is sometimes partly violated inasmuch as these members begin with the same word or form of words, for example, with
the same pronoun subject, symmetry, parallelism, and some regularity
of rhythm thus introducing themselves into a style that is designed
primarily and chiefly to express a dislike of these frivolities. It is to
be observed, however, that the members that begin with this suggestion of oratorical pattern usually break it in the words that follow.
Except for their beginnings they are as asymmetrical as we expect
them to be, and reveal that constant novelty and unexpectedness
that is so characteristic of the "baroque" in all the arts.

One illustration is to be found in the style of the "character" writings that enjoyed so great a popularity in the seventeenth century.
The frequent recurrence of the same subject word, usually *he* or
they, is the mannerism of this style, and is sometimes carried over
into other kinds of prose in the latter part of the century, as, for
instance, in writings of La Bruyère that are not included within the
limits of the "character" genre,[8] and in passages of Dryden. It is indeed so conspicuous a mannerism that it may serve to conceal what
is after all the more significant feature of the "character" style,
namely, the constant variation and contrast of form in members that
begin in this formulistic manner.

The style of the "character," however, is that of a highly specialized genre; and the form of the period with reiterated introductory
formula can be shown in its more typical character in other kinds of
prose, as, for example, in a passage from Browne describing the
Christian Stoicism of his age:

Let not the twelve but the two tables be thy law: let Pythag-
oras be thy remembrancer, not thy textuary and final instructer:
and learn the vanity of the world, rather from Solomon than
Phocylides.[9]

Browne touches lightly on these repetitions, and uses them not too
frequently. Balzac uses them characteristically and significantly. A
paragraph from his *Entretiens* may be quoted both in illustration
of this fact and for the interest of its subject matter:

Nous demeurasmes d'accord que l'Autheur qui veut imiter
Seneque commence par tout et finit par tout. Son Discours
n'est pas un corps entier: c'est un corps en pieces; ce sont des
membres couppez; et quoy que les parties soient proches les
unes des autres, elles ne laissent pas d'estre separées. Non
seulement il n'y a point de nerfs qui les joignent; il n'y a pas
mesme de cordes ou d'aiguillettes qui les attachent ensemble:
tant cet Autheur est ennemy de toutes sortes de liaisons, soit
de la Nature, soit de l'Art: tant il s'esloigne de ces bons exem-
ples que vous imitez si parfaitement.[10]

The passage illustrates exactly Balzac's position in the prose development of the seventeenth century. Montaigne is indeed—in
spite of his strictures upon him—his master. He aims, like Montaigne,
at the philosophic ease and naturalness of the *genus humile;* he
has his taste for aphorism, his taste for metaphor; he is full of
"points," and loves to make them show; in short, he is "baroque."
But by several means, and chiefly by the kinds of repetition illustrated in this passage (*c'est . . . ce sont; il n'y a point . . . il n'y a
pas mesme; tant . . . tant*), he succeeds in introducing that effect
of art, of form, of rhythm, for which Descartes and so many other
of his contemporaries admired him. He combines in short the "wit"
of the seventeenth century with at least the appearance of being
"a regular writer," which came, in the forties and fifties, to be regarded in France as highly desirable. In his political writings, and
especially in *Le Prince,* his iterated opening formula becomes too
evident a mannerism, and on page after page one reads periods of
the same form: two or three members beginning alike and a final
member much longer and more elaborate than the preceding that

may or may not begin in the same way. The effect is extremely rhetorical.

(c)

Finally, we have to observe that the typical *période coupée* need not be so short as the examples of it cited at the beginning of the present section. On the contrary, it may continue, without connectives and with all its highly accentuated peculiarities of form, to the length of five or six members. Seneca offered many models for this protracted aphoristic manner, as in the following passage from the *Naturales Quaestiones* (vii. 31):

> There are mysteries that are not unveiled the first day: Eleusis keepeth back something for those who come again to ask her. Nature telleth not all her secrets at once. We think we have been initiated: we are still waiting in her vestibule. Those secret treasures do not lie open promiscuously to every one: they are kept close and reserved in an inner shrine.

Similar in form is this six-member period from Browne's *Religio Medici*:

> To see ourselves again, we need not look for Plato's year: every man is not only himself; there have been many Diogeneses, and as many Timons, though but few of that name; men are lived over again; the world is now as it was in ages past; there was none then, but there hath been some one since, that parallels him, and is, as it were, his revived self.[11]

What has been said in a previous section of the characteristic mode of progression in *stile coupé* is strikingly illustrated in such passages as these. Logically they do not move. At the end they are saying exactly what they were at the beginning. Their advance is wholly in the direction of a more vivid imaginative realization; a metaphor revolves, as it were, displaying its different facets; a series of metaphors flash their lights; or a chain of "points" and paradoxes reveals the energy of a single apprehension in the writer's mind. In the latter part of the seventeenth century a number of critics satirize this peculiarity of the Senecan form. Father Bouhours, for instance, observed that with all its pretensions to brevity and significance this style makes less progress in five or six successive statements than a Ciceronian period will often make in one long and comprehensive construction. The criticism is, of course, sound if the only mode of progression is the logical one; but in fact there is a progress of imaginative apprehension, a revolving and upward motion of the mind as it rises in energy, and views the same point from new levels; and this spiral movement is characteristic of baroque prose.

III.   The Loose Style

(A)

In the preceding pages we have been illustrating a kind of period in which the members are in most cases syntactically disjunct, and we have seen that in this style the members are characteristically short. It is necessary now to illustrate the other type of Anti-Ciceronian style spoken of at the beginning, in which the members are usually connected by syntactic ligatures, and in which, therefore, both the members and the period as a whole may be, and in fact usually are, as long as in the Ciceronian style, or even longer.

It is more difficult to find an appropriate name for this kind of style than for the other. The "trailing" or "linked" style would describe a relation between the members of the period that is frequent and indeed characteristic, but is perhaps too specific a name. "Libertine" indicates exactly both the form of the style and the philosophical associations that it often implies; but it is wiser to avoid these implications in a purely descriptive treatment. There is but one term that is exact and covers the ground: the term "loose period" or "loose style"; and it is this that we will usually employ. In applying this term, however, the reader must be on his guard against a use of it that slipped into many rhetorical treatises of the nineteenth century. In these works the "loose sentence" was defined as one that has its main clause near the beginning; and an antithetical term "periodic sentence"—an improper one—was devised to name the opposite arrangement. "Loose period" is used here without reference to this confusing distinction.

In order to show its meaning we must proceed by means of examples; and we will take first a sentence—if, indeed, we can call

it a sentence—in which Bacon contrasts the "Magistral" method of
writing works of learning with the method of "Probation" appropriate to "induced knowledge," "the later whereof [he says] seemeth to
be *via deserta et interclusa.*"

> For as knowledges are now delivered, there is a kind of con-
> tract of error between the deliverer and the receiver: for he
> that delivereth knowledge desireth to deliver it in such form as
> may be best believed, and not as may be best examined; and he
> that receiveth knowledge desireth rather present satisfaction
> than expectant inquiry; and so rather not to doubt than not to
> err: glory making the author not to lay open his weakness, and
> sloth making the disciple not to know his strength.[12]

The passage is fortunate because it states the philosophy in which
Anti-Ciceronian prose has its origin and motive. But our present
business is with its form; and in order to illustrate this we will place
beside it another passage from another author.

> Elle [l'Imagination] ne peut rendre sages les fous; mais elle
> les rend heureux, à l'envi de la raison qui ne peut rendre ses
> amis que misérables, l'une les couvrant de gloire, l'autre de
> honte.[13]

There is a striking similarity in the way these two periods proceed.
In each case an antithesis is stated in the opening members; then
the member in which the second part of the antithesis is stated
puts out a dependent member. The symmetrical development announced at the beginning is thus interrupted and cannot be resumed.
The period must find a way out, a syntactic way of carrying on and
completing the idea it carries. In both cases the situation is met in
the same way, by a concluding member having the form of an absolute-participle construction, in which the antithetical idea of the
whole is sharply, aphoristically resumed.

The two passages, in short, are written as if they were meant to
illustrate in style what Bacon calls "the method of induced knowledge"; either they have no predetermined plan or they violate it at
will; their progression adapts itself to the movements of a mind discovering truth as it goes, thinking while it writes. At the same time,
and for the same reason, they illustrate the character of the style

that we call "baroque." See, for instance, how symmetry is first made and then broken, as it is in so many baroque designs in painting and architecture; how there is constant swift adaptation of form to the emergencies that arise in an energetic and unpremeditated forward movement; and observe, further, that these signs of spontaneity and improvisation occur in passages loaded with as heavy a content as rhetoric ever has to carry. That is to say, they combine the effect of great mass with the effect of rapid motion; and there is no better formula than this to describe the ideal of the baroque design in all the arts.

But these generalizations are beyond our present purpose. We are to study the loose period first, as we did the curt period, by observing the character of its syntactic links. In the two sentences quoted there are, with a single exception, but two modes of connection employed. The first is by co-ordinating conjunctions, the conjunctions, that is, that allow the mind to move straight on from the point it has reached. They do not necessarily refer back to any particular point in the preceding member; nor do they commit the following member to a predetermined form. In other words, they are the loose conjunctions, and disjoin the members they join as widely as possible. *And, but,* and *for* are the ones employed in the two sentences; and these are of course the necessary and universal ones. Other favorites of the loose style are *whereas, nor* (= *and not*), and the correlatives *though . . . yet, as . . . so.* Second, each of the two periods contains a member with an absolute-participle construction. In the loose style many members have this form, and not only (as in the two periods quoted) at the ends of periods, but elsewhere. Sir Thomas Browne often has them early in a period, as some passages to be cited in another connection will show. This is a phenomenon easily explained. For the absolute construction is the one that commits itself least and lends itself best to the solution of difficulties that arise in the course of a spontaneous and unpremeditated progress. It may state either a cause, or a consequence, or a mere attendant circumstance; it may be concessive or justificatory; it may be a summary of the preceding or a supplement to it; it may express an idea related to the whole of the period in which it occurs, or one related only to the last preceding member.

The co-ordinating conjunctions and the absolute-participle construction indicate, then, the character of the loose period. Like the *stile coupé,* it is meant to portray the natural, or thinking, order; and it expresses even better than the curt period the Anti-Ciceronian prejudice against formality of procedure and the rhetoric of the schools. For the omission of connectives in the *stile coupé* implies, as we have seen, a very definite kind of rhetorical form, which was practiced in direct imitation of classical models, and usually retained the associations that it had won in the Stoic schools of antiquity. The associations of the loose style, on the other hand, are all with the more sceptical phases of seventeenth-century thought—with what was then usually called "Libertinism"; and it appears characteristically in writers who are professed opponents of determined and rigorous philosophic attitudes. It is the style of Bacon and of Montaigne (after he has found himself), of La Mothe le Vayer, and of Sir Thomas Browne. It appears always in the letters of Donne; it appears in Pascal's *Pensées;* and, in the latter part of the century, when Libertinism had positively won the favor of the world away from Stoicism, it enjoyed a self-conscious revival, under the influence of Montaigne, in the writings of St. Évremond, Halifax, and Temple. Indeed, it is evident that, although the Senecan *stile coupé* attracted more critical attention throughout the century, its greatest achievements in prose were rather in the loose or Libertine manner. But it must also be said that most of the sceptics of the century had undergone a strong Senecan influence; and the styles of Montaigne, Browne, Pascal, and Halifax, for instance, can only be described as displaying in varying ways a mingling of Stoic and Libertine traits.

(B)

Besides the two syntactic forms that have been mentioned—the co-ordinating conjunctions and the absolute construction—there are no others that lend themselves by their nature to the loose style, except the parenthesis, which we need not illustrate here. But it must not be supposed that it tends to exclude other modes of connection. On the contrary, it obtains its characteristic effects from the syntactic forms that are logically more strict and binding, such as the relative pronouns and the subordinating conjunctions, by using them in a way peculiar to itself. That is to say, it uses them as the necessary logical means of advancing the idea, but relaxes at will the tight

construction which they seem to impose; so that they have exactly
the same effect as the loose connections previously described and
must be punctuated in the same way. In other words, the parts that
they connect are no more closely knit together than it chooses they
shall be; and the reader of the most characteristic seventeenth-century prose soon learns to give a greater independence and autonomy
to subordinate members than he would dare to do in reading any
other.

The method may be shown by a single long sentence from Sir
Thomas Browne:

> I could never perceive any rational consequence from those
> many texts which prohibit the children of Israel to pollute
> themselves with the temples of the heathens; we being all
> Christians, and not divided by such detested impieties *as* might
> profane our prayers, or the place wherein we make them; *or*
> *that* a resolved conscience may not adore her Creator any
> where, *especially* in places devoted to his service; *where,* if
> their devotions offend him, mine may please him; if theirs
> profane it, mine may hallow it.[14]

The period begins with a statement complete in itself, which does
not syntactically imply anything to follow it; an absolute participle
carries on, in the second member. Thereafter the connectives are
chiefly subordinating conjunctions. Observe particularly the use of
as, or that, and *where:* how slight these ligatures are in view of the
length and mass of the members they must carry. They are frail and
small hinges for the weights that turn on them; and the period
abounds and expands in nonchalant disregard of their tight, frail
logic.

This example displays the principle; but of course a single passage
call illustrate only a few grammatical forms. Some of those used with
a characteristic looseness in English prose of the seventeenth century
are: relative clauses beginning with *which,* or with *whereto, wherein,*
etc.; participial constructions of the kind scornfully called "dangling"
by the grammarians; words in a merely appositional relation with
some noun or pronoun preceding, yet constituting a semi-independent
member of a period; and of course such subordinating conjunctions
as are illustrated above. It is unnecessary to illustrate these various
cases.

(c)

The connections of a period cannot be considered separately from
the order of the connected members; and, in fact, it is the desired
order of development that determines the character of the connections rather than the reverse. In the oratorical period the arrangement
of the members is "round" or "circular," in the sense that they are
all so placed with reference to a central or climactic member that
they point forward or back to it and give it its appropriate emphasis.
This order is what is meant by the names *periodos, circuitus,* and
"round composition," by which the oratorical period has been variously called; and it is the chief object of the many revisions to which
its form is submitted.

The loose period does not try for this form, but rather seeks to
avoid it. Its purpose is to express, as far as may be, the order in
which an idea presents itself when it is first experienced. It begins,
therefore, without premeditation, stating its idea in the first form
that occurs; the second member is determined by the situation in
which the mind finds itself after the first has been spoken; and so
on throughout the period, each member being an emergency of the
situation. The period—in theory, at least—is not made; it becomes.
It completes itself and takes on form in the course of the motion of
mind which it expresses. Montaigne, in short, exactly described the
theory of the loose style when he said: "J'ecris volontiers sans project;
le premier trait produit le second."

The figure of a circle, therefore, is not a possible description of
the form of a loose period; it requires rather the metaphor of a chain,
whose links join end to end. The "linked" or "trailing" period is,
in fact, as we have observed, an appropriate name for it. But there
is a special case for which this term might better be reserved, unless
we should choose to invent a more specific one, such as "end-linking,"
or "terminal linking," to describe it. It is when a member depends,
not upon the general idea, or the main word, of the preceding
member, but upon its final word or phrase alone. And this is, in
fact, a frequent, even a characteristic, kind of linking in certain authors, notably Sir Thomas Browne and his imitators. The sentence
last quoted offers two or three illustrations of it: the connective
words *as, especially,* and *where* all refer to the immediately preceding
words or phrases; and in another period by the same author there is
one very conspicuous and characteristic instance.

As there were many reformers, so likewise many reforma-
tions; every country proceeding in a particular way and method,
according as their national interest, together with their con-
stitution and clime, inclined them: some angrily and with
extremity; others calmly and with mediocrity, not rending, but
easily dividing, the community, and leaving an honest possibility of a reconciliation;—*which,* though peaceable spirits do
desire, and may conceive that revolution of time and the mercies
of God may effect, yet that judgment that shall consider the
present antipathies between the two extremes,—their contra-
rieties in condition, affection, and opinion,—may with the same
hopes, expect a union in the poles of heaven.[15]

Here the word *which* introduces a new development of the idea,
running to as much as five lines of print; yet syntactically it refers
only to the last preceding word *reconciliation.* The whole long passage has been quoted, however, not for this reason alone, but because it illustrates so perfectly all that has been said of the order and
connection of the loose period. It begins, characteristically, with a
sharply formulated complete statement, implying nothing of what
is to follow. Its next move is achieved by means of an absolute-participle construction.[16] This buds off a couple of appositional members; one of these budding again two new members by means of
dangling participles. Then a *which* picks up the trail, and at once
the sentence becomes involved in the complex, and apparently tight,
organization of a *though . . . yet* construction. Nevertheless it still
moves freely, digressing as it will, extricates itself from the complex
form by a kind of anacoluthon (in the *yet* clause), broadening its
scope, and gathering new confluents, till it ends, like a river, in an
opening view.

The period, that is, moves straight onward everywhere from the
point it has reached; and its construction shows ideally what we
mean by the linked or trailing order. It is Browne's peculiar mastery
of this construction that gives his writing constantly the effect of
being, not the result of a meditation, but an actual meditation in
process. He writes like a philosophical scientist making notes of his
observation as it occurs. We see his pen move and stop as he thinks.
To write thus, and at the same time to create beauty of cadence in
the phrases and rhythm in the design—and so Browne constantly
does—is to achieve a triumph in what Montaigne called "the art

of being natural"; it is the eloquence, described by Pascal, that mocks
at formal eloquence.

(D)

The period just quoted serves to introduce a final point concerning
the form of the loose period. We have already observed that the
second half of this period, beginning with *which,* has a complex suspended syntax apparently like that of the typical oratorical sentence.
The Anti-Ciceronian writer usually avoids such forms, it is true;
most of his sentences are punctuated by colons and semicolons. But,
of course, he will often find himself involved in a suspended construction from which he cannot escape. It remains to show that even
in these cases he still proceeds in the Anti-Ciceronian manner, and
succeeds in following, in spite of the syntactic formalities to which
he commits himself, his own emergent and experimental order. Indeed, it is to be observed that the characteristic quality of the loose
style may appear more clearly in such difficult forms than in others.
For baroque art always displays itself best when it works in heavy
masses and resistant materials; and out of the struggle between a
fixed pattern and an energetic forward movement often arrives at
those strong and expressive disproportions in which it delights.

We shall return to Browne in a moment in illustration of the
point, but we shall take up a simpler case first. In a well-known
sentence, Pascal, bringing out the force of imagination, draws a picture of a venerable magistrate seated in church, ready to listen to
a worthy sermon. *Le voilà prêt à l'ouïr avec un respect exemplaire.*

> Que le prédicateur vienne à paraître, que la nature lui ait
> donné une voix enrouée et un tour de visage bizarre, que son
> barbier l'ait mal rasé, si le hasard l'a encore barbouillé de
> surcoît, quelque grandes vérités qu'il annonce, je parie la perte
> de la gravité de notre sénateur.[17]

Unquestionably a faulty sentence by all the school-rules! It begins
without foreseeing its end, and has to shift the reader's glance from
the preacher to the magistrate in the midst of its progress by whatever means it can. Observe the abruptness of the form of the member
quelque grandes vérités. Observe the sudden appearance of the first
person in the last member. Yet the critic who would condemn its

rhetorical form would have also to declare that there is no art in those vivid dramatic narratives that so often appear in the conversation of animated talkers; for this period moves in an order very common in such conversation.[18]

In this passage the free and Anti-Ciceronian character of the movement is chiefly due to its dramatic vividness and speed. It follows the order of life. Sometimes, however, we can see plainly that it is the mystical speculation of the seventeenth century that changes the regular form of the period and shapes it to its own ends. Sir Thomas Browne provides many interesting illustrations, as, for instance, in the period quoted in the preceding section, and in the following:

> I would gladly know how Moses, with an actual fire, calcined or burnt the golden calf into powder: for that mystical metal of gold, whose solary and celestial nature I admire, exposed unto the violence of fire, grows only hot, and liquefies, but consumeth not; so when the consumable and volatile pieces of our bodies shall be refined into a more impregnable and fixed temper, like gold, though they suffer from the action of flames, they shall never perish, but lie immortal in the arms of fire.[19]

With the first half of this long construction we are not now concerned. In its second half, however, beginning with *so when,* we see one of those complex movements that have led some critics to speak of Browne as—of all things!—a Ciceronian. It is in fact the opposite of that. A Ciceronian period closes in at the end; it reaches its height of expansion and emphasis at the middle or just beyond, and ends composedly. Browne's sentence, on the contrary, opens constantly outward; its motions become more animated and vigorous as it proceeds; and it ends, as his sentences are likely to do, in a vision of vast space or time, losing itself in an *altitudo,* a hint of infinity. As, in a previously quoted period, everything led up to the phrase, "a union in the poles of heaven," so in this everything leads up to the concluding phrase, "but lie immortal in the arms of fire." And as we study the form of the structure we can even observe where this ending revealed itself, or, at least, how it was prepared. The phrase "like gold" is the key to the form of the whole. After a slow expository member, this phrase, so strikingly wrenched from its logical position, breaks the established and expected rhythm, and is a signal of more agitated movement, of an ascending effort of imaginative realization that continues to the end. In a different medium, the period closely parallels the technique of an El Greco composition, where broken and tortuous lines in the body of the design prepare the eye for curves that leap upward beyond the limits of the canvas.

The forms that the loose period may assume are infinite, and it would be merely pedantic to attempt a classification of them. In one of the passages quoted we have seen the dramatic sense of reality triumphing over rhetorical formalism; in another, the form of a mystical exaltation. For the purpose of description—not classification —it will be convenient to observe still a third way in which a loose period may escape from the formal commitments of elaborate syntax. It is illustrated in a passage in Montaigne's essay "Des Livres," praising the simple and uncritical kind of history that he likes so much. In the course of the period he mentions le bon Froissard as an example, and proceeds so far (six lines of print) in a description of his method that he cannot get back to his general idea by means of his original syntactic form, or at least cannot do so without very artificial devices. He completes the sentence where it is; but completes his idea in a pair of curt (coupés) sentences separated by a colon from the preceding: "c'est la matiere de l'histoire nue et informe; chascun en peult faire son proufit autant qu'il a d'entendement." [20] This is a method often used by Anti-Ciceronians to extricate themselves from the coils of a situation in which they have become involved by following the "natural" order. A better example of it is to be seen in a passage from Pascal's essay on "Imagination," from which another passage has already been cited.

> Le plus grand philosophe du monde, sur une planche plus large qu'il ne faut, s'il y a au-dessous un précipice, quoique sa raison le convainque de sa sûreté, son imagination prévaudra. Plusieurs n'en sauraient soutenir la pensée sans pâlir et suer.[21]

Nothing could better illustrate the "order of nature"; writing, that is, in the exact order in which the matter presents itself. It begins by naming the subject, le plus grand philosophe, without foreseeing the syntax by which it is to continue. Then it throws in the elements of the situation, using any syntax that suggests itself at the moment, proceeding with perfect dramatic sequence, but wholly without logical sequence, until at last the sentence has lost touch with its stated subject. Accordingly, this subject is merely left hanging, and a new one, *son imagination,* takes its place. It is a violent, or rather a nonchalant, anacoluthon. The sentence has then, after a fashion, completed itself. But there is an uneasy feeling in the mind. After all, *le plus grand philosophe* has done nothing; both form and idea are incomplete. Pascal adds another member (for, whatever the punctuation, the *plusieurs* sentence is a member of the period), which completely meets the situation, though a grammatical purist may well object that the antecedent of *plusieurs* was in the singular number.

Pascal is usually spoken of as a "classical" writer; but the term means nothing as applied to him except that he is a writer of tried artistic soundness. He is, in fact, as modernistic, as bold a breaker of the rules and forms of rhetoric, as his master Montaigne, though he is also a much more careful artist. *La vraie éloquence,* he said, *se moque de l'éloquence.*

(E)

Two kinds of style have been analyzed in the preceding pages: the concise, serried, abrupt *stile coupé,* and the informal, meditative, and "natural" loose style. It is necessary to repeat—once more—that in the best writers these two styles do not appear separately in passages of any length, and that in most of them they intermingle in relations far too complex for description. They represent two sides of the seventeenth-century mind: its sententiousness, its penetrating wit, its Stoic intensity, on the one hand, and its dislike of formalism, its roving and self-exploring curiosity, in brief, its sceptical tendency, on the other. And these two habits of mind are generally not separated one from the other; nor are they even always exactly distinguishable. Indeed, as they begin to separate or to be opposed to each other in the second half of the century we are aware of the approach of a new age and a new spirit. The seventeenth century, as we are here considering it, is equally and at once Stoic and Libertine; and the prose that is most characteristic of it expresses these two sides of its mind in easy and natural relations one with the other.

IV. The Punctuation of the Seventeenth-Century Period

The "long sentence" of the Anti-Ciceronian age has received a remarkable amount of attention ever since it began to be corrected and go out of use; and there have been two conflicting views concerning it. The older doctrine—not yet quite extinct—was that the long sentences of Montaigne, Bacon, Browne, and Taylor were sentences of the same kind as those of Cicero and his sixteenth-century imitators; only they were badly and crudely made, monstrosities due to some wave of ignorance that submerged the syntactic area of the seventeenth-century mind. Their true character, it was thought, would be shown by substituting commas for their semicolons and colons; for then we should see that they are quaint failures in the attempt to achieve sentence unity.

The other view is the opposite of this, namely, that we should put periods in the place of many of its semicolons and colons. We should then see that what look like long sentences are really brief and aphoristic ones. The contemporary punctuation of our authors is again to be corrected, but now in a different sense. This is the view urged by Faguet in writing of Montaigne, and by Sir Edmund Gosse concerning the prose of Browne and Taylor.

The later view is useful in correcting some of the errors of the earlier one. But, in fact, one of them is just as false as the other; and both of them illustrate the difficulties experienced by minds trained solely in the logical and grammatical aspects of language in interpreting the forms of style that prevailed before the eighteenth century. In order to understand the punctuation of the seventeenth century we have to consider the relation between the grammatical term *sentence* and the rhetorical term *period*.

The things named by these terms are identical. *Period* names the rhetorical, or oral, aspect of the same thing that is called in grammar a *sentence* and in theory the same act of composition that produces a perfectly logical grammatical unit would produce at the same time a perfectly rhythmical pattern of sound. But, in fact, no utterance ever fulfils both of these functions perfectly, and either one or the other of them is always foremost in a writer's mind. One or the other is foremost also in every theory of literary education; and the historian may sometimes distinguish literary periods by the relative emphasis they put upon grammatical and rhetorical considerations. In general we may say, though there may be exceptions, that before the eighteenth century rhetoric occupied much more attention than grammar in the minds of teachers and their pupils. It was so, for instance, in the Middle Ages, as is clear from their manuals of study and the curricula of their schools. It was still true in the sixteenth century; and the most striking characteristic of the literary prose of that century, both in Latin and in the vernacular tongues, was its devotion to the conventional and formal patterns of school-rhetoric.

The laws of grammatical form, it is true, were not at all disturbed or strained at this time by the predominance of rhetorical motives. There was no difficulty whatever in saying what these rhetoricians had to say in perfect accordance with logical syntax because they had, in fact, so little to say that only the most elementary syntax was necessary for its purposes. Furthermore, the rhetorical forms they liked were so symmetrical, so obvious, that they almost imposed a regular syntax by their own form.

But a new situation arose when the leaders of seventeenth-century rationalism—Lipsius, Montaigne, Bacon—became the teachers of style. The ambition of these writers was to conduct an experimental investigation of the moral realities of their time, and to achieve a style appropriate to the expression of their discoveries and of the mental effort by which they were conducted. The content of style became, as it were, suddenly greater and more difficult; and the stylistic formalities of the preceding age were unable to bear the burden. An immense rhetorical complexity and license took the place of the simplicity and purism of the sixteenth century; and, since the age had not yet learned to think much about grammatical propriety, the rules of syntax were made to bear the expenses of the new freedom. In the examples of seventeenth-century prose that have been discussed in the preceding pages some of the results are apparent. The syntactic connections of a sentence become loose and casual; great strains are imposed upon tenuous, frail links; parentheses are abused; digression become licentious; anacoluthon is frequent and passes unnoticed; even the limits of sentences are not clearly marked, and it is sometimes difficult to say where one begins and another ends.

Evidently the process of disintegration could not go on forever. A stylistic reform was inevitable, and it must take the direction of a new formalism or "correctness." The direction that it actually took was determined by the Cartesian philosophy, or at least by the same time spirit in which the Cartesian philosophy had its origin. The intellect, that is to say, became the arbiter of form, the dictator of artistic practice as of philosophical inquiry. The sources of error, in the view of the Cartesians, are imagination and dependence upon sense impressions. Its correctives are found in what they call "reason" (which here means "intellect"), and an exact distinction of categories.

To this mode of thought we are to trace almost all the features of modern literary education and criticism, or at least of what we should have called modern a generation ago: the study of the precise meaning of words; the reference to dictionaries as literary authorities; the study of the sentence as a logical unit alone; the careful circumscription of its limits and the gradual reduction of its length; the disappearance of semicolons and colons; the attempt to reduce grammar to an exact science; the idea that forms of speech are always either correct or incorrect; the complete subjection of the laws of motion and expression in style to the laws of logic and standardization—in short, the triumph, during two centuries, of grammatical over rhetorical ideas.

This is not the place to consider what we have gained or lost by this literary philosophy, or whether the precision we have aimed at has compensated us for the powers of expression and the flexibility of motion that we have lost; we have only to say that we must not apply the ideas we have learned from it to the explanation of seventeenth-century style. In brief, we must not measure the customs of the age of semicolons and colons by the customs of the age of commas and periods. The only possible punctuation of seventeenth-century prose is that which it used itself. We might sometimes reveal its grammar more clearly by repunctuating it with commas or periods, but we should certainly destroy its rhetoric.

NOTES

1. *The Architecture of Humanism* (London, 1914), p. 225.
2. "Table Talk," in *Life and Letters,* ed. Logan Pearsall Smith (Oxford, 1907), II, 500.
3. For example, the *stile coupé* was sometimes called *stile serré* ("serried style"), and Francis Thompson has used this term in describing a kind of period common in Browne. For synonyms of "loose style" see section III of this paper.
4. References are as follows: Montaigne, "Des Livres," *Essais* II.x. ed. J.–V. Le Clerc (Paris, 1865), II, 122; Robert Burton, "To the Reader," *The Anatomy of Melancholy,* ed. A. R. Shilleto (London, 1893), p. 24; Owen Felltham, "Of Fear and Cowardice," *Resolves*

1. 71 (London, 1677), p. 110; Pascal, *Pensées*, ed. Léon Brunschvicg (Paris, 1904), II, 146 (section VII in 1670 Port-Royal ed.); *Pensées*, II, 269 (section XXI in Port-Royal ed.); Sir Thomas Browne, *Religio Medici*, Part II, section 11, in *Works*, ed. Simon Wilkin (London, 1846), II, 110; La Bruyère, "Des Esprits Forts," (*Œuvres*, ed. G. Servois (Paris, 1865), II, 239. These editions have been used for subsequent quotations from the authors' works.

5. The phrase comes from a midseventeenth-century work on prose style, and is there applied to *il dir moderno*: Daniello Bartoli, "Dello Stile," *Dell' Uomo di Lettere*, in *Opere* (Venice, 1716), III, 101.

6. Joseph Hall, *Heaven upon Earth*, XIII, in *Works* (Oxford, 1837), VI, 20. Note how exactly this reproduces a movement characteristic of Seneca: *Quid tua, uter* [Caesar or Pompey] *vincat? Potest melior vincere: non potest pejor esse qui vicerit.*

7. *Religio Medici*, 1.10 and 1.42, in *Works*, II, 14, 61.

8. For instance, in the famous passage "De l'Homme," 128, in *Œuvres*, II, 61, describing the beast-like life of the peasants of France.

9. *Christian Morals*, section XXI, *Works*, IV, 107. The period occurs in the midst of a paragraph in which each main member of each period begins with a verb in the imperative mood.

10. No. XVIII, "De Montaigne et de ses Escrits," in *Œuvres*, ed. L. Moreau (Paris, 1854), II, 402–403.

11. 1.6, in *Works*, II, 11. Feltham uses this manner with too much self-consciousness. See, for instance, a passage on the terse style (*Resolves*, 1.20) beginning "They that speak to *children*, assume a pretty lisping."

12. *Of the Advancement of Learning*, Bk. II, in *Works*, ed. Spedding, Ellis, and Heath (London, 1868), III, 403–404; ed. Wright, XVII.3.

13. Pascal, *Pensées*, II, 3 (section XXV in 1670 Port-Royal ed.). There should, rhetorically speaking, be semicolons after *raison* and *misérables*.

14. *Religio Medici*, 1.3, in *Works*, II, 4. Italics are mine.

15. *Religio Medici*, 1.4, in *Works*, II, 5.

16. Observe that the period from Browne quoted on p. 223 begins with movements of the same kind.

17. *Pensées*, II, 4–5 (section XXV in Port-Royal ed.).

18. It may be said that Pascal's *Pensées* should not be cited in illustration of prose form because they were written without revision and without thought of publication. But a good deal of characteristic prose of the time was so written, and the effect at which Bacon, Burton, Browne, and many others aimed was of prose written in that way.

19. *Religio Medici*, 1.50, in *Works*, II, 73.

20. *Essais*, II.x, ed. Le Clerc, II, 127.

21. *Pensées*, II, 5.

JONAS A. BARISH

Jonson's Dramatic Prose

In developing a series of assumptions about style, one might start with
the hypotheses of Benjamin Lee Whorf in his essays on "metalinguis-
tics." Whorf, inspecting such languages as Hopi, discovers that the
radical differences in structure and pattern between them and such
languages as English—"behavioral compulsions," as he calls them—
amount to radical differences in ways of interpreting reality, that
grammatical patterns are "interpretations of experience" reflecting
deep-seated habits of response to the world. Indo-European languages, for Whorf, tend to "spatialize" experience, even those aspects
of experience that on reflection have little to do with space. These
languages carve up the world into collections of discrete "things"
and "events," whereas in Hopi "events are considered the expression
of invisible intensity factors, on which depend their stability and
persistence, or their fugitiveness and proclivities"; [1] physical processes
involving motion—waves, wind, lightning—are never compartmental-
ized into units, but regarded, in the very grammar of the language,
as continuing processes. Grammar, then, is not a set of mere inert
categories through which speakers "express" "their" "thoughts" about
an "objective" reality, but is itself shot through with a highly partisan
vision of reality from which no speaker can escape. Grammatical

From *Ben Jonson and the Language of Prose Comedy* (Harvard University
Press, 1960), pp. 41–89. Reprinted by permission of the publisher and author.
For Jonson abbreviations see note 18, below.

processes have a meaning beyond any consciously intended by their
users, a meaning roughly translatable into a set of shared postulates
about the world, and such meanings vary strikingly between languages like Hopi and English.

Within the range of a language group like the Indo-European, the
differences will be smaller and more elusive. But that they exist one
can assert by appealing to the experience of learning a foreign language, which always involves, to some extent, learning to think in
a new way. The lexical habits and syntactic strategies of a new
tongue imply, and impose, new habits of perception. Erwin Panofsky
has described the salutary effect of having to learn to write in English after a lifetime of writing in German—salutary because the shift
forced him for the first time to understand some of his own terms:
"The German language unfortunately permits a fairly trivial thought
to declaim from behind a woolen curtain of apparent profundity and
conversely, a multitude of meanings to lurk behind one term"; German catchall terms like *taktisch* and *malerisch* now had to be reun-
derstood as composites of up to seven or eight distinct ideas, and
broken down accordingly.[2] The French tongue is preferred for drawing up international treaties in Europe, because French, it is felt,
by the nature of its grammar, binds the speaker (or writer) to a more
logical form of expression than any other language; it discourages
ambiguities and insists on clarity of reference. And without pretending to perceive all the terms of the comparison, one can see in the
"multiplicity" of German and the "Cartesian" qualities of French,
described by writers like Charles Bally,[3] a corollary to other significant
cultural differences.

But languages may also differ within themselves, notably from one
epoch to another, and here too the differences involve—whether as
cause or effect—differences in modes of perception. The change that
occurred when the language of the English Renaissance crystallized
into that of the Restoration is bound up with a change in the whole
form and texture of English thinking, a change symbolized by the
names of John Locke and Isaac Newton. Behind all the observable
stylistic details of the shift—the effort to make words express real
"things" on the one hand, and embody the exactness of mathematical
symbolism on the other, the narrowing range of meaning of words,
the desire to write in clear and distinct ideas, to articulate sentences
logically—"behind all the particular techniques," according to Andrews Wanning, "is a driving urge to reduce all the factors of dis-

course to tangible worldly things or to explicable abstractions from them." [4] The new view of the world embodied in the altered language expresses itself, needless to say, in virtually every phase of English culture.

But even at a given moment, within a single language, there may be a plurality of stylistic conventions, each a reduction of one or another aspect of current speech. The studies of Morris W. Croll [5] and others [6] attempt to educe from the literature of the Renaissance a set of characteristics that permits some writers to be termed "baroque" or "libertine" or "Stoic," others "Ciceronian" or "Euphuistic"—largely by virtue of the grammatical tactics these writers prefer. Complicating the situation is the fact that Croll's findings cut across linguistic boundaries to some extent. But indeed they would, in any epoch of European history: Europe shares a common past, and its languages evolve together as well as separately.

The narrowing circles of convention bring us closer and closer to the individual writer, and to conscious linguistic artistry. The gulf between Hopi and English exists on a deep, unconscious level, as does that between one Indo-European language and another until bridged (if at all) by study. Conscious purpose plays some part in the historical transformations of a single language, but here too no doubt the determining factor is still the imponderable calculus of thousands of instances of unreflecting usage. When we reach literary categories such as Croll's "baroque," we are dealing with a convention that is at the same time a collective style, since its practitioners have chosen more or less deliberately to adhere to one set of conventional practices rather than another. [7] When we move from the collective style to the individual artist, we reach the province of style *tout court*, where the writer stamps the shared style with the imprint of his own temperament. Often, however, within the limits of a collective style, individual accents may be difficult to distinguish; there are writers who simply adopt current clichés without ever conferring on them a distinctive stamp. And a powerful style may breed a race of imitations that—in fragments at least—can hardly be told apart from their parent. "Stylistic devices," one must remind oneself, "can be imitated very successfully," and "their possible original expressive function can disappear. They can become . . . mere empty husks, decorative tricks, craftsman's *clichés*. The whole relationship between soul and word is looser and more oblique than it is frequently assumed." [8]

Stylistic studies would seem to need an approach located somewhere between two pillars of unwisdom, between extreme statistic-
hunting on the one hand and rank impressionism on the other, one
that accepts the subjective basis for judgments of style but places this
under conditions of maximum control. The method of Leo Spitzer,
who urges first the scrutiny of an author's linguistic habits to discover what details of style are peculiar to him, and then—with the
aid of provisional hypotheses—the use of these elements as keys to
the artist's larger outlook,[9] seems to offer an approach at once definite
enough and flexible. Spitzer's own admirable essays of this kind,[10]
together with those of Vernon Lee,[11] Erich Auerbach,[12] Jean-Paul
Sartre,[13] Harry Levin, [14] and R. A. Sayce [15]—to name a diversified
group of brilliant performers working along similar lines—may be
mentioned, not as models, but as indications of the general direction
this study intends to pursue.

I

Since Jonson's stylistic habits differ so radically from Shakespeare's,
a rapid comparison of representative passages may serve here as a
convenient point of departure. First, the opening prose speech from
the first part of *Henry IV*:

> *Falstaff.* Now *Hal,* what time of day is it Lad?
> *Prince Hal.* Thou art so fat-witted with drinking of olde
> Sacke, and vnbuttoning thee after Supper, and sleeping vpon
> Benches in the afternoone, that thou hast forgotten to demand
> that truely, which thou wouldest truly know. What a diuell
> hast thou to do with the time of the day? vnlesse houres were
> cups of Sacke, and minutes Capons, and clockes the tongues of
> Bawdes, and dialls the signes of Leaping-houses, and the blessed
> Sunne himselfe a faire hot Wench in Flame-coloured Taffata;
> I see no reason, why thou shouldest bee so superfluous, to de-
> maund the time of the day.   (L.369; *IHIV* I.ii.1–13)

Then, two opening speeches from *Every Man out of his Humour*
and *Poetaster*:

> Come, come, leaue these fustian protestations: away, come, I
> cannot abide these gray-headed ceremonies. Boy, fetch me a

glasse, quickly, I may bid these gentlemen welcome; giue 'hem
a health here: I mar'le whose wit 'twas to put a prologue in
yond' sack-buts mouth: they might well thinke hee'd be out of
tune, and yet you'ld play vpon him too. (EMO Ind. 319–325)
Young master, master OVID, doe you heare? gods a mee! away
with your *songs*, and *sonnets;* and on with your gowne and
cappe, quickly: here, here, your father will be a man of this
roome presently. Come, nay, nay, nay, nay, be briefe. These
verses too, a poyson on 'hem, I cannot abide 'hem, they make
mee readie to cast, by the bankes of *helicon.* Nay looke, what
a rascally vntoward thing this *poetrie* is; I could teare 'hem now.

> *(Poet.* I.i.4–11)

The first thing we notice is that the rhythm of the Shakespearean
passage is slower, fuller, more oratorical, that of the Jonsonian passages more abrupt, staccato, and sharp. And these differences can
be quickly traced to the fact that Shakespeare is using not only
longer phrases, but a more oratorical, more symmetrical syntax than
Jonson. In

> Thou are so fat-witted
> with drinking of olde Sacke,
> and vnbuttoning thee after Supper,
> and sleeping vpon Benches in the afternoone,

we find not only the parisonic exactness of "drinking," "vnbutton-
ing," and "sleeping," but the fact that the three phrases are arranged
in climactic order: each succeeding one represents a more advanced
stage in Falstaff's surrender to sloth, and each is longer than its
predecessor; with "sleeping vpon Benches in the afternoone" we
reach the fullest phrase and Falstaff's final collapse into indolence.
But this sequence itself forms only a suspension, the first, or causal,
half of the "so . . . that" pattern, and leads into a resolution, the
assertion of an effect, which itself turns a somewhat intricate little
antithesis on the object of "demand." The question that follows
serves as a pause, and also to re-engage the logical machinery of the
argument. After which the Prince embarks on another periodic
sentence, more elaborate than the first, with a much more strongly
marked climax—

                              vnlesse
               houres were cups of Sacke,
               and minutes Capons,
               and clockes the tongues of Bawdes,
               and dialls the signes of Leaping-houses,
               and the blessed Sunne himselfe a faire hot Wench in
                    Flame-coloured Taffata

—and consequently a more incisive resolution, which forms a cadence
not only to the sentence itself but to the whole speech, and crowns
the argument of it at the same time. The speech has thus a beginning, a middle, and an end—an introductory flourish, a development,
and a full close—and its internal parts are constructed with similar
solidity.

By contrast, the speeches of Carlo Buffone and Luscus simulate
live language much more closely, or seem to, and the reason is that
they reject the figures of balance, parallel, and climax used by
Shakespeare. They are heavily punctuated with monosyllabic ex-
pletives like "Come, come," "gods a mee," "Nay looke," which introduce a nervous stutter into the rhythm and prevent it from
achieving any full curve. Occasional symmetrical details, such as the
"fustian protestations" and "gray-headed ceremonies" of Carlo, jab
at each other instead of acting as rhythmic pairs, or else, as in "away
with your *songs,* and *sonnets;* and on with your gowne and cappe,"
they suggest self-conscious cuteness on the part of the speaker.
Logical connectives are scarce. In "fetch me a glasse, quickly, I may
bid these gentlemen welcome; giue 'hem a health here," the expected "that" or its equivalent between the first two clauses and the
"and" that might have linked the second two have both been suppressed, so that Carlo seems to be pouncing convulsively from one
idea to another. "Giue 'hem a health here," stitched on in apposition,
has the air of a sudden afterthought. Then the malicious remarks
about the boy, who has gone off-stage to fetch a glass, consist of
three clauses glaringly unlike. Like Prince Hal in his final sentence,
Carlo pursues a single metaphor through his, but the inequality
among the members sets them tensely at odds with each other instead of engaging them in a cooperative enterprise, and the rhythm,
as a result, is jagged and discontinuous instead of round and sonorous.

At such moments, Jonson reproduces the accent of living speech
so convincingly that he seems to have abandoned rhetorical artifice.

We are indebted to Morris Croll for showing that this kind of language, which moves in streaks and flashes rather than with a steady pulsation, springs itself from a highly articulate rhetorical theory, that of anti-Ciceronianism, that it has its roots in certain philosophical attitudes, chiefly Stoic and libertine, and that it has its own preferred masters of style in Seneca and Tacitus.

The writers whom Croll calls "baroque"—a term that will be adopted here for its convenience without any insistence on its exactness [16]—shared a distrust of the Ciceronian mode of sentence formation. This is not to say that they despised Cicero, the Vitruvius of Renaissance prose, or were uninfluenced by him, but only that they reacted against his oratorical manner. Jonson's admiration of Cicero is writ large (too large) in *Catiline,* and elsewhere, but Jonson was one of the least Ciceronian of writers. Ciceronian style was marked above all by the periodic sentence, as in the passage from *Henry IV* above,[17] where the syntax remains incomplete up to some well-defined turning point, with phrases and clauses tending to mass themselves in parallel formation on both sides of the turning point. The characteristic effects of this style were achieved by advance planning: one knew from the outset of a period where it was going and how it was going to get there. When it reached its destination, it afforded the gratification of a design finally complete, every piece falling into its place in the whole. Baroque style, on the other hand, aimed to give the impression, at least, of spontaneity, and hence its first concern was to break the stranglehold of the suspended sentence, to keep its syntax unencumbered and uncommitted, so as to be free to improvise in any way at any moment.

Now it may be objected with perfect justice at this point that Hal's speech *does* give the impression of spontaneity, that far from seeming artfully composed, it sounds as casually offhand as the speeches of Carlo or Luscus. Improvisation needs ground rules, and Hal's construction of a certain syntactic frame gives him freedom: he does not have to worry about what to do with his clauses, or where to put them. Having erected a rapid scaffolding that presupposes some degree of balance and likeness, he can proceed to forget it and concentrate on the details; he can extemporize, as he does, with lordly abandon. The suspended sentence, for him, is no stranglehold, but a set of strong struts. Shakespeare may be planning his effects with the utmost care, but Hal, at least, seems to be talking with perfect naturalness. One wonders, then, whether baroque

writers were not misled, partly by abuses of Ciceronian style, partly
by its origin in formal oratory, into thinking that it contained some
intrinsic barrier to uninhibited thought; whether, tilting against the
reader's expectations, they did not find themselves conducting cam-
paigns of sabotage that involved more premeditation than the pre-
meditated style they were warring against; whether, as a result, their
own rhetoric is not parasitic in a peculiar way, unthinkable without
the background of "normal" Renaissance practice.

In any event, baroque writers regarded Ciceronianism as an invitation to glibness and insincerity, and their first aim was to replace
its logical schemes with various nonlogical maneuvers of their own,
which Croll has grouped into the two categories of the "curt style"
and the "loose style."

The curt style, illustrated above in the passage from *Every Man
out of his Humour*, owes its name, and its other names of *stile coupé*
and *stile serré*, to its abruptness and choppiness in contrast to
Ciceronian "roundness"; its characteristic device is the so-called "exploded" period, formed of independent members not linked by conjunctions but set apart by a vocal pattern of stress, pitch, and juncture
rendered typographically by a colon or a semicolon, sometimes a
comma. The members of the exploded period tend to brevity, also
to inequality of length, variation in form, and unpredictability of
order; hence they are likely to suggest the effect of live thinking
rather than of logical premeditation. The "mere fact" or main idea
of the period is apt to be exhausted in the first member; subsequent
members explore the same idea imaginatively, through metaphor or
aphorism or example, but not through ordered analysis.

> *Natures* that are hardned to *evill,* you shall sooner breake, then
> make straight; they are like poles that are crooked, and dry:
> there is no attempting them.[18]   (*Disc.* 36–38)
> They are, what they are on the sudden; they shew presently,
> like *Graine*, that, scatter'd on the top of the ground, shoots up,
> but takes no root; has a yellow blade, but the eare empty.
>   (*Disc.* 685–688)
> *The great* theeves of a State are lightly the officers of the
> Crowne; they hang the lesse still; play the Pikes in the Pond;
> eate whom they list.   (*Disc.* 1306–08)

In each of these instances, the initial member encompasses the cen-

tral idea at a single stroke; the members that follow illuminate or
particularize with metaphor. In the last example, Jonson exchanges
one metaphor for another: the officers of the crown start as thieves
of the state and end as great pikes in a pond. And if one were to
quote the period that follows, one would discover the same officers
turning into fowlers who spread nets for harmless birds but allow
the hawks and buzzards to escape. The progress of such a period,
then, is typically not a logical sequence but "a series of imaginative
moments occurring in a logical pause or suspension," [19] in which
ideas develop out of each other associatively rather than according
to any predetermined scheme. That the curt style cannot dispense
with logic altogether is perhaps too obvious to need saying. What
it can do is to excise logical ligatures, to play haphazardly and
capriciously with its elements so as to minimize the sense of logical
straitness.

Because of the freedom of its internal elements, the curt period
lends itself to the expression of quick shifts in feeling, afterthoughts,
self-corrections, unexpected interpolations or dislocations of attention,
and since in so doing it stimulates so convincingly the processes of
live thought, it becomes an ideal instrument for certain kinds of
theatrical prose.[20] Jonson uses it in a variety of ways. One characteristic way is to turn it into a vehicle for wit, allowing each successive clause, as it springs from its predecessor, to exploit the latent
potentialities of a metaphor:

> Ne're trust me, Cvpid, but you are turn'd a most acute gallant
> of late, the edge of my wit is cleere taken off with the fine and
> subtile stroke of your thin-ground tongue, you fight with too
> poinant a phrase, for me to deale with.   (CR I.i.77–81)

Here the epithet "acute" used by Mercury in the first clause prompts
its own figurative extension into the "thin-ground tongue" of the
second, after which the pointed tongue becomes the sword with
which Cupid "fights" his combats of wit. A related instance of the
curt style used for purposes of wit proves to be an "exploded" period in more senses than one. Each clause ignites a verbal fuse that
goes off as a pun in the next clause, after the manner of a chain of
firecrackers.

> He walkes most commonly with a cloue, or pick-tooth in his

mouth, hee is the very mint of complement, all his behauiours
are printed, his face is another volume of *essayes;* and his beard
an *Aristarchus.*   (CR II.iii.87–91)

The puns kindle each other by association. "Cloue" suggests a pun
on "mint," which leads to an equivocation on "printed," which gen-
erates a quibbling metaphor on "volume" and "*essayes.*"
   In such cases, the language focuses sharply on its satiric object.
The tone may be biting or not, but its primary purpose is to demolish
its object, not to define its speaker. Used more complexly, the curt
period does both at once: it sheds light on the creature being described, and it reveals the creature who is speaking.

> . . . a leane mungrell, he lookes as if he were chap-falne, with
> barking at other mens good fortunes: 'ware how you offend
> him, he carries oile and fire in his pen, will scald where it
> drops: his spirit's like powder, quick, violent: hee'le blow a
> man vp with a jest: I feare him worse then a rotten wall do's
> the cannon, shake an houre after, at the report.
>   (EMO I.ii.212–218)

Carlo Buffone, whose spiteful disposition is revealed chiefly in his
penchant for coining scurrilous similitudes, leaps here from the figure of the starved dog to that of scalding oil and fire to that of gunpowder to describe Macilente, and then to a variation of the
gunpowder figure in which he imagines himself as a rotten wall
blasted by the cannon of Macilente's wit: a good illustration of the
spiraling or rotating movement of the curt period, and of how its
sputtering rhythms may be made to define an excitable temperament
like Carlo's. The unstable tension of the curt period serves similarly
to characterize another high-strung individual, Pantilius Tucca,
whose invectives against Horace flicker back and forth between
metaphoric and literal abuse, and whose speech rhythms tend even
more than Carlo's to stumble and trip in nervous jabs of clauses.

> Hang him fustie *satyre,* he smells all goate; hee carries a ram,
> vnder his arme-holes, the slaue: I am the worse when I see him.
>   (*Poet.* III.iv. 367–369)

> A sharpe thornie-tooth'd *satyricall* rascall, flie him; hee carries
> hey in his horne: he wil sooner lose his best friend, then his
> least iest.   (*Poet.* IV.iii.109–111)

As these extracts suggest, the curt period serves especially well to
characterize angry or indignant, impatient or volatile, or merely dis-
tracted or simple-minded people. Quarlous can dismiss Edgeworth
in two irate clauses, and follow these with two more of stinging
censure on his way of life.

> But goe your wayes, talke not to me, the hangman is onely fit
> to discourse with you; the hand of Beadle is too mercifull a
> punishment for your Trade of life.   (*BF* IV.vi.26–28)

Or the curt period can portray the spluttering, almost incoherent
indignation of a Wasp, who states a proposition ("I am no Clearke")
and particularizes it in a series of nonlogical convulsions.

> That's well, nay, neuer open, or read it to me, it's labour in
> vaine, you know. I am no Clearke, I scorne to be sau'd by my
> booke, i'faith I'll hang first; fold it vp o' your word and gi' it
> mee; what must you ha' for't?   (*BF* I.iv.6–9)

Or it can reproduce the idiotic flapping about of a half-witted mind,
swayed aimlessly in opposite directions by the gusts of childish ap-
petite.

> I ha' paid for my peares, a rot on 'hem, I'le keepe 'hem no
> longer; you were choake-peares to mee; I had bin better ha'
> gone to mum chance for you, I wusse.   (*BF* IV.ii.73–75)
> S'lid, this is an Asse, I ha' found him, poxe vpon mee, what
> doe I talking to such a dull foole; farewell, you are a very
> Coxcomb, doe you heare?   (*BF* IV.ii.105–107)

It may implement the language of abuse, as we have already seen,
or it may serve to convey the disordered prattle of semisenility, as in
the speeches of Venus in *Christmas his Masque*.

> Yes forsooth, I can sit any where, so I may see [my] *Cupid* act;

hee is a pretty Child, though I say it that perhaps should not,
you will say: I had him by my first Husband, he was a Smith
forsooth, we dwelt in Doe-little lane then, he came a moneth
before his time, and that may make him somewhat imperfect:
But I was a Fishmongers daughter.   (123–129)

The scatterbrained effect is secured by the multiplicity of brief
clauses, most of them syntactically unconnected; each starts off
afresh with its own new subject, so that the result is a pepper pot
of random remarks, loosely governed by chronology but otherwise
innocent of logic. The "But" that introduces the final statement not
only lacks logical force: it is disruptive of logic, and so crowns the
effect of incoherence.

It should perhaps be emphasized that the speeches of such characters as Wasp, Tucca, and Carlo Buffone do not represent a mere
tic of punctuation on the one hand or a mere slavish transcription
of heard language on the other, but a distinct style; their barking
phrases translate into stage idiom the staccato effects of *stile coupé*.
It is true enough that people often speak so, and it is also true that
one may find patches of similar language in the popular comedy of
the 1590's. But what in earlier writers is a mere incidental twitch
Jonson transmutes into a structural principle. He takes the sprawling,
ramshackle popular language and disengages from it the strain congenial to his own rhetorical bent, thus effecting a kind of merger
between colloquial speech and his own Stoic models. The result is
a stage prose that combines the vitality of live language with the
authority and expressive potency of a formed rhetoric.

The highly impressionable Shakespeare was not likely to be im-
mune to influence from this rhetorical current, and it may be suggested that along with the primary voice Shakespeare has a subsidiary
voice that sounds much like a modified version of the curt style. One
might, however, prefer to call the Shakespearean variant something
like "plain statement," since it tends to consist of a procession of simple declarative or imperative clauses with little of the "explosiveness"
peculiar to curt style:

I haue dogg'd him like his murtherer. He does obey euery point
of the Letter that I dropt, to betray him: He does smile his face
into more lynes, then is in the new Mappe, with the augmenta-
tion of the Indies: you haue not seene such a thing as tis: I

can hardly forbeare hurling things at him, I know my Ladie will strike him: if shee doe, hee'l smile, and take't for a great fauour. (L.284; *TN* III.ii.81–89)

I would the Duke we talke of were return'd againe: this vngenitur'd Agent will vn-people the Prouince with Continencie. Sparrowes must not build in his house-eeues, because they are lecherous: The Duke yet would haue darke deeds darkelie answered, hee would neuer bring them to light: would hee were return'd. (L.92; *MM* III.ii.183–190)

Looke, th'vnfolding Starre calles vp the Shepheard; put not your selfe into amazement, how these things should be; all difficulties are but easie vvhen they are knowne. Call your executioner, and off with *Barnardines* head: I will giue him a present shrift, and aduise him for a better place.
(L.95; *MM* IV.ii.219–227)

When I bestryde him, I soare, I am a Hawke: he trots the ayre: the Earth sings, when he touches it: the basest horne of his hoofe, is more Musicall then the Pipe of *Hermes*.
(L.435; *HV* III.vii.16–19)

Leaue him to my displeasure. *Edmond,* keepe you our Sister company: the reuenges wee are bound to take vppon your Traitorous Father, are not fit for your beholding. Aduice the Duke where you are going, to a most festi[n]ate preparation: we are bound to the like. Our Postes shall be swift, and intelligent betwixt vs. (L.807; *Lear* III.vii.6–13)

Alas, the storme is come againe: my best way is to creepe vnder his Gaberdine: there is no other shelter hereabout: Misery acquaints a man with strange bedfellowes: I will here shrowd till the dregges of the storme be past. (L.27; *Temp.* I.ii.37–43)

Such speeches show certain traits of the *stile coupé*: its discontinuousness, its avoidance of logical particles, its shifts in grammatical form, perhaps above all its apparent innocence of rhetorical cunning. They differ from their Jonsonian counterparts in that the members tend to be more equal in length, and also longer, so that the rhythm is slower and gentler. Characteristically Shakespeare will insert into the middle of an otherwise highly wrought discourse one or two such clauses, which have the effect of tranquilizing the rhythm, of affording a moment's breathing-space for the actor and a pause in the forward march of the argument.

What the Shakespearean passages do not have is the bristling asymmetry of the Jonsonian speeches. George Williamson has objected to Croll's emphasis on this trait, and suggested that Croll, having committed himself to the analogy with baroque, was led to discover asymmetry in places where, in fact, symmetry predominates.[21] Williamson, by way of rejoinder, illustrates from Bacon, and with this correction, insofar as it applies to Bacon, one can only gladly agree: asymmetry, where it occurs in Bacon, remains tangential. But Jonson is another matter. "Asymmetrical" seems to define the shape of Jonson's prose so exactly that one is tempted to use it to describe the topography of his mind. Jonson delights in bending the logical axis of syntax a few degrees one way or another in order to interrupt a symmetrical pattern, to sprawl suddenly or compress unexpectedly in a way that pulls the reader up short. One may get at the difference between Bacon's style and Jonson's by comparing a passage from *The Advancement of Learning* with Jonson's adaptation of it in the *Discoveries*.

> This grew speedily to an excess; for men began to hunt more after words than matter; more after the choiceness of the phrase, and the round and clean composition of the sentence, and the sweet falling of the clauses, and the varying and illustration of their works with tropes and figures, than after the weight of matter, worth of subject, soundness of argument, life of invention or depth of judgment.[22]

The thing that impresses itself on one immediately here is the careful regularity of the sentence. The exact antithesis "more after words than matter" undergoes artful expansion in the member that follows, first into four aspects of the hunt after words:

> the choiceness of the phrase,
> the round and clean composition of the sentence,
> the sweet falling of the clauses,
> the varying and illustration of their works with tropes and
>   figures.

The four phrases fall neatly into two sets of two each. In each set the second phrase is longer than the first, and each of the phrases of the second set is longer than its counterpart in the first. One result of this strict geometrical plotting is to produce an effect of climax, to bring us to a rhythmic plateau on the phrase "with tropes and figures," after which the second half of the antithesis elaborates itself serenely into a series of five component phrases that observe exact correspondence of parts. If one were to continue quoting at this point, one would discover Bacon launching into a new sequence of parallel statements extending through five sentences: "Then grew the flowing and watery vein of Osorius the Portuguese bishop, to be in price. Then did Sturmius . . . Then did Car of Cambridge . . . Then did Erasmus . . . Then grew . . . In sum . . ." As for the sentence preceding the quoted extract, it leads up to the antithesis between words and matter by enumerating four reasons why "eloquence and variety of discourse" came to be preferred to solidity of thought. The extract from Bacon, then, not only displays a high degree of formal clarity in itself: it forms part of a sequence that is highly articulated logically, that unfolds in parallel and antithetic statements, and that preserves parisonic correspondence in many of its inner parts in order to emphasize its logical divisions.

When we turn to Jonson's paraphrase, the first thing we notice is that the period in question is no longer a complete grammatical unit. It is fused to what precedes it, by virtue of the fact that its first verb, "make," simply forms the last in a series of subordinate verbs dependent on "Wee must" in the prior sentence. The prior sentence itself issues a plea for patience in the study of style that flickers restlessly back and forth between positive and negative counsel. The plea concludes, then, with the paraphrase from Bacon:

> Then make exact animadversion where style hath degenerated, where flourish'd, and thriv'd in choisenesse of Phrase, round and cleane composition of sentence, sweet falling of the clause, varying an illustration by tropes and figures, weight of Matter, worth of Subject, soundnesse of Argument, life of Invention, and depth of Judgement. This is *Monte potiri*, to get the hill. For no perfect Discovery can bee made upon a flat or a levell.
>
> (*Disc.* 2116–24)

Jonson has eliminated Bacon's dichotomy between rhetorical curiosity and solidity of thought, and lumped together the phrases from both sides of Bacon's antithesis in a single top-heavy series. Further, he has cut away most of the articles and all the connectives, so that the period now produces an unexpected effect of abruptness. Finally, he has embedded the passage in what is itself, so to speak, an asymmetrical context, commencing with the freely zigzagging period that precedes the quoted excerpt, and ending with the two brusque periods that close the section like two hammer blows. He ends, hence, with a gnarled and knotted texture only remotely akin to the clearspun weave of the Baconian original.

One does find occasional stretches of exact or nearly exact symmetry in Jonson, but these tend to have a sledge-hammer brevity that transmits first of all a sense of power, and only secondarily the feeling of balance: "Some wits are swelling, and high; others low and still: Some hot and fiery; others cold and dull: One must have a bridle, the other a spurre" (*Disc.* 678–680). And when Jonson uses exact symmetry in his plays, he is almost always ridiculing it as an affectation on the part of the speaker. But in fact symmetrical repetition in Jonson infrequently extends—as it does here—beyond the bounds of a single clause. For the most part it is phrasal rather than clausal symmetry, which means that it appears in unpredictable clumps; and so instead of shaping the outlines of the syntax as a whole, and providing clear signposts from one unit of utterance to the next, it merely intensifies the prevailing irregularity.

> There shall the Spectator see some, insulting with Joy; others, fretting with Melancholy; raging with Anger; mad with Love; boiling with Avarice; undone with Riot; tortur'd with expectation; consum'd with feare: no perturbation in common life, but the Orator findes an example of it in the Scene.
>
> (*Disc.* 2537–43)

The violent verbal adjectives, the absence of linking terms, the heavy pointing, place a greater and greater weight on each member of the series, especially since nothing signals to us when the series will end. The series erupts, flings itself at us with steadily increasing pressure, and then gathers and collapses into the summary that follows the colon. The sentence travels through fields of force rather than through preordained paths of logic.

The fact is that although Bacon pioneered in anti-Ciceronianism, his own style remains conservative in another way. As George Williamson has shown, Baconian prose has close affinities with Euphuism,[23] and Euphuism imposes constraints of its own. If the suspensions of a Ciceronian period demand grammatical resolution, the symmetrical configurations of Euphuistic prose demand psychological resolution—the more so the more the logicality of the design becomes evident, the more the reader comes to expect for each turn a counter-turn. In a context of precise antitheses, the first half of an antithesis, no matter how self-contained grammatically, cries out for its matching other half. "The unicorn is white; the hippogriff is black. The unicorn is graceful; the hippogriff is clumsy. The unicorn is caught by maidens; . . ." One might speak of such a suspension as para-tactic, occurring after a grammatically closed unit, in the manner of a coordinate clause, in contrast to the hypotactic suspension of Ciceronian style, where the grammar remains "open" until the sus-pension is resolved. But whatever term one applies to it, one must recognize that such a technique sets up expectations as exigent as those of the more familiar Ciceronian variety. Bacon's style, on the whole, commits itself to satisfying such expectations. The baroque writers properly speaking are those who eschew both sorts of sus-pension, the hypotactic and the paratactic, or—even more important —who initiate periodic or symmetrical motions only to frustrate them.

This is precisely Jonson's procedure. Where he arouses expecta-tions of symmetry, it is usually for the purpose of violating it. When an implicitly symmetrical pattern is perpetually being disturbed and thwarted by small changes in form, we have the phenomenon of symmetry clashing with asymmetry that is at the heart of baroque stylistic practice.[24] The following passage, encompassing several pe-riods, adheres as closely as Jonson ordinarily ever does to a strict oratorical pattern:

> And an intelligent woman, if shee know by her selfe the least defect, will bee most curious, to hide it: and it becomes her. If shee be short, let her sit much, lest when shee stands, shee be thought to sit. If shee haue an ill foot, let her weare her gowne the longer, and her shoo the thinner. If a fat hand, and scald nailes, let her carue the lesse, and act in gloues. If a sowre breath, let her neuer discourse fasting: and alwaies talke at her distance. If shee haue black and rugged teeth, let her offer the lesse at laughter, especially if shee laugh wide, and open.
>   (SW IV.i.37–46)

The anaphoral "If shee" and "let her" establish a repeated figure on

which Jonson plays constant and surprising variations. The short
first member of each period undergoes its own vicissitudes: "If shee
be short," "If shee *haue* an *ill foot*," "If a fat hand, and scald nailes"
(the verb vanishes, and its object unexpectedly doubles), "If a sowre
breath" (the object becomes single again), "If shee haue black and
rugged teeth" (the verb re-enters with a new configuration of one
noun and two modifiers as object). The parallel apodoses shift form
even more fluidly, maintaining an air of exact symmetry and yet
escaping from it at every moment. The result is not symmetry but
asymmetry, perpetual displacements and dislocations of detail within
a rhythmically symmetrical framework. This, moreover, from the play
of Jonson's which more than any other simulates effects of balance
in its dialogue.

II

The loose style, Croll's other subcategory of the baroque, differs
from the curt style in that it prefers to multiply connectives rather
that to suppress them. It tends also to longer members and longer
periods, but its character is determined by its habit of heaping up
conjunctions and by the kind of conjunctions it chooses: simple
coordinates such as "and" and "or," which involve the least possible
syntactic commitment to what has gone before, and, even more
typically, the stricter relative and subordinating conjunctions used
as though they were mere coordinates. And all this, as Croll urges,
in order to free the period from formal restraints, to enable it to
move with the utmost license from point to point, to follow nothing
but the involutions of the thinking mind. For the enchaining suspensions of the Ciceronian period the loose style substitutes its own
devices, the parenthesis and the absolute construction. The usefulness of the latter especially to a writer working in a resolved style
is, as Croll has explained, that of all constructions it is "the one
that commits itself least and lends itself best to the solution of difficulties that arise in the course of a spontaneous and unpremeditated
progress." [25] It gives a writer carte blanche, enabling him to interrupt
himself at will so as to travel in any cross-direction he pleases without dictating any alteration of the original syntax. It may be thrust
in almost anywhere, and by its very nature—absolute, independent—
forces most of the burden of logical connection upon the reader.
Both the parenthesis and the absolute construction are favorites with

Jonson, and sometimes he uses the two together in the same sentence:

> . . . and presently goe, and redeeme him; for, being her
> brother, and his credit so amply engag'd as now it is, when she
> shal heare (as hee cannot him selfe, but hee must out of ex-
> tremitie report it) that you came, and offered your selfe so
> kindly, and with that respect of his reputation, why, the benefit
> cannot but make her dote, and grow madde of your affections.
>   (*EMO* V.viii.14–20)

Jonson has here made the absolute construction elliptical, by with-
holding the subject, "he," while the parenthesis intrudes with the
utmost casualness and tenuousness of reference into the middle of
a subordinate clause.

The most massive instance of Jonson's use of the absolute construction may be quoted as a curiosity of the loose style:

> Mary, your friends doe wonder, sir, the *Thames* being so neere,
> wherein you may drowne so handsomely; or *London*-bridge, at
> a low fall, with a fine leape, to hurry you downe the streame;
> or, such a delicate steeple, i' the towne, as *Bow,* to vault from;
> or, a brauer height, as *Pauls;* or, if you affected to doe it neerer
> home, and a shorter way, an excellent garret windore, into the
> street; or, a beame, in the said garret, with this halter; which
> they haue sent, and desire, that you would sooner commit your
> graue head to this knot, then to the wed-lock nooze; or, take a
> little sublimate, and goe out of the world, like a rat; or a flie (as
> one said) with a straw i' your arse: any way, rather, then to
> follow this goblin *matrimony*.   (*SW* II.ii.20–32)

In this quintessentially Jonsonian loose period, we are confronted
immediately either with a drastic ellipsis, which must be filled in
with some phrase ("Mary, your friends doe wonder, sir, *why you
do not make away with yourself at once*") in order to complete the
sense, or else with a huge series of absolute constructions that seems
to behave as a suspension and yet never leads to a resolution. Seems
to behave so, at least, to a reader. A reader is likely to demand the
completion of syntactic patterns much more stringently than a listener, who is accustomed, in talk, to hearing such patterns form,

dissolve, and drift off into others without ever fulfilling themselves. The reader awaits with a certain tension the decisive return that will close the orbit; a listener may be perfectly content to let the syntax turn into a wandering fire. And since Jonson was in this case writing for the stage, he may simply have pushed to an extreme the tendency of the baroque period to deal brusquely with its own syntactic commitments.

The absolute constructions here, it may be noticed, are in themselves, after the first, somewhat elliptical, requiring the reinstatement of the verbal phrase "being so neere" in each case. Then the extreme irregularity of the parallel members should be observed; each has its own unique configuration of subordinate clauses or modifying phrases or epithets, so that gradually the sense of parallel form all but evaporates, and we are left with a series of defiantly dissimilar constructions hooked together with "or's" and "and's," spinning freely in grammatical space and almost uncontrolled by any center of gravity. The effect of climax proceeds partly from the simple agglomeration of details and partly from the rhythmic speedup toward the end that leads into the recapitulary formula, "any way, rather, then to follow this goblin *matrimony*."

A further trait of loose style illustrated in this passage is what Croll has called the "linked" or "trailing" period, occurring "when a member depends, not upon the general idea, or the main word, of the preceding member, but upon its final word or phrase alone." [26] The effect of such tactics is, as usual, to reduce to its minimum the interdependence of the successive members, to give the period, at any moment, a thrust forward into new areas. Truewit enumerates several of the high places from which Morose may fling himself before leading up to the mention and then to the proffering of a noose. At this point a shift to the relative "which," dependent as it is solely on the word "halter," deflects the absolute constructions from their course and leaves them stranded, at the same time catapulting the period into new grammatical territory. The period now follows a trajectory determined by the verb "desire," and lands finally a great distance from its starting point. This technique of pushing a period forward into fresh syntactic domain with scarcely a backward glance at the ground already traveled is one way in which anti-Ciceronian writers avoided the oratorical or "circular" Ciceronian period with its necessary return to some initial syntactic postulate. And it was this disregard of what he considered self-evident principles of grammatical law and order that led Coleridge to describe Senecan style as a series of thoughts "strung together like beads, without any causation or progression," [27] and caused Saintsbury to complain of the abuse of conjunctions among seventeenth-century writers, who tended "apparently out of mere wantonness, to prefer a single sentence jointed and rejointed, parenthesised and post-scripted, till it does the duty of a paragraph, to a succession of orderly sentences each containing the expression of a simple or moderately complex thought" [28]—a stricture from which he unaccountably exempted Jonson.

But the writers in question intended to be wanton as the mind is wanton, to transcribe the process of thought onto the page instead of stifling it, as they thought, within prescribed logical schemes. "Je ne peints pas l'estre. Je peints le passage: non un passage d'aage en autre, ou, comme dict le peuple, de sept en sept ans, mais de jour en jour, de minute en minute." [29] Whether in fact a process of thought has any verifiable reality apart from the words that incarnate it, and whether, if so, the irregular modes of syntax preferred by most of the anti-Ciceronians are necessarily any truer to thought, any more "natural," than the suspensions of the Ciceronians or the perfected antitheses of Euphuism, are questions that Renaissance authors did not raise. They assumed that regularity was artful, irregularity natural and spontaneous, and they wrote accordingly. In the case of Jonson, a mild paradox emerges: despite his fervent belief in the hard labor of composition, for which he was both admired and ridiculed by his contemporaries, he adopted a rhetorical mode associated with improvisation. Probably—despite his own protestations to the contrary (*Disc.* 695–700)—he worked as hard to roughen and irregularize his prose as others did to polish and regularize. As George Williamson has demonstrated, imitation of Seneca could lead to something very close to Euphuism.[30] In Jonson's case it did not. He copied in Seneca only the vein of curtness and asymmetry for which he had a temperamental affinity, and in so doing produced a style more Senecan than Seneca's, insofar as Senecanism implied rebellion against rhetorical constraint.

The spontaneity implied in the loose style triumphs most decisively, as Croll points out, just when it seems most in danger of succumbing to orthodox periodicity. It falls into complex syntactic movements and then extricates itself in hairbreath fashion by improvising fresh members or absolute constructions. Jonson finds himself entangled characteristically in his own habit of multiplying relative pronouns; he escapes from his own snares not by unraveling the constructions he has initiated, but by effectively cutting the Gordian knot of the constructions and then proceeding undisturbed. He will, for example, substitute a new subject that shunts the old one onto a siding and allows the thought to advance unimpeded on a new track. In the following excerpt Crites has been exclaiming against the use of perfume by men:

> Yet, I doe like better the prodigalitie of jewels, and clothes, whereof one passeth to a mans heires; the other, at least weares out time: This presently expires, and without continuall riot in reparation is lost: which who so striues to keep, it is one speciall argument to me, that (affecting to smell better then other men) he doth indeed smell farre worse.
>
> (CR V.iv.334–340)

Parenthetically one may notice here a signal feature of the loose style in the fact that the member that elaborates the second half of the antithesis grows and grows until it outweighs everything that has preceded it, almost engulfing the period, and inhibiting all possibility of exact balance. More germane to our present purpose is the way it grows: the linking relative *which*, referring back to *this* (which in turn refers back to the perfume previously mentioned), becomes the object of a complex syntactic motion vice-governed by "who," but this motion is instantly sidetracked by the introduction of a new indefinite-pronoun subject, "it." The member commencing with "it" is elliptical, since we do not know except by implication what "it" is a special argument *of*, and it starts syntactically from scratch, so that the clause "which who so striues to keep," perilously close to the "nonchalant" anacoluthon of which Croll speaks,[31] dangles in mid-air even after the fresh start has come to its rescue and completed the period.

One may add that it is probably as much as anything else Jonson's practice with relative conjunctions that has led his editors and critics to speak of his style as "packed" and "weighty." On the one hand he will employ relative connectives that cross-refer and intertwine densely with one another, and that may, while still incomplete, sprout further subsidiary relative clauses, as in the passage just cited. But he may, on the other hand, at any moment that it pleases him, throw them overboard for new constructions and leave them ship-wrecked. Some fairly drastic instances of this kind of procedure appear in *The Entertainment at Highgate*.

> . . . vouchsafe your eare, and forgiue his behauiour, which (euen to me, that am his parent) will no doubt be rude ynough, though otherwise full of salt, which, except my pres-ence did temper, might turne to be gall, and bitternesse; but that shall charme him.   (199–203)

In this jungle of relatives and ellipses, the phrase "though otherwise full of salt" refers back to "which," itself dependent on "behauiour." A second "which," dependent solely on "salt" immediately preceding it, now makes its entry, introducing a trailing semiperiod half again as long as the member from which it springs, and subverting the initial construction entirely. The final demonstrative "that" refers back over a considerable distance to "my presence." The "packed" and "weighty" texture, then, seems to spring from the conflict of two opposing tendencies: the centrifugal force of the loose style struggling against the centripetal impulse of the Latinate conjunc-tions. A tightly integrated syntax is implied by the connectives and then carefully left unrealized.

If the curt style is peculiarly suited to expressions of quick wit, excitement, distraction, and the like, the loose style, by virtue of its greater floridity, lends itself well to purposes of formal declama-tion. It can be and is used by Jonson in a variety of ways: straight-forwardly, as in Crites' censure of perfume, or with self-conscious exaggeration and heightening, as in Truewit's tirade against matri-mony—or it may become the vehicle for the affected eloquence of fops like Amorphus and Fastidious Brisk eager to show off their aureate vocabularies. But whereas the dramatic versions of the curt style derive in part at least from prose as it was used in the popular drama of the 1590's, Jonson's theatrical adaptations of the loose style are his own original creation. Nothing in the comic prose of the preceding decade, whether in plays, novels, or pamphlets, really pre-pares us for such a baroque virtuoso piece as Fastidious Brisk's rhapsody on the court:

> A man liues there, in that diuine rapture, that hee will thinke himselfe i' the ninth heauen for the time, and lose all sense of

mortalitie whatsoeuer; when he shall behold such glorious (and almost immortall) beauties, heare such angelicall and harmonious voyces, discourse with such flowing and *ambrosian* spirits, whose wits are as suddaine as lightning, and humorous as *nectar;* Oh: it makes a man al *quintessence,* and *flame,* & lifts him vp (in a moment) to the verie christall crowne of the skie, where (houering in the strength of his imagination) he shall behold all the delights of the HESPERIDES, the *Insulae Fortunatae,* ADONIS gardens, *Tempe* or what else (confin'd within the amplest verge of *poesie*) to bee meere *vmbrae,* and imperfect figures, conferr'd with the most essentiall felicitie of your court.   (*EMO* IV.viii.18–32)

III

Having glanced at the major landmarks on Croll's baroque landscape, and having tried to show their relevance to Jonson's practice, we may carry the discussion into more particularly Jonsonian country by mentioning a few traits of style that, though not always exclusive with Jonson, are habitual enough with him to be regarded as idiosyncratic. These will in every case exemplify further the baroque syntax already outlined.

One of Jonson's customary techniques is to disturb, by one means or another, what we would ordinarily regard as logical word order. The frequent result of such tactics is to promote oddness of emphasis, to undermine expectations of "normal" arrangement; words will fail to appear in looked-for places and then emerge bizarrely where we least expect them. Jonson's simplest transposition of this sort is to add some element—subject, object, or modifier—postgrammatically, and thus to isolate it. In the statement "Men are decay'd, and *studies*" (*Disc.* 127), "Men are decay'd" forms a self-contained grammatical unit onto which Jonson has tacked an extra subject. The delayed subject comes as a kind of afterthought, and lends an improvisatory flourish to the remark. At the same time, paradoxically, it completes a rhythmic curve. If we put it back into its "normal" place in the sentence ("Men and studies are decay'd"), we make a more orderly period, and a flatter one. The same detail that roughens the syntax in one way, by separating elements that grammatically go together, smooths it out in another way by producing a cadence.

And so with most instances of this device. One might, then, tentatively add to Croll's types of baroque effect the kind of tension that arises when the syntax is doing one thing grammatically and another rhythmically. And this could be classified as a further species of asymmetry, since the grammatical logic and the rhythm are out of phase with each other, instead of synchronized as in Euphuistic or Ciceronian prose. The effect of irregularity in such cases depends on the distance between the postscripted element and its natural grammatical mate.

> A Trumpet should fright him terribly, or the Hau'-boyes?
> (*SW* I.i.160–161)
> . . . when some groome of his has got him an heire, or this
> barber . . .   (*SW* I.ii.54–55)
> Some Diuine must resolue you in that, sir, or canon-Lawyer.
> (*SW* IV.iv.148–149)
> I'll tell you, MOROSE, you must talke diuinitie to him altogether,
> or morall philosophie.   (*SW* IV.iv.81–82)
> If there bee neuer a *Seruant-monster* i'the *Fayre;* who can
> helpe it? he sayes; nor a nest of *Antiques?*
> (*BF* Ind. 127–128)

The fact that this pattern occurs so much oftener in the plays than in the *Discoveries* suggests that Jonson was seeking to vitalize his language rhythmically for the stage in ways that would have been needless for the library.

Another way of driving a wedge between two words grammatically related is to separate a relative pronoun from its antecedent by interposing a word or phrase between them:

> Come forward, you should be some dull tradesman by your pig-
> headed Sconce now, that thinke there's nothing good any
> where; but what's to be sold.   (*NNW* 12–14)
> Nor is that worthy speech of *Zeno* the Philosopher to be past
> over, without the note of ignorance: who being invited to a feast
> in *Athens* . . .   (*Disc.* 370–372)

Jonson, one observes, does not assume that a relative or subordinate clause must tread like a porpoise on the tail of its antecedent. He constantly, and sometimes perplexingly, delays the pronoun while he interpolates other matter.[32] This habit probably stems in part from Latin, a language in which, since inflected endings carry the burden of grammatical connection, the word order tends to be abstract—capable of manipulation for purposes of emphasis and design. At the same time, the cavalier distribution of elements recalls colloquial speech, which rarely pauses to pickle over the logicality of its word order. So that with this detail as with others, Jonson's "Romanizing" tendency and his fascination with living speech unexpectedly reinforce each other; the same device that on the page can suggest pressure of thought and evoke memories of classical prose, can in the theater serve to create a sense of conversational *désinvolture*.

Sometimes Jonson deliberately suppresses some grammatical element in order to avert an impending symmetry, to sabotage in advance what threatens to evolve into too fussy a balance: "But now be pleased to expect a more noble discovery worthie of your eare, as the object will be [of] your eye" (*NNW* 301–303). Here the ellipsis of an introductory *as* ("a more noble discovery, *as* worthie of your eare, *as*") leaves the reader unprepared for the exact antithesis that follows and hence unable to feel its full impact. Since symmetry depends to a large extent on preparation, and unfolding according to plan, it may be upset by a refusal to usher it in with recognizable anticipatory formulas. Conversely, a severely antithetic scaffolding may be erected in one clause only to be knocked to pieces in the next: "A woman, the more curious she is about her face, is commonly the more carelesse about her house" (*Disc.* 192–193); "His modesty, like a riding Coat, the more it is worne, is the lesse car'd for" (*Disc.* 1328–29). No reader of Euphuistic prose could have failed to expect perfect matching between the two halves of the antithesis ("the more it is worne, the lesse it is car'd for"), but Jonson wrenches askew the second member so as to produce a lopsided rather than a balanced antithesis. Or, again, the effect of balance may be undone by the interpolation of a qualifying phrase between symmetrical elements: "If I doe not, let me play the mounte-bank for my meate while I liue, and the bawd for my drinke" (*SW* IV.i.151–152).

If we leaf through Jonson for the symmetrical formulas so abundant in Shakespeare, we find that where Jonson uses them he com-

monly manages to derange their stability in one way or another.
The "as . . . so" parallelism, in Jonson, is likely to come out like
this: "In short, as Vinegar is not accounted good, untill the wine
be corrupted: so jests that are true and naturall, seldome raise
laughter, with the beast, the multitude" (*Disc.* 2657–59), where the
second half invents an entirely unforeseen syntactic combination for
itself, abandoning in particular the notion of change from sweetness
to corruption and embarking on explicit mention of those who are
judging and condemning. The "though . . .yet" antithesis is liable
to emerge in a form like this: "For though the *Prince* himselfe be
of most prompt inclination to all vertue: Yet the best *Pilots* have
need of *Mariners*, beside Sayles, Anchor, and other Tackle" (*Disc.*
1246–49), where the antithetic "yet" clause takes a sudden leap
into metaphor, and elaborates that metaphor almost to the point of
obscurity. In all of these instances, Jonson contrives to balk the kind
of satisfaction that arises from a regular design fully articulated.
Instead of a sense of fulfillment, he seeks effects of tension, instead
of the feeling of repose as the pattern rounds itself out, a feeling of
energy from the breaking of the pattern.

The asymmetry peculiar to baroque prose appears in Jonson in
still another stylistic mannerism: the coupling in parallel relation
of two elements that are either grammatically non-congruent or, if
congruent on one level, so aggressively non-parisonic as to produce
a feeling of incongruity, creating that slight sense of *offness* that
baroque writers, their ears surfeited by Lylian parison or Ciceronian
periodicity, evidently delighted in.

> . . . they find nothing new, or to seeke.   (*Disc.* 1677)
> But, beware of presuming, or how you offer comparison with
> persons so neere Deities.   (*Pan* 154–155)
> . . . to doe this with diligence, and often.   (*Disc.* 1704–05)
> . . . to taste all by degrees, and with change.
>   (*Disc.* 1654–55)
> . . . has a yellow blade, but the eare empty.
>   (*Disc.* 687–688)
> . . . with a Funnell, and by degrees, you shall fill many of
> them . . .   (*Disc.* 1794)

The parallel elements of a series may of course be set at odds with each other in the same way. In the following example, the third member rebelliously refuses to conform to the pattern of infinitives established by the first two: "*For* a man to write well, there are required three Necessaries. To reade the best Authors, observe the best Speakers: and much exercise of his owne style" (*Disc.* 1697–99). In the next, Jonson charges headlong from a past participle, "*banish't,*" to the nouns "want" and "disease": "As to wish a friend *banish't,* that they might accompany him in *exile:* or some great want, that they might relieve him: or a disease, that they might sit by him" (*Disc.* 440–443).

But irregularity need not restrict itself to a habit of interfering with symmetry, nor need it be confined within the compass of one period. Jonson's prose is marked by an almost dizzying variety of mutations of form. There are passages in which the subject changes from clause to clause, or from sentence to sentence:

> His language, (where hee could spare, or passe by a jest) was nobly *censorious.* No man ever spake more neatly, more presly, more weightily, or suffer'd lesse emptinesse, less idlenesse, in what hee utter'd. No member of his speech, but consisted of the owne graces: His hearers could not cough, or looke aside from him, without losse. Hee commanded where hee spoke; and had his Judges angry, and pleased at his devotion. No man had their affections more in his power. The feare of every man that heard him, was, lest hee should make an end.
>
>   (*Disc.* 888–898)

Despite a certain regularity here—from the steady march of subject, predicate, subject, predicate, subject, predicate—the effect of irregularity predominates because of the nervous mobility of the subject, in which respect Jonson outdoes the passage from Seneca that serves as his model. One result is to emphasize the independence and, so to speak, defiant integrity of each clause, to brace it sharply against its neighbors and force the reader to readjust his perspective at every pause. Jonson demands similar reaccommodations when he causes a subject to materialize out of thin air: "Then men were had in price for learning: now, letters onely make men vile. Hee is upbraydingly call'd a *Poet,* as if it were a most contemptible *Nickname*" (*Disc.* 279–282).

He is no less in revolt against regularity in his handling of verbs. Sometimes he pitches abruptly from the declarative mood into the imperative:

> *In Picture,* light is requir'd no lesse then shadow: so in stile, height, as well as humblenesse. But beware they be not too humble; as *Pliny* pronounc'd of *Regulus* writings: You would thinke them written, not on a child, but by a child.
>
> (*Disc.* 1541–45)

The change of pace here jolts the reader even more sharply because at the same time there erupts from nowhere the pronoun "they," for which the reader must scramble to invent an antecedent. At other times Jonson will suddenly shift gears into neutral, so to speak, by switching into the infinitive:

> A strict and succinct style is that, where you can take away nothing without losse, and that losse to be manifest.[33]
>
> (*Disc.* 1970–72)
>
> Have not I seen the pompe of a whole Kingdome, and what a forraigne King could bring hither. Also to make himselfe gaz'd, and wonder'd at, laid forth as it were to the shew, and vanish all away in a day? (*Disc.* 1404–07)

And sometimes he will without warning shift a plural verb (with its plural subject) into the singular: ". . . what Iustice or Religion is to be expected? Which are the only two Attributes make *Kings* a kinne to *Gods*; and is the *Delphick* sword, both to kill Sacrifices, and to chastise offenders" (*Disc.* 1288–91). Or he will coolly switch tenses within the space of a single period. "But the fees of the one, or the *salary* of the other, never answer the *value* of what we received; but serv'd to gratifie their labours" [34] (*Disc.* 476–478). This happens especially when he is recounting the scenic effects of a masque, as if he were aiming to convey a vivid sense of immediacy together with the precision of objective reporting: [35]

> In his hand he bore a golden censor with perfume, and censing about the altar (hauing first kindled his fire on the toppe) is interrupted by the *Genius.* (*King's Ent.* 551–553)

> When the Spectators had enough fed their eyes, with the de-
> lights of the *Scene,* in a part of the ayre, a bright cloud begins
> to breake forth.   (*Chlor.* 28–30)

And finally there is the kind of irregularity that occurs when members of a sequence not only vary internally one from another, but
from the start are launched in diverse directions by differing conjunctions:

> *Metaphors* farfet hinder to be understood, and affected, lose
> their grace. Or when the person fetcheth his translations from
> a wrong place. As if a Privie-Counsellor should at the Table
> take his *Metaphore* from a Dicing-House . . .
>
>   (*Disc.* 1905–09)

It scarcely matters, in short, what sort of regularity or continuity
one presupposes in prose style: Jonson manages to avoid them all.
Discontinuity, change of pace, interruption of design, are the materials with which he works. Despite a certain amount of incidental
symmetry, Jonson's prose is irregular on principle, and the irregularity transmits itself from the largest phenomena of style down to
the smallest, from the formation of the most massive block of loose
periods down to the parallel coupling of discongruent adverbs.
Saintsbury's dictum that Jonson "preserves—his kind cannot but
preserve—the balance of Ascham and Lyly as his chief rhetorical
instrument" [36] must then be severely emended, if indeed it is to
stand at all. If Jonson preserves balance, he does so only to upset
balance. If he deploys symmetrical patterns, he does so only to violate their symmetry. Everywhere he is restlessly interfering with the
expected structure of a phrase or clause. The asymmetrical tactics
that pervade his writing form a rhetoric distinct from, and as distinct
as, any of the more orthodox rhetorics, an antirhetorical rhetoric
that seeks to disguise itself almost as a nonrhetoric. The necessarily
stricter attentiveness of the reader to such a style, since he cannot
let his mind coast in the suspensions of a periodic sentence or in
the exact correspondences of the aculeate style, perhaps suggests
why the laborious Jonson adopts a manner apparently most congenial
to effects of improvisation. In the hands of writers like Burton,
baroque prose ambles or scampers with skittish whimsicality. Jonson,
by his reluctance to fulfill expectation, his defiance of stock responses

to syntax, creates an impression of granitic strength: the participation of the reader or listener becomes an exercise in rock-climbing over the jagged, twisted, craggy terrain of the syntax.

IV

An inquiry into the relation between these stylistic habits and larger aspects of technique might suggest rather quickly that the structure of the *Discoveries,* at least, resembles that of the curt and loose periods. Like Donne's *Devotions,* Selden's *Table Talk,* and Traherne's *Centuries of Meditations,* the *Discoveries* belong to a genre —named after the most distinguished example of it—the *pensées,* a disconnected series of jottings that explores a few dominant themes in as many ways as the writer chooses. Each *pensée* constitutes a separate quantum, a bundle of words peculiar to itself, differing in size, shape, color, and texture from all the other bundles, just as the members of the curt period differ from each other. Truth is presented in fragments, in scattered glimpses, rather than steadily and whole. There may or may not be an ordered vision behind the fragments, but the technique, at least, implies groping, exploration, tentative forays; the vision is seen only intermittently and in pieces.[37]

With the plays, the problem is more complex. It may, however, be conjectured that just as a writer who repeatedly uses causal connectives is thinking in terms of cause and effect, so a writer who shuns them is thinking in other terms, perhaps of a world so static that nothing in it is subject to change, perhaps of a world so bewildering and disintegrated that nothing in it seems causally related to anything else, a world in which the atoms of impulse, act, and event collide haphazardly in a void. It may be excessively obvious to observe that Shakespeare's plays constitute a dense network of cause and effect: but set them beside Jonson's, and the fact becomes overpowering. Coleridge's description of Iago's soliloquies as "the motive-hunting of motiveless malignity,"[38] the endless efforts to account for Hamlet's madness, Lear's folly, and the rest, suggest the extent to which we expect effects in Shakespeare to be adequately motivated. Shakespeare, by repeatedly raising the question himself, sanctions such expectations. One might compile a repertory of occasions on which characters interrogate the motives behind acts or feelings:

Why haue these banish'd, and forbidden Legges,
Dar'd once to touch a Dust of Englands Ground?
                    (L.354; *RII* II.iii.90–91)
Why do'st thou say, King *Richard* is depos'd . . .
                    (L.360; *RII* III.iv.77)
Wherefore doe you so ill translate your selfe,
Out of the Speech of Peace, that beares such grace,
Into the harsh and boystrous Tongue of Warre?
                    (L.409; *IIHIV* IV.i.47–49)
But wherefore did hee take away the Crowne?
                    (L.414; *IIHIV* IV.v.89)
Fellow, why do'st thou show me thus to th'world?
                    (L.80; *MM* I.ii.120)
Where are the vile beginners of this Fray?
                    (L.681; *Rom.* III.i.146)
Princes:
What greefe hath set the Iaundies on your cheekes?
                    (L.591; *Troil.* I.iii.1–2)
Good my Lord, what is your cause of distemper?
                    (L.777; *Ham.* III.ii.350–351)
Why brand they vs / With Base?
                    (L.793; *Lear* II.i.9–10)
Wherefore to Douer?   (L.808; *Lear* III.vii.52)
But wherefore could not I pronounce Amen?
                    (L.744; *Mac.* II.ii.31)

And this would be only the merest beginning, to be followed by
an inquiry into occasions on which characters vouchsafe explanations of acts and feelings—and still one would have barely scratched
the surface of Shakespeare's densely causal world and his dynamic
conception of character.

Jonson's world, by contrast, is not causal, and character does not
interact with character. A seeming cause produces no effect; an apparent effect springs from no discoverable cause. The archetypal
Jonsonian situation is that in which an individual pursues his humor
oblivious of everything else about him. Fungoso, his eyes fixed
greedily on Fastidious Brisk's fine suit, makes half-answers to his
uncle while privately calculating how much it will cost him to
duplicate the suit. Sogliardo, in the same moment, is too engrossed
by the prospect of vulgar pleasures in London to notice Fungoso's

inattention. Sordido, scarcely aware of the others on the stage, gazes into the sky for signs of the rain that will raise the value of his wheat. The characters remain as isolated, as blocked off from each other, as immobilized in their humors, as the members of an exploded period. Instead of a chain of circumstances, dependent one on another, the plot presents a kaleidoscopic series of characteristic stances.

Jonson modifies this technique in his mature comedies. Certainly the hoaxes and conspiracies that form the mainsprings of action in *Volpone, Epicene,* and *The Alchemist* involve causal sequence. But the sequences tend to be simple rather than multiple, and even so they often run aground and require relaunching. The fifth act of *Volpone* provides a notorious example: the mainspring of the plot having run down, Jonson must forcibly rewind it in order to bring on the catastrophe. Similarly, the denouement of *The Alchemist* depends on Lovewit's unexpected return to London, but where another playwright might have motivated the return, accounted for it through some specific circumstances connected with other facts of the plot, and where a playwright bent on suspense would have provoked our curiosity about it beforehand, Jonson characteristically allows it to come as a total surprise and then does not bother to explain it, because he cares only for the series of brilliant confusions it will produce. Even in his major comedies, that is, Jonson prefers to create his effects by means other than causal linkage: the true center of interest lies in the shifting configurations of character confronting character. Few dramatists of his stature depend so little on suspense, on tying episode to episode and evolving one incident out of another. In Shakespeare, each scene germinates out of causes planted in previous scenes, and becomes in turn the germ of future scenes. In Jonson, scene after scene has only its own existence to contemplate. In Shakespeare, people have missions, they go on errands, they seek each other out. In Jonson, they meet by accident; they just happen to turn up.

Poetaster, for instance, opens with a lively debate on the status of poetry between Ovid, his father, Tucca, Lupus, and some servants. The scene projects concisely and forcefully a whole range of attitudes toward art. But the narrative links between it and the rest of the play are exceedingly tenuous. Ovid Senior has come to visit his son—for a purpose, we assume; but we never learn what the purpose is, since when he finds his heir reciting verses, he loses his temper and forgets his errand. Then, though he threatens to disinherit his son for neglecting the law and persisting with poetry, and though Ovid Junior defies the threat, nothing further is heard of the matter. There are no repercussions for Ovid, nor does his father ever reappear on the stage. Again, Tucca has attached himself to Ovid Senior to wheedle a few drachmas out of him. The scene gives us a picturesque sample of Tucca's methods of cadging, but it also sets up a relation between the two that is never pursued. Tucca, we know, will not repay the loan; Ovid Senior, we know, will be incensed; but none of this is ever referred to again. Finally, by including Lupus, the tribune, in the scene, Jonson adds to the philistine contemners of poetry the political enemies of it. But why Lupus should happen to be a friend of Ovid Senior's, why he should meet him on this particular morning and accompany him to his son's quarters, is left wholly to conjecture: the entente between them begins and ends in the scene in question. Jonson, in short, assembles a group of characters so as to exhibit them in significant postures, but does not, except in the most perfunctory manner, account for their simultaneous presence on the stage, and does not attempt to follow through with the narrative elements planted in the scene.

Something similar may be said—and will be said in due course —concerning *Epicene*. For the moment we may pause to notice that when Marcel Achard adapted the play for Charles Dullin in 1925,[39] the chief thing he did with it was to revise it as far in the direction of the intrigue plot as it would go. By suppressing minor characters, by hooking all subsidiary action directly into the main plot, by motivating Dauphine's scheme itself more substantially, he turned the whole play into the network of cause and effect that his generation prized in the theater. Family links are specified: Achard's hero, Dauphin, is not simply Morose's nephew, but " le fils bien-aimé de sa bien-aimée soeur" (p. 149). He intrigues for Morose's inheritance not as an end in itself but to enable him to compete successfully for the hand of a rich heiress, Lady Juliet, with whom he is in love. Sir John Daw and Sir Amorous La Fool are collapsed into a single character, Sir Sottenville des Amourettes, a doltish rival of Dauphin's, whose reading of the madrigal now has the effect of inflaming Dauphin's jealousy, and whose discomfiture in the last act has the specific purpose of exposing his unworthiness before Lady Juliet, so that she will appreciate Dauphin. Truewit, now Delesprit, delivers his recommendations on fashionable folly, seduction, and feminine adornment with the precise aim of assisting Dauphin in his courtship and of reconciling him to Juliet's worldliness. The play ends, needless to say, with a triumphant union between the hero and his lady.[40]

The language reflects this new state of affairs. It now swarms with exact symmetries and logical particles. In the opening scene, Jonson's idle conversation between Clerimont and Truewit concerning the *longueurs* and secrecies of the dressing-table becomes Dauphin's complaint over the behavior of his mistress:

> Elle reçoit trop aimablement les beaux esprits, les fatuités du jour. Je ne puis pénétrer dans sa chambre qu'après une longue et terrible attente. Elle m'accueille le dernier parce que je n'ai pas l'esprit chargé de madrigaux et que je ne la sais pas comparer habilement à la lune aux étoiles et au soleil. J'attends donc les deux heures encore qu'elle consacre à parer, baigner, peindre, parfumer et ajuster sa noble personne. Car elle donne dans le travers du temps, et se défigure par des poudres, des crèmes et des onguents. (p. 143)

The sense of motive, intention, and causality that figures so strongly in the adaptation appears in the multiplication of causal conjunctions, in the "parce que," "donc," and "car." Lady Juliet's behavior is ascribed to a certain set of attitudes; its effects on Dauphin are equally specific. Or, for the more conventional symmetry of Achard's style, one might compare Truewit's boast, "If I doe not, let me play the mountebank for my meate while I liue, and the bawd for my drinke," with Delesprit's, "Je la rendrai amoureuse de toi, ou je veux gagner mon pain sur la place publique et mon vin dans un mauvais lieu" (p. 147), with its reiteration of purpose and its more pat antithesis. Finally, to see how Achard alters the Jonsonian loose period, one might compare the long passage quoted earlier (in section II) with its equivalent from Delesprit:

> Vos amis s'étonnent, Monsieur, que la Tamise étant si près, où vous pouvez vous noyer si agréablement, ou bien le pont de Londres, d'où une belle chute peut vout précipiter au fond de la rivière; qu'ayant à votre disposition nos jolis clochers de la ville, tel que celui de Bow, celui de Saint-Paul dont la hauteur vous offre encore un saut plus rapide; ou si vous préfèrez un endroit plus près de votre maison, les fenêtres de ce grenier qui

donne sur la rue; qu'ayant dans ce même grenier une poutre, et
cette corde que vos amis vous envoient, ils s'étonnent, dis-je, et
préfèreraient vous voir commettre votre tête vénérable à ce
noeud coulant qu'à celui du mariage. Ils aimeraient certes vous
voir prendre du sublimé et mourir comme un rat ou comme
une mouche,—dit-on,—d'une paille au derrière, . . .

(p. 166)

The major change here is precisely the break-up of the long winding
baroque movement into a series of rationally ordered members, pe-
riodically reintroduced by a "que," reconfirmed by a "dis-je," and
then halted entirely and recommenced afresh when it begins to grow
top-heavy.

La femme silencieuse, in short, reintroduces logical *engrenage*
into the language and causal continuity into the lives of the characters. In Jonson, the avoidance of logical particles and the preference for the exploded period reflect the discontinuous plot structure;
society is conceived as a collection of disconnected atoms, in which
each character speaks a private language of his own, pursues ends
of his own, collides from time to time with other characters, and
then rebounds into isolation.

It goes without saying, but it must be said nevertheless, that none
of this is meant to imply inferior workmanship, second-rate drama-
turgy, or a deficient sense of the "dramatic" on Jonson's part. Jonson's sentences, Jonson's plots, are not undramatic: they are dramatic
in a special and somewhat uncommon, perhaps a Joycean, sense.
They constitute a series of epiphanies. Their pictorial fullness and
verbal density embody a vision: they show us that the things we
see are those things that they are and no other things. Harry Levin
has appropriately urged us to criticize Shakespeare in terms of
"movement and warmth," Jonson in terms of "pattern and colour." [41]
Disapproving the heavy plotting of most Elizabethan drama, Jonson
replaces it with something akin to the kaleidoscope, where blocks
of color are put in strange conjunction, then shaken to produce
new conjunctions, or, as Levin has suggested, to the chess game, in
which each character "has only his characteristic move, . . . and
the object of the game is to see what new combinations have been
brought about." [42] One might compare this emphasis on abstract
design with that in Gabrieli's brass *canzone* for St. Mark's, or Stra-
vinsky's *Agon,* where the manipulation of textures, contrasting

sonorities, competing rhythms, resembles the clash of jargons, the shrill rivalry of character pitted against character, of the Jonsonian stage.

For an analogy that included more of the expressive and realistic content of Jonsonian theater, one might cite Eric Bentley in defense of Brecht. Speaking of the lack of suspense in Brecht's plays, Bentley likens them to paintings by Brueghel, where the dramatic whole is conceived as an aggregate of small dramas, as a picturesque assemblage of minor tensions rather than as a single dominant tension. Brueghel's "Battle between Carnival and Lent" offers a swarming villagescape in which the queer little figurines engage in dozens of diverse activities—watching a Lenten play, dancing in a ring, huddling around a bonfire—activities related for the most part only analogically to the weird combat taking place in the foreground. In Bosch's "Temptation of St. Anthony," the saint himself is only a spectator to the eerie scene, in which snouted creatures, astride mooncalves, strum harps, or wizened homunculi go fishing from dolphins rigged as boats. Similarly, in Brecht's patchwork of the Thirty Years' War, or Jonson's crazy quilt of Bartholomew Fair, "swift, strong sensation" is avoided. The eye is invited "to linger on this detail or that. The eye that accepts the invitation discovers one 'drama' after another in the picture and even a total drama of the whole." [43]

What is true of the design as a whole obtains for the smaller unit of the period or sentence: instead of the closely woven, climactic effect of the Ciceronian period, Jonson's prose affords the clash of clause against clause, the abrupt reversals and unexpected prolongations, that defeat the wish for suspense but gratify the craving for "pattern and color"; instead of the single, imperious tension, the diffracted tension that allows the ear "to linger on this detail or that."

V

To detect the "psychological etymon" [44] behind this stylistic behavior is not easy, far less easy, certainly, than for other baroque writers. One can, of course, point to Jonson's neo-Stoicism, his admiration for the anti-Ciceronian prose of Seneca and Tacitus. But Bacon revered Tacitus and writes a prose akin to Euphuism. Seneca himself is more Euphuistic, more word-catching, than Jonson. One can point also to Jonson's mimetic preoccupation, his fascination with the sounds of live language. But one has still not explained why he preferred the stutter of the curt style to the rotunder poly-syndetic effects equally common—one supposes—in Elizabethan speech. What follows, then, is to be regarded as speculative and exploratory.

If we assume that the restlessness of baroque style expresses some restlessness within the writer, some inner conflict or war with the world at large, we can see that it lends itself admirably to the needs of authors like Donne, Browne, Milton, Burton, Montaigne, and Pascal. Donne's tensions are not merely obvious: they form the subject matter of his art. In sermon and poem alike he dramatizes his own paradoxes of feeling, his struggles between carnal love and religious devotion, his craving to unite matter and spirit. There are the obvious doubts and the obvious suffering. *Mutatis mutandis,* much the same may be said of Pascal. In Sir Thomas Browne we have a milder personality, but one still caught between different kinds of belief: committed on the one hand to hieroglyphic mysteries like the quincunx, and on the other to the sober reappraisal of popular errors. *Religio medici* expounds the writer's theology with such minute particularity, such pondering of every nuance, that despite its orthodoxy as a whole it becomes an absolutely private vision. In Milton—verse and prose alike—we have the passionate assertions of a spirit whose Protestant self-sufficiency leads him steadily further from the center of orthodoxy into an area of belief uniquely his own, and recognized by him as such. In *The Anatomy* of *Melancholy,* individualism takes the form of eccentricity; Burton revels in his own crotchets, and makes out of the baroque rhetoric an appropriately crotchety style in which to do so, just as his philo-sophical master, Montaigne, reveled in the oddities of *his* tempera-ment.

The common denominator among these writers seems to be an intense, sometimes rebellious subjectivity, for which the skittishness of baroque prose provides an ideal instrument. But when we ap-proach Jonson with similar expectations, we seem to run into a blank wall. Jonson goes through no dark night of the soul like that of Donne or Pascal, nor does he feel impelled to record his own configuration of belief and discriminate it from those of others, as do Browne and Milton. Unlike Montaigne, Jonson would never have admitted to any pleasure in reading his own entrails. Far from courting eccentricity, like Burton, Jonson satirizes it scornfully, the whole theory and dramatic practice of "humors" comedy being an attempt to scourge deviations from the social norm. Instead of listening to the inner voice, the private idiosyncrasy, Jonson respects only the standards of the humanist tradition, the consent of the learned, the congress of the good, and he never expresses the slightest doubt that he speaks for the learned and the good of all ages. What distinguishes the *Discoveries* from the *Devotions,* the *Pensées,* the *Table Talk,* and the *Centuries of Meditations* is precisely the suppression of all doubt and personal revelation—the frequent paraphrases, marginally acknowledged, from other authors, giving the work more the air of a compilation than of a private meditation.

In short, where the other baroque writers explicitly dramatize their tensions, in Jonson the tensions remain buried. The other writers manage to relate their private disturbances to large cultural crises, theological, ecclesiastical, or political, but Jonson, by refusing to acknowledge his, can express them only in oblique and devious ways, which makes them less easy to isolate. But no one has ever doubted their existence. The presence of tension in Jonson reveals itself most obviously in his insistent claim to be without tension; the oftener he protests his imperturbabiilty, the less we are inclined to believe it. Jonson cannot, like the stoic he longs to be, remain indifferent to the vicissitudes of fortune. He cannot despise the acclaim or the scorn of others; he exults in approval and smarts painfully under criticism. He cannot cleanse himself of the petty passions he would like to disown.

Nor can he find the post in society that he claims as his due, that of the teacher-poet standing at the elbow of the monarch, unfolding wise and sane counsel, instructing his peers in the good life and flicking off the insect malice of envious rivals. The casting of himself in just such a role in *Cynthia's Revels* and *Poetaster* is in both cases an act of extravagant wish-fulfillment, yet even in these fantasies of Crites and Horace, the serenity is only skin-deep: just below the surface lurks the marsh of insecurity, envy, and suspicion. If it would be rash to suggest that Jonson is exorcising his own eccentricity in the fops and fools of the comical satires, he is certainly doing something like it with Morose, Wasp, and other characters of the mature comedies. Jonson himself cannot believe in the ideal image of himself to which he would like the world to subscribe; he can only inch toward it by loading onto the gulls and victims of the comedies his own hampering tensions, and casting them out.

The result is that Jonson's most successful art is that in which unmasking and casting out have fullest scope. More and more often into the ceremoniousness of the masques intrude outbreaks of the critical spirit that cannot credit the reality of the vision being created. Satiric comedy affords the only lightning rod by which Jonson's high tension can release itself in ordered, concentrated form. The massive voltage streaks down in the great comedies, igniting everything in its path, creating by destroying and destroying by creating. The positive standard, the ethical humanism and solid sense to which he is always appealing, remains for the most part in the background, and every effort to incarnate it dramatically (Bonario, Surly, Grace Wellborn) is a failure.

In Jonson, in short, we have a subjectivity as intense as Donne's masquerading as its opposite, a thin-skinned suspiciousness masking itself as a benign imperturbability, and an acute social insecurity clothing itself in the mantle of achieved status, in a fashion similar to that in which the social-climbing citizens of Jonson's own comedies clothe themselves in the jargon and gestures of a superior class in order to be accepted by it. And it is dissonances like these, no doubt, within Jonson himself, that lead him to adopt baroque style, with its broken rhythms and perilous balances, rather than the stabler rhetorics of Euphuism or Ciceronianism, with their implicit sense of integration into a harmonious, ordered cosmos.

NOTES

1. Benjamin Lee Whorf, *Language, Thought, and Reality*, ed. John B. Carroll (New York, 1956), pp. 137, 147. For a stimulating, if inconclusive, discussion of the Whorf hypothesis see *Language in Culture*, ed. Harry Hoijer (Chicago, 1954).
2. *Meaning in the Visual Arts* (New York, 1955), pp. 329–330.
3. E.g., *Linguistique générale et linguistique française*, 2d ed. (Berne, 1944), esp. pp. 339–370, "Formes générales de l'expression," and *Le langage et la vie*, 3d ed. (Paris, 1952), pp. 53–57 and *passim*.
4. "Some Changes in the Prose Style of the Seventeenth Century," unpubl. diss. (Cambridge, 1938), p. 109. See also F. W. Bateson, *English Poetry and the English Language* (Oxford, 1934), a more

speculative and impressionistic essay on the relations between linguistic change and literature, with special reference to poetry.

5. Especially " 'Attic Prose' in the Seventeenth Century," *Studies in Philology*, XVIII (1921), 79–128; "Attic Prose: Lipsius, Montaigne, Bacon," in *Schellling Anniversary Papers* (New York, 1923), pp. 117–150; "Muret and the History of 'Attic' Prose," *Publications of the Modern Language Association*, XXXIX (1924), 254–309; "The Baroque Style in Prose," in *Studies in English Philology*, ed. Malone and Ruud, pp. 427–456, reprinted above.

6. Especially George Williamson, *The Senecan Amble* (London, 1951).

7. On convention, see Harry Levin, "Notes on Convention," in *Perspectives of Criticism*, Harvard Studies in Comparative Literature, No. 20 (Cambridge, Mass., 1950), pp. 55–83.

8. René Wellek, "The Concept of Baroque in Literary Scholarship," *Journal of Aesthetics and Art Criticism*, V (1946), 96.

9. *Linguistics and Literary History* (Princeton, 1948), Ch. i.

10. For prose, see especially the chapters on *Don Quixote* and Diderot.

11. *The Handling of Words* (London, 1923).

12. *Mimesis*, trans. Willard R. Trask (Princeton, 1953).

13. *Situations I* (Paris, 1947), esp. "La temporalité chez Faulkner," pp. 70–81; "M. Jean Giraudoux et la philosophie d'Aristote," pp. 82–98; and "Explication de *l'etranger*," pp. 99–121.

14. "Observations on the Style of Ernest Hemingway," *Kenyon Review*, XIII (1951), 581–609.

15. *Style in French Prose* (Oxford, 1953).

16. The struggles to convert this concept from art history into a meaningful term for literary history have not been entirely happy. The further attempt to differentiate, as the art historians do, between "baroque" and "mannerist" in literature has only compounded confusion and darkened counsel. René Wellek's caveat against the promiscuous use of "baroque" ("The Concept of Baroque in Literary Scholarship," pp. 77–109) has not prevented the appearance of more speculation concerning the baroque *Zeitgeist,* more freewheeling analogies between the arts, more attempts to define "baroque" in narrowly stylistic terms, as well as a generous quota of rebukes from the cautious. The present study will use the term "baroque" because Croll used it, because there is no satisfactory substitute, and because —for all its uncertainties—it still seems a useful way of suggesting stylistic procedures that may, in the last analysis, transcend the bounds of a single art and relate to a whole cultural conformation.

17. Of course the Shakespearean passage is not really Ciceronian, but only relatively or approximately so in contrast with Jonson. "The Ciceronian style," as Croll has pointed out, "cannot be reproduced

in English, or indeed in any modern language. The ligatures of its comprehensive period are not found in the syntax of an uninflected tongue; and the artifices necessary to supply their function must produce either fantastic distortion or insufferable bombast." ("Attic Prose," *Schelling Anniversary Papers*, p. 134.)

18. Citations from Jonson throughout are to the edition of C. H. Herford and Percy and Evelyn Simpson, 11 vols. (Oxford, 1925–1952). The following abbreviations are used in the present chapter:

> *Disc.: Timber, or Discoveries*
> *CR: Cynthia's Revels*
> *EMO: Every Man out of his Humour*
> *Poet.: Poetaster*
> *SW: Epicene, or The Silent Woman*
> *BF: Bartholomew Fair*
> *NNW: News from the New World Discovered in the Moon*
> *Pan: Pan's Anniversary*
> *King's Ent.: The King's Entertainment in Passing to His Coronation*
> *Chlor.: Chloridia*

In Shakespeare references, 'L' refers to Sir Sidney Lee's facsimile of the First Folio.

19. Croll, "Baroque Style," p. 433.

20. The transference of language from the printed page to the speaking voices of actors in a theater involves, necessarily, many accommodations. Most of these, however, occur on the level of phonology, and hence are properly analyzable only by microlinguistic techniques, including scrutiny of phonetic sequences, stresses, pitch, juncture, and the like. Even for a contemporary text, it is doubtful whether such an analysis would produce very satisfactory results. George L. Trager and Henry Lee Smith, Jr. (*An Outline of English Structure*, Studies in Linguistics, Occasional Papers 3 [Norman, Oklahoma, 1951], pp. 50–51) list at least eight different ways of saying "How do they study?" where the variations are confined entirely to pitch, stress, internal juncture and terminal juncture, and even so are not exhaustive. When we deal with such far more complex utterances as Jonson's sentences, when we take into account the problems of declamation in a theater whose declamatory techniques are at best only half understood, in a language three hundred years old whose phonology has been only fragmentarily reconstructed, we are facing a set of variables so formidable as to make any meaningful phonological appraisal a will-o'-the-wisp. One must, then, renounce formal discussion of this problem and confine oneself to repeating truisms, such as the fact that a good playwright somehow contrives to make his dialogue speakable, that—as actors know—an intricate sentence

of Congreve's can be pronounced more trippingly on the tongue than a simpler one from William Archer's translation of Ibsen, because the former was written by a master of theatrical speech and the latter was not.

In Jonson's case, one can of course point to certain details of phonetic realism—his growing tendency to substitute the "-s" ending of third person singular verbs for the more literary "-eth" inflection, his use of clipped forms (as he would have thought them) such as "hem" for "them"—and to his employment, on a massive scale, of modish phrases and cant terms that he would have scorned to use in his own person. But in sentence structure, if it can be separated from the rest, significant differences between the stage prose and the non-dramatic prose are few, partly because of the very nature of the baroque rhetoric to which Jonson was committed. What Jonson does, in fact, as this chapter is trying to show, is to take syntactic strategies normal in his critical prose and use them in the theater for specifically theatrical purposes, for characterization and effects of realism and satire.

I should like here to thank my former colleague James Sledd for turning the gimlet eye of a trained linguist on an earlier version of this chapter. In so doing, he rescued it from many errors. What errors it now contains have been perpetrated since he read it.

21. *The Senecan Amble,* p. 145, p. 156, n. 1.
22. *The Advancement of Learning,* Everyman ed., p. 24.
23. *The Senecan Amble,* pp. 89, 115, 118, 120, 184, and *passim.*
24. Croll, "Baroque Style," p. 437.
25. "Baroque Style," p. 443.
26. "Baroque Style," p. 447.
27. *Miscellaneous Criticism,* ed. Thomas Middleton Raysor (Cambridge, Mass., 1936), p. 217.
28. "English Prose Style," in *Miscellaneous Essays* (London, 1892), p. 7.
29. Montaigne, "Du repentir," *Essais,* ed. Albert Thibaudet, Bibliothèque de la Pléiade (Paris, 1958), p. 899.
30. See note 23 above.
31. "Baroque Style," p. 452.
32. For the "possessive as antecedent of a relative pronoun," a peculiarity of Elizabethan syntax in general, see A. C. Partridge, *Studies in the Syntax of Ben Jonson's Plays* (Cambridge, 1953), pp. 46–47, and for the (baroque) use of "a common relative with different case functions," p. 70. Jonson's own *English Grammar* (Herford and Simpson, VIII, 453–553), it might be added, is, disappointingly, of little help. The section on syntax (pp. 528ff.) devotes itself mainly to combinations required by idiom (agreement of noun and verb,

position of article and noun, etc.) and a few minor variations. It deals only hastily and perfunctorily with connectives, and it ignores (as do other grammars, for that matter) the whole area of the "probable" and "possible" in syntax, of acutest interest to stylistic study.

33. The fact that these lines form part of a long excerpt borrowed almost intact from John Hoskins does not invalidate them as evidence of Jonsonian style. It is, in fact, remarkable how smoothly the extract from Hoskins (itself an adaptation of Lipsius) fits into Jonson's own prose. On Hoskins, and the borrowings in the *Discoveries,* see the *Directions for Speech and Style,* ed. Hoyt H. Hudson (Princeton, 1935).

34. Here, as in the quotation above from *Disc.* 1404–07, I have restored the Folio reading. Herford and Simpson correct "hither. Also" to "hither also," and "serv'd" to "serve." The original reading in both cases strikes me as thoroughly Jonsonian. While certainty in such matters is impossible—Jonson *may* have intended "serve"—I trust that the evidence of this chapter as a whole will suffice to leave the benefit of the doubt with the text as it actually stands. It seems as rash to force Jonson's grammar to conform to modern practice as it was for earlier editors of Shakespeare to correct Shakespeare when he followed a plural subject with a singular verb or took other liberties later regarded as unorthodox. For tense shift as a characteristic of baroque poetry see Lowry Nelson, Jr., "Góngora and Milton: Toward a Definition of the Baroque," *Comparative Literature,* VI (1954), 53–63.

35. The fact that other writers do the same thing in similar circumstances leads one to suspect a special convention at work. See, for example, Dekker, *The Magnificent Entertainment,* lines 67–76, 175–179, 309–312, 456–465, 497–500, 831–845, in *The Dramatic Works,* ed. Fredson Bowers, 3 vols. (Cambridge, 1953–1959), II, 253–303; Middleton, *The Triumphs of Truth* and *Civitatis Amor* in *Works,* ed. A. H. Bullen, 8 vols. (Boston, 1886), VII, 239, 284–285, etc.; and Carew, *Coelum Britannicum,* in *Poems,* ed. Rhodes Dunlap (Oxford, 1949), pp. 154, 168, 176.

36. *A History of English Prose Rhythm* (London, 1912), p. 205.

37. It is uncertain how far this view would have to be modified if one were convinced, with Ralph S. Walker, *Ben Jonson's Timber or Discoveries* (Syracuse, 1953), pp. 1–13, that Jonson's editor, rather than Jonson, was responsible for the haphazard grouping of the *Discoveries,* and that even such disorder as may have existed in the manuscript merely reflected the incomplete state in which Jonson left it. The method of composition in either case remains the same: that of the gradual accretion of discrete fragments. And Digby's cavalier editorial practice would seem to reflect the general feeling

of the time about what constituted a "work," or a publishable unit of writing. It is at least arguable that had Jonson himself confronted publication, he might have been guided by his own motto, *tanquam explorator,* and left the fragments in something like their present tentative, exploratory form.

38. *Shakespearean Criticism,* ed. Thomas Middleton Raysor, 2 vols. (Cambridge, Mass., 1930), I, 49.

39. *La femme silencieuse* (with *Je ne vous aime pas*), Editions de la Nouvelle Revue Française (Paris: Librarie Gallimard, 1926).

40. The treatment would be similar in another modern version, proposed but not, apparently, executed, by a Mr. Elmer Harris, a dramatist. Mr. Harris would introduce "love-passages between Epicoene and the two puppets, La-Foole and Daw," so as to provoke mutual jealousy and thus motivate the quarrel between them. The Ladies Collegiate, too, "must be motivated" (Gayley, *Representative English Comedies,* II, 120–121). "Motivate! Motivate!" seems to be the rallying cry of the adapters of Jonson. What cannot be "motivated," or made to produce further action, is discarded as "irrelevant."

This would be the place to speak of Stefan Zweig's adaptation of *Epicene* into a libretto, *Die schweigsame Frau,* for Richard Strauss (1935), if that were relevant. But it is not relevant, Zweig having altered the plot so radically as to make comparison purposeless. He has, of course, "motivated" his own new plot at every point, "explained" Morose's hatred of noise in terms of a traumatic naval battle, and so forth.

41. *Ben Jonson: Selected Works* (New York, 1938), p. 25.

42. Page 30.

43. Eric Bentley, *In Search of Theater* (New York, 1954), p. 147.

44. Spitzer, *Linguistics and Literary History,* p. 11.

GEORGE WATSON

✒

The Language of the Metaphysicals

The "metaphysical" style of English in the early and mid-seventeenth century is a classic example of a language known to posterity best through its enemies. That it is a language rather than a form is plain: it exists in the long poem as well as in the short, and in prose as well as in verse. But the earliest comments that easily come to mind are all hostile. Samuel Butler's foolish Puritan knight, though he has nothing to say, can chop logic with the rest of his kind and knows the names of all the figures of speech:

> He could distinguish, and divide
> A hair 'twixt south and southwest side:
> On either which he would dispute,
> Confute, change hands, and still confute . . .
> For rhetoric, he could not ope
> His mouth, but out there flew a trope.[1]

Dryden, a few years later, has one of his characters in the dialogue *Of Dramatic Poesy* (1668) talk deflatingly of a style he calls Clevelandism, or "wresting and torturing a word into another meaning"; and Pope, in the first book of the *Dunciad* (1728), devastatingly summarizes the extended metaphor as "ductile Dulness" (I.64). It is no surprise, then, if the subject is a battle-ground: or rather, a field from which several armies have now departed, leaving their weapons scattered. This was once no easy cause. The claims made for the metaphysical style in the 1920s and 1930s, at the height of its modern vogue, were for understandable reasons framed in controversial terms; and poets and critics like T. S. Eliot saw the style in its potential influence on Anglo-American poetry as the best hope for a civilized Modernism. Nobody, in all probability, thinks that now: indeed nobody now sees the Metaphysicals as a cause at all. The creative use of literary history by the Modernists in the early twentieth century has itself become a part of the history of another age.

It is now plain, what is more, that the Metaphysical School is an invention—admittedly an intelligent invention, and one of long standing—on the part of English literary historians, rather than a phenomenon of which men could easily take note at the time. There is no reason to suppose that any Renaissance Englishman ever saw the Metaphysicals as a school, as he may have seen the University Wits or the Tribe of Ben as a school. There are no contemporary manifestoes and no contemporary critiques. Even as late as 1779, when Johnson identified these poets as such, in his Life of Cowley ("a race of writers that may be termed the metaphysical poets"), probably drawing his term from a hint of Dryden's, the name did not take easily or without opposition. And in the place where one would most naturally expect contemporary identification to occur, in the writings of Elizabethan rhetoricians, nothing of the sort seems clearly to happen. In spite of an intense interest in the language of poetry in that age, and especially in its figurative elements, nobody seems to have thought that the use of the metaphysical conceit, or extended metaphor—or the use of any other figure, for that matter—distinguished one school of poets from another.

To turn to the poetry itself, however, is to realize that Dryden, Johnson, and the Modernists were after all on firm ground. In an age as language-conscious as the late Elizabethan and Jacobean, awareness does not need to wait upon critical comment: it is there, and very explicitly there, in the poems themselves. Much poetry in that age is directly critical in its concern: not just illustrative of the possibilities of poetic language, that is, but positively assertive about them. In Love's Labour's Lost Shakespeare confidently expected his audience to share with his actors a witty apprehension of a range of styles. A point can be made conceitedly and at length, so the play shows, if time and social occasion permit, or in quick,

literal terms if action is afoot. Berowne, in his speech on Love as
a Hercules (4.3), extravagantly exploits a whole battery of figures
to prove a paradox of love, "It is religion to be thus forsworn," and
the King joins in exultantly with a military conceit, "Soldiers, to the
field!", which Berowne continues:

> Advance your standards, and upon them, lords!
> Pell-mell, down with them! but be first advis'd
> In conflict that you get the sun of them,

whereupon Longaville bluntly cuts through rhetoric with a curt demand for literal speech:

> Now to plain-dealing; lay these glozes by;
> Shall we resolve to woo these girls of France?

Benedick in *Much Ado,* and Malvolio in *Twelfth Night,* both
comically misinterpret what they take to be messages from their
mistresses by applying what Benedick calls the "double meaning"
(2.3) of love-language. In exchanges of love, as Elizabethans knew,
what seems to be literal is never just that. Duplicity is a habit of
fortune-tellers, too: Bertram, in *All's Well,* refers contemptuously
to Parolles as having deceived him "like a double-meaning proph-
esier" (4.3); and Macbeth, catastrophically deceived by the proph-
ecies of the witches, discovers the double function of language to
his cost only in the last scene of the tragedy:

> And be those juggling fiends no more believed
> That palter with us in a double sense;
> That keep the word of promise to our ear
> And break it to our hope.

Herbert, in the first "Jordan" poem in the *Temple* (1633), sees two
large possibilities in poetic language, a complex-figurative and a
simple-literal:

> Who says that fictions only and false hair
> Become a verse? Is there in truth no beauty?
> Is all good nature in a winding stair?

> May no lines pass, except they do their duty
> Not to a true, but painted chair?

and when he writes of "catching the sense at two removes" he offers a succinct account of conceited language in the very act of rejecting it. Traherne, no less paradoxically, makes a claim of his own for literal diction in an introductory poem "The Author to the Critical Peruser," a claim which the poems in the rest of the manuscript do remarkably little to justify:

> No curling metaphors that gild the sense,
> Nor pictures here, no painted eloquence . . .

Milton, in the second and third books of *Paradise Lost* (1667), illustrates the contrast between a muddled and divided Hell, a place of vexed and unending debate, where the fallen spirits

> found no end, in wandering mazes lost (2.561)

and the serene clarifications of cosmic intent offered by God to the Son and angels in the following book. But this is already past the end of the story. The last years of the monarchy, together with the Cromwellian interregnum, must be considered here in stylistic terms as a Great Divide. By the Restoration of 1660 the doubleness of language is seen more sharply than ever, but seen now in retrospect, as a dangerous toy. Language is no longer a game, for the most part: the literal has won.

One or two arguments concerning the Renaissance doctrine of double speech will have to be stated here in summary form. The first is that, as a doctrine, it is false. Language is not simple to the extent that it is literal and complex to the extent that it is figurative. The assumption, fundamental as it is to the writings of Renaissance rhetoricians, is after all nothing more than that, and it can be made to yield under critical examination to arguments like Mr. Barfield's. When the rhetoricians of the sixteenth century indulge their favourite sport of categorizing figures of speech like metaphor and simile, metonymy and synecdoche, they are explaining features of language that are genuinely there, though perhaps not always or usually there in the strict and isolable sense they seem to suppose.

It would have been perfectly natural for Herbert, who was appointed a Reader of Rhetoric in the University of Cambridge in 1618, to assume with all educated men of his age that figures of speech are properties superadded to language, like a wig to a head ("fictions only and false hair"); but this view satisfies now neither historically nor logically. Historically, because it now seems highly implausible to suggest that language began as literal and became figurative only with the sophistications of civilization; and logically, because it is plain that the translation-game which the Metaphysicals often invite us to play in their poems is not in the last analysis a possible one. Figurative language cannot always be translated into literal without loss of sense. Those who "plainly say 'My God, my king,'" as Herbert demands at the end of his poem, may be behaving unexceptionally in a theological sense; but they cannot pretend that their language is doing all the work that Herbert's *Temple,* or Donne's "Holy Sonnets" before it, can be shown to do.

The point is not as remote from modern concerns as it may at first appear. If Renaissance rhetoricians are subject to easy assumptions about the nature of language, so are those modern scholars who revive their memory in the hope that rhetoric will help to solve the mysteries of Renaissance poetic style. A work as distinguished as Rosemond Tuve's *Elizabethan and Metaphysical Imagery* (1947) is a case in point, and its erudition has inevitably inspired many admiring successors. It is always tempting in scholarship to suppose that a case based on an abundant use of evidence from contemporary sources and on rich archaeological investigation is more authentic than one argued anachronistically, so to speak, with the equipment of modern knowledge. But in the sphere of language, at least, this can hardly be so. For one, it assumes that the Renaissance poet's use of rhetoric, considered as a deliberate use, is of greater interest than those aspects of his language for which he would be incapable of offering explanations based on contemporary rhetorical theory. This seems very unlikely. One might admit that school-rhetoric is a genuine element in what the Metaphysicals do, and as such worthy of some critical attention. But to suppose that it explains all or most of what they do with language is merely utopian. It is significant that Miss Tuve, in her epoch-making analysis of the logical structure of the metaphysical conceit, is compelled to use arguments of her own making: arguments, one is tempted to add here, which a Renaissance poet would not readily have understood. But then the notion that a poet usually understands the whole of what he is doing with a language as he writes it seems no more plausible than to suppose that a cyclist understands, or needs to understand, the balance of forces that keeps him from falling off.

Another argument of even wider scope may be found helpful here. Modern linguists, if they are performing their function with full historical rigour, know what other ages have known about language and more besides. They know what Plato said in the *Cratylus,* Cicero in the *Rhetoric,* and Puttenham in the *Art of English Poesy* (1589), and they also know what Saussure, J. R. Firth, and Professor Chomsky have said. In this contest, it hardly needs to be emphasized, the Renaissance rhetorician is at a grave disadvantage. He knows his Cicero and his own immediate predecessors, and not much else. To suppose that with such equipment he can yet see more than we can see in a Renaissance poem, linguistically considered, is to suppose an extreme improbability. No doubt something has to be conceded to the view that contemporaries often see and take for granted in works of art features which later ages can only laboriously and with learned difficulty perceive. But then I am not denying that a study of Renaissance rhetoric may be of some limited use in the study of Renaissance poetry. What needs to be denied here is that such a study can answer all or most of the questions which, as modern readers, we may properly pose.

The function and duty of the modern analyst of poetic language, then, is to use anachronistic arguments boldly, as far as they may help him; and he need not be intimidated by archaeological fanaticisms or parades of erudition. What is there in a poem is there independently of whether the poet or his contemporaries knew it to be there or not; and still more, independently of whether they could have explained it or not. But does a modern theory of language like twentieth-century structuralism do the work any better? The absence of positive examples here is admittedly a suspicious circumstance. There are examples of archaeological analysis (if one may so dub the works of Miss Tuve and her successors) which undeniably reveal certain features in metaphysical poems which would otherwise have remained unnoticed, and the only issue can be whether these are major or minor features. With structural linguistics in the last half century, however, the cupboard seems a good deal barer. Can one point to a single example of such analysis of a metaphysical poem? No doubt the structuralist will wish to retort

that his subject is a new one, and that the literary critic had better
wait and see. But the critic has been waiting now for decades, and
what he is given to see amounts to little or nothing. It is a question
of continuing delicacy in intellectual history to know at what point
an enquiring openmindedness in the face of new intellectual movements has a right and a duty to turn into something less amiable:
a blunt demand to match pretension with performance. Structural
linguistics, in a dawning awareness that the intellectual world in
general, and literary critics in particular, are now less patient than
they once were towards their claims for the indulgence due to a
new science, now tend to moderate their enthusiasm for what their
discipline has to teach the historians of literature. Tempers are
cooler, and claims more moderate, than in years past, and a conference of linguists and critics would now probably content itself with
mutual admissions that the contribution of either discipline to the
other must for the time being remain modest and undramatic. And
perhaps an agreement to go one's separate ways, with occasional
interchanges of information, may be the best that circumstances
here afford.

The truth is that there is no strictly linguistic way to take intellectual possession of metaphysical poetry, and that this judgment
must apply, though in differing measure, to Renaissance and to
modern methods of linguistic analysis. The literary historian has
no alternative outside himself, no tool-kit he can borrow from another. He must simply look harder. I propose here to take a harder
look at one or two metaphysical poems, with a view to testing
ancient and accepted assumptions about the ways that language
works in them.

It is now widely held that the distinguishing mark of the metaphysical style is the conceit or extended metaphor. Miss Tuve laid
her emphasis firmly here, in a complex account of an historical movement from the "intrinsically decorative images" (p. 69) of much
Elizabethan verse towards the "multiple logical bases" (p. 264) that
characterize the imagery of the Metaphysicals. Professor Helen
Gardner, in a masterly introduction to her anthology *The Metaphysical Poets* (1957, revised 1966), puts the case more succinctly:

> What differentiates the conceits of the metaphysicals is not the
> fact that they very frequently employ curious learning in their

comparisons. Many of the poets whom we call metaphysical, Herbert for instance, do not. It is the use which they make of the conceit and the rigorous nature of their conceits, springing from the use to which they are put, which is more important than their frequently learned content. A metaphysical conceit . . . is not indulged for its own sake. It is used . . . to persuade, or it is used to define, or to prove a point. . . . (p. 21)

and she goes on to describe how the seventeenth-century conceit "aims at making us concede justness while admiring ingenuity."

I wish to juxtapose two poems to this account, which is convincing enough in its own terms to bring many a metaphysical poem vividly to mind, and influential enough, in any case, to be worth testing against real cases. Only one of them (Herbert's) appears in Professor Gardner's anthology, but this is not likely to be because she doubts the metaphysical status of the other, which is from Donne's *Songs and Sonnets*.

"Negative Love"
JOHN DONNE

I never stoop'd so low, as they
Which on an eye, cheek, lip can prey,
    Seldom to them which soar no higher
    Than virtue or the mind to admire,
For sense and understanding may
    Know what gives fuel to their fire.
My love, though silly, is more brave,
For may I miss, whene'er I crave,
If I know yet what I would have.

If that be simply perfectest
Which can by no way be express'd
    But *negatives*, my love is so.
    To all, which all love, I say no.
If any who deciphers best
    What we know not, ourselves, can know,
Let him teach me that nothing: this
As yet my ease and comfort is,
Though I speed not, I cannot miss.

"Vertue"

GEORGE HERBERT

Sweet day, so cool, so calm, so bright,
The bridal of the earth and sky:
The dew shall weep thy fall tonight;
    For thou must die.
Sweet rose, whose hue angry and brave
Bids the rash gazer wipe his eye:
Thy root is ever in its grave,
    And thou must die.
Sweet music, full of sweet days and roses,
A box where sweets compacted lie:
My music shows ye have your closes,
    And all must die.
Only a sweet and virtuous soul,
Like season'd timber, never gives;
But though the whole world turn to coal
    Then chiefly lives.

Both poems are undeniably metaphysical, for whatever reason, and it is not merely because they happen to be by Donne and Herbert that we wish to call them so. But they do not easily bear out the view that the grand characteristic of such poetry is its use of figurative language. The Donne poem, indeed, approaches very nearly to the purely literal, and is probably as literal as most twentieth-century expository prose; and the point may be worth emphasizing, since the fallacy that poetry distinguishes itself from prose by virtue of imagery is still widely held. The imagery of "Negative Love" amounts after all to nearly nothing: *stoop'd, prey, soar, fuel to fire*—these four almost exhaust the possibilities in eighteen lines. They are all metaphors, and all unemphatically so, belonging to that numerous class of metaphors in English which are in process of disappearing, by sheer familiarity, into the pattern of literal usage. It seems fair to say that if they were not there, the poem would not for that reason alone be radically different; and the second of the two stanzas, it may be noted, is totally non-figurative, unless a desperate case is to be made in favour of *deciphers*. It seems unlikely that any literary work in English comes much closer to the purely literal than "Negative Love."

Herbert's "Vertue" is something else, but it is doubtful whether its figurative features, which are more abundant, are its characteristic strength. The structure is tightly and ingeniously wrought, and can most easily be grasped by summarizing the refrain: *day must die, rose must die, all must die, soul lives.* Bluntly stated like this, the pattern seems astonishingly lucid, and misrepresents the poem only by omitting the delicate distractions of Herbert's fourfold elaboration on day, rose, music, and the virtuous soul. The metre, as so often in the *Temple,* is neatly binding, and separates with its "die"-rhymes the first three stanzas from the fourth. A severe logic, as Coleridge would have said; and indeed he quotes the poem as a model, with two others by Herbert, at the end of the nineteenth chapter of the *Biographia Literaria.* But is the poem conceited? In attempting to answer this question, the incidental or decorative images in the poem may safely be neglected. In fact they must for this purpose be neglected, since it is often emphasized that the distinguishing feature of the metaphysical conceit is its structural function. If Herbert says that a fine day is like the marriage of heaven and earth, this is only a conceit if he chooses to continue the comparison. And it is clear that he does not.

> The dew shall weep thy fall tonight

is hardly a continuation of the metaphor in "bridal": it is more like a fresh start. Much the same can probably be said of the rest of "Vertue," and emphatically needs to be said of the last stanza, since the leap from "timber" to "coal" is in its essence daring and unheralded. Plainly, if any sort of case is to be made for the conceit here, it cannot be made in respect of images internal to individual stanzas: it can only be made, if at all, for the structure of the whole poem.

The poem is about virtue, which alone among earthly things, being God-given, does not decay. It is hard to see that the unity of the poem can be called a matter of imagery at all, let alone of conceited imagery. An image is a comparison or analogy considered as a rhetorical device. Where is the comparison here? No doubt Herbert's day, rose, and music *illustrate* those worldly things which, in contrast to virtue, are subject to decay. But illustration is barely a form of comparison. It is indeed a rhetorical device, but not the device required by those who attribute a decisive importance to the place of the conceit in metaphysical poetry. In both these poems, indisputably metaphysical as they are, the conceit seems to be totally absent.

Nothing in this argument, it should be said at once, is fatal either to the intelligent study of the conceit as such, or to the view that it is a significant, even a dominating, aspect of many a metaphysical poem. Donne's compasses in "A Valediction Forbidding Mourning," which image the parting and reunion of two lovers, have done a traditional service in most previous discussions of the question and will rightly serve their turn again; and they occupy in the last three stanzas of the "Valediction" a place which justifies the established view of how conceits can notably function in the School of Donne. What is in question here is not whether all this happens, but rather whether it needs to happen. If the critic could raise his eyes from the conceit for long enough to notice functions of language in these poems of which the conceit is only one example, he might find issues of more compelling interest than the mere identification and analysis of a single and only doubtfully characteristic figure of speech.

Certain common (though not universal) aspects of metaphysical poems, some familiar and some not, may be grouped together here as a reminder of the experience they offer. Many metaphysical poems, it is not often noticed, are narrative. Donne's "Valediction Forbidding Mourning," which has been so earnestly tested for its rhetorical properties, tells a little story of a man leaving a woman and assuring her of his return. His "Ecstasy" tells another story of two lovers lying on a flowery bank, hands clasped and with gazing eyes, unspeaking and yet communicating by means of a "dialogue of one" a shared doctrine of Platonic love. The first poem is framed as a dramatic monologue; the second, in the past tense, as an historical incident with a large interpolation of speculation on the philosophy of love. The dramatic monologue is a continuing device in the school; it is used by Herbert in "The Collar," for instance, and by Marvell, in a purer form, in "To his Coy Mistress." Since most English metaphysical poems are about either God or a mistress, the monologue and the dialogue are highly appropriate forms: the lover or sinner may naturally plead, expostulate, and woo. The famous opening device of certain among these poems, by which the poet starts the action of his story *in medias res,* is easily accountable here, like the opening of Donne's "Canonization" ("For Godsake hold your tongue, and let me love . . ."), since both love and religion are familiar social rituals in which the reader can well be expected to seize the dramatic essence of the situation after the slightest of hints. A metaphysical poem may say surprising things, but it is commonly about an unsurprising subject. It often recounts an incident lifted for a moment out of the familiar web of two large complexes of human behaviour, man's love of God and his love for woman. It is a story taken from a larger story, and that larger story is one which poet and reader share before the poem begins.

The shared experience of poet and reader which characterizes much of metaphysical poetry may help to bring the language of these poems into sharper focus and clarify the nature of the change that overtook English poetry in the mid-seventeenth century, at the end of the epoch. "Sharing" here means something very simple: it means that for the reader the end of the poem is known or guessed, in outline at least, soon after the poem begins. The coy mistress will come to bed, the sinner will repent, lovers will die, the old lessons of grace and mortality will be better understood. The question in a metaphysical poem is not whether but how: just as in a bull-fight it is not usually a question whether the bull will die, only the manner of his death exciting expectation. Some of Donne's poems, and especially the Platonic poems in the *Songs and Sonnets,* place a heavy strain on this interpretation, and may even be thought to violate it altogether; and certainly the argument of "Negative Love" or of the "Ecstasy" is unfamiliar to the uninstructed and heavily compounded with paradox. But then the uninstructed were hardly meant to see poems like these, designed to be passed from hand to hand in manuscript and left unpublished in the poet's lifetime; and the sophisticated minority who knew something of Renaissance Platonism may have savoured these poems all the more because they offered a special interest in the esoteric. Minority culture is not an invention of the last hundred years; and Donne's language here, though not exactly secret or private, plainly belongs to a coterie. He is rather fond of suggesting that the neighbours will not easily understand what he says, or future ages either:

> I would that age were by this paper taught
> What miracles we harmless lovers wrought.

But "love's riddles," as he calls them in another poem, are after all there to be solved; they are not meant to "tease us out of thought As doth Eternity," but to tease only for the instant. Even Donne's most difficult poems were probably meant to be like this; and if some of the problems they pose are now unanswerable, this is more likely to arise from the lapse of time than from any intended effect of impenetrability.

The language of the Metaphysicals, then, though shared, is shared with a degree of deliberate difficulty: designed, as riddles and puzzles are designed, to offer a kind of teasing clarity. The general temper of Elizabethan poetry (and especially love poetry) out of which the style was born favoured the paradox of a language which is clear, but not clear all at once. Allegory is the perfect instance: it is interpretable, but not without effort, and the effort is what makes the experience of reading. Spenser, in his introductory letter to Ralegh placed before *The Faerie Queene* in 1590, calls his poem a "dark conceit," a thing devised to offer a degree of difficulty. Another favourite analogy of the age, and one which strikes the modern mind with a sense of oddity, is between the poet and lawyer or public orator. Puttenham regarded the poet as a "pleader" (3.7.19), and speaks of the "certain novelty and strange manner" (3.1) which the language of poetry requires. Sidney makes a similar point, and with greater variety and amplitude, in the course of the *Apology*. He makes no bones about the essential familiarity of material in the Elizabethan short poem, "that lyrical kind of songs and sonnets." Writing about God, at least, is a matter of finding new words to fit old truths: "we might well want words, but never matter; . . . we could turn our eyes to nothing, but we should ever have new-budding occasions." Love poetry, he goes on, is poetry designed to persuade; and he warns against extravagance and alliteration, against an excess of "forcibleness," "courtesan-like painted affectation" in language, "coursing of a letter," and "figures and flowers extremely winter-starved." [2] These temptations are not to poets alone: they afflict, so Sidney says, writers of prose, including scholars and preachers. The proper business of the poet is not mechanically to collect and reproduce in their poems the figures of Cicero's oratory, or Demosthenes's, but rather to " devour them whole"; and he approvingly instances Cicero's trick of imitating rage in an oration by means of the figure of repetition, "and so do that artificially which we see men do in choler naturally." Sidney is not a Metaphysical, and much of his argument concerning the proper diction of poetry is a reasoned resistance against the widening variety of linguistic devices which, even as soon as the early 1580s, seemed to him to threaten the fabric of English. But he shares with his successors a sense of the interconnections between lyric poetry and more utilitarian uses of language: the statesman's in the senate, the lawyer at the bar are not easily separable from the poet's, as they are for us, in the diction they employ. A poem is a kind of argument, and its end is to win and convince.

Is the argument of a metaphysical poem real or fictional? This is probably one of those questions of literary history which are problematical now precisely because the matter seemed so natural at the time. It would be tempting, and probably not altogether mistaken, to suppose that these poems were offered to their first readers as fictions, and that the arguments they embody, expounded often through little narratives in well defined and often familiar dramatic situations, would have seemed to those first readers as essentially impersonal, independent of real events, and technically competitive. "The writers represented in the three volumes of Saintsbury's *Caroline Poets*," it has been shrewdly observed, "seem at times to be involved in a kind of never-ending *New Statesman* competition." [3] This must be true of many, and perhaps most, of these poems, and it is strongly tempting to argue that metaphysical language in its essence is not so much an argument as a mimesis of an argument, where the rules of logic are deliberately but subtly violated as a challenge to the reader. They are spot-the-fallacy tests, at times, and it may be part of their fascination to use them in this way. Marvell's "To his Coy Mistress," for instance, like other seduction-poems of the age, is presumably written against a background of assumption that what it proposes contravenes in the end both decorum and morality. To suppose that Marvell thinks the arguments good arguments seems absurd; and if he had thought so, one is inclined to add, he would have been the less likely to show his hand by writing the poem. On the other hand, he plainly thinks them persuasive arguments, which is something else. They might work, in a given situation, without deserving to work.

A Renaissance Englishman, on the other hand, would probably have thought this view over-solemn and (what matters more) at least partly mistaken. It is often a precarious business to define the relation between poetry and life in another age, and Renaissance love poetry is among the trickiest of all examples. Perhaps the modern confessional novel is an analogy here. Twentieth-century novels about sexual decorum and morality often traverse the same territory as Donne or Marvell, in the sense of analysing and interpreting the range of permitted and unpermitted acts. If a total outsider to this tradition were to ask whether these novels are autobiographical or not, we should be rightly puzzled how to answer, and certain that a yes or no answer would not do. It is not that we doubt that these novelists hold views about behaviour, and convey them; and it is hardly to be denied that they exploit their private experiences when they write. It may even be among the special pleasures enjoyed by their acquaintances to spot the resemblances between fact and fiction. But we also know that these novels are technically competitive, as metaphysical poems often were, and that most of their readers are legitimately indifferent to questions of autobiographical reference.

It may be that metaphysical poems existed in just such a relationship to their own world as this: with the important difference that in their case private reference may have been vastly more significant than in any modern novel, and perhaps even an exclusive interest in the first instance. But the brief history of metaphysical poetry, from the 1590s down to the Restoration, seems to be a progress towards public status. This is a language that begins in relative secrecy among friends, and turns decisively towards public utterance with Herbert's *Temple*. It is true that the *Temple* is a posthumous publication, by a matter of weeks or months. But this is likely to be an accidental fact, arising from the early death of the poet at the age of forty; and the *Temple* seems in retrospect just the sort of collection a clergyman might publish, though Herbert may first have intended these poems for use in manuscript within a limited circle like the religious community at Little Gidding. Earlier cases are more strictly private. Sir Walter Raleigh, if he may now be accepted as the first Metaphysical, left his poems unpublished at his death in 1618, and they remained uncollected till the nineteenth century; and Donne's *Songs and Sonnets* and divine poems were left in manuscript until after his death in 1631. Marvell and Traherne continue, for whatever reason, the old Elizabethan reticence, and though Marvell lived till 1678 his poems did not see print till three years later, while Traherne's were unprinted before this century. But volumes of metaphysical verse are common during the Civil War and Protectorate, and Crashaw and Vaughan both publish verse in their lifetimes. It may be that the making public of this highly private or coterie language is a powerful reason for its sudden demise in English poetry after 1660. A strain is imposed which is hardly to be borne. The matter may be viewed under several aspects: literary, philosophical, and political.

The literary reasons for the decay of the metaphysical are perhaps the most powerful of all, but they are the least amenable to discussion. I think it is clear, however, from what Butler, Dryden, and others write on the subject in the early and mid-1660s, that the new poets of the Restoration are above all things *bored* with the old style. It has become a kind of fribbling, a way of saying nearly nothing in as many words as possible: worse still, a way of almost saying something but not quite, a kind of poetic torment-of-Tantalus. Dryden in the *Essay of Dramatic Poesy* speaks of "the ghost of a jest" which "flies before the poet, never to be caught," and compares the old style of poetry to swallows catching gnats on the Thames: "how seldom they touch it; and when they do, 'tis but the surface: they skim over it . . ." The sudden turning away by English poets from the complexities of Dylan Thomas's diction soon after his death in 1953 is a similar case. All languages die, and in a dynamic literary tradition like the English they tend to die fast. In a sense, no other explanation is needed.

The philosophical aspect can best be studied in Hobbes, in his anonymous appendix to Descartes's *Meditationes* (1641) and in the chapter of the *Leviathan* (1650) entitled "Of Speech" (I.4). In his Life of Hobbes, Aubrey speaks of Dryden as a "great admirer" of Hobbes, adding that he "oftentimes makes use of his doctrine in his plays." The remark is open to various interpretations, but it certainly encourages the assumption that Dryden read Hobbes with approval. And Hobbes's nominalism is extreme: "What is nowhere, is not, and therefore has not a being, or any nature," he writes in opposition to Descartes's hypothetical instance of a perfect triangle. Language, he insists in the *Leviathan,* consists simply of names:

> The first author of speech was God himself, that instructed Adam how to name such creatures as he presented to his sight; for the Scripture goeth no further in this matter.

Adam was later encouraged to add more names,

> and so by succession of time so much language might be gotten as he had found use for; though not so copious as an orator or philosopher has need of. For I do not find anything in the

Scripture out of which directly or by consequence can be
gathered that Adam was taught the names of all figures, numbers, measures, colours, sounds, fancies, relations . . .

So much for rhetoric. So much, indeed, for any delicate play of
language, literal or figurative. Dryden was not a linguistic doc-
trinaire, like Sprat and some other early members of the Royal
Society. But it seems natural to suppose that he was influenced by
a climate of opinion hostile to all uses of language other than the
severely descriptive. "So likewise," Hobbes continues his attack,

> if it be false to say that virtue can be poured, or blown up and
> down, the words *inpoured virtue, inblown virtue,* are as absurd
> and insignificant as a round quadrangle.

The political aspect is more speculative in its wider implications.
There is the plain and highly significant fact that by 1660 "wrested
meanings," especially of Scripture, were heavily associated by Eng-
lishmen with Puritanism and regicide. This prejudice affected styles
of preaching in a direct sense, notably by reducing or abolishing
figurative references to the Divinity. No doubt all this worked
towards simplicity in the language of poetry too, though in a far less
pure and simple sense. But another effect of the Civil War upon
language has been less noticed. I spoke earlier of the highly equivocal
status of argumentative language in many metaphysical poems—a
language neither clearly private nor clearly public in its reference,
neither plainly good as argument nor yet altogether bad, as if imitating or parodying at close distance the writings of the Schools.
Donne's "Negative Love" is very like this. It is a serious argument
in favour of Platonic love: but to ask if it is serious for Donne is
to ask what cannot easily be answered, and what even Donne's
most intimate friends might have found difficult to answer. Compare with this an example of poetic argument from after the Restoration. Dryden, in a poem of Catholic apologetics entitled *The Hind
and the Panther* (1687), is arguing against the view that the senses
are still the grounds of religious belief, as they were in the age of
miracles:

> But winnow well this thought, and you shall find
> 'Tis light as chaff that flies before the wind.

Were all those wonders wrought by pow'r divine
As means or ends of some more deep design?
Most sure as means, whose end was this alone,
To prove the godhead of th' eternal Son.
God thus asserted: man is to believe
Beyond what Sense and Reason can conceive,
And for mysterious things of faith rely
On the Proponent, heaven's authority.
If then our faith we for our guide admit,
Vain is the farther search of human wit,
As when a building gains a surer stay,
We take th' unuseful scaffolding away.

(I.112–125)

This is a whole world away from the language of the Metaphysicals. And what removes it is not its extreme literalness, which is admittedly sustained here without flagging from the end of the first couplet to the beginning of the last. Sustained literalness can be paralleled, after all, though not easily paralleled, in the poems of the old style. What counts here is a different sort of literalness from the mere absence of imagery. Dryden's argument, to put it bluntly, means what it says. Language has assumed a function which, in the previous age, would usually have been felt too simplistic to merit the title of poetry. A confidence has been achieved in the expository function of verse, a confidence which the next century was to exploit in Pope's *Essay on Man,* Cowper's *Task,* and Wordsworth's *Prelude.* A generation that had lived through the controversies of the 1640s and 1650s, and the violence attendant on those controversies, may easily have felt that no other function for language could any longer be seriously regarded. It is equally natural that, with the death of these controversies, the nineteenth and twentieth centuries should regret the loss of something that Dryden and his contemporaries could view only with the harsh distaste of survivors. The play of speech in which the Renaissance delighted has not ceased to puzzle, as it was always meant to do, but it has long since ceased to provoke. It endangers no one. A lapse of time has returned it to its original condition of a language conscious of its own dimensions, working boldly within familiar themes and anxious to share with others a sense of how much and how variously it can perform.

NOTES

1. *Hudibras: the First Part* (London, 1663), I.67–70, 81–2.
2. *An Apology for Poetry,* ed. Geoffrey Shepherd (London, 1965), pp. 137–8.
3. Anne Righter, "John Wilmot Earl of Rochester," *Proceedings of British Academy,* LIII (1967), p. 59.

HUGH SYKES DAVIES

✍

Milton and the Vocabulary of Verse and Prose

✦

These phrases have been collected from one writer:

> endorse him on the backside of posterity: apostate scarecrows:
> asinine feast of sowthistles and brambles: fadge together: the
> bar will blush at this incogitant woodcock: ignoble hucksterage
> of piddling tithes: belching sour crudities: ruefull bellowing
> of enthymemes: chip of the old block: make a national war of
> a surplice brabble: rumple the bobbins of your oratory: wince
> and fling: spend their youth in bezzling: though this barrow
> grunt at the word: lay snares for your own bitterns: pangs and
> gripes of a boiling conscience: ragged infantry of the brothels:
> your buzzard idol: brutish hopes of a fat deanery: broken-
> winded tizzick: ravished by a troop of camping housewives:
> canonist with a foppish fardel of matrimonial cases: such a
> cock-brained solliciter: cockering and wanton impulses: poor
> transformed heffer of the commonwealth: phlegmy clod of an
> antagonist: grind in the mill of a servile copulation: courtesy
> of a night-walking cudgeller: cullionly paraphrase: those sanc-
> tified cutthroats: a coy, flirting style: a sucking satyr that ought
> to use his coral: the gamut of every municipal fiddler: the set-
> tled mud of his fancy: fustiest and flashiest that ever corrupted
> in an unswilled hogshead: greasy clutch of high feeding:
> finical goosery of your neat sermon-actor: prog and pander for

fees: matters not for folkmooters to babble in: truckage of
perishing coin: fine sophistical boulting-hutch: tankard drollery:
a venereous pargetory for the stews: say no more to a snout in
this pickle: wading up to his auditors in deep shallows that wet
not the instep: not content with the wonted room of his margent, he must cut out large docks and creeks from his text
wherein to unload the unseasonable frigates of his authorities:
wipe your fat corpulencies out of our light.

The list, which could easily be lengthened in the same style, is from
the writer whose language, in Addison's view, was "too much laboured," so that "our language sunk under him." It is the writer
whose style, according to Johnson, was "formed by a perverse and
pedantic principle," and the writer too whom Arnold found the
supreme exemplar of "the Grand Style" in English. But they, of
course, were talking of his verse, and this list is from his prose. The
difference between their views, and the general impression which
would probably be formed about the style of the phrases in the list
is due, not to a difference of opinion, but to a difference in the
selection of material. Milton is, in fact, something of a leading case
in the matter of "poetic diction," a conspicuous and very eminent
example of a writer who used one register of vocabulary in his verse,
and another in his prose. The case is not only important in itself.
It raises questions of method in literary and linguistic studies, and
suggests problems which are central to the history of the language.
The problem of method may be put in some such way as this.
If "poetic diction" can be broadly defined as a group of words used
by a particular author, or group of authors, fairly frequently in verse,
but rarely or not at all in their prose, then it is theoretically possible to list these words. Is this likely to be worth doing? And if
so, can it actually be done? The answers to these questions are
much more complex than the questions themselves, for they depend
upon a rather delicate balancing of probable or possible gains
against a vast deal of work, some of which, but by no means all,
might be mechanized. All that is proposed in this paper is to give
a number of guesses and approximations, illustrating from the particular, and probably particularly rewarding case of Milton, what
might be gained, and how.
The characteristic method of literary criticism is, of course, subjective. In a broad sense, it belongs to the realm of rhetoric rather

than to that of logic; its purpose is to persuade, for it can rarely prove; and its chief weapon is the enthymeme, not the proposition. When it deals with the larger aspects of literature, these are the appropriate, because the only possible methods. Descriptions and comparisons of plots and characters, the relation between content and its historical background, the manner in which style and content mutually interact—for these, and many other of its customary tasks, criticism can do no other than follow subjective methods. From a succession (it is to be hoped) of careful readings, some general impressions will emerge, to be tested and clarified and illustrated by examples from the text itself. And since these are usually those passages which were most active in creating the general impressions of the critic, there is inevitably something circular in the whole process. The conclusions were already implied in the choice of examples; or perhaps conclusions based on earlier readings, or the opinions of others, determined the choice of examples. This danger is regrettable, and not only in theory; but it must be accepted, since there is no other way of dealing with materials of this kind. The only way of avoiding the danger is not to deal with them at all. In discussions of the verbal aspect of literature, on the other hand, other methods exist, and the arguments in favour of at least considering them are the greater because it is precisely in this field that subjective judgments based upon unsystematically chosen examples are the strongest.

There is, in the first place, the greatest number of items between which choice may be made. The vocabulary of any text forms a population, in the statistician's sense, much larger than that of the ideas, the images, or the relations with other writers and ideas of the time in which the text was written; the dangers of unsystematic choice are correspondingly greater. Worse still, it is clear that within it, the commonest words are those which have the least chance of catching the attention of the unsystematic chooser, while the rarest are the most likely to catch his eye and memory. This follows directly from the central law governing the relation between words and their meanings: that words occurring frequently tend to have many meanings, while those which occur rarely have few meanings. Or—to vary the terms of the description slightly—frequently occurring words convey very little "information," while rarely occurring words convey much. It is for this reason that a reader whose method is unchecked by any theoretical knowledge of the relation between frequency of use and other aspects of words, and of the characteristic frequency-structures found in the vocabularies of texts, is liable to make choices of examples on principles which escape his attention, and thus evade questioning. He might, for example, be a good deal struck by the word "amphibologie" in Chaucer, or "mazarin" in Emily Dickinson, or "incarnadine" in Shakespeare. But if he were to go on to make anything of the special quality of these words, without observing that each of them is used only once by each writer, and not at all by the other two, he would unwittingly commit himself to an assumption which he might not wittingly accept: that in the vocabulary of any author, the words which occur only once are of exceptional importance.

For these reasons, and for some others which will suggest themselves as we proceed, the present methods of literary criticism in dealing with problems of vocabulary are clearly unsatisfactory. But what is involved in adopting methods which are theoretically better?

Perhaps the obvious improvement is to replace a subjective choice of examples for an objective one: to use samples instead of examples. If the whole vocabulary were thought to be too large a population for investigation, this would no doubt be the best expedient. Random sampling, or perhaps spread sampling, along the lines so familiar in statistical work, would be some improvement on selection by undefined personal hunches. But unless the samples taken were very large, they might well fail to reveal some significant aspects of the whole population. For example, suppose that the occurrence of some particular class of word were very patchy, so that several members of this class were often found in close proximity to each other, but very rarely in the rest of the text, then random sampling might well miss most, or all, of these patches. If this were to happen, the effect on estimates of the proportions of the special class of word to the whole vocabulary would be affected considerably, but this would matter comparatively little, since figures of this kind are rarely significant save as broad indications; what would matter much more would be that the existence of these special patches might escape notice, and that an important feature of the style would thus be missed. It will be seen below that patches of this kind are found in Milton's verse and prose. Random sampling has its uses in the study of vocabulary: it is, for example, a handy way of estimating the total number of word-occurrences in any text. But for more delicate and intricate investigations, nothing short of a complete concordance is of much use.

Fortunately, it is now possible to make new concordances by means of computers; and new ones are being published, not speedily, but steadily. The chief obstacles to their usefulness are the lack of any clear agreement about the kinds of numerical information they should contain, and the lack of concordances to prose, above all for those authors whose verse has been provided for.

The first of these defects is the more irritating, because the older concordances were not only lacking in numerical information, but compiled on a plan which did not even see any possible use for it. For example, the Wordsworth concordance by Professor Lane Cooper, which has so often been praised as a model of its kind, omits completely 52 of the commonest words, and gives only "partial lists" of 156 more. Few of the words omitted, it is true, would be of much use to a critic concerned with Wordsworth's vocabulary; but their omission or partial listing means that it is impossible, from this concordance, to make any estimate of the total number of word-occurrences in his verse, or of the proportion within this total of any particular class of word. And it is often essential to know both, if the study of the vocabulary as a whole, or of any part of it, is to be carried on meaningfully. For it is well known that some important aspects of any vocabulary vary, not only according to the individual usages of the author, but with the size of the text under investigation. Any text longer than a hundred words or so has two main components, when its vocabulary is listed and counted. There is on the one hand a relatively short list of words, of about 100, which occur very often, and on the other hand a very long list of words which occur more rarely. Indeed the class of words which occur only once each is invariably much the largest single class. In a fairly short sample of text, say of 10,000 words (or, more precisely, 10,000 word-occurrences), all of the first group will be found, most of them many times over; as the sample increases, say to 100,000 word-occurrences, very few new words will be added to this group, for the same old words will go on appearing again and again, like a revolving stage army. With the increase in the sample, however, the second group of words will continue to grow, and will only reach a standstill when the author has written enough to exhaust his whole vocabulary. In between these two main components of any vocabulary is a much smaller one, made up of relatively few words intermediate between the very frequent and the rare, and behaving, as a group, in the same intermediate manner. Every sample of text, in fact, has its own frequency-distribution, varying not only in size but also in shape. If the sample is increased, the shape will change. This is of the greatest practical importance, for it means that comparisons between two samples of text can be made only if they are of about the same size, so that differences and resemblances between them are likely to be real, not merely reflections of the size of the samples. If comparisons are to be made between texts of different lengths, affecting single words or groups of words, it is essential to know these lengths, and to make the somewhat complicated estimates needed to allow for their effects. For example, "balm" (with "balmy") occurs 20 times both in Shakespeare and in Emily Dickinson. Obviously it is relatively more common in the latter, since her text is much smaller. It is, very roughly, only one-fifth of Shakespeare's. But this does not mean that she uses the word five times as often as he does. Keats uses the same word 15 times, Wordsworth 12. But nothing much can be deduced from these figures in isolation. It is an unfortunate fact that the older concordances cannot be made to yield the information which is needed to interpret the vast store of information they contain, because they are incomplete. Sooner or later they will have to be re-made, if any progress is to be made in this field of study.

The more modern, machine-made concordances often fail to make this basic numerical information readily available, even though they may include it. For example, the Cornell concordance to Emily Dickinson does not record the total number of word-occurrences on which it was based, though it lets fall, in passing, the vague observation that it was "more than 100,000." [1] It can, of course, be calculated from the concordance itself, since the words are all included in the list; but much multiplication and addition is involved, and it is, to say the least, irritating to know that the computer had all these figures at its digit-tips. The only concordance made so far which has adequate numerical summaries of its entries is that to *Ulysses*.[2] So good is it that there may be some danger of its exercising an undue influence on the statistical studies of vocabulary; it is so very convenient to use, and yet it may not be typical.

There is, then, much lacking in the concordances now available. The older ones are seriously incomplete, the newer ones are lacking in numerical information. Worst of all, however, those dealing with English texts have dealt almost entirely with verse, and in no single case is there a concordance to the prose of the writers of this verse. This very seriously limits the usefulness of the verse concordances themselves, for it is impossible to survey systematically the vocabularies of writers like Donne, Milton, Dryden, Wordsworth, Coleridge, Keats, or Arnold while little or nothing can be discovered about their uses of words in their prose. Certainly the problems of poetic diction cannot be explored in any objective way until these prose concordances are made, either in general or in relation to particular authors.

Apart from the more obvious practical inconveniences of having no prose concordances of this kind, a serious problem of basic method is involved. Udny Yule, one of the founding fathers of the statistical study of vocabulary, showed that frequency-distributions of words conformed broadly with Poisson series, and that the study of word-occurrences could be compared with the distributions of accidents, about which a good deal was already known. He pointed out, however, that there were some awkward differences between word and accident distributions, and none worse than this:

> . . . there is another and more troublesome point of difference. Our distributions are incomplete: they do not give the number of words that have *not* met with the "accident" or "happening" of being used. In other terms, since we do not know this number, we do not know the total number of words "at risk," the number of words subject to the "risk" of being used by the author. The distributions of words are so to speak *decapitated*, lacking the leading frequency f_0: the distributions are incomplete. For the development of any theory of word-distribution we must, however, assume the total number of words "at risk" to be known, as theory can only consider the complete distribution.[3]

This is bad enough, and there seems to be no remedy for it but to makes estimates, as Yule did (p. 73), of the total vocabulary of Macaulay: oddly enough it was about the same as his estimate of his own vocabulary. But the position is much worse if we try to deal with the vocabulary of a poet, for whose prose no concordance has been made. The word-distributions are not only "decapitated":

they are also based on a sample which has been split in some accidental fashion, into a part which is known, and a part which is
unknown.

It is very evident, then, that there is no immediate prospect of
displacing the subjective approach to the problems of poetic diction.
For some time ahead, the literary critics are likely to have it to
themselves. Yet it is not clearly premature to consider, in a very
tentative and preliminary fashion, the manner in which the accumulation of concordances may eventually open the way to a more
objective attack on these problems. There is, indeed, something to
be said for making an imaginative exercise of it. By defining some
of the ways in which the evidence could be arranged, if mechanical
devices were readily available, we can throw a little light on the
kinds of word-list likely to be useful. We may even, though with
still greater caution, allow ourselves to make some vague hypotheses
about the patterns which might emerge from them.

It so happens that in the case of Milton alone an exercise of this
kind need not start quite from scratch. The Index to the Columbia
edition (New York, 1940), though very far from being a concordance to the prose, offers a fairly large if incomplete body of
material. It is, as its editor explains, more of an Index Rerum than
an Index Verborum, and it is no fault of his that it omits many
words completely and has incomplete entries for most of the rest.
It is certainly no basis for really systematic work, and yet its mere
existence is a great temptation: not only because it offers a starting
point, however shaky, for a comparison of a verse with a prose
vocabulary, but even more because, if one had to choose just one
writer for a guessing-game of this kind, that writer should, on historical grounds, be Milton. That is why I have allowed myself to
make, with the aid of this Index, the list of words from which we
started, and with its further aid, to explore its possible significance.

This list of words is no more than illustrative or exemplary, and
of a general quality, which certainly cannot yet be quantified. But
the quality is fairly obvious, and it may be convenient to call it
"demotic," for this word has not, so far as I know, any specialized
or precise application in linguistic studies, and will serve the better
for a confessedly vague and provisional purpose. This demotic quality is suggested by such features as these:

(i) Extensive involvement in alliteration. In English this is one of the most reliable signs of the presence of a popular or colloquial vocabulary.

(ii) Side by side with "hard words" of conspicuously Romance origin (*apostate, enthymemes, incogitant,* etc.) are many words redolent and stinking of low and rural life: asses really do consume sowthistles and brambles, a barrow is a castrated boar, and it grunts indefatigably, bitterns were snared—though less readily than woodcock, a buzzard was of no use in falconry.

(iii) There is a high proportion of words beginning with the markedly Teutonic letters of the alphabet, *b, f* and *p*. Many of them are, according to the *OED,* without respectable etymologies, and are dismissed as "prob. echoic." I should like here to draw attention to those nearly forgotten classics of linguistic science—the prefaces to the earlier volumes of the *OED.* Unfortunately the editors, or their successors, gave up writing them quite early in the alphabet, though they continued to give, volume by volume, some statistical information which is invaluable in studies of vocabulary. Some of the early prefaces, however, are full of profitable observations. Thus the very first, A–B (1888), points out that while words under A are mostly of certain origins, those under B are often new and echoic. The preface to F notes the almost total absence of scientific and learned terms under this letter, and the large proportion of onomatopoeic words, like *fizz, flip,* and *flop.* (Perhaps this is why the term *flip-flop,* used to describe the basic component of a computer, strikes the layman as slightly odd, especially when encountered in the title of a Ph.D. dissertation like "The Use of Ferrite Cores in Flip-Flops.") By the time they reached P, the editors were less communicative, but few English users are under any illusions about the general respectability of words beginning with this letter.

(iv) In a few cases, the *OED* yields information about the status or register of words in the list. For example, *flirt* is recorded as a verb meaning to flick or jerk in the late sixteenth century, but the meaning "to practise coquetry" is dated 1732 (and as a noun). But there is little doubt that Milton is using it in this sense, because it is made to accompany *coy* (a "coy, flirting style"), and there is no doubt either as to his use of *coy,* for Eve

> Yielded with coy submission, modest pride,
> And sweet reluctant amorous delay.

It looks rather as if the OED had dated this meaning of *flirt* too late, but nevertheless the entry suggests that Milton was one of the earlier users of the word in this sense: and that is as much as to say that it was at least highly colloquial.

If "demotic" can now be taken as a reasonably accurate description of the words in the list, we can go on to see how many of them, and of what kinds, are also found in Milton's verse. Numbers may be used here, as a passing convenience, but it must not be forgotten that they are nothing more, since the list on which they are based is far from being an unbiased sample; they will, in fact, do no more than describe this bias in another way.

The first group of words is that of structurals, and they are ignored, since they all occur as frequently in the verse as in the prose—or nearly so.[4]

These are the words from the remainder found both in the verse and in this selection of phrases from the prose:

> backside, posterity, apostate, feast, blush, ignoble, belching, sour, rueful, bellowing, old, make, national, war, oratory, fling, spend, youth, word, lay, snares, pangs, gripes, boiling, conscience, ragged, infantry, idol, brutish, hopes, fat, troop, huswives, matrimonial, cheeks, makes, fitter, wanton, impulses, poor, transformed, clod, antagonist, see, end, follies, grind, mill, servile, present, coy, satyr, use, settled, mud, fancy, flashiest, corrupted, neat, fees, matters, babble, perishing, coin, church, say, wading, deep, wet, content, wonted, room, cut, large, unseasonable, wipe, corpulencies, light.
>
> Total: 78

These are found only in the selection of prose:

> endorse, scarecrows, asinine, sowthistles, brambles, fadge, bar, incogitant, woodcock, hucksterage, piddling, tithes, crudities, enthymemes, chip, block, surplice, brabble, rumple, bobbins, wince, bezzling, barrow, grunt, bitterns, brothels, buzzard, deanery, broken-winded, tizzick, ravished, camping, canonist, foppish, fardel, cases, inflate, cock-brained, solliciter, cockering,

heiffer, commonwealth, phlegmy, copulation, courtesy, night-
walking, cudgeller, cullionly, paraphrase, sanctified, cutthroats,
flirting, style, sucking, coral, gamut, municipal, fiddler, fustiest,
unswilled, hogshead, greasy, clutch, high feeding, finical,
goosery, sermon-actor, prog, pander, folkmooters, truckage, fine,
sophistical, boulting-hutch, tankard, drollery, venereous, pargetory, stews, snout, pickle, auditors, shallows, instep, margent,
docks, text, unload, frigates, authorities.

Total: 91

Such lists as these have their crude uses, and perhaps the most
important of them is to remind us forcibly that even when they
are produced quickly and comprehensively, all will not be beer and
skittles. There is still a great deal of editing and interpreting to be
done, and it is not at present possible to imagine that much of this
work could be mechanized. It is so often necessary to consider not
the word only, but the particular meaning in its context. For example, *margent* has been counted as not occurring in the verse,
because it is here equivalent to the modern word *margin;* but it is
found in the verse in its other meaning of "river-bank." The first
list illustrates this difficulty more extensively, and in still more recalcitrant forms. *Clod,* for example, is used in the verse in its literal
sense of a lump of earth; but how should it be classified when it
is joined with *phlegmy* and applied to *antagonist?* Still more difficult
(and therefore instructive) are those cases in which the whole
demotic force of the expression is due to the fact that the words have
been brought together in a particular order. For example, *settled,
mud,* and *fancy* are all found separately in the verse, but there is
no phrase in it to compare with "the settled mud of his fancy."
Similarly, *wipe, fat, corpulency,* and *light* are all found separately
in the verse, which nevertheless contains no phrase remotely comparable with "Wipe your fat corpulencies out of our light," in which
the verse-meanings of every word have been transformed. *Wipe*
has a sense very different from that which it bears in

Som natural tears they drop'd, but wip'd them soon.

In the verse *fat* occurs only twice, and literally of animal fat; here
it refers to the gluttonous obesity of bishop-fed ecclesiastics. *Corpulency* is in *Paradise Lost,* but in its literal sense, of the body of a

serpent. As for "light," it is, of course, much used in the verse, and in some very famous contexts, but never there with a reference to the highly colloquial phrase "Get out of my light!"—the phrase which has been so skilfully modified into "Wipe your fat corpulencies out of our light."

Clearly many modifications are necessary to the mere lists of words; some of them might end in transferring items from the second list to the first, but rather more, from the examples chosen, would be transferred from the first list to the second. So far as these examples go, then, they suggest that the vocabulary of Milton's prose is more demotic than that of his verse, both in the choice of words and in the choice of meanings.

This subjective impression can be made a shade more objective by a happy accident in Milton's dealings with words. In his little book *The Making of English* (1904), Henry Bradley, no doubt relying on his vast experience of the language as one of the editors of the *OED,* commented on the apparent lack of verbal originality in Milton, when compared with Shakespeare: "That Milton had a genuine faculty for word-making, even though he chose to exercise it sparingly, is sufficiently proved by his invention of *anarch* as a designation for the personification Chaos" (p. 234). It is possible to do a little better for him than that, by looking at his uses of the prefix *be-*. This very interesting prefix can, of course, perform mainly grammatical functions, often descended from, or extended by analogy with, its use in Old English, e.g., *believe, bereft.* But in seventeenth-century English, it was still "alive," "unbound," forming intensive verbs with the sense "thoroughly, soundly, conspicuously, to excess, ridiculously," as the *OED* says. Of words made in this fashion, Milton was apparently fond, but he indulged his taste for them very differently in his verse and in his prose. In the former, he confined himself to the more usual combinations and the less pejorative: *bedecked, begirt, beguile, benumbed, bestuck* ("Truth . . . bestuck with slandrous darts"). In the prose, however, he wielded the prefix in much livelier fashion: *bedewed* (= drunk), *bescrawl, bescribbled, bespurted* ("with his own holy water"), *bejade, bejesuited, belepered, bespaul, be-law-given.* The last of these is not in the *OED;* the preceding four are given as first uses in Milton, at any rate in figurative senses.

Shakespeare—to pick up Bradley's comparison—used the prefix

freely and often, but with less originality than Milton. This usage is the more instructive because, on the whole, Milton was unlikely to have been fully conscious of it. The segregation of certain forms, the more violently novel and perjorative, as being fit for prose but unfit for verse was probably due rather to "feeling," a vague sense of "decorum," than to deliberate choice on each occasion.

Let us now pretend that a computer had provided the three lists described above for the whole of Milton's text, and that the lists had been edited so as to correct any errors made by the machine, and in particular to classify correctly particular uses of words according to their meanings in their contexts—a task at the moment beyond any machine-programme. Suppose now that we are to examine more closely the role of demotic words in his vocabulary, and that we have duly informed the computer of those that have been classed in this way. One of the many interesting questions we may now have answered will be this: in which groups of x words are y demotic words found? We should then have the material for making a good estimate of the extent to which the demotic words were bunched together in both verse and prose, and it may be added that without good information about local variations in the density of demotic occurrences, no overall figures describing their occurrence would be of much value.

In a general way, we can probably guess something about these variations. It is clear from our initial examples that Milton called on the demotic part of his vocabulary especially for the purpose of "railing," in terms of his own time. That is to say, he described the objects of his dislike in words recognized to be low, vulgar, involving taboos of one kind and another, so that the things or people described were smeared with the nastiness of the words. The status, the register of the words, is determined by the use to which they are put. The chief objects of Milton's dislike are well known: Pope, King, bishops, bishop-minded clergy, ecclesiastical luxury, ceremonial and discipline. He was also against sin. All of these topics, when they arose in verse or in prose, were likely to involve the use of demotic words.

So far as the prose is concerned, this is obvious enough. The most demotic language is to be found, broadly speaking, in the *Smectymnuus* pamphlets and *Colasterion*—though it would be more than useful to have this impression checked by a computer. The *Areo-*

pagitica is much more restrained. One would expect it to show a substantially higher correlation with the vocabulary of the verse. In the verse itself, the intrusion of the characteristic "vituperative" topics bring with them their train of dirty words, often rather unexpectedly. For example, *flashiest* was placed above in the list of words common to the prose and verse solely because it occurs in the anti-episcopal remarks of Comus, "their lean and flashy songs." There are several other examples in the same speech. "Such as for their bellies' sake": "belly" was used often in the prose in association with the clergy, as "the proud clergy have glutted their ingrateful bellies," "the clergy set up two gods, Mammon and their belly." The "lean and flashy songs" in "Lycidas" are "grated on scrannel Pipes," and their singers "scramble at the shearers' feast." These are the only occurrences of *scrannel* and *scramble* in the verse, but they are found in the prose in such contexts as "so foul a scrannel mouth as yours," "the bishops will fall to scrambling after the ruin of the pope."

A similar intrusion of demotic words characterizes the speech of Comus to his coy guest, and of course their purpose is to indicate Milton's condemnation of sinful arguments—possibly too to show how they must have struck the young lady, so that her rejection of them was never for a moment in doubt. *Spawn, budge, tub, shops, hutch't* are all worth looking up in the Columbia Index (it is often wise to check the findings with one of the older verse concordances).

In *Paradise Lost*, of course, a very much larger field for study is opened, but it will yield many examples of the same kind. Thus *leer*, a pretty demotic word, occurs only once in Milton (unless it is omitted from the Index), in a description of Satan at his sinning when, "with jealous leer Ey'd them askance," he spied on the conjugal felicity of Adam and Eve. And Death, another bad hat, after the Fall "with delight snuff'd the smell of mortal change," this being the only occurrence of *snuff* in Milton. Many other examples could be given, showing that the occasional appearance of demotic words in *Paradise Lost is* restricted to passages of vituperation, and that they are more or less freely used in the prose.

Another obvious question would be much easier to answer if a computer had produced a complete list of all the passages in which demotic words occurred at a fairly high density. It is this: how far, or in what terms, was Milton conscious of his own practice of segregating the demotic part of his vocabulary from his more usual verse diction?

The wary beginnings of an answer can be found in the obvious places. The Index gives a number of contexts for the crucial word *decorum,* and several of them show that he was familiar with the usual doctrines associated with it in Puttenham and others: that low words should be used in writing of low subjects and persons, lofty words of lofty topics, medium ones of middle things and persons. His own use of vituperation shows that he was entirely at one with Shakespeare in seeing it as dependent upon what we should now call registers defined by social class:

> O thou thing,
> Which I'll not call a creature of thy place,
> Lest barbarism, making me the precedent,
> Should a like language use to all degrees,
> And mannerly distinguishment leave out
> Betwixt the prince and beggar.[5]
> (*The Winter's Tale,* II. 1)

But though Milton knew all about this rhetorical doctrine, it was very characteristic of him to develop a doctrine of his own, based on the Bible rather than on Aristotle and Cicero. His fullest exposition of it is in *An Apology against a Pamphlet:*

> If therefore the question were in oratory, whether a vehement vein throwing out indignation, or scorn upon an object that merits it, were among the aptest *Ideas* of speech to be allow'd, it were my work, and an easie one to make it cleare both by the rules of the best rhetoricians, and the famousest examples of the Greek and Roman Orations. But since the Religion of it is disputed, and not the art, I shall make use only of such reasons and authorities, as religion cannot except against.[6]

The first of these authorities was Christ himself, who used all kinds of discourse, "mild and familiar . . . plaine and impartiall home-speaking . . . bitter and ireful rebukes." The Bible itself, and through it the Spirit of God, had not avoided the occasional use of obscene words, "words not civill at other times to be spoken." These, and many other precedents, authorize this principle:

And thus I take it to be manifest, that indignation against men and their actions notoriously bad, hath leave and autority oft times to utter such words and phrases as in common talk were not so mannerly to use. That ye may know, not only as the Historian speaks, *that all those things for which men plough, build, or saile, obey vertue,* but that all words and whatsoever may be spoken shall at some time in an unwonted manner wait upon her purposes.[7]

Within this framework of ideas, then, Milton was fully conscious of the issues raised by his "railing," and of its necessary association with scornful attacks on all kinds of evil.

There is, however, another factor probably at work, of which he was less directly conscious. Again, we sorely need to interrogate our imagined computer, to give us the respective dates at which the main demotic passages were written. For there is some prima facie reason to believe that Milton used the demotic register most freely in that period of the Civil War, up to about 1646, in which he felt the greatest confidence in the good sense of the common people:

> No my *matriculated confutant* there will not want in any con-gregation of this Island, that hath not beene altogether famisht, or wholly perverted with Prelatish leven, there will not want divers plaine and solid men, that have learnt by the experience of a good conscience, what it is to be well taught, who will soone look through and through both the lofty nakednesse of your *Latinizing* Barbarian, and the finicall goosery of your neat Sermon-actor.[8]

As the sympathies of these plain and solid men changed, over the next ten years, so that they were no longer of Milton's mind in religion and politics, they turned, before his very eyes and in his very words, into an "inconstant, irrational, image-doting rabble, a credulous, hapless herd, begotten to servility, enchanted with tyranny." [9] Feeling this about them, and well knowing that his audience had drifted away from him, it would have been very natural if the demotic side of his language were less used, less required, and that he should, in his later prose as well as in the verse, have moved more exclusively among the higher registers of his vocabulary.

In so far as this connection between Milton's abandonment of demotic words might be proved to be related with his political position, in relation to that of English society, the way would lie open to proving, by a wide range of similar analyses, a much larger hypothesis: that his case, though very demonstrative and fully documentable, was typical, not unique, and that this abandonment of demotic words, their degradation to the level of cant and slang, was a characteristic of the English language itself during and after the Civil War. The way would be opened, in fact, to doing several things that have been said to need doing. For example, Professor Wyld, in his *History of Modern Colloquial English,* pointed out that surprisingly little was known about the effects on the language of the Civil War. And I have somewhere come across a striking phrase describing the literary and linguistic changes of the seventeenth century as a "dissociation of sensibility"; it might be possible, by a careful study of the processes of segregation at work on the vocabulary of English, to give this fine phrase a definite meaning.

But these are very distant prospects, just discernible as eventual possibilities, but at present far beyond our materials and ability to process them. Nevertheless, having indulged so far in what I know to be a guessing-game, I will conclude with two hypotheses, one mainly concerned with Milton himself, the other with the development of the language in general.

Milton's language has often been described as "Latinized," as being more dependent than that of other English writers on Romance words and Latin idioms. This may be largely true of his verse, but it is certainly untrue of his prose. The really distinctive aspect of his language is the strict segregation which he practised, more or less knowingly, between its upper registers (often predominantly Romance) and its lower ones, Teutonic, often of unknown etymology, echoic, and colloquial. The language of the verse is, indeed, much more accurately described negatively than positively. It is not the presence of long and rare Romance words that distinguishes it from Shakespeare; there is no single line in Milton more heavily "Latinized" than "multitudinous seas incarnadine." What distinguishes it is the absence of the balancing colloquial easy diction of "making the green one red." Yet the exclusion of this element must be seen as the more remarkable, the more in need of explanation by real linguistic research, and by reference to the political and social changes then working on the language, because the prose shows that Milton was no mean master of its resources—that many words emphatically of the lower, indeed of the lowest registers, were "at risk" in his writing. Indeed, on his own remarkable admission in *Colasterion*, they were at high risk, because he relished using them, always provided that he could do so with a clear conscience, on subjects and occasions not of his own choosing, but luckily forced on him by his opponents:

> Since my fate extorts from mee a talent of sport, which I had thought to hide in a napkin. . . .[10]

It is the essence of Milton's special interest for the historian of English that he knew the "sport" of railing and the words that went with it, enjoyed them, relished them when he had a pretext, and yet despised and rejected them for what he regarded as all weighty ends of expression.

The broader hypothesis bears on the problem which English, among the major languages of the world, presents most fully, that of a vocabulary not merely fringed with a small proportion of words resulting from contact with other languages, but divided right down the middle, so to speak, by the distinction between the older Teutonic and the newer Romance elements. It is obvious that, from the twelfth century onwards, the Romance words formed increasingly an upper register of the vocabulary, in terms of social prestige, educational panache, and the like. Yet it was still very possible, in the time of Shakespeare, to use both registers together, and even to exploit the contrasts and tensions between them. What appears to happen in the seventeenth century, and in close relation with the social and political changes brought about in the Civil War, is that the tendency to segregation is suddenly intensified. The lower register loses esteem with the sudden lurch that accompanies a change of balance. It was, of course, only what would be expected. A language, as Saussure explained long ago, is a system, not an aggregation of independent parts. There is no such thing as a mere addition to such a system, like the addition of an annexe to an hotel. The addition of the vast stock of Romance words to the system of English changed the whole language, and in particular, it led, as it was bound to lead at some time, to the degradation of many of the old Teutonic words into lower and yet lower registers—from the colloquial to the slangy, from the slangy to the forbidden, and so to the obsolete. The special interest of Milton is that he gives such a clear indication of the very moment when this balance was actually tipped. And it is, of course, all the more interesting because it has never since been restored.

NOTES

1. *A Concordance to the Poems of Emily Dickinson*, ed. Stanford P. Rosenbaum (Ithaca, 1964), p. xvii.
2. A brief comparison between the "shapes" of the word-frequency distributions of *Ulysses* and *Finnegans Wake* is made on p. 3 of the Introduction to the latter (ed. Clive Hart [Minneapolis, 1963]). It shows very clearly that the two main components of such distributions, as described above, fall into two very different patterns. The commonest 141 words in both account for 46 per cent of the total word-occurrences. The "rare" component, however, is very different. Words occurring only once account for only 6.2 per cent of *Ulysses,* but for 27.8 per cent of *Finnegans Wake.* The difficulty found in reading the latter is due, not only to the complex nature of many of the words themselves, but also to the unusual shape of the frequency-distribution. The human brain is not used to such a density of information and is probably incapable of dealing with it.
3. G. Udny Yule, *The Statistical Study of Literary Vocabulary* (Cambridge, 1944), p. 44.
4. The qualification is put in because I have often found from my frequency-lists of verse that the proportion of structurals/lexicals is lower than that in lists of prose. If generally true, this would be a very interesting difference.
5. I have often had reason to wish that Shakespeare had given his own definition of tragedy as succinctly and indisputably as he here tells us of his theory of diction.
6. *An Apology against a Pamphlet* . . . Columbia edition, III, 312.
7. Ibid., 316.
8. Ibid., 348.
9. *Eikonoklastes,* V. 309.
10. Columbia edition, IV, 272.

RICHARD FOSTER JONES

↙

Science and English Prose Style, 1650–75

Literary style, like human personality, is a compound exceedingly difficult of analysis, for when its more obvious constituents are made clear, there still remains an illusive element, consciousness of which leaves the analyst with the unpleasant sensation of not having reached the bottom of the matter. As the most complex phenomenon in literature, style is the resultant of all the forces, known and unknown, underlying literary development, and the method and extent of the contribution made by each of these forces are a matter of probable inference rather than of positive demonstration. For that reason, any attempt, however ambitious, to account for the style of a literary epoch must be content with pointing out those more obvious influences that are combined and reflected in speech and writing, and with ignoring other factors which may escape detection. Under the protection of this confession I shall attempt to make manifest what seems to me the most important influence instrumental in changing the luxuriant prose of the Commonwealth into that of a diametrically opposite nature in the Restoration.

To one who is familiar with the writers of the Puritan regime, it would be rash to maintain that the style of this period is homogeneous, but probably every one can agree that the dominating

From *The Seventeenth Century* (Stanford University Press and Oxford University Press, London, 1951), pp. 75–110. Reprinted by permission of the publishers. First published in *PMLA*, XLV (1930), pp. 977–1009.

manner of writing was that revealed in the great figures of Jeremy Taylor, Sir Thomas Browne, and John Milton, and lesser writers like Nathanael Culverwell. As is well known, this style is characterized by various rhetorical devices such as figures, tropes, metaphors, and similes, or similitudes, to use a term of the period. The sentences are long, often obscurely involved, and rhythmical, developing in writers like Browne a stately cadence, which, in the studied effect of inversions, is the prose counterpart of Milton's blank verse. The penchant for interlarding a work with Latin and Greek quotations is also apparent. The diction reveals a host of exotic words, many Latinisms, and frequently poetic phraseology of rare beauty. Against this style there arose a movement which later became an organized revolt, and which in the course of its condemnation of the old developed for itself a new standard of expression. The spirit animating the revolt had its origin in the scientific movement that determined the intellectual complexion of the seventeenth century. It is the purpose of this article to show that the attacks on the old, as well as the formulation of a new, style find consistent expression in those associated with the new science, that the first organized scientific body in England, the Royal Society, definitely adopted a linguistic platform which exerted a powerful influence on the style of its members even in writings other than scientific, and that the foremost exponents of the new style were members of this society and in most cases deeply interested in science.

Since Bacon stimulated and, to a certain extent, determined the scientific development of this period, one should search first in his writings for evidence of a stylistic standard. Without insisting upon a direct connection between his views and the movement that arose near the middle of the century, it would be foolish to underestimate the possible influence of one whose words were reverenced by later scientific reformers of style. At the very outset, however, we may say that his own style was quite different from that advocated by the scientists. "Ornamented with the riches of rhetoric," as it is, it everywhere reveals tropes, figures, and similitudes. For this reason his followers, though worshiping his ideas, never refer to his manner of expression as a model. Sprat, it is true, cites him as an example, but for poets and wits, not for writers of serious prose.[1] Rawley, Bacon's chaplain and biographer, represents his patron as opposed to fine writing, and tells us that in composing his works, the philosopher "would often ask if the meaning were expressed plainly enough, as being one that accounted words to be but subservient or ministerial to matter, and not the principal." [2] Yet even Rawley must have been aware that plainness is not a characteristic quality of Bacon's prose, for he immediately adds the rather meaningless statement, "And if his style were polite, it was because he would do no otherwise." Regardless of his own style, however, Bacon attacks all manner of rhetorical devices because they lead to the first distemper of learning, "when men study words and not matter," and he holds that similitudes and ornaments of speech render the detection and correction of errors very difficult.[3] Moreover, near the beginning of the *Magna Instauratio* he reveals a stylistic attitude which, though not apparent in his own practice, is essentially the same as that later maintained by his followers. "It being part of my design," he says, "to set everything forth, as far as may be, plainly and perspicuously (for nakedness of the mind is still, as nakedness of the body once was, the companion of innocence and simplicity), let me first explain the order and plan of the work." [4] While his antagonism to rhetoric and his advocacy of a naked style may not have inspired the stylistic revolt, they had their origin in the same scientific spirit that animated the later reformers of prose, who express views similar to his.

The immediate influence of Bacon's words must have been slight, for the exuberant prose of the Elizabethans continued on to the more highly developed and poetic style of the Commonwealth. In 1646, however, is heard again the plea for a plain style; this time in John Wilkins' *Ecclesiastes, or a Discourse Concerning the Gift of Preaching*. Wilkins, who later became the prime mover in the establishment of the Royal Society, had been for a number of years deeply interested in science, and was at this moment an enthusiastic member of a small group of men who met weekly in London to put into practice the Baconian experimental philosophy. It was the spirit of the latter that prompted him to say, as regards the "phrase" that should be used in preaching,

> It must be plain and naturall, not being darkned with the affectation of Scholasticall harshnesse, or Rhetoricall flourishes. Obscurity in the discourse is an argument of ignorance in the minde. The greatest learning is to be seen in the greatest plainnesse . . . When the notion it self is good, the best way to set it off, is in the most obvious plain expression . . . And it

will not become the Majesty of a Divine Embassage, to be garnished out with flaunting affected eloquence. How unsuitable it is to the expectation of a hungry soul, who comes unto this ordinance with a desire of spiritual comfort and instruction, and there to hear onely a starched speech full of puerile worded Rhetorick? 'Tis a sign of low thoughts and designs, when a mans chief study is about the polishing of his phrase and words. . . . Such a one speaks onely from his mouth, and not from his heart.

The same opinion is continued in another passage, concerning which we must remember that the epithet "solid" was so consistently applied to the new philosophy as opposed to the old that the expression "solid business" is equivalent to scientific matters. "It must be full, without empty and needlesse Tautologies, which are to be avoided in every solid business, much more in sacred. Our expressions should be so close, that they may not be obscure, and so plain that they may not seem vain and tedious." [5] A glance at Wilkins' own writings discovers a practice consistent with his theory, and William Lloyd, in a funeral sermon on him, truly says,

He spoke solid truth, with as little shew of Art as was possible. He exprest all things in their true and Natural colours; with that aptness and plainness of Speech, that grave Natural way of Elocution, that shewed he had no design upon his hearers. His plainness was best for the instruction of the simple . . . He applied him self rather to their understanding than Affections . . . In his Writings he was Judicious and plain, like one that valued not the Circumstances so much as the substance.

Two years later the same contempt for the superficial fineries of verbal dress appears in William Petty, one of the outstanding members of the little group which, about the middle of the century, met weekly in Petty's lodgings at Oxford for the purpose of carrying on experiments, a group that later merged with a similar body in London to form the Royal Society. Petty was especially interested in the practical aspect of science, devoting much of his time to inventions of various sorts. In communicating some matters of scientific nature to Samuel Hartlib, he says,

I shall desire you to shew them unto no more than needs you must, since they can please only those few that are real Friends to the Design of Realities, not those who are tickled only with Rhetorical Prefaces, Transitions and Epilogues, and charmed with fine Allusions and Metaphors.[6]

The expression "Friends to the Design of Realities" is interesting in this case, for it means nothing more than subscribers to the new philosophy, and thus the quotation shows that Petty makes style a distinguishing mark between the experimental philosophers and those who held to the old tradition. This remarkable sensitiveness to matters of style on the part of the scientists, which is revealed in their thinking it necessary to confess, and vindicate, their lack of rhetorical ornament, appears again in a work by Francis Glisson, a famous physician of the time, and a prominent member of the London group of Baconians which was formed in 1645. He concludes his Preface in the following manner:

Finally expect no flashes of Rhetorick and Courtly-Language;
        Nobis licet esse tam dicertis,
        Musas qui colimus severiores.

And indeed the conditions of the matter forbids all such painting; in such a manner,

Ornari res ipsa negat, contenti doceri.[7]

The next opposition to rhetorical ornament is discovered in Hobbes's Leviathan, 1651. Though now chiefly remembered for his psychological and political philosophy, Hobbes was, according to his own statement, most interested in natural science.[8] His philosophical interests were developed in France along with Descartes, Gassendi, and Mersenne, but in his earlier years he had been a companion of Bacon, and from the latter he may have caught his scientific enthusiasm. In his characteristically blunt fashion, Hobbes tells us that there is nothing he distrusts more than elocution, and that he has rejected the ornament of classical quotations because there is no longer any virtue in ancient authority.[9] He permits a counselor to use only significant, proper, and brief language, and forbids them *"obscure, confused,* and *ambiguous Expressions, also all metaphoricall Speeches, tending to the stirring up of Passion,"* which are useful only to deceive.[10] In speaking of that antithetical pair dear to the seventeenth-century critic—judgment and fancy—he lays down the law, as the Royal Society did later, that—

> In Demonstration, in Councell, and all rigourous search of Truth, Judgement does all; except sometimes the understanding have need to be opened by some apt similitude; and then there is so much use of Fancy. But for Metaphors, they are in this case utterly excluded. For seeing they openly professe deceipt; to admit them into Councell, or Reasoning, were manifest folly.

And again, "in a Sermon, or in publique, or before persons unknown, or whom we ought to reverence, there is no Gingling of words that will not be accounted folly." [11] Among the four abuses of speech, he lists the metaphorical use of words, "that is, in other sense than that they are ordained for; and thereby deceive others." [12] He insists that "Metaphors and Tropes of speach" are no true grounds for reasoning, and one of the causes for absurd conclusions he ascribes "to the use of Metaphors, Tropes, and other Rhetoricall figures, in stead of words proper." [13] He concludes by saying:

> The Light of humane minds is Perspicuous Words, but by exact definitions first snuffed, and purged from ambiguity; *Reason* is the *Pace;* Encrease of *Science,* the *way;* and the benefit of man-kind, the *end.* And on the contrary, Metaphors, and sensless and ambiguous words, are like *ignes fatui;* and reasoning upon them, is wandering amongst innumerable absurdities.[14]

The same scientifically induced materialism so characteristic of Hobbes appears in John Webster's *Academiarum Examen,* 1653. Webster was a chaplain in the Parliamentarian army, and an early and ardent follower of Bacon. In the work mentioned above he vehemently attacks the old philosophy, and fervently recommends a reformation of the universities in the way of the substitution of experimental science for the Aristotelianized divinity and natural philosophy dominant there. But he is not content with attacking these only; he would place distinctly below the new science such subjects as rhetoric, oratory, and the like, which, he says,

> serve for adornation, and are as it were the outward dress and attire of more solid sciences; first they might tollerably pass, if there were not too much affectation towards them, and too much pretious time spent about them, while more excellent and necessary learning [i.e., experimental philosophy] lies neg-lected and passed by: For we do in these ornamental arts, as people usually do in the world, who take more care often time about the goods of fortune, than about the good of the body it self or the goods of the mind, regarding the shell more than the kernel, and the shadow more than the Substance.[15]

A similar dislike for an ornate style and a corresponding approval of plainness in expression may be found in Robert Boyle, a scientist so illustrious it would be impertinent to comment on his connection with the new movement. In his *Some Considerations Touching the Style of the Holy Scriptures,* written about 1653 though not pub-lished until 1661, he expresses the view that when verbal ornaments are spared, they are not missed, and that some writings expressed in the plainest language outshine other subjects decked with the gaudi-est expressions. Nor does he ascribe any importance to an objection that the Bible is destitute of eloquence and unadorned with the flowers of rhetoric, an objection which, he says, "a philosopher [i.e., a scientist] would not look upon as the most considerable." [16]

We also find the Baconian spirit stirring in out-of-the-way places. In 1660 Joshua Childrey published his *Britannia Baconia,* which is in reality a natural history of England, Scotland, and Wales, and the title of which indicates its connection with the new science. The author worshiped Bacon, and regarded his words with almost superstitious awe, trying in all humility of spirit to put into practice the precepts of the great master. He, too, was imbued with a scorn of fine language, and with a feeling that science demanded a style more suited to its purposes. "I have endeavour'd," he says in the Preface, "to tell my tale as plainly as might be, both that I might be understood of all, and that I might not disfigure the face of Truth by daubing it over with the paint of Language." He then proceeds to emphasize the fact that clear and accurate expression is just as essential to the communication of truth as careful observation is to its discovery, and he implies his conviction that the prevailing style was inimical to its proper presentation. A like attitude continues to be manifested in this branch of science, if for the moment we may step beyond the chronological limits of this article. Robert Plot, in the *Natural History of Oxfordshire*, 1676, says,

> And these [natural and artificial phenomena] I intend to deliver as succinctly as may be, in a plain, easie unartificial Stile, studiously avoiding all ornaments of Language, it being my purpose to treat of Things, and therefore would have the Reader expect nothing less than Words.[17]

Ten years later, in the *Natural History of Staffordshire*, he is still making the same stylistic pronouncement, though the need for it had long ceased to exist. Certainly hostility to the style of the Commonwealth must have been deeply imbedded in scientists to cause this one to say in 1686, at a time when rhetoric was no longer in favor with any one of importance,

> I shall make all *Relations* (as formerly) in a plain familiar Stile, without the Ornaments of *Rhetorick,* least the matter be obscured by too much *illustration;* and with all the imaginable brevity that perspicuity will bear.[18]

The foregoing quotations are sufficiently numerous and emphatic to indicate that repugnance to the prevailing style and a feeling for the need of a simpler, more direct manner of expression were a characteristic feature of the new science from its very inception. To us it seems quite natural that science should be antipathetic to rhetoric, but in this period some unique factors tended to accentuate this antipathy. Above everything else, the experimental philosophy was characterized by a savage attack upon "Aristotelity," to use Hobbes's term, in the course of which the chief charge was brought against the wordiness of Peripateticism.[19] Again and again the new scientists stigmatized the traditional philosophy for being concerned only with words having no concrete significance and representing only figments of the imagination. Thus verbal superfluity became suspect. Allied to this attitude was the feeling for concrete reality, which naturally eschewed the verbal luxuriance of figurative language and the more subtle effects of imaginative expression. All this led to an insistence upon a direct, unadorned style which should be concrete in idea, and clear and economical in expression, in short, to use a phrase of the period, "the marriage of words and things." [20]

When the experimental philosophers were joined in a royally protected society, 1662, it was inevitable that what had been the more or less sporadic and scattered, but still representative, attacks on prose expression should be combined and strengthened into an organized revolt. So we are not surprised to find that in the statutes of the Royal Society, published in 1728, Chapter V, Article IV, reads:

> In all Reports of Experiments to be brought into the Society, the Matter of Fact shall be barely stated, without any Prefaces, Apologies, or Rhetorical Flourishes, and entered so into the Register-Book, by order of the Society.

But the full importance of this requirement is not revealed until we read Thomas Sprat's *History of the Royal Society,* 1667, in an oft-quoted passage of which the author makes clear the Society's intense opposition to rhetorical prose, and outlines the ideal of a new style which had already crystallized and upon which it was vehemently insisting. Sprat's words throw so much light on the movement which we are tracing that I shall give them in full, even at the risk of bringing before the reader's eye that with which he is already familiar.

> Thus they have directed, judg'd, conjectur'd upon, and improved *Experiments.* But lastly, in these, and all other businesses, that have come under their care; there is one thing more, about which the *Society* has been most sollicitous; and that is, the manner of their *Discourse:* which, unless they had been very watchful to keep in due temper, the whole spirit and vigour of their *Design,* had been soon eaten out, by the luxury and redundance of *speech.* The ill effects of this superfluity of talking, have already overwhelm'd most other *Arts* and *Professions;* insomuch, that when I consider the means of *happy living,* and the causes of their corruption, I can hardly forbear recanting what I said before; and concluding, that *eloquence* ought to be banish'd out of *civil Societies,* as a thing fatal to

Peace and good Manners. To this opinion I should wholly incline; if I did not find, that it is a Weapon, which may be as easily procur'd by *bad* men, as *good:* and that, if these should onely cast it away, and those retain it; the *naked Innocence* of vertue, would be upon all occasions expos'd to the *armed Malice* of the wicked. This is the chief reason, that should now keep up the Ornaments of speaking, in any request: since they are so much degenerated from their original usefulness. They were at first, no doubt, an admirable Instrument in the hands of *Wise Men:* when they were onely employ'd to describe *Goodness, Honesty, Obedience;* in larger, fairer, and more moving Images: to represent *Truth,* cloth'd with Bodies; and to bring *Knowledg* back again to our very senses, from whence it was at first deriv'd to our understandings. But now they are generally chang'd to worse uses: They make the *Fancy* disgust the best things, if they come sound, and unadorn'd: they are in open defiance against *Reason;* professing, not to hold much correspondence with that; but with its Slaves, *the Passions:* they give the mind a motion too changeable, and bewitching, to consist with *right practice.* Who can behold, without indignation, how many mists and uncertainties, these specious *Tropes* and *Figures* have brought on our Knowledg? How many rewards, which are due to more profitable, and difficult *Arts,* have been still snatch'd away by the easie vanity of *fine speaking?* For now I am warm'd with this just *Anger,* I cannot with-hold my self, from betraying the shallowness of all these seeming Mysteries; upon which, *we Writers,* and *Speakers,* look so bigg. And, in few words, I dare say; that of all the Studies of men, nothing may be sooner obtain'd, than this vicious abundance of *Phrase,* this trick of *Metaphors,* this volubility of *Tongue,* which makes so great a noise in the World. But I spend words in vain; for the evil is now so inveterate, that it is hard to know whom to *blame,* or where to begin to *reform.* We all value one another so much, upon this beautiful deceipt; and labour so long after it, in the years of our education: that we cannot but ever after think kinder of it, than it deserves. And indeed, in most other parts of Learning, I look on it to be a thing almost utterly desperate in its cure: and I think, it may be plac'd amongst those *general mischiefs;* such, as the *dissention* of Christian Princes, the *want of practice* in

Religion, and the like; which have been so long spoken against, that men are become insensible about them; every one shifting off the fault from himself to others; and so they are only made bare common places of complaint. It will suffice my present purpose, to point out, what has been done by the *Royal Society*, towards the correcting of its excesses in *Natural* Philosophy; to which it is, of all others, a most profest enemy.[21]

This earnest indictment of the earlier mode of expression does not represent the sentiments of Sprat only. The *History* was written at the instigation and under the auspices of the Royal Society, was closely followed by the members during its composition, and when finished was heartily approved by the same body, so that we may look upon Sprat's attitude as typical of that of his colleagues.[22] Furthermore, in the next paragraph Sprat describes in terse and effective manner the style required by the Society of all papers presented to it.

They have therefore been most rigorous in putting in execution, the only Remedy, that can be found for this *extravagance:* and that has been, a constant Resolution, to reject all the amplifications, disgressions, and swellings of style: to return back to the primitive purity, and shortness, when men deliver'd so many *things,* almost in an equal number of *words.* They have exacted from all their members, a close, naked, natural way of speaking; positive expressions; clear senses; a native easiness: bringing all things as near the Mathematical plainness, as they can: and preferring the language of Artizans, Countrymen, and Merchants, before that, of Wits, or Scholars.[23]

The great importance of this discussion of style relative to other matters canvassed in Sprat's *History* is made clear by comments upon the book itself, in which the manner of expression is the characteristic most remarked. In an ode which was prefixed to the *History,* and which will later be treated more in full, Cowley notices, and with great praise, only the style of the work. In the next year Glanvill thinks it necessary to praise its stylistic qualities in a passage which expresses the desired ideal as elucidated by Sprat and renders a fairly accurate criticism of the latter's prose. The book, he says, is writ in a way of so *judicious* a *gravity* and so *prudent* and *modest* an *expression,* with so much *clearness* of *sense,* and such a *natural fluency* of *genuine eloquence:* So that I know it will both *profit* and entertain you. And I say further, that you may remember to do your self this right, That the *Style* of that Book hath all the *properties* that can recommend any thing to an *ingenious relish:* For 'tis *manly,* and yet *plain; natural* and yet not *careless:* The *Epithets* are *genuine,* the *Words* proper and *familiar,* the *Periods smooth* and of *middle* proportion: It is not *broken* with *ends* of *Latin,* nor *impertinent Quotations;* nor made *harsh* by *hard* words, or *needless terms* of *Art;* Not rendred *intricate* by long *Parentheses,* nor *gaudy* by *flanting* [sic] *Metaphors;* not *tedious* by *wide fetches* and *circumferences* of *Speech,* nor *dark* by too much *curtness* of *Expression:* 'Tis not *loose* and *unjointed, rugged* and *uneven;* but as *polite* and as *fast* as *Marble;* and briefly avoids all the *notorious defects,* and wants none of the *proper* ornaments of Language.[24]

It is remarkable how sensitive the scientists were to the problem of expression. We may say without exaggeration that their program called for stylistic reform as loudly as for reformation in philosophy. Moreover, this attitude was in the public mind indissolubly associated with the Society.[25]

Such, then, was the stand firmly taken by the first scientific society in England as regards expression in prose composition. Naturally its stylistic ideal was reflected in the scientific writings of its members.[26] The question next arises, did it actually influence the style of nonscientific writings of the day? Fortunately we have two examples, one of which is remarkable, of men whose style was radically changed under the pressure exerted by the Society. In 1661 Joseph Glanvill, later the most ardent defender of the Royal Society, published his *Vanity of Dogmatizing,* the contents of which time prevents me from describing, except to say that within its narrow compass it gathered all the new threads of philosophical thought that traversed the mid-seventeenth century. It is written in a highly rhetorical, exuberant, one might even say flamboyant, style, animated by an enthusiasm great enough to justify the charge of its being rhapsodical. The modern note sounded by Glanvill, however, must have brought him into sympathetic contact with some fellows of the

Royal Society, and thus have whetted his desire to become a member of that body. At any rate, when, near the end of 1664, he published a second edition entitled *Scepsis Scientifica*,[27] he prefixed an "Address to the Royal Society," in which he eulogized the new philosophy in general and that company in particular. This composition has all the earmarks of being a bid for an invitation to join the philosophers, and such an inference is borne out by the fact that on December 7, 1664, Lord Brereton presented the book to the Royal Society, and, after the "Address" had been read, proposed the author as a candidate for membership.[28] What especially interests us in the dedication is the following passage found near the conclusion:

> I found so faint an inclination [toward publishing the work again] that I could have been well content to suffer it to have slipt into the state of *eternal silence* and *oblivion*. For I must confess that *way* of *writing* to be less agreeable to my *present relish* and *Genius;* which is more gratified with *manly sense*, flowing in a *natural* and *unaffected Eloquence,* than in the *musick* and curiosity of *fine Metaphors* and *dancing periods*. To which measure of my present humour, I had indeavour'd to reduce the style of these Papers; but that I was loth to give my self that trouble in an Affair, to which I was grown too *cold* to be much concern'd in. And this *inactivity* of temper perswaded me, I might reasonably expect a pardon from the *ingenious,* for faults committed in an immaturity of *Age* and *Judgment,* that would excuse them.[29]

Here we have a man desiring admission to the Royal Society, who with humility of spirit apologizes for his past sins, and with obvious alacrity swears allegiance to a stylistic creed that might otherwise have barred his entrance. I would not wish, however, to insinuate that his conversion was not sincere, for later events prove otherwise. But though he had evidently come under the influence of the scientists, and had experienced a true change of heart in stylistic matters, his open apology was evidently intended to serve a purpose. When we remember that less than four years separated the two editions, the reference to the immaturity of youth provokes a smile. It is significant that a man seeking admission into the Society considered it necessary to place himself in the proper position as to style.[30]

A number of changes are introduced into the *Scepsis,* but, as the author states, very few as regards style, and they are concerned only with the substitution of simpler and more usual words for coined words or unusual Latinisms.[31] This change, however, reveals that he was moving in the direction of the new manner of expression demanded by the scientists. It is a stroke of good fortune for our purposes that in 1676 Glanvill published a third abbreviated version of the *Vanity of Dogmatizing,* as the first of seven essays combined to form a volume with the title, *Essays on Several Important Subjects in Philosophy and Religion.*[32] A comparison of this essay with the first version affords nothing short of a revelation. Under the influence of the Royal Society the author's changed stylistic standards had established complete control over his writing, and had caused him to revise with a ruthless hand work written under the inspiration of the great prose writers of the Commonwealth. Furthermore, though in the second edition he had contented himself with an apology, leaving the style little changed, he would not permit the treatise to go forth again until it had become "quite changed in the way of writing." It is hardly necessary to do more than display parallel passages to show what science was doing to prose.

That all bodies both *Animal, Vegetable,* and *Inanimate,* are form'd out of such particles of matter, which by reason of their figures, will not cohære or lie together, but in such an order as is necessary to such a specifical formation, and that therein they naturally of themselves concurre, and reside, is a pretty conceit, and there are *experiments* that credit it. If after a decoction of *hearbs* in a Winter-night, we expose the liquor to the frigid air; we may observe in the morning under a crust of Ice, the perfect appearance both in *figure,* and *colour,* of the *Plants* that were taken from it. But if we break the *aqueous Crystal,* those pretty *images* dis-appear and are present[ly] dissolved.

And there is an experiment . . . That after a decoction of Herbs in a frosty Night, the shape of the Plants will appear under the Ice in the Morning: which Images are supposed to be made by the congregated *Effluvia* of the Plants themselves, which loosly wandring up and down in the Water, at last settle in their natural place and order, and so make up an appear-

Now these *airy Vegetables* are presumed to have been made, by the reliques of these *plantal emissions* whose avolation was prevented by the *condensed inclosure*. And therefore playing up and down for a while within their liquid prison, they at last settle together in their natural order, and the *Atomes* of each part finding out their proper place, at length rest in their methodical Situation, till by breaking the *Ice* they are disturbed, and those counterfeit *compositions* are scatter'd into their first *Indivisibles. Vanity,* p. 46.

ance of the Herbs from whence they were emitted. *Essays,* p. 11.

Gone is the Brownesque "swelling" sentence at the beginning of the first passage, and the touch of beauty that adorned the account of the experiment has vanished; while the "vicious abundance of phrase" and "volubility of tongue" that characterize the remainder of the quotation have given way to the "plain and familiar words" and the "close, naked, natural way of speaking" of the latter version.

But this is so largely prosecuted by that wonder of men, the Great *Des-Cartes,* and is a Truth that shines so clear in the Eyes of all considering men; that to goe about industriously to prove it, were to light a candle to seek the Sun. *Vanity,* p. 28.

Upon which position all the Philosophy of *Des-Cartes* stands: And it is so clear, and so acknowledg'd a Truth, among all considering Men, that I need not stay to prove it. *Essays,* p. 5.

For body cannot act on any thing but by motion; motion cannot be received but by quantative dimension; the soul is a stranger to such gross substantiality, and hath nothing of quantity, but what it is cloathed with by our deceived

For *Body* cannot act on anything, but by *Motion; Motion* cannot be receiv'd but by *Matter,* the *Soul* is altogether *immaterial;* and therefore, how shall we apprehend it to be subject to *such Impressions. Essays,* p. 6.

phancies; and therefore how can we conceive under a passive subjection to material impressions. *Vanity*, p. 29.

If we will take the literal evidence of our Eyes; the *Æthereal Coal* moves no more than this *Inferior clod doth. Vanity*, p. 78.

To *Sense* the *Sun stands still* also; *and no Eye* can perceive its *Actual* motion. *Essays*, p. 20.

And thus, while every age is but another shew of the former; 'tis no wonder, that Science hath not out-grown the dwarfishness of its *pristine stature*, and that the *Intellectual world* is such a *Microcosm. Vanity*, p. 138.

And thus while every Age is but an *other shrew* of the *former*, 'tis no wonder that humane science is *no more* advanced above it's *ancient* Stature. *Essays*, p. 25.

In these passages there is an obvious change from "specious tropes" and "vicious abundance of phrase" to a "primitive purity and shortness," in which "positive expressions" and "native easiness" are manifest. The reduction of these "wide fetches and circumferences of speech" to a direct and "natural way of speaking" brings out in vivid relief not only the way in which the scientific spirit was destroying the sheer joy in language, but also how the definite linguistic stand taken by the Royal Society was producing results.[33]

Nor is the composition of our Bodies the only wonder; we are as much non-plust by the most contemptible *Worm*, and *Plant*, we tread on. How is a drop of Dew organiz'd into an Insect, or a lump of Clay into animal Perfections? How are the Glories of the Field spun, and by what Pencil are they limn'd in their unaffected bravery? By whose direction is the nutriment so regularly distributed unto the respective parts, and how are they kept to their specifick uniformities? If we attempt Mechanical solutions, we shall never give an account, why the Woodcock doth not sometimes borrow colours of the Mag-pye, why the Lilly doth not exchange with the Daysie, or why it is not sometime painted with a blush of the Rose? Can *unguided matter* keep it self to such exact conformities, as not in the least spot to vary from the *species?* That divers Limners at a distance without either copy, or designe, should draw the same *Picture* to an undistinguishable exactness, both in form, colour, and features; this is more conceivable, then that *matter,* which is so diversified both in quantity, quality, motion, site, and infinite other circumstances, should frame it self so absolutely according to the Idea of it and its kind. And though the fury of that *Appelles,* who threw his Pencil in a desperate rage upon the Picture he had essayed to draw, once casually effected those lively representations, which his Art could not describe; yet 'tis not likely, that one of a thousand such præcipitancies should be crowned with so an unexpected an issue. For though *blind matter* might reach some elegancies in individual effects; yet specifick conformities can be no *unadvised* productions, but in greatest likelyhood, are regulated by the immediate efficiency of some *knowing* agent. *Vanity,* pp. 44 ff.

Blind Matter may produce an elegant effect for once, by a great Chance; as the Painter accidentally gave the Grace to his Picture, by throwing his Pencil in rage, and disorder upon it; But then *constant* Uniformities, and Determinations to a *kind,* can be *no Results* of *unguided Motions."* *Essays,* p. 11.

Here, indeed, is merciless pruning. The "amplification of style" found in the extended illustrations, touched with beauty, of the composition of bodies, has been unhesitatingly cut away, for Glanvill's changed standard reveals in it only a "trick of flaunting metaphor," "specious tropes and figures," and he now feels that the discussion has been rendered "tedious by wide fetches and circumferences of speech." Certainly condensation could go no further than is manifested in the later version. How completely has vanished the feeling for beauty in language, as well as a spirit of enthusiasm and imaginative activity!

The process that had been inaugurated in the *Scepsis Scientifica* of reducing exotic and unusual words, or "hard words," to more natural terms, as well as a constant striving for a simpler, more direct expression, is carried still further in this last version, as is made clear by the foregoing quotations and may be emphasized by further passages. "Which to us is utterly occult, and without the ken of our Intellects" becomes "to which we are altogether stranger"; "those abstrusities, that lie more deep, and are of a more mysterious alloy" = "the Difficulties that lie more deep"; "those principiate foundations of knowledge" = "the Instruments of knowledge"; "Plato credits this position with his suffrage; affirming" = "Plato affirms"; "is a difficulty which confidence may triumph over sooner, then conquer" = "is hardly to be conceived"; "is but as the Birth of the labouring Mountains, Wind and Emptiness" = "stands yet unresolved"; "preponderate much greater magnitudes" = "outweigh much heavier bodies." [34] And there are many verbal changes, always making for greater simplicity or brevity, which may be represented by the following: "our employed mindes" = "we"; "material $\epsilon\iota\delta\omega\lambda\alpha$ = "material Images"; "bodily distempers" = "diseases"; "doth much confer to" = "makes"; "education-prepossessions" = "first opinions"; "præterlapsed ages" = "past ages"; "world's Grand-ævity" = "greatest antiquity"; "midnight compositions" = "dreams."

Although it is true that Glanvill is reducing a book to the dimensions of an essay, and thus omits many ideas *in toto,* the comparisons placed before us reveal not a change in or omission of ideas, but an alteration in treatment and expression only.[35] In sentence structure the Brownesque inversions, as well as Browne's habit of overloading the first part of a sentence at the expense of the latter, are ironed out and straightened into a natural order in which verb follows subject, and object verb. Exclamatory sentences and rhetorical questions are subdued to direct assertions, the length of sentences is perceptibly decreased, and oratorical cadence has almost disappeared. The verbal reform, begun in the *Scepsis,* is continued in the substitution of simpler, more current words for the unusual Latinisms and exotic terms characteristic of Browne, while emotional and extravagant expressions are greatly tempered. There is general condensation in expression, an economy of words which deflates the verbosities and superfluous terms of the earlier style. Figurative language and poetic imagery, whether extended or brief, are abolished, curtailed, or restrained. Illustrations, in the description of which Glanvill had shown a feeling for beauty, are purged of all qualities except the essential one of expository clearness. All the glories of enthusiastic expression and all joy in beauty have faded into the common light of day. We find in a comparison of the two versions not only a change in style but also a vivid picture of the spirit of one age yielding to that of another.[36]

We have in the essays of Abraham Cowley what I take to be another example of the direct influence which the sentiments and regulations of the Royal Society were exerting upon writers. That there was a decided change in style between his early and later prose has been recognized by more than one scholar. Mr. A. A. Tilley in the *Cambridge History of English Literature* asserts that Cowley furnished a complete transition from the old to the new style in prose, his early work revealing stiff, cumbrous, and involved sentences, nearer to Jeremy Taylor than to Dryden, and unlike the conversational ease of the later essays composed during the last four or five years of his life. Mr. Tilley calls especial attention to the fine example of rhetorical prose in the latter part of *A Vision Concerning Oliver Cromwell,* published in 1661 though composed in 1659, contrasting with that the style of the *Essays,* which is neither stiff nor slovenly, and in which the use of metaphors is restrained, and the sentences are well turned.[37] Dr. A. B. Gough, in his edition of Cowley's prose works, also thinks that the style of the *Essays* reveals a decided advance in clarity and ease over the earlier prose.[38] Cowley's first biographer, in the year after the former's death, pointed out "that in the Prose of them [the *Essays*], there is little Curiosity of Ornament, but they are written in a lower and humbler style than the rest, and as an unfeigned Image of his Soul should be drawn without Flattery." Several passages in the essays themselves bear witness to the author's acquired depreciation of eloquence, in one of which he speaks slightingly of "Figures and Tropes of Speech" as only adorning discourse,[39] and in another he refers scornfully to the "tinckling" of oratory.[40] But the best expression of his changed attitudes appears in "The Garden," composed in 1666 and addressed to John Evelyn, where, after an opening paragraph, which misses much of being as rhetorical as the *Vision,* the author says, "You may wonder, Sir (for this seems a little too extravagant and Pindarical for *Prose*) what I mean by all this Preface." [41]

This change has generally been attributed to French influences, especially Montaigne, but we must remember that when the *Vision* and earlier prose works were written, Cowley had for some years been exposed to French influence without results. What possible factor comes into play between 1659, when the *Vision* was composed, and the composition of the *Essays?* In February 1660, Cowley was proposed for membership in, and in the following March was elected to, the "invisible college" that was soon to become the Royal Society.[42] In 1661 he published a *Proposition for the Advancement of Experimental Philosophy,* which was an elaborate plan for a "Philosophical College," and to which the structure of the Royal Society owed much. Upon his retirement into the country he severed formal relations with the Society, since he could no longer attend the meetings, and was not reckoned a member after the passing of the second charter of April 22, 1663. But his contact with the members was by no means broken nor his interest in science lost. In fact, Sprat says, "This labour about Natural Science was the perpetual and uninterrupted task of that obscure part of his Life." On December 7, 1664, at the same meeting at which Glanvill's *Scepsis* was presented to the Society, a committee was appointed to improve the English tongue, composed of more than a score of men, among then Dryden, Evelyn, Sprat, and Waller.[43] Naturally, Cowley, not being a member, does not appear in the list, but we learn from excellent authority that he met with them. On August 12, 1689, Evelyn wrote to Pepys,

> And in deede such [improving the English tongue] was once design'd since the Restauration of Charles the Second (1665), and in order to it three or fowre Meetings were begun at Grey's Inn, by Mr. Cowley, Dr. Sprat, Mr. Waller, the D. of Buckingham, Matt. Clifford, Mr. Dryden, & some other promoters of it. But by the death of the incomparable Mr. Cow-

ley, distance & inconvenience of the place, the Contagion &
other circumstances intervening, it crumbled away and came to
nothing.

The important place here granted Cowley in the scheme is borne
out by what Sprat says in his *Life* of the poet: "we [Clifford and
Sprat] had persuaded him . . . to publish a Discourse concerning
Style." At the very time Sprat was writing the *History of the Royal
Society* with its pronounced opinions on style, he was conferring
with Cowley about improving the language and persuading him to
write a discourse on style. Certainly Cowley must have been brought
into direct and stimulating contact with the stylistic convictions of
the new philosophers. This is made all the clearer by his "Ode to
the Royal Society," prefixed to Sprat's history, in which he ardently
praises Bacon, the new philosophy, and the Society. One stanza,
however, is devoted to praise of Sprat's work,

> And ne're did Fortune better yet
> Th' Historian to the Story fit:
> As you [Royal Society] from all old Errors free
> And purge the Body of Philosophy;
> So from all Modern Folies He
> Has vindicated Eloquence and Wit.
> His candid Stile like a clear Stream does slide
> And his bright Fancy all the way
> Does like the Sun-shine in it play;
> It does like *Thames,* the best of Rivers, glide
> Where the God does not rudely overturn,
> But gently pour the Crystal Urn,
> And with judicious hand does the whole Current guide.
> T'has all the Beauties Nature can impart,
> And all the comely Dress without the paint of Art.

From this stanza we see that the only aspect of Sprat's volume which
the poet notices is its style, that he attributed to his future biographer credit for purifying prose as the scientists had purified natural
philosophy, and that he evidently approved Sprat's indictment of
the traditional prose style and subscribed to the new standard that
the scientists had formulated. Thus Cowley must have been keenly
and sympathetically aware of the efforts made by the experimental

philosophers to discredit the old methods of expression, and he must have come under the same influence that metamorphosed Glanvill. To seek for the cause of his stylistic evolution in any other quarter seems to me farfetched, if not futile.

With the example of Glanvill and Cowley before us, may we not infer that the same pressure toward stylistic reform must have been brought to bear upon all members of the Society,[44] and through them even upon the world outside? Furthermore, when we consider the notable array of men of affairs, noblemen, clergymen, and writers who were members of the Society, we must believe that the influence of the latter was indeed far-reaching. The many-sided Isaac Barrow, divine, mathematician, and classical scholar, by virtue of being professor of geometry at Gresham College, Lucasian professor of mathematics at Cambridge, 1663, and a very early member of the Royal Society, could hardly have escaped being influenced by the stylistic attitude of the Society. John Tillotson, another great exponent of the new style, "whose sermons at Lincoln's inn and St. Lawrence Jewry attracted large congregations," and became a stylistic pattern for the whole nation, was not elected a member of the Society until 1672.[45] Yet in another way he had come under its influence. As a son-in-law of John Wilkins, he was associated with the latter in the composition of *An Essay towards a Real Character and a Philosophical Language,* 1668 [46] This remarkable project had long been in Wilkins' mind, and in 1662 he was prodded to develop it by the Royal Society, the members of which were deeply interested in the matter.[47] The study of language naturally involves consideration of style, and we are not surprised to find the stylistic attitude of science reflected in various parts of the *Essay.*[48] In this way Tillotson must have had impressed upon him the stylistic values of the new philosophy.[49]

Finally, Dryden, who asserted that whatever talent he had for English prose was due to his having often read the works of Tillotson,[50] was in a position to be even more directly influenced by the persistent efforts of the scientists to purify prose expression. He joined the Royal Society the same year in which it received the patronage of Charles II, and the poem addressed to Dr. Charleton bears eloquent testimony to his admiration of and interest in the new science. He, too, was a member of the committee appointed to improve the tongue, at the meetings of which, we may infer, he discussed stylistic matters with Cowley, Clifford, and Sprat. That

he was no indifferent listener to the scientific discussions of the Society is revealed in his answer to the charge of being magisterial,
preferred against him by Sir Robert Howard: "I must crave leave
to say, that my whole discourse was sceptical, according to the way
of reasoning which was used by Socrates, Plato, and all the Aca-
demics of old . . . and which is imitated by the modest inquisitions
of the Royal Society." [51] If he was so influenced in the method of
presenting his ideas, would he not likewise be influenced in the
manner of his expression, a matter considered no less important by
the scientists?

Before concluding this article it may be advisable to distinguish
between the revolution in style which we have outlined and another
stylistic movement of the century.[52] The Anti-Ciceronian movement
was the rhetorical counterpart of the revolt against that body of
orthodox ideas, gathered largely from antiquity, in which the Renaissance was complacently resting. The rationalistic spirit of inquiry,
especially in moral and political matters, which demanded a turning
away from what appeared to be only the forms of knowledge to
direct observation and the realities of life, also found it necessary
to revolt against the Ciceronian style that was closely associated with
orthodox philosophies. In the same way, the scientific movement, in
the main engineered by Bacon, represented the abandonment of
empty theories of nature for observation and experiment. It also
announced a stylistic program, but one distinctly different from the
Anti-Ciceronian. In short, the desire to discover knowledge which
would more fully satisfy the demand for reality was responsible for
both revolutions, but the stylistic movements that accompanied them
pursued different and divergent courses. The Anti-Ciceronian style
found its theories in Aristotle and its models in such Latin writers
as Lucan, Juvenal, Persius, Tacitus, Pliny, and especially Seneca;
science renounced Aristotle and all his works, and sought for no
models in the ancients. Instead of a conscious literary style, such
as the other movement was developing, the new philosophy found
in the very nature of its material a manner of expression characterized by the lack of literary qualities. The former style, which was
far from denying itself the assistance of rhetoric, made use of aphorism, antithesis, paradox, and especially metaphors; the latter, which
eschewed all rhetorical flourishes, laid not the slightest claim to these
qualities, and against metaphors, as this article has revealed, carried
on constant and uncompromising warfare. Again, neologizing was

a distinct characteristic of the Anti-Ciceronians, and freakish Latin-isms and strange words were admitted into their works; the scientists, on the other hand, abhorred all such importations, preferring "the language of Artizans, Countrymen, and Merchants" to the "hard" words of scholars. Bacon, Hall, Johnson, and Wotton have been considered the Anti-Ciceronian leaders in England, but there is nothing that relates the last three to the stylistic propaganda of sci-ence. Bacon, it is true, attacked the study of style for its own sake, which, he claimed, was fostered by study of the classics, and his own style reveals Anti-Ciceronian characteristics, but in at least one passage in his works [53] he condemns this style—in fact, he considers it one of the distempers of learning—and elsewhere, as revealed near the beginning of this article, he states with approval the character-istics which were later embodied in the stylistic ideal of the scientists, and which do not belong to the other movement. Other examples of Anti-Ciceronianism in England are Donne, Burton, and Browne, with the first of whom the scientists were in no way concerned, while against the style of the latter two they were in open revolt. In fact, the inclusion of these men among the Anti-Ciceronians coerces the belief that one object of the scientific attack was not Ciceronianism but Anti-Ciceronianism. Finally, the absence of any reference on the part of the scientific reformers either to the move-ment in general, or to single representatives of the movement, strongly argues their indifference to, if not ignorance of, the move-ment as such.

There are, to be sure, certain resemblances between the two sty-listic attitudes. In both "reality" is emphasized, but with the sci-entists the term generally means a material reality, while the Anti-Ciceronians used it to refer much more widely to rationalistic explanations of human experience. Though in both "things" are preferred to "words," the experimental philosophers had concrete objects in mind, while the others were thinking of intellectual or moral conceptions. Indeed, as has been said, both attitudes had their origin in that element in the Renaissance which turned from reli-ance on the authority of the ancients and their unsatisfying philos-ophy to a rationalistic examination of actual experience, but they developed in quite different directions. Neither is it significant that both object to musical phrases and pronounced rhythm in prose, though the Baconians were consistent in their practice, as cannot be said of the Anti-Ciceronians. Likewise, the former constantly emphasize clearness, which together with plainness was the cardinal tenet in their creed, but the latter, though sometimes including the word in their terminology, frequently did not exemplify it in their practice. To the scientist brevity meant the excision of all rhetorical devices; to the others it meant studied brevity such as aphorisms, point, and the like. Again, appropriateness, propriety, is a term so general and common that its use by both parties is hardly indicative of any relationships, and, in fact, it signified one thing in science and another in moral matters, which constituted the most important element in the revolt against Cicero. One must be cautious in arguing a relationship from the mere occurrence of similar terms, for terms have a way of detaching themselves from their use and of becoming common property, a fact which may be illustrated by examples given earlier in this article. Alexander Ross objects strenuously to the "Tullian pigments" in Browne's style, an expression that seems immediately to identify him with the Anti-Ciceronians, but Ross was the most orthodox of the orthodox, vociferously opposed to everything new in science and philosophy, and so by no stretch of the imagination can he be included in that group. Browne, on the other hand, was not a Ciceronian, as the charge would imply, but an Anti-Ciceronian. Another example is revealed in the passage quoted from Samuel Parker, in which the expression "scheme of words" is used, and which thus would seem to place him among the enemies of Cicero, since the latter especially objected to the *schemata verborum* in Ciceronian style. But Parker employs the term with reference to metaphors, which are one of the *figurae sententiae*, and these latter are characteristic of the Anti-Ciceronians.

By far the clearest and most consistent explanation of the attacks of science upon rhetorical prose is discovered in the nature of the scientific movement. Above everything else the new science insisted upon the necessity of abandoning the empty notions of traditional philosophy, which seemed far removed from material objects, and of observing carefully and recording accurately all physical phenomena. In the concrete nature of the experimental philosophy is to be found the secret of the craving for a clear, accurate, plain style and the belief that such a style was essential to the attainment of scientific goals.[54] This obsession with the actual nature and appearance of things caused them to resent the interposing of any possible obstruction between observation and description, and gave rise to a stylistic taste which decreed that a rhetorical style, with its figurative language and musical cadence, was the product of folly, vanity, and immaturity, and was not appropriate to serious discourse. Furthermore, the interest in science, together with the wider growth of rationalism, tended to create a distrust of the imagination, a distrust which in some cases was deepened by the growing feeling that fancy was associated with the passions, and, therefore, was a dangerous faculty of the mind. This latter attitude appears infrequently in the scientific revolt, but plays a great part in the attack on pulpit eloquence. Finally, scientific materialism exerted a distinct influence on ideas regarding the nature of language. A suggestion of this appears in Bacon, but it finds clear and definite expression in Hobbes, who claims that words are only the marks of things.[55] Thus the connotative value of words and their power to invest the creations of the imagination with life and being are summarily cast into the discard. Hobbes's idea is implied in the words of many of the scientists, and in Samuel Parker is again clearly stated.[56] Its most remarkable manifestation, however, is in John Wilkins' *Essay towards a Real Character and a Philosophical Language*, 1668, in which words are literally reduced to marks, and which frankly confesses to making no provision at all for such creatures of the imagination as fairies, fauns, and the like on the ground that they have no existence in nature. With this conception of language in the background, is it strange that science came to grips with imaginative prose?

There were, of course, other factors co-operating with science in the simplification of English prose. Rationalism and the steady growth of the classical spirit made against all extravagancies. In explaining the attacks on intricacies of style, Mr. Spingarn mentions the substitution of general for technical terms, the preference for sceptical as opposed to dogmatic modes of thought and speech, the horror of pedantry, the trend toward precision of word and idea, and the attempt to make literature approximate conversation. In most of these matters the presence of the two factors just mentioned may be noted, but it should be remarked that science also was very much concerned with all but the last. Two characteristics of the scientific revolt, however, distinguish it from other stylistic influences, and justify the opinion that science exerted by far the most powerful force upon prose. First, the thoroughgoing nature of the stylistic reform advocated by the experimental philosophers, which, rejecting any compromise whatsoever with rhetoric, insisted upon

an undefiled plainness and caused the issue at stake to be outlined
sharply and distinctly. Perhaps of greater importance is the fact that
reformation of style was a very significant part of a definite program adopted by a closely organized society of prominent men who
were aggressively active in promulgating their views. The extent
to which Glanvill's style changed under their discipline is a fair
gauge of the influence that must have been exerted upon all members of the society, and, through them, upon the outside world.

NOTES

1. *History of the Royal Society*, pp. 416–17. Earlier in the volume he
   had found in Bacon's prose traits quite different from those demanded by the Royal Society. See p. 36. See also R. Boyle, *Works*,
   ed. T. Birch, V, 39.
2. *The Works of Francis Bacon*, ed. Spedding, Ellis, and Heath, (new
   ed., 7 vols., 1879–90), I, 11.
3. *Ibid.*, III, 282–84. The first reference contains his famous explanation of, and attack on, Ciceronianism. Though his own prose reveals
   elements that ally him to the Anti-Ciceronians, his emphasis upon
   a plain style is quite foreign to them; furthermore, as will be noted
   later, he was so far from approving their style that he considered it
   one of the distempers of learning.
4. *Ibid.*, IV, 22. In a *Preparative towards a Natural and Experimental
   History* he lists rhetorical ornaments among the factors which increase the difficulty of, while adding nothing to, the work. "And for
   all that concerns ornaments of speech, similitudes, treasury of eloquence, and such like emptinesses, let it be utterly dismissed." IV,
   254.
5. *Ecclesiastes, or a Discourse concerning the Gift of Preaching as it
   falls under the Rules of Art*, 1646, p. 72.
6. *The Advice of W. P. to Mr. Samuel Hartlib, for the Advancement
   of some particular Parts of Learning*, London, 1648; *Harleian Miscellany*, 1810, VI, 2.
7. *A Treatise of the Rickets*, 1651. (This is a translation of the Latin
   edition which appeared the preceding year.) Mention might here
   be made of John Dury's *The Reformed School* (c. 1649), a passage
   from which (p. 49) reads: "Whatsoever in the teaching of Tongues
   doth not tend to make them a help unto Traditionall knowledge, by
   the manifestation of Reall Truths in Sciences, is superfluous, and
   not to be insisted upon, especially towards Children, whence fol-
   loweth that the Curious study of Criticismes and observations of
   Styles in Authors and of straines of wit, which speak nothing of

Reality in Sciences, are to be left to such as delight in vanityes more than in Truths." Dury belonged to that group of educational reformers which centered around Comenius, and to which Samuel Hartlib also belonged. Their philosophy, which is shot through with the spirit of scientific utilitarianism, was largely inspired by Bacon, and properly falls in the scientific movement. Dury's emphasis upon "reality" manifests the same attitude as is revealed in the quotation from Petty, and clearly indicates that the materialistic nature of the new science, with its insistence upon direct sense-observation of natural phenomena, was the chief source of this craving for a plain style. For an extended discussion of the influence of the Baconian philosophy upon educational theory, see Foster Watson, *The Beginning of the Teaching of Modern Subjects in England,* chap. vi.

8. See end of the *Leviathan.*
9. *Leviathan,* ed. A. R. Waller, pp. 526–27.
10. *Ibid.,* p. 185.
11. *Ibid.,* pp. 43–44.
12. *Ibid.,* pp. 14–15.
13. *Ibid.,* pp. 21, 25.
14. *Ibid.,* p. 26.
15. *Ibid.,* p. 88.
16. See Boyle's *Works,* ed. T. Birch, II, 92, 136; III, 2, 512; V, 54.
17. P. 2.
18. P. 1.
19. Numerous references might be given to support this statement, but I shall quote only one writer, who figures in this study. *"Aristotelian Philosophy* is a huddle of *words* and *terms insignificant."* And again, speaking of entities, modes, and formalities, "What a number of words here have nothing answering them? . . . To wrest names from their known meaning to Senses most alien, and to darken *speech by words without knowledge;* are none of the most inconsiderable faults of this *Philosophy* . . . Thus these *Verbosities* do emasculate the Understanding; and render it slight and frivolous, as its objects." Joseph Glanvill, *Vanity of Dogmatizing,* 1661, pp. 150 ff. He also speaks of the verbal emptiness of Aristotle's philosophy.
20. One stylistic vice obviously came under the ban of the experimental philosophers. The latter's violent attack upon the ancients and upon authority in general did much to depreciate the value of Latin and Greek quotations. Glanvill, in the *Vanity of Dogmatizing,* attacks this habit on the ground that reliance on antiquity is no longer to be countenanced, so that appeals to it are impertinent and futile. " 'Twas this vain Idolizing of Authors, which gave birth to that silly vanity of *impertinent citations;* and inducing Authority in things neither re-

quiring, nor deserving it. That saying was much more observable, *That men have beards, and women none;* because quoted from *Beza;* and that other *Pax res bona est;* because brought in with a, *said St. Austin."* (Pp. 142 ff.) In 1678 he says that "the custom is worn out everywhere except in remote, dark corners." (*An Essay Concerning Preaching,* pp. 18 ff.) See also Hobbes's view of the same matter given earlier in this article.

21. Pp. 111–13.

22. Cf. Thomas Birch, *History of the Royal Society,* II, 3, 47, 51, 138, 161, 163, 197 (hereafter cited as *Hist. Roy. Soc.).*

23. P. 113. Sprat believed that English writers in general were freer from stylistic vices than the French. "There might be," he says, with an eye on France, "a whole Volume compos'd in comparing the Chastity, the newnesse, the vigour of many of our *English* Fancies, with the corrupt, and the swelling Metaphors, wherewith some of our Neighbors, who most admire themselves, do still adorn their books." And again, "We have had many Philosophers, of a strong, vigorous, and forcible judgment, of happy and laborious hands, of a sincere, a modest, a solid, and unaffected expression, such who have not thought it enough to set up for Philosophers, only to have got a large stock of fine words, and to have insinuated into the acquaintance of some great Philosophers of the age." (*Observations on Monsieur de Sorbier's Voyage into England,* 1665, pp. 265, 271. See also Sprat, *History of the Royal Society,* pp. 40–41.) Evelyn expresses the same sentiment, only he makes a luxuriant prose style a characteristic of the whole French nation. "The Reader will find," he remarks in the Preface to his translation of a French treatise on painting, "in this discourse (though somewhat verbose, according to the style of this overflowing nation) divers useful remarks." (*Miscellaneous Writings of John Evelyn,* ed. W. Upcott, 1825, p. 559.) Another sturdy Englishman expresses the same sentiment in more emphatic words: "And indeed however our smoother tongued Neighbours may put in a claim for those bewitcheries of speech that flow from Gloss and Chimingness; yet I verily believe that there is no tongue under heaven, that goes beyond our English for speaking manly strong and full." (Nathaniel Fairfax, *A Treatise of the Bulk and Selvedge of the World,* 1674, "To the Reader.") In view of the common opinion that French influence played a great part in the simplification of English prose, these quotations are worthy of note. Furthermore, not a single stylistic reformer in England, as far as my knowledge extends, ever refers, directly or indirectly, to any influence from across the Channel.

24. *Plus Ultra,* p. 84.

25. The following quotation from Sprat's *History* clearly evinces the im-

portant place granted style in the obligations of the scientists. In fact, it shows that the experimental philosophers considered a reformation in current methods of expression essential to the advancement of science. "Their [members of the Royal Society] purpose is, in short, to make faithful *Records*, of all the Works of *Nature*, or *Art*, which can come within their reach: that so the present Age, and posterity, may be able to put a mark on the Errors, which have been strengthened by long prescription: to restore the Truths, that have lain neglected: to push on those, which are already known, to more various uses: and to make the way more passable, to what remains unreveal'd. This is the compass of their Design. And to accomplish this, they have indeavor'd, to separate the knowledge of *Nature*, from the colours of *Rhetorick*, the devices of *Fancy*, or the delightful deceit of *Fables*." Pp. 61–62.

26. See P. H. Hembt, "The Influence of Early Science on Formative English, 1645–1675," *Journal of Chemical Education*, III, 1051, and C. S. Duncan, *The New Science and English Literature*, pp. 147–54.

27. This version is accessible in a modern edition by John Owen, 1885. All references are to this edition.

28. See Birch, *Hist. Roy. Soc.*, I, 500. Glanvill's purpose is also suggested by a change introduced in the body of the work. A passage in the *Vanity*, p. 240, reads, "And the sole Instances of those illustrious Heroes, *Cartes, Gassendus, Galileo, Tycho, Harvey, More, Digby;* will strike dead the opinion of the worlds decay, and conclude it, in its *Prime*." In the *Scepsis*, p. 209, there is substituted for the names given above "that Constellation of Illustrious Worthies, which compose the Royal Society."

29. In an earlier passage he gives another excuse for this style though at the same time suggesting the immaturity of youth as one. After speaking of some ingenious people laboring under the prejudices of education and customary belief, he says, "For Such it was then that the ensuing *Essay* was designed; which therefore wears a dress that possibly is not so suitable to the graver *Geniuses*, who have outgrown all *gayeties of style and youthful* relishes; But yet perhaps is not improper for the persons, for whom it was prepared. And there is nothing in *words* and *styles* but *suitableness*, that makes them *acceptable* and *effective*. If therefore this Discourse, such as it is, may tend to the removal of any *accidental* disadvantages from *capable Ingenuities*, and the preparing them for *inquiry*, I know you have so noble an *ardour* for the benefit of Mankind, as to pardon a *weak* and *defective* performance to a *laudable* and *well-directed* intention." (P. liv.) In still another passage he touches upon this all-important matter: "And 'Tis none of the least considerable expectations that

may be reasonably had of your Society, that 'twill discredit that *toyishness* of *wanton fancy;* and pluck the misapplyed name of the *Wits,* from those conceited Humorists that have assum'd it; to bestow it upon the more *manly spirit* and *genius,* that playes not tricks with *words,* nor frolicks with the *Caprices* of *froathy imagination."* (P. lxv.) These words clearly indicate the popular association of stylistic reform with the Society, and the important place such a reformation occupied in the scientific movement.

30. This case furnishes strong support to Herford's contention that Browne's style was the obstacle in the way of his joining the Royal Society. Browne had early become notorious for his style. In *The Philosophicall Touchstone, or Observations upon Sir Kenelm Digbe's Discourses,* 1645, an attack on the *Religio Medici,* Alexander Ross says, "Your Rhetoricall descriptions (which are both uselesse in and destructive of *Philosophy*) make the soule sometimes equall with God, sometimes no better than a corruptible body; . . . If you lay the fault of this upon your *Rhetoricall* expressions, I must answer you, that *Rhetorick* in such a subject may be well spared: use your *Rhetorick* when you will work upon the *affections,* but not when you will *informe* the *understanding.* Rhetorick . . . ought not to be used, but with great discretion, especially in abstruse questions . . . If you will dispute like a *Philosopher,* you must lay aside *Rhetorick,* and use *Philosophicall* termes; otherwise you will do as the fish *Sepia,* to wit, you'l so thicken the waters of your discourse, with the *liquor* that cometh out of your mouth, that you will make your self *invisible,* and delude the Reader, which is the fashion of those, who dare not confide in the strength of their arguments; whereas *naked* truth cares not for such *dressings,* nor seeks she after such *corners."* (P. 92.) Ross has nothing but scorn for "Rhetoricall flourishes" and "Tullian pigments." See C. H. Herford's edition of Browne's works, Everyman's Library, p. xiv.

31. Ferris Greenslet in *Joseph Glanvill,* 1900, pp. 200–201, has listed all such verbal changes, which amount to less than a score. Dr. Greenslet notices the difference between Glanvill's early and later work in the matter of diction, clearness, and simplicity, as well as in the quality of imagination. But since he failed to compare the *Vanity* with the version that appeared in the *Essays,* he did not perceive the extent or fully understand the nature of the author's stylistic evolution. Though he attributes the change in part to the influence of science, he failed to perceive the conscious and decisive nature of the influence which the Royal Society exerted on Glanvill. He is correct in detecting Bacon in the concrete imagery and balanced brevity of sentence structure, but he limits Browne's influence too narrowly to words. Though he accurately characterizes Glanvill's later style as

simple, plain, reasonable, he is not sufficiently aware of the profound change that had taken place.

32. Concerning this essay, "Against Confidence in Philosophy," a passage in the preface to the volume reads: "[It] is quite changed in the way of Writing, and in the Order. Methought I was somewhat fetter'd and tied in doing it, and could not express my self with that ease, freedom, and fulness which possibly I might have commanded amid fresh thoughts: yet 'tis so alter'd as to be in a manner new." A comparison of the two versions reveals that chapters xvi, xvii, xviii, and xix, attacking Aristotle and the Peripatetic philosophy, as well as chapters i, ii, vi, xi, xx, xxi, and xxii, have been omitted almost *in toto*; that there is much beneficial rearrangement of material; and that much other material has been either left out or highly condensed. These changes, together with the compression in style, have caused the treatise to shrink to a fourth or a fifth of its first dimensions. A passage in the "Epistle Dedicatory" again calls attention to a change in his stylistic taste: "They [the essays] were some of them written several years ago, and had trial of the World in divers Editions: Now they come abroad together (with some things that are *new*) reduced to such an Order, as is most agreeable to my present judgment."

33. Likewise, the enthusiastic, exclamatory, and picturesque elements of the following passage are strangely subdued to a quieter level. "What cement should untie [unite] heaven and earth, light and darkness, natures of so divers a make, of such disagreeing attributes, which have almost nothing, but *Being,* in common; This is a riddle, which must be left to the coming of *Elias.* How should a thought be united to a marble-statue, or a sun-beam to a lump of clay! The freezing of the words in the air in the northern climes, is as conceivable, as this strange union. That this active spark, this συμψυτον πνευμα [as the Stoicks call it] should be confined to a Prison it can so easily pervade, is of less facill apprehension, then that the light should be pent up in a box of Crystall, and kept from accompanying its source to the lower world: And to hang weights on the wings of the winde seems far more intelligible." (*Vanity,* p. 20.) "So that, what the *Cement* should be that unites *Heaven* and *Earth, Light* and *Darkness,* viz. Natures of so divers a make, and such disagreeing Attributes, is beyond the reach of any of our Faculties: We can as easily conceive how a thought should be united to a Statue, or a Sun-Beam to a piece of Clay: How words should be frozen in the Air, (as some say they are in the remote North) or how Light should be kept in a Box; as we can apprehend the *manner* of this *strange Union.*" *Essays,* p. 4.

34. *Vanity,* pp. 26, 27, 29, 53, 137; *Essays,* pp. 5, 6, 13, 25.

35. It would be easy to quote many more parallel passages illustrating this change, but the reader should compare the two versions himself in order to realize fully the transformation that has taken place. It is hardly necessary to point out that all Glanvill's later works reveal the same stylistic evolution.

36. Later Glanvill joined in the attack on pulpit eloquence, which arose about 1668, and his words show that science was by no means without its influence upon this attack. Furthermore, the terms used by the reformers of the pulpit are startlingly similar to those with which the scientists have made us familiar. (See Glanvill, *Philosophia Pia*, pp. 73, 90–91; the last essay in *Essays on Several Important Subjects*, 1676, and *An Essay Concerning Right Preaching*, 1678, pp. 11–51.) For an account of Glanvill's vigorous defense of the Royal Society, consult the present writer's "The Background of *The Battle of the Books*," *Washington University Studies*, VII, Humanistic Series II (1920), 125–29.

37. VIII, 431–33.

38. P. 310.

39. Abraham Cowley, *The Essays and Other Prose Writings*, ed. A. B. Gough, 1915, p. 143.

40. *Ibid.*, p. 199.

41. *Ibid.*, p. 169.

42. Birch, *Hist. Roy. Soc.*, I, 17.

43. *Ibid.*, I, 499. The late Professor Emerson in "John Dryden and A British Academy" (*Proceedings of the British Academy*, X, 1924) calls attention to the fact that Cowley was not a member of this committee, and thinks that Evelyn's memory had played him false in mentioning Cowley. But we must remember that Evelyn does not say that Cowley and the others were members of the committee, and that there is no reason why both the poet and Clifford, who also was not a member, should not have met with the committee.

44. Another possible example of the influence of the Royal Society in sobering the style of its members is found in Samuel Parker, later bishop of Oxford, who in 1666 published *A Free and Impartial Censure of the Platonick Philosophie*, dedicated to Bathurst, then president of Trinity College, Oxford, and formerly a member of the Oxford group of Baconians, to which reference has already been made. Both in the dedication and in the body of the work (pp. 2, 64) Parker expresses his gratitude to Bathurst for turning him from the unprofitable study of the old scholastic philosophy to the new experimental science. Though disclosing the influence of both Hobbes and Descartes, the *Censure* reveals chiefly the influence of Bacon and his followers. Parker brings to bear upon Platonism the same arguments which the experimental philosophers had used, and were

using, against Aristotelianism, namely, that, as regards natural phenomena anyway, its empty notions could not be tested by sense
observations or experiments, the criteria of truth. From this attack
on a philosophy which presumably is mainly words, he passes naturally to an onslaught upon a wordy and figurative style, which is
fully in keeping with the attitude of the scientists, and in the composition of which he undoubtedly had an eye on the Cambridge
Platonists. These latter, he says, "put us off with nothing but rampant
Metaphors and Pompous Allegories, and other splendid but empty
Schemes of speech . . . true Philosphie is too sober to descend to
these wildernesses of Imagination, and too Rational to be cheated by
them. She scorns, when she is in chase of Truth, to quarry upon
trifling gaudy Phantasms: Her Game is in things not words . . . I
remember I had not long conversed with Platonick Authors, when
I took occasion to set it down as a note to my self, that though a huge
lushious stile may relish sweet to childish and liquorish Fancies, yet
it rather loaths and nauceats a discreet understanding then informs
and nourishes it . . . Now to discourse of the Natures of things in
Metaphors and Allegories is nothing else but to sport and trifle with
empty words, because these Schemes do not express the Natures of
Things, but only their Similitudes and Resemblances." (Pp. 73 ff.)
And he continues his attack on metaphors at great length. But in
spite of this expressed antipathy to rhetorical prose, the style of the
Censure is far from being bare and unadorned. (Note, for instance,
the following: "But when they pretend to be Natures Secretaries,
to understand all her Intrigues, or to be Heavens Privadoes, talking
of the Transactions there, like men lately drop'd thence encircled
with *Glories*, and cloathed with the Garments of *Moses* & *Elias*,"
etc., p. 73.) He had been for only a short time a member of the
Royal Society, and perhaps its influence had not had time to bear
fruit. In his next important works, however, *A Discourse of Ecclesiastical Politie*, 1671, we note a decided toning down of his enthusiastic
language, though he himself claims that he is pursuing a middle way
between a bare and an ornate style. (*A Defence*, pp. 97–98.) Parker
is treated more at length in my article on pulpit eloquence.

45. *Cam. Hist. of Eng. Lit.*, VIII, 346, 423.
46. "His [Tillotson's] joining with Dr. Wilkins in perfecting the scheme
of a *real character and philosophical language*, the *essay* towards which
was publish'd in 1668, led him to consider exactly the truth of language and style, in which no man was happier, or knew better the
art of uniting dignity with simplicity, and tempering these so equally
together, that neither his thoughts sunk, nor style swell'd; keeping
always a due mean between flatness and false rhetoric. Together
with the pomp of words he cut off likewise all superfluities and need-

less enlargements. He said what was just necessary to give clear ideas of things, and no more. He laid aside long and affected periods. His sentences were short and clear; and the whole thread was of a piece, plain and distinct. No affections of learning, no torturing of texts, no superficial strains, no false thoughts, nor bold flights. All was solid and yet lively, and grave as well as elegant . . . he retrench'd both the luxuriances of style, and the length of sermons." Thomas Birch, *The Life of the Most Reverend Dr. John Tillotson*, 2d ed., London, 1753, pp. 21–22.

47. Birch, *Hist. Roy. Soc.*, I, 119; II, 265, 281, 283.

48. In the Dedication a passage reads, "To which it will be proper for me to add, That this design will likewise contribute much to the clearing of some of our Modern differences in Religion, by unmasking many wild errors, that shelter themselves under the disguise of affected phrases; which being Philosophically unfolded, and rendered according to the genuine and natural importance of Words, will appear to be inconsistencies and contradictions. And several of those pretended, mysterious, profound notions, expressed in great swelling words, whereby some men set up for reputation, being this way examined, will appear to be, either nonsence, or very flat and jejune." Later he speaks of "the Common mischief that is done, and the many impostures and cheats that are put upon men, under the disguise of affected insignificant Phrases." On pp. 17–18, he says, "As for the ambiguity of words by reason of *Metaphor* and *Phraseology,* this is in all instituted Languages so obvious and so various, that it is needless to give any instances of it; . . . And though the varieties of Phrases in Language may seem to contribute to the elegance and ornament of Speech; yet, like other affected ornaments, they prejudice the native simplicity of it, and contribute to the disguising of it with false appearances. Besides that like other things of fashion, they are very changeable, every generation producing new ones; witness the present Age, especially the late times, wherein this grand imposture of Phrases hath almost eaten out solid knowledge in all professions; such men generally being of most esteem who are skilled in these Canting forms of speech, though in nothing else." The same values that appear in the previous discussions of style also appear in the use of such terms as brevity, perspicuity, significancy, and facility of expression, and the like. See pp. 319, 443, 447.

49. That the Royal Society looked upon Wilkins as specially qualified for the study of language or style is revealed in the fact that, though he was not appointed on the committee to improve the language, perhaps because he was too busy with the *Essay,* he was ordered to attend the first meeting of the committee and outline to them the proper method of procedure. Birch, *Hist. Roy. Soc.*, II, 7.

50. Congreve's dedication of *Dryden's Dramatic Works*, quoted by Ker, *Essays of John Dryden*, I, xxvii, n.

51. "Defence of an Essay of Dramatic Poesy," *Essays of John Dryden*, ed. Ker, I, 124. Dryden in the Preface to *Religio Laici* called himself a sceptic in philosophy, and Ker, I, xv, speaks of him as "sceptical, tentative, disengaged." How much of this quality was due to the scepticism of science that stretched from Bacon to the Royal Society? See Bredvold's "Dryden, Hobbes, and the Royal Society," *Mod. Phil.*, XXV (1928), 417–38.

52. In discussing this paper, a fraction of which was read before one of the groups of the Modern Language Association at Toronto in 1928, one scholar maintained that there was some relation between the two movements and referred to Professor Morris Croll's very able articles on Anti-Ciceronianism. During my own investigations I had discovered no such relationship, and a close study of the problem has confirmed me in the belief that the two movements were separate and distinct in that the scientific demand for stylistic reform neither had its origin in, nor drew support from, the Anti-Ciceronian revolt. For Professor Croll's theories consult the following: "Juste Lipse et le Mouvement Anti-Cicéronien," (*Revue du Seizième Siècle*, Vol. II [1914]); " 'Attic' Prose in the Seventeenth Century," (*Stud. in Philol.*, Vol. XVIII [1921]); "Attic Prose: Lipsius, Montaigne, Bacon," (*Schelling Anniversary Papers*, 1923); "Muret and the History of 'Attic Prose,' " (*PMLA*, Vol. XXXIX [1924]).

53. See *Schelling Anniversary Papers*, pp. 138–39.

54. Probably the most remarkable example of this passion for concrete, material reality in language as well as in philosophy, is discovered in the startling proposal advanced by Nathaniel Fairfax in the preface to *A Treatise of the Bulk and Selvedge of the World*, 1674. Fairfax displays a violent antipathy to all imported words in the English language, and in his own work he tries as far as possible to substitute English coinages for words of foreign origin, with grotesque results in some cases. Since he was a great admirer of the Royal Society and the experimental philosophy, which impressed him with its practical and utilitarian character, it is not strange to find him proclaiming an interest in things, not words. Thus he advocates the purification and enlargement of the English vocabulary, made necessary by the activities of the new scientists, through the introduction of plain, homely words, gathered from the fields and shops. He wishes to realize literally Sprat's "so many things in the same number of words," not difficult Latinisms but the common words of daily use, "words that answer works, by which all Learners are taught to do, and not make a Clatter." More of his sentiments are worth quoting: "Now the *Philosophy* of our day and Land being so much workful

as the world knows it to be, methinks this of all times should be *the* time, wherein, if ever, we should gather up those scatter'd words of ours that speak works, rather than to suck in those of learned air from beyond Sea, which are as far off sometimes from the things they speak, as they are from us to whom they are spoken. Besides, it may well be doubted, whether Latine can now be made so fit to set forth things the writings of a *Working Philosophy* by, as our own Speech. —For we must know that almost all the old pieces of good Latine that we draw by, have been taken up by that sort of learning that is wont to be worded in the Schools, and spent in the setting to sale of such things as could best be glazed with the froth of ink, by the men of Closets. Whence he that is best skill'd in it, is so hard put to it, in the Kitchin, the Shop, and the Ship; and ever will be, though *Plautus* should be as well understood as *Tully*. For the words that are every day running to and fro in the Chat of Workers, have not been gotten into Books and put aboard for other Lands until this way of Knowing by Doing was started amongst us.—But as Learnings being lockt up in the Tongues of the Schools, or Love's being lickt up in more the womanly simprings of the lips, and the smiling kissing speeches of some others abroad, have been enough to enkindle in us a panting after, and fondness for some of those Out-landish dynns: So if the works of our own men shall be shipt over by words of our own tongue, it may happily make others who have love enough for the things, to seek as much after our words, as we upon other scores have done after theirs; the first draught being *English,* name and thing, doing and speaking." Cf. what Sprat says about the Royal Society's "preferring the language of Artizans, Countrymen, and Merchants, before that of Wits, or Scholars."

55. *Leviathan,* ed. A. R. Waller, p. 14.
56. *A Free and Impartial Censure,* p. 61.

W. P. KER

The Style of Dryden's Prose

Dryden's prose has been described by Dr. Jonson in one of the
pleasantest passages in the *Lives*: "Criticism, either didactic or de-
fensive, occupies almost all his prose, except those pages which he
has devoted to his patrons; but none of his prefaces were ever
thought tedious. They have not the formality of a settled style, in
which the first half of the sentence betrays the other. The clauses
are never balanced, nor the periods modelled: every word seems
to drop by chance, though it falls into its proper place. Nothing
is cold or languid; the whole is airy, animated, and vigorous; what
is little, is gay; what is great, is splendid. He may be thought to mention himself too frequently; but while he forces himself upon our
esteem, we cannot refuse him to stand high in his own. Every thing
is excused by the play of images and the spriteliness of expression.
Though all is easy, nothing is feeble; though all seems careless, there
is nothing harsh; and though since his earlier works more than a
century has passed, they have nothing yet uncouth or obsolete."

   To this account of Dryden's style there is little to be added except
in the way of illustration. It is a paragraph in which the great master
of formal periods has taken occasion to salute the master of the
other sort of prose, and in so doing to pay honour to both styles.
Nowhere has the grace of Dryden's free elocution been better de-

From *Essays of John Dryden,* 2 vols. (Clarendon Press, 1900), introduction,
pp. xxvi–xxxi. Reprinted by permission of the publisher.

scribed. Dryden's sentences are like sentences of good conversation, in which it is not necessary that every point should be deliberated. They run on easily, clauses are added to qualify the chief proposition, and in one case at least there is so much freedom and exuberance in the dependent clauses that the grammar of the sentence is left helpless in the tangle and thicket of relative pronouns.

In his revision of the *Essay of Dramatic Poesy*, Dryden came to believe that he ought to put some restraint on his tendency to leave hanging phrases at the end of his sentences. As he tells us himself, he noted as a fault the preposition left at the end of a clause and belonging to a relative understood; and in the revised version of his Essay he carefully corrected "the end he aimed at" into "the end at which he aimed," and "the age I live in" to "the age in which I live," and so on. But this correction and restriction, though it was a move towards greater propriety of language, was very far short of conversion to the periodic structure of sentences, and Dryden's prose remains in the Preface to the *Fables* in 1700 essentially what it was in the Essay of 1668; no less "airy and animated," and no more stately and dignified.

Dryden's prose, which is intended for the greatest number, which is meant to be popular, loses nothing of its value by being compared with his contemporaries, though it may be found to be not altogether exceptional nor new in character. Dryden himself, according to Congreve's well-known evidence, acknowledged Tillotson as his master in the art of familiar discourse; [1] and there were others; before all, there was Cowley, whose style obtains from Dr. Johnson little less than the praise given to the *Essays* of Dryden for their lightness, grace, and ease. There were also the French authors. However much the influence of France may have been abused by historians as an explanation of the new fashions of literature at the accession of Charles II, there is no reason why it should be disallowed or refused its due in accounting for the changes of taste. French criticism, French talk about literature, had already found the right kind of expression thirty years and more before the *Essay of Dramatic Poesy*. The ancestors of Dryden's prose are to be traced in Chapelain's Preface to the *Adone* of Marino, in Mesnardière's *Poëtique,* in the Dialogues and Essays of Sarrasin, in the Prefaces of Scudéry, in the Discourses and *Examens* of Corneille. In all these different authors, and in others, there was to be found, with differ-

ent faculties, the same common quality of clearness in exposition and argument, which even without genius may be pleasing,
and with genius is the most valuable auxiliary, as in the essays
of Dryden and Corneille. What criticism might be without the
example of the French is shown in the Preface to *Samson Agonistes*.
In date it is some years later than Dryden's *Essay*; in temper it
belongs to the Italy of a hundred years before; it is like one of the
solemn sermons before an Italian learned society, in which the
doctrine of Poetry used to be expounded more gravely than any text
of St. Thomas. The difference between an Italian and a French
education in their influence on prose may be seen by comparing
Milton and Chapelain, authors much alike in ambition, self-respect,
and solemnity of mind; in everything but poetical genius and the
circumstances of their lives. Milton writing his opinions about
Tragic Poetry writes like an Italian contemporary of Tasso, with
grave magnificence; Chapelain, by nature no less grave, and as much
inclined as Milton to walk with the gait of "the magnanimous
man," is obliged by his associates to let his dignity go and to speak
like other people. Between the scholar who was also a wit—Ménage
—and the man of the world who was also a student—Sarrasin—there
was no more room for declamation than there is in a reading party
in summer. Chapelain the pedant has written a dialogue with
Ménage and Sarrasin the wits taking part in it, and it is as easy
and pleasant as the writing of the wits themselves, as fresh as anything of Dryden's; a defence of Lancelot and the library of Don
Quixote, a delightful apology for Romance, by the great champion
of literary authority, the patron if not the inventor of the Unities.
It is no small part of the attraction of Dryden's essays that they
bring their readers into acquaintance with that new world of France
in the age of Louis XIII, when all the world and the Dramatic
Unities were young, when Corneille at the Hôtel de Bourgogne
scarcely knew himself as yet for anything different from Hardy,
when Scaramouche and Jodelet were getting things ready for
Molière, and when the cloak and sword of Madrid, and the Castilian
Point of Honour, were mingled in the visions of the dramatic poet
with an idea of some unattained perfection, a sort of inaudible
dramatic music, a harmony partly moral, partly imaginative, which
should constitute the absolutely faultless play. It is from this world,
so adventurous yet so decorous, so strangely mixed of "Gothic" tra-

ditions and pedantic authority, Spanish comedies and classical learning, and through all of it the zest and interest of a society which
sees a long day before it and much to be won, that the spirit of
Dryden's essays is in great measure derived.

Much also is native to them in England; they inherit from Ben
Jonson's *Discoveries* as well as from the Discourses of Corneille.
But it is from the language and the manners of Corneille and his
fellows that the essays of Dryden have caught their style and accent.

There is little that is peculiarly French in the details of Dryden's
prose. In a well-known passage of *Marriage à la Mode* (1673), Act
iii. sc. 1, there is a satire on the importation of French phrases and
their use in the warfare of conversation. "They began at *sottises*
and ended *en ridicule*"; they include *foible, chagrin, grimace, em-
barrasse, double entendre, equivoque, eclaircissement, suitte, beveue,
façon, penchant, coup d'etourdy, languissant.* Dryden does not allow
himself to be led very far on this way in his own practice. In the
Dedication of the Rival Ladies (1664) he protests against the abuse
of foreign terms, and in the Preface to the *Second Miscellany*
(1685) he even seems to note the word *diction* as not completely
naturalized. But Dryden was not the man to make any fanatical opposition to a prevailing fashion, and he uses French words as they
come convenient.

If there is anything old-fashioned in his style it is perhaps that
liking for conceits, which fortunately never disappears from his
verse nor from his prose. He is indeed more temperate than the men
moribus antiquis, such as Butler must be reckoned in spite of Butler's affection for lucidity and good sense. But there are many places
where Dryden seems to be writing for a sentence or two in the manner of Butler or Cleveland. So in the Dedication of *Love in a
Nunnery:*

> For this reason I have often laughed at the ignorant and
> ridiculous descriptions which some Pedants have given of the
> Wits, as they are pleased to call them, which are a generation
> of men as unknown to them as the people of Tartary or the
> *Terra Australis* are to us. And therefore as we draw giants and
> anthropophagi in those vacancies of our maps, where we have
> not travelled to draw better, so these wretches paint lewdness,
> atheism, folly, ill-reasoning, and all manner of extravagancies
> amongst us, from want of understanding what we are.

NOTE

1. "I have heard him frequently own with pleasure that if he had any talent for English prose, it was owing to his having often read the writings of the great Archbishop Tillotson." Congreve, Dedication of *Dryden's Dramatic Works*.

J. P. W. ROGERS

✍

Pope and the Syntax of Satire

Spence is of course invaluable. It is a shame, though, that we should have to rely on him so heavily. Anecdotes can possess charm as well as graphic immediacy, but there is a limit to the amount of serious enlightenment which they can provide. Pope must have tangled with the grammarians in his earliest youth, long before the last book of *The Dunciad* was set down. Unhappily we know very little of this stage in his development. Spence cites a remark to the effect that it was the family priest (one Banister, alias Taverner) who "taught [him] the figures, accidence and first part of grammar." Such nuncupatory testimony is proverbially suspect; and it would be better for this essay—which constitutes, roughly, the first part of a poetic grammar of Pope's work—if we had fuller evidence.[1] It would be nice even to have as much to go on as in the case of Martinus Scriblerus.

Martinus, it may be recalled, sampled parts of both the trivium and the quadrivium, not to mention metaphysics and gymnastics. But in Chapter VII, where one might have expected a formal analysis of the Scriblerian trivium, rhetoric and logic are joined by metaphysics. This is a pointed substitution, and we may guess at Martinus's deficiencies from the parallel information that rhetoric, too, is passed over briefly—it has already been covered in *Peri Bathous*. That Martinus did learn some grammar, doubtless of a pedantic kind, we know from his association with Conradus Crambe. This was the schoolfellow carefully chosen for him by his deluded father: a word-chopper by hereditary right. Chapter IX of the treatise, which describes "How *Martin* became a great Critic," thus descibes the influence of "the puns of Crambe . . . on the Mind and Studies of Martinus":

> He conceiv'd, that somewhat of a like Talent to this of Crambe, of *assembling parallel sounds,* either *syllables,* or *words,* might conduce to the Emendation and Correction of *Ancient Authors,* if applied to their Works, with the same *diligence,* and the same liberty . . .

Here is the hint for *Virgilius Restauratus* and the various attacks on Bentley.[2] But something more than the over-niceties of classical scholarship is at issue. This is the satiric tip of an iceberg: for Pope throughout his life was vitally concerned with words, their interactions, their bumps and jars, their contrast or alignment, their phonetic weight, semantic range, and structural role. For Pope, as for any other practising poet, "the Dance of Numbers, and the Change of Rime" (Savage's phrase) came down ultimately to questions of verbal shape.

There are surprisingly few commentators on the structure of Pope's language. Professor Tillotson has invoked a Euclidean image to describe what might be called the geometry of syntax.[3] That phrase recalls certain others used by Professor Davie in his absorbing book, *Articulate Energy.* Indeed, Davie speaks at one point of "a diagram of forces" in a line of Pope's, prolonging the same metaphor.[4] However, he has little to say directly on Pope; and in addition, as Miss Christine Brooke-Rose has pointed out, the book is finally about conceptual processes rather than syntax in the narrow sense. Miss Brooke-Rose, in her turn, confines herself to metaphor, somewhat stringently defined, and her analytic method comes uncomfortably close in places to downright parsing; besides producing statements like "He [Shakespeare] is very good indeed on Intransitive Verbs. . . ."[5] These are, needless to say, gaps which are prescribed by the declared scope of each book. Much more disappointing is Mrs. Parkin's study of Pope's "workmanship." Her chapter on "Parallelism, Antithesis, and Paradox," could hardly be further from linguistic concerns. The antithesis is that of subject-matter or intention, not syntax; and in any case antithesis is a deliquescent thing for Mrs.

Parkin, always on the point of melting into paradox. We are indeed
told that "good poems may and do exist in which paradox is lacking
or negligible"—a concession hardly wrung from the author—but paradox has itself softened into something larger and hazier than a
rhetorical figure. As with the modern use of "irony," we are dealing
with psychological rather than lexical effects—paradox has become
a state of mind. There are some interesting observations at the outset: "Antithesis is a special kind of parallelism, and paradox may
be defined as a special case of antithesis in which both halves of
the antithesis are stated to be true." But soon the hunt for "tension"
begins, as unending and as self-enclosed as the quest for the grail.

According to Mrs. Parkin, the predominance of antithesis and
parallelism "in neoclassical English poetry, and particularly in the
poetry of Pope, has long been acknowledged and commented on." [6]
That would have been my own impression until recently. But as
far as Pope goes, the truth seems to be that the detailed applications
of these resources have seldom been considered. Pope's imagery,
his diction, his versification, even his rhyming, have found able
analysts. But on his poetry as a verbal structure we have little: linguistics, not an over-modest science in general, has kept unusually
silent, and criticism at large has exhibited less valour than discretion.
To be blunt, Professor Wimsatt is the only guide offering his services
on this expedition, apart from those who promise an easy day for
a lady.

I

Wimsatt distinguishes between "verse, where patterns of form do
not . . . support parallels of stated meaning, but run counter to
meaning": and prose, where symmetrical syntax "comes fairly to
the aid of logic." In his view, it is rare to find "equalities of verse"
coinciding with "parallels of meaning." [7] On this showing, it is rhyme
especially which dislocates the potential logic of the verse form by
means of its irrational and irrelevant congruence. My own view is
that a distinction has indeed to be drawn between the two modes
of discourse, but that it should be drawn on different grounds. The
basic fact is that in prose syntax any degree of parallelism is willed
and therefore noticeable. It is a patterning imposed on recalcitrant
material, or at least on neutral material. By contrast poetry is ductile,
its inherent structure being hospitable to repetitive statements of

any kind. To put this in concrete historical terms, we may distinguish (1) the typical symmetries of Renaissance prose, whether Ciceronian, Senecan, Euphuistic, "baroque" or however labelled; and (2) the equivalences, positive or negative, achieved by Pope and others in the heroic couplet. In the first case, even where there is a deliberate attempt "to avert an impending symmetry, to sabotage in advance what threatens to evolve into too fussy a balance," [8] there is a more or less regular effect attained by setting one member of a sentence against another. The sentence carves out its own channel, and it is within the control of the writer to fix its external bounds, as the ideas conveyed seem to demand. But Pope is working with another independent variable, the couplet itself. And even if we disregard rhyme for the moment, it is plain that many syntactical parallels will be swimming with the tide of the verse. The line unit in its own form asserts an identity and a balance. It follows that symmetry, either of sound, of meaning or of construction, is less immediately apparent: the congruence may be put down to the pressure of the verse rhythm, or may even go unobserved insofar as it is a separate entity from that rhythm.

An example will help. In his dialogue with Fortescue (Hor. *Sat.* ii.i) [9] the satirist replies to his friend's hint that excessive boldness will call out physical assault in retaliation:

> *P.* What? arm'd for *Virtue* when I point the Pen,
> Brand the bold Front of shameless, guilty Men,
> Dash the proud Gamester in his gilded Car,
> Bare the mean Heart that lurks beneath a Star;
> Can there be wanting to defend Her Cause,
> Lights of the Church, or Guardians of the Laws?
> Could pension'd *Boileau* lash in honest Strain
> Flatt'rers and Bigots ev'n in *Louis'* Reign?
> Could Laureate *Dryden* Pimp and Fry'r engage,
> Yet neither *Charles* nor *James* be in a Rage?
> And I not strip the Gilding off a Knave,
> Un-plac'd, un-pension'd, no Man's Heir, or Slave?
> I will, or perish in the gen'rous Cause.

> (ll. 105–117)

An attentive reader will be alive to the successive questions incorporated within the third, fourth, fifth, and sixth couplets here. The effect Pope seeks is to imply that his desire to speak out is as well justified as that of earlier satirists, and that his situation is broadly equivalent. The parallelism in the construction asserts the social and moral identity which Pope is claiming. And, of course, the sudden shift to a blunt affirmative style ("I will . . .") carries all the more impact because of the successive queries—rhetorical as they are— which have preceded this line. What might easily escape observation is an earlier series of equivalent statements. From the second line to the fourth Pope places a strong stress on the first syllable of each verse. Again, every one of these stresses falls on an active transitive verb, occupying the first part of a trochaic (i.e. inverted) foot. Following this verb we get a direct object in the formula "the + moral adjective (monosyllabic) + noun," and then a phrase qualifying that object. The total effect is to distract attention from the line unit as such. The parallelism runs across the couplet form; the rhymes are in any case rather flat and unassertive; and the emphasis on the initial verb also contributes to this process. It might be said that Pope achieves an eloquent syntactical form by modifying and even impairing his basic metrical scheme.

This passage gives us, in fact, a disguised parison, as the rhetoricians would say: that is, a series of clauses using the same parts of speech in the same order. Analysts of Renaissance prose often set down the structure of sentence in a kind of visual lay-out.[10] There is some point in doing that, since the diagram enacts the reader's response; its contours are a fact additional to the plain prose utterance. But the verse parison just looked at already contains its own diagrammatic statement: indeed, arguably, it offers a formal tautology. Pope's use of the standard symmetrical forms which Puttenham and others catalogue allows for that fact. Generally he avoids simple repetitive formulae, since the ineluctable repetition of the verses themselves provides a mode of continuity—any naked parallelism superadded can only appear jejune. So we find him indulging in what Tillotson calls "significant variation"; that is, bending versification or sentence-structure so as to produce some uncovenanted or even discordant effect.

Another subdued version of the parisonic device (this time involving a train of direct objects) is found in the "Epistle to Arbuthnot." It occurs during Pope's celebrated vindication of his own career— immediately after the couplet describing his conversion from "Fancy's Maze" to "moraliz'd . . . song":

> . . . That not for Fame, but Virtue's better end,
> He stood the furious Foe, the timid Friend,
> The damning Critic, half-approving Wit,
> The Coxcomb hit, or fearing to be hit;
> Laugh'd at the loss of Friends he never had,
> The dull, the proud, the wicked, and the mad;
> The distant Threats of Vengeance on his head,
> The Blow unfelt, the Tear he never shed;
> The Tale reviv'd, the Lye so oft o'erthrown;
> Th' imputed Trash, and Dulness not his own;
> The Morals blacken'd when the Writings scape;
> The libel'd Person, and the pictur'd Shape;
> Abuse on all he lov'd, or lov'd him, spread,
> A Friend in Exile, or a Father, dead;
> The Whisper that to Greatness still too near,
> Perhaps, yet vibrates on his SOVEREIGN's Ear—
> Welcome for thee, fair Virtue! all the past:
> For thee, fair Virtue! welcome ev'n the *last!*

> (ll. 342–359)

Commentators have been so busy explaining the allusions that they
have scarcely had time to remark the subtle technique or the ends
it serves. The long catalogue of nouns may be regarded as in apposition to the initial object "Foe." That places a huge emphasis on the
verb "stood," which has to carry all the rest of this swollen predicate
on its back. I take the meaning to be "withstood," with a hint of
the modern sense, "put up with"—the nobly suffering satirist's Christ-
like capacity to forbear every ill done to him thus indicated. All
these can be endured for the sake of virtue.

In moving from grammar to rhetoric, however, it is noteworthy
that the passage involves a sort of anaphoric construction. That is
to say, the repeated phrases almost all start with the word "the."
Now this is of course the greyest-looking word in English, though
recent analysts have shown that the definite article is neither as
definite nor as innocent as that. The result is to be scarcely aware
of the parallelism set up by its use; when the passage is abstracted
from its context, as I have just abstracted it, the repetition may be
obvious, but in normal reading I doubt if many are conscious other
than in the dimmest way of its anaphoric basis. And that is as Pope
would wish it. Iterative constructions generally carry a hectoring

air with them. Here the poet is seeking a more muted kind of symmetry. His employment of phrases introduced by "the" performs several functions. (1) It lends a certain impersonality to the catalogue of outrages; "the Writings" are those of "one Poet" (line 336) rather than those simply of the actual Alexander Pope. This not only deflects the charge of egotism: it serves wider imaginative purposes, by suggesting that others might have been in Pope's situation and might not have behaved as stoically as he did. This effect is strengthened by the participle phrases, of which more in a moment. (2) It implies a factuality, an agreed historicity, in the events to which it refers. A grammarian has written that "*the* assumes familiarity or previous knowledge." Pope exploits the article to suggest that there is no argument about the threats, say, having been offered; he insinuates the idea that the only debate is about what exactly they constituted or why they were offered. (3) At the same time the formula conveys a measure of generalization; *the* tale is one of many, *the* lie "often" encountered. (The article comes to the aid of the adverb; it is almost as if a continuous tense of the verb, such as the imperfect, were used.) The coxcomb is any coxcomb, not worth identifying more closely. An entire line is built up of these emblematic forms ("The dull, the proud . . ."), making it sound almost like a modern movie title. These are representative men, and women: Pope's syntax asserts that there are many more where they came from. (4) In this context any noun without an article, or with a different form of the article, will stand out. With line 346, "the Friends" would suggest that they really were friends if only for a moment: the omission of "the" indicates "the loss of such so-called friends . . ." "Dulness" is a sprawling mass not to bear the definition even of a simple article; the chiasmic line allows "Dulness" to be qualified not merely by the symmetrically placed "not his own," but also by the original epithet "imputed"—which would not be possible if "the" were repeated before the second noun. Abuse is scattered casually, piecemeal. And finally there is the sudden shift to "a Friend," the special case of Atterbury, and "a Father," the unique parental role. In a manner both economical and moving, Pope has switched from the general or public case to the intimate: grammar directs the change.

Nor is this the only interesting feature of the syntax. A cursory reading will disclose the fondness for participles: more especially, for past participles serving as predicative adjectives. Or rather, the

strict grammatical form is predicative, the implied sense is perhaps
equivalent to that of an absolute construction. So "imputed Trash"
has the force of a passive verb; trash has been and is still being
imputed to the poet. So too with "hit," "unfelt," "reviv'd," "o'er-
thrown," "blacken'd, "libell'd," "pictur'd," and so on. Each of these
words could be expanded into a full predication. The pattern would
be: "I do not feel these blows," and "They continue to libel my
person and to depict my physical appearance." But Pope's refusal to
commit himself to such a positive assertion is deliberate; the poetry
gains because it leaves the reader with an agent-less process of de-
nunciation and terrorism. A sinister third-person anonymity attaches
to the oppressors of Pope—they are everywhere. If the satirist had
come straight out and named his enemies, the impression would be
so much the less threatening. Speaking of the passive voice in a
different context, Miss Brooke-Rose has well said: "The very help-
lessness of the subject, even in metaphoric relation to the verb, em-
phasises the instrumental . . . force of the indirect object which is
really responsible for the metaphoric change." [11] Similarly, Pope
uses an implied passive, built into the actual syntactical function of
the participle, to convey his own open, though not vulnerable, position before the onslaughts of his detractors. Once more, grammar
enacts a complete human situation. If not quite "a little tragic plot,"
the repetitive construction does much in its own structural identity
to make Pope's imaginative point.

This kind of pseudo-parallelism is among the commonest effects
of Pope's verse. There is likewise a pseudo-antithesis, an opposition
which turns out to be less and less complete the longer it is sustained. In a short form this trick can be seen when Pope unleashes
his famous couplet on Lady Mary Wortley Montagu:

> From furious *Sappho* scarce a milder Fate,
> P-x'd by her Love, or libell'd by her Hate . . .[12]

Here the grammar supplies a suggestion of alternatives, but the sense
is clearly "it's all the same either way." Pope is fond of such spurious
adversative constructions: in the epistle "To Augustus" we get

> But those who cannot write, and those who can,
> All ryme, and scrawl, and scribble, to a man.
>
> (ll. 187–188)

There *ought* to be a difference between the two groups, Pope is saying, but in practice they both contribute to the flood of unwanted
book-making. Similarly, at the end of that harsh yet beautiful vision
of the condition of woman, which Pope inserts in his "Epistle to a
Lady":

> See how the World its Veterans rewards!
> A Youth of frolicks, an old Age of Cards,
> Fair to no purpose, artful to no end,
> Young without Lovers, old without a Friend,
> A Fop their Passion, but their Prize a Sot,
> Alive, ridiculous, and dead, forgot!
>
> (ll. 243–248)

Pope employs what is generally called the antithetical style, yes.
But he does so to assert an equivalence rather than an antimony.
The alternatives set out on either side of the caesura ought to be
contradictory: the sad reality is that they are not contradictory at
all. As a result the perversity and mutability of this world stand
forth all the more plainly. Life, in belying the expectations of the
heroic verse form,[13] exposes the shallow optimism of those who
look to find human felicity wherever they go. The last line but
one, with its beautiful phonetic architecture, carries within its own
grammar the clue to the entire technique. Really the word "but"
is a fraudulent usage. The genuine link to connect such indistinguishable fates would be "and." In the final line, however, there is
an authentic choice offered. Such an old age of tedium and dis-
honour may be a living death. But presumably most women would
prefer to be alive and ridiculous than dead and forgotten. The conjunction we might have anticipated in this case is "but." That the
connotations of such basic linguistic particles has been blurred is
no accident. This is the grammar of paradox, these are the language-
games played by satire.[14]

In Chapter X of *Peri Bathous,* Pope indulged himself in a little
fun at the expense of Lee, Ambrose Philips, Blackmore, and others,
with a section called "The Antithesis, or Seesaw." The trope was
defined as the figure "whereby Contraries and Oppositions are
balanced in such a way, as to cause a reader to remain suspended
between them, to his exceeding delight and recreation." [15] The ex-

amples cited show that Pope had in mind a sort of mechanical
oxymoron—"The Gods look pale to see us look so red." Pope himself
never fell victim to this functionless mode of opposing things, any
more than he did to the mindless parallelism which lesser writers
exacted from the couplet form; except that, as Peter Dixon has
neatly illustrated, he can employ "deliberately mechanical balance
and repetition" for a special purpose.[16] We rarely see Pope "culti-
vating expressive forms for their own sake." [17] He resists the easier,
more automatic effects of the heroic couplet in favour of a more
inward method. Once more the "Epistle to Arbuthnot" will provide
an instance:

> Yet then did *Gildon* draw his venal quill;
> I wish'd the man a dinner, and sate still:
> Yet then did *Dennis* rave in furious fret;
> I never answer'd, I was not in debt:
> If want provok'd, or madness made them print,
> I wag'd no war with *Bedlam* or the *Mint*.
> (ll. 151–156)

Initially one supposes that Gildon represents poverty, Dennis madness. Yet in the second line quoted, Pope emphasizes his own pas-
sivity—which in turn suggests the fury of Gildon, not of Dennis.
Similarly the fourth line constitutes in effect an answer to the first:
Pope's freedom from poverty allows him to escape the "raving" of
Dennis. In the last couplet appears a typical chiasmic sequence,
want/madness/Bedlam/Mint. Moreover want "provokes," that is,
stirs up and excites—the postponement of the composite object
"them" means that the verb attains an absolute or intransitive force.
This last is a common device in Pope. The total effect of this degree
of interplay is to indicate that madness and poverty are very near
allied. In Pope's world of Dunces, the Bedlamite and the pauper
are of imagination all compact. By the time we reach line 155, the
word "or" has become little more than a sign of equation. Behind
the superficial antithesis lies an inescapable identity. Behind the
conscious iteration used to mark Pope's own position ("I wish'd
. . . I never answer'd . . . I wag'd") lies a complex series of adjustments which go to illustrate the *unlikeness* of Pope from his oppressors.[18]

II

If, then, Pope is not confined to the cruder mechanisms of Augustan
verse, there is much in the satiric tradition that he does exploit. He
was not one to reject valuable effects simply because they were obvious or close at hand. The inheritance he enjoyed was one descend-
ing primarily from Waller, Dryden, and perhaps Prior.[19] Now, "The
facility provided by the couplet is that it requires the deployment
of specific meanings, moment by moment: every shot has to
count." [20] In other words, the couplet—unlike, say, the Pindaric
ode as then understood and practised—tends to deal with one thing
at a time. Its structure imposes a type of serial form on the material.[21] Hence the readiness with which it accommodates itself to
itemization: one thinks of the "receipt" or recipe pattern which
Pope used more than once. But yet again Pope's inclination is to
turn the inventory into something else. His lists, which at first
appear to follow passively the sequence of the line-units, generally
prove to have more autonomy, more life of their own. One might
instance the description of Narcissa ("Now deep in Taylor . . .
Now drinking citron . . . Now Conscience chills her . . .").[22] Or
take this passage from the "Epistle to Cobham":

> See the same man, in vigour, in the gout;
> Alone, in company; in place, or out;
> Early at Business, and at Hazard late;
> Mad at a Fox-chace, wise at a Debate;
> Drunk at a Borough, civil at a Ball,
> Friendly at Hackney, faithless at Whitehall.
>   (ll. 130–135)

The alternatives start off mildly enough, with each side capable of
an innocent interpretation—gout did not necessarily imply dissolute
living. As we move on, the more aggressive meanings force their
way to the surface. But at least, if it is unworthy always to be
gaming late into the night, there is the corresponding virtue of
being "early at Business." At this point, the stress is on the "puzzling
Contraries" which Pope has been anatomizing. By the last couplet,
our reaction has grown more suspicious. If the man is drunk at his
constituency, then doubtless that is because he has been spending
his time (to quote Bubb Dodington's immortal phrase) "in the in-

famous and disagreeable compliance with the low habits of venal wretches." [23] That he is civil at the mayoral ball, then, suggests no very honourable motive. This impression is confirmed in the last verse quoted. The members for Middlesex were nominated at Hackney, so the sense is patent: the man is ready with promises before the election, faithless afterwards. Both the alternatives offered are ignoble. Under cover of suggesting the variety of human character, Pope has insinuated one of his miniature exempla to reveal the present state of political morality.

The duplicity of this technique rests on a simple psychological fact. Augustan heroic verse is constructed around near-recurrences, elements which seem to resemble their predecessors but do not quite. In reality the poem is moving on, but the almost-congruous members (rhyme, metric pattern, often syntax) lull us into believing that no advance has been made. As Donoghue says, the ode delights in postponement. [24] The couplet, whatever its putative delays, entails constant progression. This is promoted partly by internal workings. With the line, "Poxed by her Love, or libell'd by her Hate," much of the impetus derives from the placing of the two crucial words at either end of the verse. The whole metrical scheme springs shut, with the hinge after the fourth syllable. Pope uses all kinds of means to give his lines this self-enclosed energy. Other poetic techniques, in other historical circumstances, have been designed to blur the divisions between separate units, to allow free movement back and forth among the constituent parts of the poem. But the entire aesthetic of Augustan England was ranged against such a practice—its entire ethic, too, one might almost say. The strength of eighteenth-century poetry at its best is that it is good at knowing the syntactic moment to leave. Pope's verse, above all, gains momentum and life from its refusal to merge one statement into another. Typically he achieves continuity by linguistic signals, by partial repetition or by some kind of verbal gesture ("Now . . . now/Hence . . . / Hear this! and . . ."). What he does *not* do is dislocate the structure of his language so that the sequence of ideas fluctuates or turns back on itself. [25]

The phrase "verbal gesture" perhaps calls for explanation. At its simplest, this takes the form of mimetic construction, where the connectives act out grammatically the relationship described. Sometimes this is done with prepositions, as with this passage from a satiric prose work of Pope, *A Further Account of the most Deplor-*

able Condition of Mr. Edmund Curll (1716). A porter is sent to find Curll's authors at various addresses, including "At the Laundresses, at the Hole in the Wall in *Cursitors* Alley, up three Pairs of Stairs, the Author of my *Church History*—if his Flux be over—you may also speak to the Gentleman who lyes by him in the Flock Bed, my *Index-maker*." Or again: "At a Tallow-chandlers in Petty *France*, half way under the blind Arch . . ." or "At the Bedsted and Bolster, a Musick House in *Morefields*, two Translators in a Bed together." [26] Now what Pope does with physical locations here, by means of prepositions and adverbs mainly, he does with moral relations elsewhere. And not necessarily in a context of satire: a straightforward case is the celebrated opening to *Windsor Forest*:

> The Groves of Eden, vanish'd now so long,
> Live in Description, and look green in Song:
> *These*, were my Breast inspir'd with equal Flame,
> Like them in Beauty, should be like in Fame.
> Here Hills and Vales, the Woodland and the Plain,
> Here Earth and Water seem to strive again,
> Not *Chaos*-like together crush'd and bruis'd,
> But as the World, harmoniously confus'd:
> Where Order in Variety we see,
> And where, tho' all things differ, all agree.
> Here waving Groves a chequer'd Scene display,
> And part admit and part exclude the Day;
> As some coy Nymph her Lover's warm Address
> Nor quite indulges, nor can quite repress.
>
> (ll. 7–20)

And so on. Obviously the controlling fact in this passage is the care with which the integrity of the line-unit is preserved. The major syntactical divisions all coincide with line-endings; minor breaks in the sense fall at the caesural pause. More remarkable, however, is something which does not necessarily follow from that state of affairs. In every case the beginning of the verse (after the very first, announcing the subject) conveys the relation of the ideas presented to those which have gone before. On occasions the relationship is spatial (here/where, and so on); sometimes it is one of analogy (like/as); sometimes the link is negative or restricted (not/and part). Throughout, the connectives provide us with a conducted tour not merely of the literal forest but also of its imaginative significance for Pope—its historical and mythopoeic identity. And these verbal signals emphasize the discrete nature of the units, structural or metrical, by the very act of describing their mutual relationship.

A more complex instance occurs in the delightful poem to Teresa Blount, on her banishment to the country after the coronation in 1714. The theme of the girl exiled from the pleasures of the town was a stock satiric occasion: *Rambler,* numbers 42 and 46, take it up. In Pope's version, fair Zephelinda is wafted away from gay sparks to "old-fashion'd halls, dull aunts, and croaking rooks":

> She went from Op'ra, park, assembly, play,
> To morning walks, and pray'rs three hours a day;
> To pass her time 'twixt reading and Bohea,
> To muse, and spill her solitary Tea,
> Or o'er cold coffee trifle with the spoon,
> Count the slow clock, and dine exact at noon;
> Divert her eyes with pictures in the fire,
> Hum half a tune, tell stories to the squire;
> Up to her godly garret after sev'n,
> There starve and pray, for that's the way to heav'n.
>
> (ll. 13–22)

Pope begins by reiterating the change enacted in Zephelinda's journey: she went "to plain-work, and to purling brooks . . ." Having accustomed us to this transition, he shifts from the prepositional "to" and drifts, inconsequentially as it seems, into the infinitive. A series of verbs, strictly in this same form, is now employed in the succeeding lines: muse/spill/trifle/count/dine/divert/hum/tell. Their frequency answers to the tedious routine of life: the absence of a subject robs them of the activity we associate with a verb. They are things going on without Zephelinda's conscious agency, almost without her connivance. Three of these truncated infinitives mark the opening of three lines in a row; then the miserable article "up"— again a verbless directive, appropriate to trance-like states such as sleepwalking. Then two more grey non-activities, as Zephelinda sees them: starve and pray. The fulcral point occurs at the strange cacophonous juncture "Or o'er cold coffee . . ." In the light of what has already been said, it should be no surprise that this grammatical

alternative turns out to be for Zephelinda no human alternative
at all.

Geoffrey Tillotson has written of Pope's poems that "they assemble
the least fluid parts of speech and yet escape congestion either of
meaning or metre"—an observation recalling Owen Barfield's similar
description of "architectural" poetry, where "the poet is working in
solid masses, not in something fluid." [27] The fact is that Pope was
not after fluidity, insofar as that represents a poetic virtue to us
today. He wanted poetry, just as Dr. Johnson did, to render the
existing categories of reality, and not to blur those essential differences in nature or in magnitude which were present in every sphere
of life—moral, social, physical, or metaphysical. The duty of language was to overcome the inarticulate energy of mere flux.

III

It is possible to distinguish broadly between two methods of organization in poetry: I will call these closed and open syntax. The
extreme form of open syntax is found in such modes of verse as
imagism, where prose logic has been abandoned and the only continuum is one of figurative association. But the method is found
in a good deal of older poetry, and it does not necessarily imply a
breakdown of all "logical" sequence. The differentia lies in the fact
that, where the syntax is open, there may be more than one separate
—indeed competing—manner of linking the units of sense, each of
which is logically feasible and poetically convincing.

One index of this state of affairs is the employment of light
punctuation. Of Puttenham's three "intermissions of sound," open
syntax characteristically utilises the comma as against the colon or
the period.[28] The reason is obvious. The comma is a fluid stop; it
may mark a break in thought, but it may not. And whereas a full
stop firmly closes one segment and introduces another, the comma
vacillates—its effect may, so to speak, stretch forward or back. The
words it governs (I do not think that is too strong a term) may be
affected in quite different ways. To this extent, it offers one more
type of ambiguity: but an ambiguity dependent not on the semantic
role of the words in question so much as on their structural role.

To speak again in general terms, I would regard open syntax as
the preferred mode of what might be styled the poetry of contemplation. By this I mean poetry which is absorbed by the sheer grandeur

or beauty or multiplicity of things as they are. It belongs to the
literature of *rapture,* more than anything else. In short, open syntax
is appropriate to a verse where relationships are in doubt, where
the simple quiddity or mere existence of things is more important
than the way in which they interact. The presence or immanence of
any object or idea can be rendered by nouns, even if the connectives
are in doubt or removed. To express a *state* requires no propositions
or verbs. As with the project in the Laputan Academy, the poet
need carry round with him only names for *things*—provided we take
that word to cover abstractions too. The poetry of contemplation
tends to move in a series of jerks from one object or essence to another; it operates like one of those guide-books which dilates im-
pressively on the merits of each tourist-attraction, but never explains
how the traveller can get from one to the next. It is a poetry of
localized celebration, not one of direction-finding.

To put the matter in this way is to invite the suspicion that a
hostile judgment is intended. In order to eliminate that impression,
I will cite briefly three outstanding examples of the style I have
attempted to describe. Firstly, the eleventh stanza of Milton's "Na-
tivity Hymn":

> At last surrounds their sight
> A Globe of circular light,
>   That with long beams the shame-fac't night array'd,
> The helmed Cherubim
> And sworded Seraphim
>   Are seen in glittering ranks with wings displaid,
> Harping in loud and solemn quire,
> With unexpressive notes to Heav'ns new-born Heir.

Writing of such sustained elevation and majesty needs no routine
critical commendation, which can only usurp the function of a
formal vote of thanks. It is noteworthy, however, that nouns and
adjectives dominate the stanza. The main verbs are few and rather
colourless: *surrounds, array'd* (in subordinate clause), *are seen.* All
the glitter and all the dignity proceed from the evocative or surprising
epithets (*shame-fac't, unexpressive*), as well as the clear ringing
nouns, usually rhyme-words. It is generally dangerous to place too
much reliance on punctuation in early texts, but we know enough
of Milton's own intentions to be sure that his best effects were not

achieved through the drunken invention of apprentice compositor
X or Y. It is interesting, then, to note the total absence of heavier
stops. The stanza was not, of course, chosen at random. But it is
not untypical. Stanzas xiv and xv also restrict themselves to commas
as far as intermediate punctuation goes: and so do the second and
third stanzas.

Not altogether dissimilar is the technique of this portion of Blake's
Jerusalem (c. 4, lxxxix). Here there are three colons, but they
divide off parts of a list, rather than serving their habitual grammatical end of marking syntactically discrete statements.

> Tho' divided by the Cross & Nails & Thorns & Spear
> In cruelties of Rahab & Tirzan, permanent endure
> A terrible indefinite Hermaphroditic form,
> A Wine-press of Love & Wrath, double, Hermaphroditic,
> Twelvefold in Allegoric pomp, in selfish holiness:
> The Pharisaion, the Grammateis, the Presbiterion,
> The Archiereus, the Iereus, the Saddusaion: double
> Each withoutside of the other, covering eastern heaven.
> Thus was the Covering Cherub reveal'd, majestic image
> Of Selfhood, Body put off, the Antichrist accursed,
> Covern'd with precious stones: a Human Dragon terrible
> And bright stretch'd over Europe & Asia gorgeous.
> In three nights he devour'd the rejected corse of death.

The very real power this stanza develops is generated by a sort of
galvanic running, jumping, and standing still—on the spot. There
is throughout a marked preference for heaping up and simply presenting: and so lists of nouns, avoidance of main verbs, particularly
active, transitive forms, and repeated appositional devices. Open
syntax often figures itself as a search for covert methods of achieving
the force, if not the reality, of apposition. Until the last line, Blake
confines himself to indicating and naming.

Finally, a familiar instance from Hopkins: the fourth stanza of
"The Wreck of the Deutschland":

> I am soft sift
> In an hourglass—at the wall
> Fast, but mined with a motion, a drift,
> And it crowds and it combs to the fall;

> I steady as a water in a well, to a poise, to a pane,
> But roped with, always, all the way down from the tall
> Fells or flanks of the voel, a vein
> Of the gospel proffer, a pressure, a principle, Christ's gift.

The peculiar lurching motion of this verse is aided by a number of technical features, notably the stanza-form (an impeded expansive movement) and the alliteration. There is a slightly garbled style of repetition, as though produced by a speech defect—the strange locution "*a* water in a well" has something of the effect of an involuntary reiteration, found in a Spoonerism or a tongue-twister: just as people will say, after a number of rapid attempts, "The Poleith police dismisseth uth." The net result is a series of parallel forays, a crab-wise advancement towards the final two words, where the spluttering alliteration is at length resisted. In Hopkins's case, the syntax is at once more complex, more interesting and more important than in either Milton or Blake. Nevertheless, it is evident that key moments of transition are marked by a comma; that, apart from line four, verbs play virtually no part in the organization; and that the line unit has little to do with the developing sense of the stanza.

Hopkins, to take another famous example, is interested in the windhover for what the bird is in itself. The falcon may represent the glory of God as mediated to us in "Brute beauty and valour and act": but the poet is not concerned with its position in the scale of things, earthly or divine. Augustan poetry, on the other hand, is very often about social intercourse, "conversation," ideas of hierarchy and subordination, of reciprocity—trade is the great image of moralists, poets and dramatists alike, as in *George Barnwell*. These mutual dealings can be on an abstract level: there is the interplay of private vice and public virtue in Mandeville's morality, which at times reads strangely like an algebraic sum. The poets of this age needed a form which could do more than assert that things are, or are not, the verse of wrapt contemplation or wonder. They sought an idiom that could define and illustrate *connections,* which might be causal or temporal or anything else. It was with this aim in view that they developed a style placing strong emphasis on connective particles and repetitive signals. The language is gestural; it conducts the reader along an intelligible itinerary, like a good cicerone, instead of simply showing him the sights.

One side effect of this elective affinity for sequentiality is that eighteenth-century poetry makes full use of the verse-form as given. The style allows the ideas of expressive units to flow with the tide. Now the fact is that any series of lines in themselves impose a chain of subsequence, which naturally hovers on the edge of a consequence by a *post hoc ergo propter hoc* trick in the reader's mind. The Augustan poets capitalized on this fact. It is an ineluctable feature of all poetry set out in consecutive lines—even freaks of the "Easter Wings" kind—that one verse follows another in a repeated wave-like motion. Even some forms of concrete poetry fall in with this pattern. A good many writers ignore this fact of aesthetic life as a tiresome contingency; others go so far as to make a positive effort to counteract its malign presence. The characteristic energy of Augustan verse is devoted to accepting and gratifying the need as one native to the condition of poetry. The couplet form, primarily, is a machine in which to live consecutively.

I say advisedly "couplet," without specifying the closed variety. Quite a high proportion of eighteenth-century poetry handles the couplet with some degree of licence. But the pentameter line and the emphatic rhyming normally found make for regularity, even where the sense floods over from one couplet to the next. Syntax, too, makes its contribution when parallel sentence-shapes are used —with a similar proviso, that semantically the parallelism may be a spurious one. Paul Fussell has said that "Pope customarily endstops tightly, and his endstopping helps enact his customary analytic view of his materials." [29] This is true; but the same one-thing-at-a-time manner of discourse can be achieved even where enjambement is rather free. The epistle to Bolingbroke will furnish an example:

> But when no Prelate's Lawn with Hair-shirt lin'd,
> Is half so incoherent as my Mind,
> When (each Opinion with the next at strife,
> One ebb and flow of all follies all my Life)
> I plant, root up, I build, and then confound,
> Turn round to square, and square again to round;
> You never change one muscle of your face,
> You think this Madness but a common case,
> Nor once to Chanc'ry, not to Hales apply;
> Yet hang your lip, to see a Seam awry!
>
> (ll. 165-174)

This passage beautifully renders the comic indecision Pope is, with studied mock-modesty, attributing to himself. The ideas play deftly in and out of the couplet. The sentence is organized around two long subsidiary clauses (concessive in effect, though introduced by "when"—the force is almost that of "*quand même* . . ."), followed by a series of verbs describing Bolingbroke's reaction. The main statement is delayed by the generalizing parenthesis, which brings Pope's whole biography into account. The "ebb and flow of follies" are exemplified in two casually analogical lines. In line 169, the repetition of the personal pronoun before "build," as against its omission before the surrounding verbs, adds to the impression of feckless vacillation. With the next line, Pope reverts to a rocking-horse measure which acts out a pointless turnabout:

> Turn round to square, and square to round again.

After this long catalogue of aimless meandering, Pope presents Bolingbroke's attitude as firm and straightforward: the syntax correspondingly abjures the finicky adjustments of parenthesis and antithetical phrasing. This is a beautiful piece of poetic workmanship; but it has little to do with those engines of tension which Mrs. Parkin describes so enthusiastically.

On most occasions, however, Pope does take advantage of the "facility" provided by the couplet: Donoghue's word is suggestive, in conveying the idea (along with that of capacity) of a trading arrangement, an understanding by which certain benefits can be obtained on agreed terms. An instance of the more usual method is the splendid peroration on Vice in the Epilogue to the Satires, I. Suddenly, with the ejaculation "Lo!" the calm prose logic is disrupted, and the tight endstopping is momentarily overset:

> *Virtue* may chuse the high or low Degree,
> 'Tis just alike to Virtue, and to me;
> Dwell in a Monk, or light upon a King,
> She's still the same belov'd, contented thing.
> *Vice* is undone, if she forgets her Birth,
> And stoops from Angels to the Dregs of Earth:
> But 'tis the *Fall* degrades her to a Whore;
> Let *Greatness* own her, and she's mean no more;
> Her Birth, her Beauty, Crowds and Courts confess,

Chaste Matrons praise her, and grave Bishops bless:
In golden Chains the willing World she draws,
And hers the Gospel is, and hers the Laws:
Mounts the Tribunal, lifts her scarlet head,
And sees pale Virtue carted in her stead!
Lo! at the Wheels of her Triumphal Car,
Old *England's* Genius, rough wtih many a Scar,
Dragg'd in the Dust! his Arms hang idly round,
Our Youth, all liv'ry'd o'er with foreign Gold,
Before her dance; behind her crawl the Old!
See throning Millions to the Pagod run,
And offer Country, Parent, Wife, or Son!
Hear her black Trumpet thro' the Land proclaim,
That "Not to be corrupted is the Shame."

(ll. 137–160)

With verse of such astonishing resource, one scarcely knows where to begin commentary. Confining attention to linguistic issues, however, one could point to the couplet,

Her Birth, her Beauty, Crowds and Courts confess,
Chaste Matrons praise her, and grave Bishops bless . . .

The inversion in the first line, with the mention first of the qualities, then the response, gives the reaction a sense of inevitability; phonetic likenesses in the second half of the verse subtly reinforce the impression of an automatic and mindless falling into line. When we come to the next line, the heavy assonance goes to produce a prim, tight-lipped air. Moreover, the omission of "her" at the end of the statement, where it would appear in prose, adds to the feeling that the bishops do not really know what it is they are blessing. This trick is used, incidentally, in the "Epistle to a Lady," where we are told of Atossa:

So much the Fury still out-ran the Wit,
The Pleasure miss'd her, and the Scandal hit.

(ll. 128–129)

where the identical notion of random and uncontrolled effect attaches to the second verb.

Even more interesting are lines 155–156 of the Epilogue, which run:

> Our Youth, all liv'ry'd o'er with foreign Gold,
> Before her dance; behind her crawl the Old!

Youth and age are isolated at the extreme edges of the couplet. They strain towards one another like jousting knights about to tilt; the remaining ideas are forced inwards and receive a new stress. This placing also sharpens the contrast between the antithetical verbs "dance" and "crawl." It thrusts attention on the rhyme word "Gold," which Pope wishes to get in the centre of our mind, as carrying the real moral urgency. Youth and age are examples of the subjects of Vice; they emphasise the range of humanity affected. Their banishment to the extreme limits of the couplet is symbolically appropriate.

IV

I have argued that closed syntax was peculiarly suited to the ends which eighteenth-century poets set themselves. It ministers to that coherence they habitually sought—that variety of precision which takes the form of knowing when you are moving from one thing to the next, and knowing too in what direction that move takes you.[30] This aptness could be explained by a number of factors. There is, for example, the continuing prestige of formal logic. The study of logic may not have occupied such an important place in education around 1700 as a century or more earlier. Yet one has only to recall R. S. Crane's persuasive argument that "old-fashioned textbooks in logic" still penetrated Swift's imagination sufficiently to set up the first vague stirrings of Book IV of *Gulliver*—the first distant prospect of Houyhnhnmland.[31] And apart from logic, there was the master-science of the seventeenth century, geometry. Descartes, Hobbes, Leibniz, and others had converted men to the view that the human condition could best be explained, literally or morally, in spatial terms. It is with Locke, however, that psychology becomes openly a *relational* subject; and this is where the Augustans got not merely an idiom but a way of disposing that idiom.

A glance at the contents page of the *Essay Concerning Human Understanding* immediately shows Locke's mind as operating across antimonies, as so many eighteenth-century poems do. Ideas "of

Sensation" are contrasted with those "of Reflection." There are ideas
of pleasure and pain, of duration and of expansion; ideas of cause
and effect, identity and diversity. There are clear and obscure ideas,
real and fantastical, distinct and confused, true and false. There are
abstract and concrete terms, and much else. As well as the antithetical habit of mind, the schematization illustrates a trick of thinking of ideas as combinations or dispersals of simpler essences.[32] The
alignment of moral and mathematical here is highly suggestive; this
is one version of the ethical calculus. But more to the point is the
stress Locke lays on that form of interaction which can be expressed
as a *dependency*.

Later on in his *Essay*, Locke comes to write of "Relation." The
understanding, he says, is not confined, in the consideration of anything, to that precise object: "it can carry any idea as it were beyond
itself, or at least look beyond it, to see how it stands in conformity
to any other."[33] He goes on to show how many words directly express a "reciprocal intimation," such as husband and wife; and
further, that certain words, apparently absolute, "do conceal a tacit,
though less observable, relation." *Old* and *imperfect* are cited as
cases in point.[34] Later still, Locke in his chapter "Of other Relations" describes various modes of comparison. These include "ideas
of proportional relations" (simple comparison, in effect); "natural
relation," arising out of "the circumstances of . . . origin or beginning" (blood ties and the like); "moral relations"; and "instituted
or voluntary relations." The last are especially interesting. These
have to do with "a moral right, power, or obligation to do something." Examples are a general's right to command an army, a citi-
zen's right to certain privileges. Locke defines this class of relation
in his normal contractual terms, as "depending upon men's wills,
or agreement in society." Then follows the significant passage:

> Now, though these are all reciprocal, as well as the rest, and
> contain in them a reference of two things one to the other;
> yet, because one of the two things often wants a relative name,
> importing that reference, men usually take no notice of it, and
> the relation is commonly overlooked: e.g. a patron and client
> are easily allowed to be relations, but a constable or dictator
> are not so readily at first hearing considered as such. Because
> there is no peculiar name for those who are under the com-
> mand of a dictator or constable, expressing a relation to either

of them; though it be certain that either of them hath a certain power over some others, and so is so far related to them, as well as a patron is to his client, or general to his army.[35]

There could be no more representative expenditure of energy, in the age, than an effort of this kind. Locke is attempting to uncover relationships of mutual obligation, based on patterns of dominance and submission. And Pope too was a child of his age. He could only make sense of things if he could see them in some sort of vertical, generally hierarchical, scheme. To understand how one man or one act "stands in conformity to any other" is to seize the moral, psychological, and social significance of those compared—i.e., both terms of the comparison.

An important rider follows from this. If a poetry of relational statements is one specially fitted for a particular historical context, it is also uniquely suitable for one literary form. Recently the phrase "situational satire" has gained some currency. But it is a redundant expression. All satire is a placing activity; it rests on the writer's being sure how one thing stands in relation to the next. The basic stance of the satirist is of one who knows a hawk from a handsaw. More pertinently, Augustan satire was built on a long tradition of *laus et vituperatio*: it dealt out praise or blame in accordance with standards which might be personal or public. Moreover, it commonly utilized devices such as mock-heroic, burlesque, parody, imitation—all of which imply a *dependency* of one thing upon another, all of which involve a locational activity by which one thing (the "parasite") is set against another (the "host").[36] Satire, in short, is inalienably comparative as regards both intent and method. Its style and literary structure reflect the fact.

Pope's poetry is one of sharply defined transitions, and its central merit is that it always knows where it is going. To put it in a slightly different way, ideas in Pope never hang about on the doorstep; if they are leaving, they leave. Some of the credit for this cleanness of outline may go to the heroic couplet, with its Miesian economy of design. A larger factor, I would contend, was the poet's unrelaxing vigilance in the matter of grammatical links and copulatives. The nature of his syntax—unambiguous, transparent, compact —was an essential precondition of his critique of the world: for satire, in describing how things stand in relation to one another, demands a language which likewise connects and locates.[37]

Yet I would not wish to end by merely adapting Lytton Strachey, and seeming to assert that closed syntax is Pope's criticism of life. Deft, shapely and high-pressured as his language is, it is only because of the higher imaginative ends it serves that we notice it at all. Bethel's sermon on temperance (*Sat.* II.ii) is astonishingly concise ("You know my Laconic Style," wrote Pope in a cable-ese letter to Dr. Cheselden).[38] But it is not the language poets use which confers immortality: in the end, it is ripeness of judgment which is all, in satire as in every sort of literature.

> How pale, each Worshipful and rev'rend Guest
> Rise from a Clergy, or a City, feast!
> What life in all that ample Body say,
> What heav'nly Particle inspires the clay?
> The Soul subsides; and wickedly inclines
> To seem but mortal, ev'n in sound Divines.
> On morning wings how active springs the Mind,
> That leaves the load of yesterday behind?
> How easy ev'ry labour it pursues?
> How coming to the Poet ev'ry Muse?
> Not but we may exceed, some Holy time,
> Or tir'd in search of Truth, or search of Rhyme.
> Ill Health some just indulgence may engage,
> And more, the Sickness of long Life, Old-age:
> For fainting Age what cordial drop remains,
> If our intemp'rate Youth the Vessel drains?
>
> (ll. 75–90)

NOTES

1. Joseph Spence, *Observations, Anecdotes and Characters of Books and Men,* ed. J. M. Osborn (Oxford, 1966), I, 8–10, §14–17. Spence quotes Pope's remark, "I did not follow the grammar [in the earliest reading of the classics he attempted], but rather hunted in the authors for a syntax of my own." (I, 11: §22.) See also George Sherburn, *The Early Career of Alexander Pope* (Oxford, 1934), pp. 38–41.

2. *Memoirs of Martinus Scriblerus,* ed. C. Kerby-Miller (New Haven, 1950), pp. 118–124, 129: see also notes, pp. 243–271. "Crambe" was defined by Nathaniel Bailey as "a Repetition of Words, or say-

ing the same Thing over again." A cognate form was "Crambo," a rhyming game; Kerby-Miller, p. 247.

3. Geoffrey Tillotson, *Augustan Poetic Diction* (London, 1964), pp. 14, 124.

4. Donald Davie, *Articulate Energy* (London, 1955), p. 82. Cf. "Syntax like Mathematics," pp. 91–95. Davie's phrase "the path of an energy through the mind" (p. 157) is a peculiarly apt one, for Pope just as much as for Wordsworth, whose poetry calls forth the expression.

5. Christine Brooke-Rose, *A Grammar of Metaphor* (London, 1958), pp. 21, 296. Pp. 303–305 are devoted to a summary of Pope's practice, based on the rather limited sample afforded by *Eloisa to Abelard*.

6. Rebecca Price Parkin, *The Poetic Workmanship of Alexander Pope* (Minneapolis, 1955), pp. 66–84.

7. See for example W. K. Wimsatt, "One Relation of Rhyme to Reason," in *The Verbal Icon* (Lexington, 1967), pp. 154 ff. Wimsatt's other valuable contributions to this broad field of study include *The Prose Style of Samuel Johnson* (New Haven, 1941), esp. chs. i, ii, on parallelism and antithesis, as well as ch. iv, "The Consistency of Johnson's Style," reprinted below; and his edition of *Alexander Pope: Selected Poetry and Prose* (New York, 1951), esp. pp. xxii–xxxiii.

8. Jonas A. Barish, *Ben Jonson and the Language of Prose Comedy* (Cambridge, Mass., 1960), p. 71. Much of Barish's excellent discussion is germane to the present essay: see for instance his comments on the "slight sense of *offness*" favoured by baroque writers (p. 73), which tallies with many of Tillotson's observations on the fondness in Pope for "unequal balance"—*On the Poetry of Pope* (Oxford, 2nd ed., 1950), pp. 127–128. For the Renaissance background, see also Brian Vickers, *Francis Bacon and Renaissance Prose* (Cambridge, 1968), ch. iv, "Syntactical Symmetry."

9. Quotations and line-references follow the one volume edition of the Twickenham text, published as *The Poems of Alexander Pope*, ed. J. Butt (London, 1963). I have disregarded *The Dunciad* in this essay, as I have commented extensively on the poem in my book on *Grub Street* and a forthcoming article on "Proper Nouns in *The Dunciad*."

10. See for instance Vickers, pp. 115–140. For the rhetorical figures alluded to in the text, see Vickers, p. 97, and Wimsatt, *Verbal Icon*, pp. 176–177.

11. Brooke-Rose, pp. 229–230. The same writer comments, "Pope . . . really lets himself go with verbs. He uses proportionately more intransitive verb metaphors than any other poet" (p. 235). Even where

the strict grammatical form is not that of a verb, Pope often manages to get an active propulsive force into other parts of speech.

12. Hor. *Sat.* ii.i.84–85. There is a kind of alliterative chiasmus here. very common in Pope: cf. "Riches that *vex*, and *vanities* that *tire*." The only reference to such a device I have seen is that of F. W. Hilles, "Johnson's Poetic Fire," *From Sensibility to Romanticism*, ed. Hilles and H. Bloom (New York, 1965), p. 72.

13. Tillotson writes that the Augustans "saw man as an oxymoron, a cross-hatching, a contradiction in terms . . . To say what they saw inevitably required the couplet" (*Augustan Poetic Diction*, p. 15). Arguably the last sentence overstates the matter. But in any case it is clear that the couplet is capable of expressing both massive certainties and prim compromise. According to W. H. Auden ("Pope," *From Anne to Victoria*, ed. B. Dobrée [London, 1937], p. 100), "no form will express everything, as each form is particularly good at expressing something. Forms are chosen by poets because the most important part of what they have to say seems to go better with that form than any other; there is generally a margin which remains unsaid . . ." In my view Pope often gains effects by playing off what the couplet *seems* to assert against what reality proclaims. For brief but excellent comments on the passage from the "Epistle to a Lady" quoted in the text, see Allan Rodway, "By Algebra to Augustanism," *Essays on Style and Language*, ed. R. Fowler (London, 1966), pp. 63–69.

14. For interesting comment on the use of these conjunctions, cf. Barish, p. 17; Brooke-Rose, pp. 80–87, 303. John Dennis sensed in an obscure way Pope's fondness for pseudo-linkage, whereby "he seems to take pains to bring *something* into a Conjunction Copulative with *nothing,* in order to beget *nothing.*" See his *Remarks on the Rape of the Lock* (1728), extracted by J. D. Hunt (ed.), *Pope: The Rape of the Lock/A Casebook* (London, 1968), p. 64. On Pope's deceptive use of the word "but," see A. L. Binns, " 'Linguistic' Reading," in Fowler, p. 125.

15. Quoted from Wimsatt, *Pope,* p. 334.

16. Peter Dixon, *The World of Pope's Satires* (London, 1968), p. 88. See also p. 96, on the "persistent balancing of the half-lines" in an imitation of Donne, so as to mime "the minuet-like progression of . . . court ritual."

17. Wimsatt, *Johnson,* p. 49.

18. Pope habitually breaks up lists by one means or another. A fair example would be the beginning of "Sober Advice from Horace," where the transition from common to proper nouns serves to fix the roster in the here and now (i.e. to resolve it), and yet paradoxically to disrupt the previous smooth sequence:

> The Tribe of Templars, Play'rs, Apothecaries,
> Pimps, Poets, Wits, Lord *Fanny's,* Lady *Mary's.*
>
> (ll. 1-2)

A double response is called for. Actually Hervey and Lady Mary are unmistakable, unique; but there is a subliminal idea of *"et hoc genus omne,"* so that the fearsome couple both belong to the list and subvert its reality. The repeated heavy stresses aid the process. "Lord" is actually in a weak position, metrically, but like "Pimps" it receives a fairly strong emphasis. We are drawn to feel that it is the lordship and ladyship of the couple (as well as their peculiar demerits) which align them with the rest of the tribe. For the use of the plural number, cf. my essay on "Proper Nouns in *The Dunciad."*

19. It is often forgotten that Prior's use of octosyllables in *Alma* by no means represents an invariable choice. *Solomon* antedates the greater part of Pope's major work, excluding the *Rape* and the *Iliad.*

20. Denis Donoghue, "Swift as Poet," in *Swift Revisited,* ed. Donoghue (Cork, 1968), p. 81.

21. Atterbury characteristically deplored the fact that there was "no distinction of parts" in English writers before Waller: see Geoffrey Tillotson, *Pope and Human Nature* (Oxford, 1959), p. 186. One recalls, too, Johnson's complaint that Prior's glorified Spenserian stanza became "unnecessarily tedious"—"an uniform mass of ten lines thirty-five times repeated, inconsequential and slightly connected, must weary both the ear and the understanding" (*Life of Prior*). The "want of method" which is the "great defect" of *The Seasons* (*Life of Thomson*) may likewise have been produced by the inconsequentiality of blank verse, as opposed to the "connectedly various" couplet—a misappropriation of Tillotson's phrase for Pope himself (*On the Poetry of Pope,* p 159).

22. "Epistle to a Lady, ll. 63–68: cf. Hor. *Ep.* ii.i.156–160.

23. *The Political Journal of George Bubb Dodington,* ed. J. Carswell and L. A. Dralle (Oxford, 1965), p. 264.

24. Donoghue, p. 79.

25. One of the most misleading passages in Pope occurs in what is perhaps an over-discussed poem today, the "Epistle to Burlington." We need, it may be, a new Laokoon in Pope criticism. Certainly the poet has the skill "decently to hide": but he pleasingly confounds us by quite other methods than varying and concealing the bounds of his verse. Or at least: if the limits of the couplets resemble a ha-ha, they do so all the more because you cannot after all get rid of a boundary, or move it, just be concealing it from the curious gaze.

Pope's description of Stanton Harcourt, in a letter to Lady Mary Wortley Montagu (dated 1718 by George Sherburn in his edition of the *Correspondence* [Oxford, 1956], I, 505) illustrates very clearly the *puzzled* reaction which men of the time display when "the whole is so disjointed, & the parts so detacht from one another, & yet so joining again one can't tell how." To this degree a house, like a poem, ought to be an organized arrangement, a configuration whose parts should relate to one another in an intelligible fashion. But by quoting this instance I am no doubt breaking the self-denying ordinance I have just set out.

26. *The Prose Work of Alexander Pope*, ed. N. Ault (Oxford, 1936), I, 278–279.

27. Tillotson, *On the Poetry of Pope*, p. 104; Owen Barfield, *Poetic Diction* (London, 2nd ed., 1952), p. 96.

28. There are some useful remarks on this topic in Ian A. Gordon, *The Movement of English Prose* (London, 1966), pp. 20–22.

29. Paul Fussell, *Poetic Meter and Poetic Form* (New York, 1967), p. 117.

30. One might adapt a passage from *Rambler* no. 137 to the poetic context: "The chief art of learning . . . is to attempt but little at a time. The widest excursions of the mind are made by short flights frequently repeated; the most lofty fabricks of science are formed by the continued accumulation of single propositions." The phrase omitted and replaced by dots was "as Locke has observed."

It is because he fails to appreciate this aggregative intention, I think, that Francis Berry presents so unfavourable a view of Pope's linguistic effects. In Pope, he writes, "the Verbs have only local application. Though they perform their logical and syntactical purpose with a marvellous efficiency, having served that immediate purpose they do not act on the Verbs of other passages, or on passages as a whole, whether adjacent or distant. Having served their immediate purpose their energy expires"—*Poets' Grammar* (London, 1957), p. 122. Quite so: but this is precisely the aim of analytic poetry and of closed syntax.

31. R. S. Crane, "The Houyhnhnms, the Yahoos and the History of Ideas," *Reason and the Imagination*, ed. J. A. Mazzeo (London, 1962), pp. 243 ff.

32. "Essences" is used in the non-technical sense. It is of course a slippery term, as Locke himself recognised (III.iii.12.)

33. *Essay*, II.xii.4. In fact all three sorts of idea seem to involve relations; but I am concerned simply with what Locke himself says.

34. *Essay*, II.xxv.1–3.

35. *Essay*, II.xxviii.1–4.

36. Johnson characteristically defines burlesque in terms of disproportion (*Life of Butler*). It is instructive to contemplate, too, the distortions of scale which underlie so much satire, notably *Gulliver's Travels*.

As a final observation, one may adduce the fact that within Pope's lifetime Johnson was busy composing parliamentary debates. The closest student of this undertaking has noted that "Johnson tends to treat each speech as a unit, to give each . . . a carefully turned beginning and an end." Again, "Johnson, when he writes a succession of short speeches, tends to treat it as a series." In fact the real debates contained more forensic interplay and cross-cut exchange. Johnson's speeches depart from reality under this very aspect; they "have little relation to one another." See B. B. Hoover, *Samuel Johnson's Parliamentary Reporting* (Berkeley and Los Angeles, 1953), pp. 61, 135–136.

37. As regards the larger organizational units in the poem, one may set alongside this account Earl Wasserman's description of the "disjunctive blocks" which make up Pope's "Ode for Musick": quoted in Maynard Mack (ed.), *Essential Articles for the Study of Alexander Pope* (London, 1964), p. 167. If the Jacobean nightmare was that things would fall apart, the primal Augustan terror was that everything would *merge*. A contrast might also be drawn with Milton. Ronald D. Emma has this to say of *Milton's Grammar* (The Hague, 1964), "He was seldom in a hurry to leave an idea . . . Where we would now require periods Milton often uses colons, semicolons, or commas, perhaps with a rhetorical rather than a strictly logical objective. It is a patience-trying task to determine where one sentence ends and another begins according to our conventions" (p. 142). Emma calls Milton "a poet of qualification more than of predication" (p. 142). This recalls Josephine Miles's distinction between phrasal and clausal poetry: see *Eras and Modes in English Poetry* (Berkeley and Los Angeles, 1957). In Professor Miles's scheme, Pope emerges as a "balanced" poet, along with Hopkins, as against the "phrasal" Milton and Blake (pp. 8–9). There is not space to argue out my disagreements with Professor Miles, which spring chiefly from the method she has chosen to adopt. But my own view is that a less crude apparatus than the simple count of the adjective-verb ratio would show Pope to be a highly predicative poet. Finally his imaginative technique is one of assertion rather than description.

38. Pope, *Correspondence*, IV, 372.

LOUIS T. MILIC

Swift and Syntactical Connection

"A close reasoner and a good writer in general may be known by his pertinent use of *connectives*." [1] Although Coleridge illustrated this opinion with a reference to the seventeenth-century Whig, Samuel Johnson, it is especially applicable to Swift. His way with conjunctions and related words is a fundamental aspect of his writing.

Curme traces the history of the modern use of subordination and connection (hypotaxis) from a primitive stage of communication, in which related propositions were simply laid side by side, the relationship to be discerned by the reader (parataxis). [2] Proverbs still retain that paratactic feature: "Easy come, easy go." The intermediate stage between parataxis and full hypotaxis is one in which *and* is made to serve all kinds of connective uses, as in such dialects as Irish English, for example: "Did you not hear his reverence, and he speaking to you now?" [3] It is possible to see a remnant of this earlier syntax in the still common omission of such relatives as *which* or *that* in modern English prose; and paratactic clauses are not always considered reprehensible even in formal writing. Nonetheless, the avoidance of connectives is the exception in modern English.

Though it may be surmised that the extensive use of connectives

From *A Quantitative Study of Swift's Style* (Mouton, The Hague, 1967), pp. 122–35. Reprinted by permission of the publisher and author.

has rendered English less direct and perhaps less colorful, there is no gainsaying that the language has increased in clarity and logical power since their emergence. But more than one writer has probably become aware of the suspicion expressed by the eighteenth-century rhetorician George Campbell: "Of all the parts of speech, the conjunctions are the most unfriendly to vivacity." [4] Perhaps as a product of these conflicting trends, there is a wide variation in the use of connectives in such matters as choice and range of types, positioning, frequency. In this stylistic feature, it may be expected that mature writers will express a consistent preference which may be isolated by careful examination.[5]

The problem of connectives is closely related to the questions of transition and of reference. A writer articulating his thought wishes to indicate the relationship of each segment to the next and to suggest at intervals how far he has gone in the argument, as well as to set at rest any questions that may arise in the mind of the reader. The solution to this problem is in part structural, a matter of organizing the parts of the discourse into a rational and coherent order. But to do so provides only a partial solution, given the complexity of human thought and the unwillingness of many readers. Connective signposts provide the reader with the author's own key to the relation of the materials and throw the entire composition into focus. Good writers must always be concerned about the appropriateness of their connectives, as Locke suggests:

> The words whereby [the mind] signifies what connexion it gives to the several affirmations and negations, that it unites in one continued reasoning or narration, are generally called *particles*: and it is in the right use of these that more particularly consists the clearness and beauty of a good style. To think well, it is not enough that a man has ideas clear and distinct in his thoughts, nor that he observes the agreement or disagreement of some of them; but he must think in train, and observe the dependence of his thoughts and reasonings upon one another. And to express well such methodical and rational thoughts, he must have words to show what connexion, restriction, distinction, opposition, emphasis, &c., he gives to each respective *part* of his discourse. To mistake in any of these, is to puzzle instead of informing his hearer: and therefore it is, that those words which are not truly by themselves the names of any ideas are

of such constant and indispensable use in language, and do much contribute to men's well expressing themselves.[6]

A plausible place to begin the search for connectives is the beginning of a sentence. Swift had a predilection for coordinating conjunctions at the head of his sentences. A rough preliminary count was made of the first word in several hundred sentences from the works of Swift and a selection of authors whose styles had considerable reputations: Addison, Johnson, Gibbon, Macaulay, Samuel Butler, and Hemingway.[7] The predominant impressions emerging from an inspection of the results are these: Gibbon begins forty per cent of his sentences with articles, Swift only ten per cent of his, the others falling between, near the low end, conversely, only ten per cent of Gibbon's sentences begin with pronouns, whereas nearly half of Hemingway's do, Swift being second with thirty per cent; as might have been expected, Hemingway uses fewest introductory conjunctions, but the other writers, headed by Johnson and Swift, are quite uniform in this category. Gibbon and Hemingway, it seems, represent polar extremes in introductory habits; Swift and Butler are remarkably similar, except for conjunctions. The most interesting finding, however, is that Swift uses more than twice as many coordinating conjunctions as Gibbon and Johnson, the runners-up. This count, tentative as it is, supports the observation I had made while reading *Gulliver's Travels* that Swift seemed to begin many sentences with coordinating conjunctions. A more precise count was now in order to test the accuracy of the observation with more significant data.

For this tabulation, the authors are limited to Addison, Johnson and Macaulay, in addition to Swift.[8] Only three classes of introductory words are counted: coordinating conjunctions, subordinating conjunctions, and conjunctive adverbs and phrases.[9] The results of this test are gratifyingly conclusive.[10] Table 5.1 gives the details. Altogether, Swift's use of the connectives in these three classes is more than twice as great as that of any of the three other writers.[11] To the reader of Swift, it would appear that he begins one sentence in five with a coordinating conjunction and one in three with a connective of some sort. The details of the tabulation further reveal that Swift makes unusually heavy use of *and, but* and *for,* half his connectives consisting of these three, the favorite being *but.*[12] This

Table 5.1

Percentage of initial connectives in 2000-sentence samples of Addison, Johnson, Macaulay and Swift

Connective	Addison	Johnson	Macaulay	Swift
C	5.5	5.8	7.4	20.2
S	7.1	6.2	4.1	5.4
SC	3.3	1.4	1.5	8.3
TOTAL	15.9	13.4	13.0	33.9

pattern of preference is surely a striking peculiarity of his style.[13] Perhaps this peculiarity is most striking because of the limitation it implies. A writer who begins one-sixth of his sentences in much the same way will seem monotonous and repetitious. Moreover, it might be difficult to imagine how he could readily adapt such a mechanism to the necessity of varying his transitions from point to point, unless he wrote always about the same subject or unless his arguments followed a rigidly similar pattern.

But limitation seems unlikely. A glance at the list of Swift's writings reveals a wide range of interests: politics, religion, economics, manners, language, history, even "Thoughts on Various Subjects," which may be taken as a symbol of his wide-ranging mind. Neither is it true that his method of argument is always the same. Some works are expository and some persuasive; some operate by *reductio ad absurdum,* some by irony, some by paradox, sarcasm, even vilification; some are satirical, some parodic, some homiletic, some narrative. In this storehouse of matters and manners one can readily detect what no one seems inclined to deny him: a flexible and versatile mind, unlikely to be dully bound to a minute repetory of introductory devices, especially a mere triad of conjunctions.

The three coordinating conjunctions in question (*and, but, for*) may from the "notional" point of view be considered as additive, adversative, and causal. It is true that these three functions seem to represent the major types of links between related propositions. But it is unlikely that they would alone offer adequate subtlety of nuance for an ingenious reasoner like Swift. I speculated that in some manner these conjunctions were varied, were given a different coloring from one use to the next in order to accomplish the variety of tasks that connectives are used for. A possibility that seemed likely, on the basis of an earlier observation I had made, was the linking of the introductory word with some following word in order to produce a suitable range of compounds, such as *and* plus another connective. An examination of a number of Swift's works reveals that a coordinating conjunction is indeed often followed by another word which may be classified as a connective or which has connective quality.[14]

In English it is normal to expect to find the subject (a noun or nominal) near the beginning of a sentence. When the sentence begins with a connective, it is safe to expect that the next word will be a nominal or a determiner. But a surprising number of times [15] the subject is deferred to make way for a connective or transitional word. Such collocations may be found on almost any page of Swift's works.[16] It is possible to infer, after one has gathered a sufficient number of illustrations of this procedure, that Swift does not use his introductory *and, but* or *for* in the customary way, in order to impart the logical aspect of the connection between one sentence and the next. Rather, he seems to use it as a kind of neutral connective, that is, a word which shows only that one sentence is connected with another without reference to the nature of the connection.[17]

Despite Swift's considerable dependence on a limited number of coordinating conjunctions, his use of connectives of all types is less limited than his contemporaries'. This hypothesis was tested by counting the number of connective types that appear in consecutive 1000-word samples of Addison, Johnson, Gibbon and Swift. The results, which are merely indicative, are given in Table 5.2.

Table 5.2

Number of different connective types in two 1000-word samples of
Addison, Johnson, Gibbon and Swift

	Addison	Johnson	Gibbon	Swift
Types	20,20	12,21	19,12	22,25

In a thorough study of Swift's vocabulary, we should expect to find a large number of the standard connectives, a number of words used as connectives which are not primarily connectives (*now, then, again*) and a variety of phrases serving as connectives (*'tis true, for these reasons*). This range of variety together with his predilection for introductory connectives and his dependence on a favorite triad of conjunctions implies a pattern of use which is quite consistent, both with itself and with as much of his personality as it may be relevant to refer to.

The classification of connectives into grammatical types on the basis of their function is a well-established practice, both in traditional grammars and in modern works. The logical or "notional" classification has been set aside, however, with much of the terminology of traditional rhetoric.[18] It is perhaps that readers and especially writers realized that such notional concepts as "causal," "concessive," "adversative," "alternative" and the like did not say enough about the types of relationships possible between propositions. Connectives themselves are mere shorthand means to that end. Obviously, complicated relationships require more than a mere *but* or *however* can provide. Such connections must be outlined with all the logical facilities inherent in discursive prose. But for the purpose of moving the reader's attention in the direction of a certain type of expectation or disappointment, these *buts, fors* and their more elaborate brethren have their use. Curiously enough, the most sophisticated writers have sometimes sedulously avoided making use of any more of these than the inevitable *and,* suggesting in this way that their subtlety of thought transcended mechanical means of showing relationships or perhaps that the relation was so inescapable that marking it would be anti-climactic. Conversely, it is possible to use connective words without reference to their notional significance. It is this that Swift does quite frequently with his *ands, buts* and *fors,* as well as with some others.

Normally, when a sentence begins with *for* (in itself rather uncommon), it is expected that the relationship between the previous sentence and the present one will be causal or resultative or the like, "Introducing the ground or reason of something previously said." [19] Swift, however, begins a sentence with *for* which opens a paragraph containing an announced digression from the main line of narrative:

But all would not suffice, and the Ladies aforesaid continued still inflexible: To clear up which Difficulty, I must with the Reader's good Leave and Patience, have recourse to some Points

of Weight, which the Authors of that Age have not sufficiently
illustrated.

For, about this Time it happened a Sect arose, whose Tenents
obtained and spread very far . . .[20]

It is evident that the purpose of this *for* is merely to supply a connection between the matter being dwelt on and the matter now introduced as illustrative of it. The conjunction *for* in that location might
very readily be replaced by *thus* or *so* or even the bare indefinite
article ("A sect arose . . ."), and in the prose of another writer
might well have been, but Swift prefers to suggest a specious causality as a means of directing his reader.

In the same way, Swift uses the conjunction *nor* in the first paragraph of Section IX of *A Tale of a Tub* ("A Digression concerning
Madness"): "nor shall it any ways detract from the just Reputation
of this famous Sect, that its Rise and Institution are owing to such
an Author as I have described Jack to be." [21] The promise made by
that initial *nor* is that the writer will continue to give reasons why
the Aeolists' ("this famous Sect") reputation should not be attacked.
In fact, in the previous section Swift has introduced the Aeolists
and ironically proposed to do them justice but has not given any
reasons for the depreciation of their reputation. Instances of this
sort, where the notional aspect of the connective is either wholly
disregarded or distorted or made use of for the purpose of suggesting
a relationship which has not been presented, are very frequent. To
this might be added those uses of connectives which exaggerate or
intensify beyond what seems reasonable the relationship between the
current statement and a previous or remote one.

As an illustration, the two paragraphs which follow may be cited:

Lord Peter was also held the Original Author of Puppets and
Raree-Shows; the great Usefulness whereof being so generally
known, I shall not enlarge farther upon this Particular.

But, another Discovery for which he was much renowned,
was his famous Universal Pickle. *For* having remark'd how
your Common Pickle in use among Huswives, was of no farther
Benefit than to preserve dead Flesh, and certain kinds of Vegetables; Peter, with great Cost as well as Art, had contrived a
Pickle proper for Houses, Gardens, Towns, Men, Women,
Children, and Cattle; wherein he could preserve them as

Sound as Insects in Amber. *Now,* this Pickle to the Taste, the Smell, and the Sight, appeared exactly the same, with what is in common Service for Beef, and Butter, and Herrings (and has been often that way applied with great Success) *but* for its many Sovereign Virtues was a quite different Thing. *For* Peter would put in a certain Quantity of his Powder Pimperlim pimp, after which it never failed of Success.[22]

In this passage, five connectives are italicized, of which four might very easily be spared as guides to the notional relationship between the elements they govern. This is not to say that they might altogether be spared, because they perform a function of a special nature, unlike the interior *but* whose function is precisely adversative, opposing the sovereign virtue of the pickle with its common appearance. However, the initial *but* implies that the discovery of the pickle will be enlarged on, unlike that of Puppets and Raree-shows which will not, but it actually opposes the dismissal of further discussion about the two items with another discovery for which Peter is renowned. Although this appears to be a mere rhetorical error, it is wholly in the spirit of Swift's irregular use of these introductory particles. This is fully shown by the initial *for* which follows the antecedent *but*. Its value seems closest to *thus* or other illustrative connective, fulfilling a function designed to display a stage or point in the argument, like the *now* which follows it, and whose notional value is approximately null. The final *for* possesses a hint of indispensability, as it pretends to connect the unexpected sovereign virtue of the pickle with an explanation of its operation. Nonetheless, its presence is supererogatory, as can be demonstrated by a re-writing of the passage without the four dispensable connectives:

Lord Peter was also held the Original Author of Puppets and Raree-Shows; the great Usefulness whereof being so generally known, I shall not enlarge farther upon this Particular.

Another Discovery for which he was much renowned, was his famous Universal Pickle. Having remark'd how your Common Pickle in use among Huswives, was of no farther Benefit than to preserve dead Flesh, and certain kinds of Vegetables; Peter, with great Cost as well as Art, had contrived a Pickle proper for Houses, Gardens, Towns, Men, Women, Children and Cattle; wherein he could preserve them as Sound as Insects in Amber. This Pickle to the Taste, the Smell, and the Sight, appeared exactly the same, with what is in common Service for Beef, and Butter, and Herrings, (and has been often that way applied with great Success) but for its many Sovereign Virtues was quite a different Thing. Peter would put in a certain Quantity of his Powder Pimperlim pimp, after which it never failed of Success.

This passage in the revised version can be understood as readily as the original and is perhaps a little more compact. The change that took place points to the unorthodox use of these connectives. The omission of two *fors,* a *but* and a *now* does not so much obscure the relationship of the parts, which is obvious enough, as it removes the emphasis, the continuity, what might be called the entrainment of the passage. Such use of more words than are strictly necessary, however it may resemble pleonasm, because it is directed toward the more accurate reception of the message, is in the spirit of the redundancy valued by communications engineers.

A similar pseudo-pleonastic use of connectives is found where two are used instead of one. Usually these combinations consist of a coordinating conjunction followed by a conjunctive adverb. The most common, one for which eighteenth-century rhetoricians and lexicographers castigated Swift, is *but however,*[23] as in, "But however, such great Frenzies being artificially raised . . ."[24] Other adversative combinations present *but* with a phrase, as in "But on the other side, whoever should mistake the Nature of things so far . . ."[25] Additive pleonasms are common with *and:* "and, indeed, if the former Danger . . .";[26] "And besides there was already in the Town . . .";[27] "And likewise because too great an Affectation of Secrecy . . .";[28] Other combinations may be found of varying rarity: "But still, there is in this Project a greater Mischief . . ."[29] "Or perhaps they scare us . . ."[30] A cursory examination reveals that of the cited pairs either word alone would suffice. That Swift uses both should lead us to wonder whether he intends the particular effect or whether the mechanism and the resultant effect were beyond the reach of Swift's consciousness.

Another type of connective use may help to elucidate this question. It has been shown that introductory connectives (usually coordinating conjunctions) are used as mere links or joints in the syntactic architecture of Swift's prose. The actual task of specifying a notional relationship is handed over to a pleonastic or redundant pair. More often, however, the introductory group of connectives is made up of two or more from different notional classes. These usually consist of *and, but, for* followed by a conjunctive adverb or a subordinating conjunction, though others appear as well.

The most common combination is the one beginning with *and*, which is found with a very wide variety of companions: *and after all, and although, and as, and if, and therefore, and thus*. Some more elaborate examples may be unearthed: *and indeed if*,[31] *and likewise because*,[32] *and therefore as*,[33] *and therefore when*,[34] and perhaps most interesting, *and therefore if notwithstanding!* [35] There is a large number of *but if, but though, but when, but whether*, and *but while* combinations, not to mention all the derivatives of *for, or, nor, so, neither, yet*.

If it is recalled that these groupings occur at the head of sentences, it may be inferred that Swift is availing himself of two rhetorical opportunities. He is modifying the plain and rather bare character of the unadorned connective, especially the favored triad, and presenting it in such a variety of guises that his prose achieves a highly diversified appearance, far more so than could be guessed by the frequency with which these particular three recur. Moreover, he presents his reader, at the beginning of each sentence headed by this kind of grouping, with a set of guides to the relationships involved in the thought which is often contradictory, for example, *for although* in "For although he were at last undeceived and reconciled to her, yet I lost all Credit with him." [36] The combination of causal with concessive, pretending to adduce a result of some antecedent happening but diluting it was a concession or diminution of the explanation, is confusing if not contradictory. But in the sentence cited it may be seen that both *for* and *yet* do not function except for emphasis. The sentence makes perfect sense without them. They are not confusing because they are, as before, merely emphatic or redundant.[37]

A concatenation such as *and therefore if notwithstanding*, which consists of three essential elements, each one promising the later introduction of a relevant clause, would burden the reader's mind with an excess of difficulty before permitting him to proceed with the argument. Actually, the sentence in which that grouping occurs, even out of context and without punctuation is not difficult to understand:

and therefore if notwithstanding all I have said it shall still be
thought necessary to have a bill brought in for repealing Christianity I would humbly offer an amendment that instead of the
word Christianity may be put religion in general which I conceive will much better answer all the good ends proposed by
the projectors of it.[38]

To say that something is not difficult to understand is not to say
that it is especially clear. The clarity with which Swift has always
been credited is not helped by this proceeding. It is well-known that
Swift favored clarity as a characteristic of style, and it seems therefore likely that he would have eschewed what in his writing might
be inimical to it. It can hardly be supposed that he would think the
multiplication of non-essential connectives at the beginning of sentences a help to clarity. The conclusion cannot be escaped that Swift
was not aware of the extensiveness or the idiosyncrasy of his practice
in this regard. Even his manuscript corrections and textual variants
do not show any curbing of this trait, but rather a juggling of *yets*
and *fors*.[39] He revised the surface but could not modify the fundamental structure. One of his recent editors, commenting on the
ineffectiveness of Swift's revisions, specifies it accurately: "He was
struggling against a tendency to write in just the way he disliked." [40]
This observation is supported by the constant gap between Swift's
ideals of style and his practice.

A prose which is as extensively connected as Swift's has been
shown to be cannot fail to impress the reader. His attention is inevitably called to the connective tissue between sentences, although
the effect must be to a great extent below the hreshold of consciousness, judging by the lack of comment about this feature of Swift's
writing. Nonetheless, the connectives must diffuse an appearance of
great logic, convey the picture of a writer whose material is so ready
to his mind that he distributes concessions, hypotheses, causes, results with such freedom that he can scarcely fit them all into his
sentences. But, in spite of the forbidding aspect of some of these
mounds of connectives, the reader has no difficulty in understanding;
in fact, he is not at all put off by the complex web of inter-relation-
ships. Because he does not realize that his understanding is due to
the redundant nature of the connective guides, he reaches the conclusion that the writer is eminently logical, transpicuously clear, and
economical with words to the point of terseness.

Clarity of language, it has often been said, results when clarity of thought is adequately translated into words. That this is an inadequate concept scarcely needs documentation. Swift's reader is permitted to glimpse the complexity of a question or event and given a succession of interrelated data providing a semblance of inevitability, in a manner exuding vigor and confidence. Because the randomness of events has been given form, the reader feels enlightened by order and clarity.

But it is persuasiveness, not clarity, which results from Swift's use of connectives.[41] The enchainment of sentences by means of connectives carries the reader along with great mobility and induces him to believe in the clarity and simplicity of what he has read.[42] He has been moved rapidly through Swift's line of argument, has become persuaded by it and has emerged feeling that everything is clear. And Swift's handling of connectives is an important factor in that success.

NOTES

1. Samuel Taylor Coleridge, *Table Talk*, 15 May 1833.
2. George O. Curme, *Syntax* (Boston, 1931), p. 170.
3. *Ibid.*, p. 172, a quotation from J. M. Synge, *The Well of the Saints*.
4. *The Philosophy of Rhetoric* (London, 1776), III.iv.1.
5. The study of individual preferences in the choice of particles is one that has had much vogue in classical scholarship. See, for example, J. D. Denniston, *The Greek Particles*, 2d ed. (Oxford, 1954), pp. lxxviii–lxxxii. Cf. Gilbert Highet, *Poets in a Landscape* (Harmondsworth, 1959): "It is possible . . . to learn much about Plato by studying something apparently so insignificant as his use of particles —the little almost-meaningless words of emphasis and qualification like, 'of course,' 'certainly', 'at least', in which the Greek language is so rich, and which (in written prose) perform the same function as gestures, voice-tones, and facial expressions in conversation" (p. 157). *Particles* is a broader term than *connectives,* but some of the connectives considered below have only ill-defined connective functions.
6. John Locke, *An Essay Concerning Human Understanding,* ed. A. C. Fraser (Oxford, 1894), II, 98–9.
7. The sample of Swift included material from his "signed" and his "anonymous" material and was about 1300 sentences in extent. The material for the other authors included about 400 sentences for each. The grammatical categories are the conventional ones. The evidence

is not presented in any detail because no conclusions are drawn from the figures.

8. Samples are two-thousand periods long.

9. Examples of coordinating conjunctions (C), *and, but, or;* subordinating conjunctions (S), *after, when, if;* conjunctive adverbs, or sentence-connectors (SC), *however, therefore, in the meantime, in short.*

10. With a standard deviation of 8.8, the results are significant at the five per cent level, though there are only four sub-samples.

11. It would be interesting to be able to compare these figures with those of some other worker. But the only possible comparison is not very instructive. Robert R. Aurner, "Caxton and the English Sentence," *Wisconsin Studies in Language and Literature,* No. 18 (1923), does not define *connective* and uses samples of 100 sentences. He finds that Addison begins 2 sentences with connectives, Macaulay 16, and Johnson 17 in the *Rambler* and 5 in the *Lives* (p. 50).

12. Of the 2,000-sentence sample, Swift begins 678 with a connective and 354 with *and, but* or *for.*

13. It seems to be a practice frowned on by the more puristic rhetoricians. See, for instance, James Harris, *Hermes* (London, 1751): ". . . in the modern polite Works . . . scarce such a thing as a Particle, or Conjunction is to be found." Even more particular is *The London Universal Letter-Writer* (c. 1800): "I hate particles where they are avoidable; be therefore sparing in your *fors,* your *buts,* and your *ands.*" Both are quoted in *English Examined,* compiled by Susie I. Tucker (Cambridge, 1961), pp. 81, 146-7. See also Campbell, *Philosophy of Rhetoric,* III.v.1-2.

14. Expressions with such connective quality include, apart from conjunctive adverbs, a number of adverbs, such as *perhaps, then, surely,* and phrases like *of course, to be sure, on the other hand.*

15. On the basis of a rough count without statistical pretensions, I would say between a quarter and a third of the time.

16. In *Prose Works,* ed. Herbert Davis, 14 vols. (Oxford 1939-64), III, the following examples were found: "But, although" (58), "And first" (58), "But then" (59), "But, at present" (59), "But, by the Way" (60), "And for that Reason" (61), "And indeed" (63), "But as" (63), "And, not to mention more" (65), "But however" (65), "Or else" (66), "But beside" (67), "And so" (69), "But after all" (71), "For where" (75).

17. It is possible to observe a similar use in the King James version of the Bible and in some other seventeenth-century stylists. Swift was, it must be recalled, thirty-three before the century ended, and it is not unreasonable to suppose that he was subject to the same influences as affected the other writers of his time. That is, if he uses introductory conjunctions in the same way as the King James version, it

need not be because he imitated the Biblical style, though he was doubtless subject to its influences. It is more probable that he responded to the challenge of connection in the same way as the translators of the Bible did.

18. Both classifications are used in two such different books as George O. Curme, *English Grammar* (New York, 1947), and Harold Whitehall, *Structural Essentials of English* (New York, 1956).

19. *Oxford English Dictionary*, s.v. *For*, conj.

20. *A Tale of a Tub, Works*, I, 45–6.

21. *Works*, I, 102.

22. *A Tale of a Tub, Works*, I, 67–8, italics supplied.

23. Sterling A. Leonard, *The Doctrine of Correctness in English Usage 1700–1800* (Madison, 1929), p. 280.

24. *Examiner, Works*, III, 65.

25. *A Tale of a Tub, Works*, I, 31.

26. *Examiner, Works*, III, 63.

27. *History of the Four Last Years of the Queen, Works*, VII, 142.

28. *Free Thoughts, Works*, VIII, 81.

29. *Argument, Works*, II, 30.

30. *Examiner, Works*, III, 17.

31. *Examiner, Works*, III, 63.

32. *Free Thoughts, Works*, VIII, 81.

33. *Freemen of Dublin, Works*, XIII, 85.

34. *Hatred of Clergy, Works*, XIII, 124.

35. *Argument, Works*, II, 37.

36. *Gulliver, Works*, XI, 50.

37. This closely resembles what Denniston, p. xli, calls the "corresponsive use of particles" in Greek: "Coherence of thought is adequately secured by the presence of a backward-pointing particle. The reader or listener, when he has reached a certain point, meets a particle which looks back to the road he has traversed, and beckons him on in a certain direction. But greater coherence is attained if in addition a forward-pointing particle warns him in advance what path he will soon have to travel, the connexion being expressed reciprocally, from rear to van and from van to rear."

38. The original, punctuated, version follows: "And therefore, if, notwithstanding all I have said, it shall still be thought necessary to have a Bill brought in for repealing Christianity; I would humbly offer an Amendment, that instead of the Word *Christianity*, may be put Religion in general; which I conceive, will much better answer all the good Ends proposed by the Projectors of it" (*Argument, Works*, II, 37).

39. E.g., the textual notes to *Gulliver's Travels* in *Works*, XI.

40. Jonathan Swift, *An Enquiry into the Behavior of the Queen's Last*

Ministry, ed. Irvin Ehrenpreis (Bloomington, 1956), p. xxxi. Ehrenpreis notes a number of amplifications serving to introduce smoothness by means of additional introductory conjunctions.

41. Johnson well says: "it will not be easy to find . . . any inconsequence in his connections, or abruptness in his transitions." *Lives of the Poets,* ed. Hill, III, 52.

42. To discover how successfully, see Johnson's famous comment on Swift's pamphlet, "The Conduct of the Allies," in *Boswell's Life of Johnson,* ed. Hill-Powell, II, 65: "He had to count ten, and he has counted it right."

WAYNE C. BOOTH

✍

Irony in Eighteenth-Century Fiction

Confusions of distance did not begin with modern fiction. In all
periods and in many different genres we find speakers who win
credence when they should be doubted, or who lead critics to dispute the precise degree of their untrustworthiness. In drama (Is the
villain always trustworthy in soliloquy?), in satire (Where does
Rabelais stand in his work?), in comic fiction (Is Sterne laughing
at his narrator in *A Sentimental Journey?*), in the dramatic monologue (What is Browning's precise judgment upon his many vicious
and foolish spokesmen?)—in short, wherever explicit judgment has
been unavailable, critical troubles, as well as some extraordinary delights, have ensued.

If we are to see what is distinctively troublesome about modern
fiction, we should be quite clear about the causes of earlier difficulties with distance.

Lack of adequate warning that irony is at work.—Most successful
irony before the modern period gave unmistakable notice, in one
form or another, that the speaker could not be trusted. In Lucian's
True History, for example (about A.D. 170), the narrator introduces
himself as a liar like other historians: "When I come across a
writer of this sort, I do not much mind his lying; the practice is
much too well established for that. . . . I see no reason for resigning
my right to that inventive freedom which others enjoy; and, as I

From *The Rhetoric of Fiction* (Chicago University Press, 1961), pp. 316–23.
Reprinted by permission of the publisher and author.

have no truth to put on record, having lived a very humdrum life, I fall back on falsehood—but falsehood of a more consistent variety; for I now make the only true statement you are to expect—that I am a liar." [1] While such a warning does not guarantee that the ironies will be easily decipherable, it at least insures that the reader will be working on the right line.

The warning need not be a direct statement, of course. Any grotesque disparity between word and word or word and deed will serve. Though one might, for example, be deceived by the opening of *Jonathan Wild* (1743), the deception does not last long.

> As it is necessary that all great and surprising events, the designs of which are laid, conducted, and brought to perfection by the utmost force of human invention and art, should be produced by great and eminent men, so the lives of such may be justly and properly styled the quintessence of history. In these, when delivered to us by sensible writers, we are not only most agreeably entertained, but most usefully instructed; for, besides the attaining hence a consummate knowledge of human nature in general; of its secret springs, various windings, and perplexed mazes; we have here before our eyes lively examples of whatever is amiable or detestable, worthy of admiration or abhorrence, and are consequently taught, in a manner infinitely more effectual than by precept, what we are eagerly to imitate or carefully to avoid.

Up to this point one has no unequivocal reason for questioning the reliability of Fielding's narrator. It is easy enough to imagine an author talking in such a way. And we are not absolutely disabused until the fifth paragraph.

> But before we enter on this great work we must endeavor to remove some errors of opinion which mankind have, by the disingenuity of writers, contracted: for these, from their fear of contradicting the obsolete and absurd doctrines of a set of simple fellows, called, in derision, sages or philosophers, have endeavoured, as much as possible, to confound the ideas of greatness and goodness; whereas no two things can possibly be more distinct from each other, for greatness consists in bringing all manner of mischief on mankind, and goodness in removing it from them.

With this passage, whatever weak suspicions have been aroused by the inflated style of the first paragraphs are turned into certainties. Unless we are willing, without irony, to allow him to divorce greatness and goodness, unless we think, with the narrator, that a man who "brings all manner of mischief on mankind" is made truly great by doing so, we are forced to move behind the overt beliefs of the narrator to the implicit beliefs of the author. By the end of the chapter, no one can believe that the author himself takes goodness in a great man to be "meanness and imperfection," or that, like his narrator, he wants the reader to "concur with us in allowing" Jonathan Wild the title of "*The Great.*"

Without such unmistakable clues, irony has always given trouble, and there is no *a priori* reason for assuming that the fault is the reader's. We may be tempted to laugh at the foolish Tories who were taken in by Defoe's impersonated Tory as he argued for extermination in *The Shortest Way with the Dissenters* (1702). But since Defoe gives us a realistic impersonation, without providing the evidences for his unmasking, it is hardly surprising that none of its first readers "did imagine it could be wrote by a *Whigg.*" [2] An intelligent reader, whether high churchman or dissenter, could easily read every word without having his suspicions aroused, because Defoe's mock-Tory presents no single argument that might not have been advanced by a real fanatical Tory. A careful student of polemic would of course recognize even on first reading that the arguments are specious; but so are the arguments of much serious polemic. The dialectical route by which Defoe's speaker reaches the conclusion that true charity dictates the extermination of the dissenters is, after all, common in form with much fanatical rhetoric: " 'Tis Cruelty to kill a Snake or a Toad in cold Blood, but the Poyson of their Nature makes it a Charity to our Neighbours, to destroy those Creatures, not for any personal Injury receiv'd, but for prevention; not for the Evil they have done, but the Evil they may do." "*Moses* was a merciful meek Man, and yet with what Fury did he run thro' the Camp, and cut the Throats of Three and thirty thousand of his dear *Israelites*, that were fallen into Idolatry; what was the reason? 'twas Mercy to the rest to make these be Examples, to prevent the Destruction of the whole Army." [3]

To us, knowing the full story of the pamphlet, the signs of Defoe's intentions may seem obvious. How could his contemporaries have failed to recognize the absurdity of this argument? But if we com-

pare Defoe's masterful impersonation with the more fully developed
satire of Swift's *A Modest Proposal* (1729), we see that the argument for mass cruelty in Defoe is very different from the similarly
cruel proposal in Swift. The cruelty advocated by Defoe's Tory, in
the name of Mercy, is not unheard of, incredible, absolutely beyond
human experience; heretics have been exterminated before, as all
his readers knew, and they will be again. Thus the argument, which
to any dissenter must have seemed fully as infuriating and outlandish as Swift's argument for child-cannibalism, was not incredible
even to the dissenters; on the contrary, it was frightening, and for
them the irony failed. For the Tories, on the other hand, it must
have been both frightening and exhilarating; even for the moderate
Tories, it would not, on first reading, seem impossible that an extreme Tory could argue in this manner.

What is even more deceptive is that his factual claims are not by
any means outright lies. He accuses the dissenters of having been
cruel, immoderate, and unjust. Most dissenters must have suspected
that the charge was at least in part true. Thus the argument, *"No
Gentlemen,* the Time of Mercy is past, your *Day of Grace is over;*
you shou'd have practis'd Peace, and Moderation, and Charity, if
you expected any your selves" (p. 3), is, within its own limits, perfectly sound; and unlike the "sound" arguments with which Swift
begins *A Modest Proposal,* it does not give way, as the pamphlet
progresses, to arguments that are patently absurd to all reasonable
men of both parties.

Finally, there is no statement within the pamphlet of a positive
program which, if read properly, would reveal the true position of
the author. Even after we are alerted to irony, we cannot discover
from the pamphlet alone what Defoe's position is. Compare this
method with Swift's inverted statement of his own beliefs at the
conclusion of *A Modest Proposal:* "Therefore let no man talk to me
of other Expedients: *Of taxing our Absentees at five Shillings a
Pound: of using neither Cloaths, nor Houshold Furniture except
what is of our own Growth and Manufacture: of utterly rejecting
. . .*"—the tabulation of Swift's true proposals, as rejected by his
speaker, goes on, in full italics, for half a page. There is nothing of
this sort in Defoe. If we read his pamphlet unwarned, with its absolute consistency of tone and sincerity of purpose showing on every
page, we might easily make the mistake made by Defoe's contemporaries.

Now the curious thing about this comparison with Swift is that in terms of realistic consistency alone, Defoe's method might seem the better one. He maintains a dramatic, realistic impersonation throughout, and he does not engage in any of Swift's winking or rib-punching. If we judge according to abstract criteria of tone or distance, Defoe's piece is the better one. It is certainly more significant as a forerunner of modern fiction.[4] But if we are willing, as I think we must be, to judge realized intentions as revealed in total structure, Swift's work is superior in its very willingness to sacrifice consistency to satiric force. Our comic delight is less in Defoe, even if we know that the pamphlet is ironic, because we have fewer objects of ridicule: (1) no reader could conceivably be ridiculous for failing to understand; and (2) the speaker himself is less absurd than Swift's. The more realistic his impersonation, the less ridiculously exaggerated he will be, and the less right we will feel to laugh at him or at readers deceived by him.

Excessive complexity, subtlety, or privacy of the norms to be inferred.—Even when the reader is properly alerted, he will always have trouble if the unspoken norms are not fairly simple and generally agreed upon. The debate about where Swift stands in the fourth book of *Gulliver's Travels* is apparently as much alive today as it ever was—not because Swift has left any doubt about the presence of irony, but because it is very hard to know how much distance there is between Gulliver and Swift and precisely which of the traveler's enthusiasms for the Houyhnhnms is excessive. Whatever Swift's satirical point, it is neither sufficiently commonplace nor sufficiently simple to be easily deciphered. Does he agree with Gulliver that "these noble Houyhnhnms are endowed by nature with a general disposition to all virtues" (chap. viii), or is Swift attacking, behind Gulliver's back, the "absurd creatures" who, in their cold rationalism, "represent the deistic presumption that mankind has no need of the specifically Christian virtues?"[5] As Professor Sherburn says, it is unlikely "that there will ever be unanimous agreement as to what Swift is doing in . . . Gulliver's fourth voyage" (p. 92). Unless there has been some permanent loss of clues to meanings which were clear to Swift's contemporaries, we must conclude either that Swift's norms are too complex or that their relations with Gulliver's opinions are too complicated.

Even if we conclude that the fourth book has been left to some degree indecipherable, we may follow the current of fashion and praise Swift for his ambiguities rather than condemn him for his inconclusiveness. But whichever side we fall on, ambiguity will be paid for by a loss of satiric force. Unless Swift valued subtleties and ambiguities more than effectiveness in conveying a simpler message, we must entertain the possibility that somebody—whether author or reader—has gone astray.

Fortunately my main point here does not depend on an assessment of blame: whenever an impersonal author asks us to infer subtle differences between his narrator's norms and his own, we are likely to have trouble.

We certainly meet this difficulty in *Moll Flanders*. It would be a clever reader indeed who could be sure just how much of Moll's behavior is consciously judged and repudiated by Defoe. Ian Watt, one of the most helpful commentators, finds many passages in which he cannot decide whether the reader's judgment works against Moll alone or against Defoe as well. Moll tells her lover, for example, that she would never willingly deceive him, and adds, "Nothing that ever befell me in my life sank so deep into my heart as this farewell. I reproached him a thousand times in my thoughts for leaving me, for I would have gone with him through the world, if I had begged my bread. I felt in my pocket, and there I found ten guineas, his gold watch, and two little rings." [6] Does Defoe intend this final sentence as Moll's unconscious self-betrayal, as I am inclined to think, or is Defoe himself betrayed by it? Watt concludes that, though Defoe *reveals* Moll's sophistries which conceal her dual allegiance here to the lover and to her own economic preservation, "he does not, strictly speaking, portray them," since he is himself their victim; "consequently *Moll Flanders* is undoubtedly an ironic object, but it is not a work of irony" (p. 130). Everyone finds some examples of intended irony in the novel; everyone finds moments when Defoe seems to be giving himself away. But there is a large tract of Moll's behavior where most of us would be hard put to decide whether the inconsistencies we are amused by were intended by Defoe.

The reader who is untroubled by such problems may argue that his opinion of the book does not depend on whether the artist was on top of its ironies. But for most of us the question is an important one: if we find ourselves laughing at the author along with his characters, our opinion of the book as art must suffer. In any case, whether we read *Moll Flanders* in Watt's manner or join those who see Defoe as a great ironist, it is clear that Moll's point of view has given us difficulties that Defoe could not have intended; the very quality of our interest in the book depends on decisions which even now, more than two hundred years after the event, cannot be made with any assurance.

Vivid psychological realism.—A prolonged intimate view of a character may work strongly, as in *Emma,* against our capacity for judgment. One of the troubles in *Moll Flanders* is that this effect works to soften our judgment of her worst misdeeds and to confuse us about her minor faults. Trollope reported that even a character as vicious as the protagonist of Thackeray's *Barry Lyndon* (1844) produced this effect on him. The comic villain who tells his own tale is guilty of every conceivable meanness, deliberately harming almost everyone else in the book; he engages in the most outlandish arguments in self-justification, and unlike Moll he dies unrepentant. And yet, as Trollope says, "his story is so written that it is almost impossible not to entertain something of a friendly feeling for him. . . . The reader is so carried away by his frankness and energy as almost to rejoice when he succeeds, and to grieve with him when he is brought to the ground." [7] It was not only Trollope who almost grieved; many readers were caught in the net of Barry Lyndon's rhetorical vitality. It baffled them to find themselves excusing his crimes, and they then complained about Thackeray's immorality.[8] Presented with a kind of indomitable mental reality, and presented with it at first hand, they found themselves, like Thackeray himself, "filled full with those blackguards." [9]

Richardson was distressed to learn that his readers admired even that case-hardened sinner, Lovelace. But once Lovelace has been given a chance to speak for himself, as the epistolary form allows him to do, our feeling toward him even at the moment when we fear for Clarissa most intensely is likely to be double-edged. Unlike our response to villains presented only from the outside, the experience is a combination of natural detestation and natural fellow feeling: bad as he is, he is made of the same stuff we are. It is not surprising that Richardson's intentions have often been overpowered by this effect.[10]

NOTES

1. *Works,* trans. H. W. and F. G. Fowler (Oxford, 1905), II, 137.
2. From a pamphlet published in London in 1703: *The New Associa-*

tion, Part II, With farther Improvements, As Another and Later Scots Presbyterian-Covenant, Besides that mention'd in the Former Part. . . . An Answer to some Objections in the Pretended D. Foe's Explication, in the Reflections upon the Shortest Way . . . (p. 6). I owe this reference to my colleague, Leigh Gibby. For a discussion of the difference between impersonation and the kind of irony that plays fair with the reader, see Ian Watt, *The Rise of the Novel* (Berkeley, 1957), p. 126.

3. *The Shortest Way with the Dissenters* (London, 1702), pp. 18, 20. Cf. Voltaire's *"pour encourager les autres."*

4. See Robert C. Rathburn, "The Makers of the British Novel," in *From Jane Austen to Joseph Conrad,* ed. Robert C. Rathburn and Martin Steinmann, Jr. (Minneapolis, Minn., 1958), pp. 3–22, esp. p. 5: "Defoe used the device of a persona so well that his satire had a doubly ironic effect in that the persons satirized took him seriously. . . . The pamphlet brought Defoe to the pillory, but it also showed his skill in writing from an assumed point of view."

5. Irvin Ehrenpreis, *The Personality of Jonathan Swift* (London, 1958), p. 102. For a rejection of this ironic reading, see George Sherburn, "Errors concerning the Houyhnhnms," *Modern Philology,* LVI (November, 1958), 92–97. See also William Bragg Ewald, Jr., *The Masks of Jonathan Swift* (Oxford, 1954). A substantial bibliography of the controversy can be found in Kathleen Williams, *Jonathan Swift and the Age of Compromise* (Lawrence, Kansas, 1958), p. 177 n. Again I feel required to confess myself as on the side of the less elaborately ironic reading, but the real point is that decision is difficult.

6. *The Rise of the Novel,* p. 125. Watt provides a thorough discussion of recent interpretations of Defoe as a conscious ironist. For a more favorable treatment of Defoe's ironies, see Alan D. McKillop, *The Early Masters of English Fiction* (Lawrence, Kansas, 1956), ch. i.

7. *Thackeray* (London, 1879), p. 71.

8. See Gordon N. Ray, *The Buried life* (Cambridge, Mass., 1952), pp. 28 ff.

9. Trollope, *Thackeray,* p. 76. For a report of similar difficulties in Smollett, see McKillop, *Early Masters,* pp. 147–50.

10. See Watt, *The Rise of the Novel,* p. 212: "Balzac, for example, thought it appropriate in 1837 to illustrate the point that there are always two sides to a question by asking, with what was certainly meant to be a rhetorical flourish—'Who can decide between a Clarissa and a Lovelace?' "

W. K. WIMSATT

✍

The Consistency of Johnson's Style

I

More perhaps than any other English prose writer, Johnson is said
to have changed his style as he grew older, to have bettered it.
Macaulay says:

> Since Johnson had been at ease in his circumstances he had
> written little and had talked much. When therefore he, after
> the lapse of years, resumed his pen, the mannerism which he
> had contracted while he was in the constant habit of elaborate
> composition was less perceptible than formerly, and his diction
> frequently had a colloquial ease which it had formerly wanted.
> The improvement may be discerned by a skilful critic in the
> *Journey to the Hebrides,* and in the *Lives of the Poets* is so
> obvious that it cannot escape the notice of the most careless
> reader.[1]

And within the era of tabulation Professor Taylor has offered cor-
roboratory evidence in one respect, that of sentence length.[2] The
only voice raised in emphatic dissent has been that of Dr. Birk-
beck Hill.[3] It must be apparent that in some sense Macaulay is
right, that in some way Johnson's writing is "lighter" in the *Lives*

From *The Prose Style of Samuel Johnson* (Yale University Press, 1941), pp.
74–88. Reprinted by permission of the publisher and author.

of the Poets than in the *Rambler*. The question to be decided, then, is one of classification or definition. Is the greater "lightness" of the *Lives* of a sort that should be referred to Johnson's style? It is just this that Dr. Hill denies, and his denial is what I wish to sustain and elaborate.

As a preliminary, something may be said of Johnson's conversation itself, which Macaulay praises highly before making it the source of Johnson's improvement in writing. "When he talked, he clothed his wit and his sense in forcible and natural expressions." [4] "As respected style, he spoke far better than he wrote. Every sentence which dropped from his lips was as correct in structure as the most nicely balanced period of the *Rambler*. But in his talk there were no pompous triads, and little more than a fair proportion of words in *-osity* and *-ation*. All was simplicity, ease and vigour." [5] Macaulay's description fits a good deal of the recorded conversation of Johnson. There are many shorter conversational passages in the *Life* in the same style as the sustained monologue of 20 July 1763:

> In civilized society, personal merit will not serve you so much as money will. Sir, you may make the experiment. Go into the street, and give one man a lecture on morality, and another a shilling, and see which will respect you most. If you wish only to support nature, Sir William Petty fixes your allowance at three pounds a year; but as times are much altered, let us call it six pounds. This sum will fill your belly, shelter you from the weather, and even get you a strong lasting coat, supposing it to be made of good bull's hide. Now, Sir, all beyond this is artificial, and is desired in order to obtain a greater degree of respect from our fellow-creatures. And, Sir, if six hundred pounds a year procure a man more consequence, and, of course, more happiness than six pounds a year, the same proportion will hold as to six thousand, and so on as far as opulence can be carried. [6]

In this extraordinary piece of reporting, if we may believe it is not an assemblage of pieces, but represents Johnson's unbroken discourse, [7] we have something like a spoken essay, and it must be admitted it is something quite unlike a *Rambler*. Here is the method by example rather than generality, the swift tide of unelaborated short statement, the deft insertion of subordinate matter without recourse to periodicity. The style of Johnson the writer appears in a few philosophic words, "procure," "opulence"; but most of the words are plain and blunt, the outcrop of the underlying specific vein of meaning. The tone is the dogmatic cynicism of the conversational Johnson (when he talked to be contradictory), like the dogmatism of his essays, but not like their more hopeful castigation of vice and folly. Emphasis is secured, not by balanced antithetic words (though there is antithesis) or by weighty groups of big words, but by conversational methods, by short independent clauses, syntactic isolation, by "Sir," "Now, Sir," "And, Sir." [8]

Grant, then, that Macaulay's description of Johnson's talk is a fair statement of some of the truth. There is on the other hand the fact that Johnson frequently did speak just such philosophic words as appear in his writing. "There is a good deal of Spain that has not been perambulated." "In the description of night in Macbeth, the beetle and the bat detract from the general idea of darkness,—inspissated gloom." "A speech on the stage, let it flatter ever so extravagantly, is formular." "There is in it such a *labefactation* of all principles, as may be injurious to morality." "It has been maintained that this superfoetation, this teeming of the press in modern times, is prejudicial to good literature." "Sir, among the anfractuosities of the human mind, I know not if it may not be one, that there is a superstitious reluctance to sit for a picture." "He might have *exuberated* into an Atheist." [9] Mr. S. C. Roberts has made what seems a just observation, "that while long words and laboured phrases may well be a source of weariness or irritation in a familiar essay, they may nevertheless provide entertainment in conversation." Phrases which in the *Rambler* would be "quoted as illustrating the verbal elaboration of Johnson's literary style . . . are typical of the kind of sentence that readers of Boswell delight to quote." [10] But it may be added that we read such utterances with delight in Boswell only because we hear the great moral essayist speaking as he writes; it is intimate, revealing, surprising, and funny. There is a shade of self-parody that Johnson himself seems to feel and exploit. [11]

JOHNSON. "Every society has a right to preserve publick peace and order, and therefore has a good right to prohibit the propagation of opinions which have a dangerous tendency. To say the *magistrate* has this right, is using an inadequate word:

it is the *society* for which the magistrate is agent. He may be
morally or theologically wrong in restraining the propagation
of opinions which he thinks dangerous, but he is politically
right." [12]

Johnson admitted that "he made it a constant rule to talk as well as
he could both as to sentiment and expression," "to impart whatever
he knew in the most forcible language he could put it in." [13] And
we have clear evidence that to his contemporaries his conversation
did seem like his essays. Sir John Hawkins wrote that Johnson
talked "in such language, that whoever could have heard and not
seen him, would have thought him reading." [14] "Johnson spoke as he
wrote," recollected Sir Brooke Boothby. "He would take up a topic,
and utter upon it a number of the *Rambler*." [15] His conversation is
the same as his writing," wrote Mrs. Harris of Salisbury in 1775.[16]
The young lady from America, Miss Beresford, who was fortunate
enough to hear Johnson in the coach to Oxford in 1784, said to
Boswell aside, "How he does talk! Every sentence is an essay." [17]
    Miss Burney had just been reading the *Life of Cowley* when she
reflected:

> how very like Dr. Johnson is to his writing; and how much the
> same thing it was to hear or to read him; but that nobody could
> tell that without coming to Streatham, for his language was
> generally imagined to be laboured and studied, instead of the
> mere common flow of his thoughts. "Very true," said Mrs.
> Thrale, "he writes and talks with the same ease, and in the
> same manner." [18]

If we suppose that Miss Burney's notion of Johnson's writing was
at this moment formed chiefly from reading the *Life of Cowley*,
then this passage supports Macaulay's contention that there is a
connection between Johnson's conversation and his later style. But
one may wonder whether her recent reading of this work was sufficient to alter a notion of Johnson's writing that must have been
formed over a number of years by the reading of the *Ramblers* and
other works of his middle period. And the same may be said of Mrs.
Thrale. Both these ladies, while praising Johnson's talk as natural
and easy, are struck with the resemblance between his talk and

his writing. What they seem to mean is that Johnson's writing itself is easy, not only the *Lives,* which they are just reading, but the *Ramblers* and *Rasselas,* the works which they would think of as characteristic. *"The Rambler,"* Mrs. Thrale was to say in the *Anecdotes,* ". . . expressed in a style so natural to him, and so much like his common mode of conversing." [19] And: "We used to say to one another familiarly at Streatham Park, Come, let us go into the library, and make Johnson speak *Ramblers.*" [20]

It appears to me unlikely that Johnson's conversation was a source of whatever lightness appears in his later writings, or that as he grew older and wrote and talked more he talked himself into a simpler way of writing. What is more tenable is that all his life Johnson exhibited different degrees of his own peculiar style both in his talk and in his writing, and that especially in his writing this is to be referred to differences of subject-matter.

II

We may begin to illustrate this from a body of Johnson's writing which lies closest to his conversation, his letters. Macaulay noticed the lightness of some of the letters, particularly those from the Hebrides. "His letters from the Hebrides to Mrs. Thrale are the original of that work of which the Journey to the Hebrides is the translation." [21] And Macaulay compares a sentence from the *Journey:*

> Out of one of the beds, on which we were to repose, started up, at our entrance, a man black as a *Cyclops* from the forge.[22]

and what Johnson had written to Mrs. Thrale:

> When we were taken upstairs a dirty fellow bounced out of the bed where one of us was to lie.[23]

Macaulay could have cited a number of other passages of this kind.[24] Where the letters to Mrs. Thrale and the *Journey* touch on the same subjects, it is true that the *Journey* is cast in more emphatic patterns and is more serious or philosophic—that is, the "style" is heavier. The purpose of the *Journey* is certainly not that of the letters to Mrs. Thrale; its whole intended meaning is not the same.

What is of more importance to note in Johnson's collected *Letters* is the clean cleavage between his essay style and at least two other styles, the factual and the playful, all three of which occur side by side almost from the beginning to the end.[25] Dr. Hill says, "In his letters little change in his diction can be traced from the first one to the last." [26] Little change from first to last, but abrupt changes within the space of a single letter at any time from first to last. In December 1755 we find him writing to Miss Boothby:

> Of the fallaciousness of hope, and the uncertainty of schemes, every day gives some new proof; but it is seldom heeded, till something rather felt than seen, awakens attention. This illness, in which I have suffered something and feared much more, has depressed my confidence and elation; and made me consider all that I have promised myself, as less certain to be attained or enjoyed. I have endeavoured to form resolutions of a better life; but I form them weakly, under the consciousness of external motive. Not that I conceive a time of sickness time improper for recollection and good purposes, which I believe diseases and calamities often sent to produce, but because no man can know how little his performance will answer to his promises; and designs are nothing in human eyes till they are realized by execution.

But in the same letter:

> Mr. Fitzherbert sent to-day to offer me some wine; the people about me say I ought to accept it, I shall therefore be obliged to him if he will send me a bottle.[27]

What has become of the Rambler? What has affected him so suddenly? The answer is certainly not that he has lost his style. Rather he has lost his subject. Even the Rambler cannot make antitheses and parallels out of Mr. Fitzherbert and his bottle of wine, or at least does not try.

Twenty-eight years later the same contrast appears. In November 1783 he writes to Mrs. Thrale:

> Those that have loved longest love best. A sudden blaze of kindness may by a single blast of coldness be extinguished, but that fondness which length of time has connected with many circumstances and occasions, though it may a while [be] suppressed by disgust or resentment, with or without a cause, is hourly revived by accidental recollection. To those that have lived long together, every thing heard and every thing seen recals some pleasure communicated, or some benefit conferred, some petty quarrel, or some slight endearment. Esteem of great powers, or amiable qualities newly discovered, may embroider a day or a week, but a friendship of twenty years is interwoven with the texture of life.[28]

His next letter to the Thrale household, one to Susanna, begins:

> Here is a whole week, and nothing heard from your house. Baretti said what a wicked house it would be, and a wicked house it is. Of you however I have no complaint to make, for I owe you a letter. Still I live here by my own self, and have had of late very bad nights; but then I have had a pig to dinner, which Mr. Perkins gave me. Thus life is chequered.[29]

The whole collection of Johnson's letters is a patchwork of this sort. The pieces of Ramblerism are usually short, sometimes no more than a phrase or sentence containing an inversion, a philosophic term, or a balance. "That I have answered neither of your letters you must not impute to any declension of good will, but merely to the want of something to say." [30] "Some supervenient cause of discord may overpower this original amity." [31] "He had raised money and squandered it, by every artifice of acquisition, and folly of expence." [32] The longest, as long as a *Rambler*, is the carefully written letter on books to Dr. Barnard, the King's librarian.[33] Passages of factual simplicity are to be found in almost all the letters and toward the end of even the most discursive ones. Playful or antic passages are most typical of the letters to Mrs. Thrale or her daughters, though giving way to a strain of melancholy after Mr. Thrale's death in the spring of 1781.[34] Johnson's letters, with their abrupt changes in topic, mood, and style, their juxtaposition of paragraphs of wholly different consistency, exhibit in miniature the differences which are to be found in his writing career.

III

The passages which are to follow, illustrating the consistency of
Johnson's style from the Preface to *Lobo* to the *Lives of the Poets,*
have not been selected at random. The analysis of elements of style
cannot be a blind experiment by which we discover some quality
in the writing which we could not discover by reading. Analysis
can be only a corroboration and detailed appraisal of some quality
perceived by the reader as part of meaning. Some passages from
Johnson's early and some from his late prose have been culled with
great care as examples of *Ramblerism;* others have been chosen for
their lightness. The purpose has not been to show averages in the
different periods. One must admit that there are more *Ramblers* in
the *Rambler* period, that in the late period there is more of the opposite kind of writing.

We have an early forecast of the *Rambler* in the Preface to *Lobo,*
1735.[35] The narrative translation itself of course offered not much
opportunity for Johnson to exercise himself.[36] But the Preface, or
at least part of it, was an original, discursive composition, an essay.[37]
If a count is made of parallels and antitheses, it will be found to
have about the weight of a moderately heavy *Rambler.* The very
second sentence contains a chiasmic antithesis of type II with two
parallel elements: "his attempt stands in need of no apology, whatever censures may fall on the performance." Boswell quotes three
paragraphs which gave Edmund Burke particular delight, the last
of which is as follows:

> The reader will here find no regions cursed with irremediable
> barrenness, or blest with spontaneous fecundity; no perpetual
> gloom or unceasing sunshine; nor are the nations here de-
> scribed either devoid of all sense of humanity, or consummate
> in all private and social virtues: here are no *Hottentots* without
> religion, polity, or articulate language; no *Chinese* perfectly
> polite, and completely skilled in all sciences: he will discover
> what will always be discovered by a diligent and impartial en-
> quirer, that wherever human nature is to be found, there is a
> mixture of vice and virtue, a contest of passion and reason;
> and that the Creator doth not appear partial in his distribu-
> tions, but has balanced in most countries their particular incon-
> veniencies by particular favours.[38]

The *Debates in Parliament*, 1740–3, again exhibit the Johnsonian style, this time almost unmixed. Here there was no hindrance of facts or narrative; he might luxuriate in abstract emphasis. "They are commonly formed," says Dr. Hill, "of general statements which suit any one speaker just as well as any other. The scantier were the notes that were given him by those who had heard the debate the more he had to draw on his imagination. But his was an imagination which supplied him with what was general much more readily than with what was particular." [39] Here one may pick almost at random. The following passage from the "Debate on Addressing His Majesty for Removing Sir Robert Walpole" is written in a style that is sustained with little variation through the whole of the two volumes. It is an uninteresting puffy prose, that of Johnson expressing other men's opinions, without the moral conviction and spirit of the *Ramblers*.

> To endeavour, my Lords, to remove from places of publick trust all those who appear to want either the virtues or abilities necessary for executing their offices, is the interest of every member of a community. And it is not only the interest but the duty of all those who are either by the choice of the people, or by the right of birth, invested with the power of inspecting publick affairs, and intrusted with the general happiness of their country. That therefore every motive combines to make it the duty, and every argument concurs to prove it the privilege of your Lordships, is too evident to be doubted. [40]

If Johnson could be heavy before the *Ramblers,* he could also be (and it is equally relevant to our purpose to note it) light during the period of the *Ramblers.* [41] Dr. Hill has maintained that this is evident in Johnson's miscellaneous writings. "The Preface to the Dictionary, the Life of Sir Thomas Browne, the Review of Jonas Hanway's Journal, and of Soame Jenyns's Nature and Origin of Evil . . . are free from any excess of mannerisms." [42] But one may find the principle better illustrated even within the *Ramblers*. A topic on which Johnson was always forced to employ his lightest style was specific literary criticism. The reference to this poem and that, the quotation of passages and reference to them, the use of technical terms, "verse," "foot," "syllable," "long" and "short," all conspired to prevent Johnson's logic from taking hold of the theme and carrying it to the realm of elaborate generality. This sort of subject matter in a great measure accounts for the lightness of the *Lives*. Johnson has no sooner done with the recital of biographical events than comment on particular works claims his attention. He manages to insert only interludes of essay, of general appraisal of literary character. And if we look at such a *Rambler* as No. 88, on Milton's versification, we see the complete anticipation of many sections of the *Lives*.[43] How could Johnson be most Johnsonian when he had such as the following to write?

> The great peculiarity of *Milton's* versification, compared with that of later poets, is the elision of one vowel before another, or the suppression of the last syllable of a word ending with a vowel, when a vowel begins the following word. As
>
> Knowledge——
> Oppresses else with surfeit, and soon turns
> Wisdom to folly, as nourishment to wind.
>
> This license, though now disused in *English* poetry, was practised by our older writers, and is allowed in many other languages ancient and modern, and therefore the criticks on *Paradise Lost* have, without much deliberation, commended *Milton* for continuing it.[44]

Passages of the same lightness are to be found in *Rasselas,* except that here the occasion is not literary criticism but narrative. Such a passage as that running through Chapters XIII–XV, a continuum of rather pure narrative, has a marked difference in weight from philosophic conversation such as that of Chapters XXVII–XXVIII. The following is from Chapter XIII.

> As they were walking on the side of the mountain, they observed that the conies, which the rain had driven from their burrows, had taken shelter among the bushes, and formed holes behind them, tending upwards in an oblique line. "It has been the opinion of antiquity, said Imlac, that human reason borrowed many arts from the instinct of animals; let us, therefore, not think ourselves degraded by learning from the coney. We may escape by piercing the mountain in the same direction. We will begin where the summit hangs over the middle part, and labour upward till we shall issue up beyond the prominence."

The eyes of the prince, when he heard this proposal, sparkled with joy. The execution was easy, and the success certain.[45]

Contrast it with the following from Chapter XXVII.

The highest stations cannot therefore hope to be the abodes of happiness, which I would willingly believe to have fled from thrones and palaces to seats of humble privacy and placid obscurity. For what can hinder the satisfaction, or intercept the expectations, of him whose abilities are adequate to his employments, who sees with his own eyes the whole circuit of his influence, who chooses by his own knowledge all whom he trusts, and whom none are tempted to deceive by hope or fear? Surely he has nothing to do but to love and to be loved, to be virtuous and to be happy.[46]

Sixteen years later the same mixture of styles is to be observed. The *Journey to the Western Islands* consists for the most part of paragraphs of narrative or description alternate with paragraphs of discussion. We find on one page a passage like the following:

But it must be remembered, that life consists not of a series of illustrious actions, or elegant enjoyments; the great part of our time passes in compliance with necessities, in the performance of daily duties, in the removal of small inconveniencies, in the procurement of petty pleasures; and we are well or ill at ease, as the main stream of life glides on smoothly, or is ruffled by small obstacles and frequent interruptions. The true state of every nation is the state of common life. The manners of a people are not to be found in the schools of learning, or the palaces of greatness, where the national character is obscured or obliterated by travel or instruction, by philosophy or vanity; nor is publick happiness to be estimated by the assemblies of the gay, or the banquets of the rich.

And on the next page:

Finding nothing to detain us at *Bamff*, we set out in the morning, and having breakfasted at *Cullen*, about noon came to *Elgin*, where, in the inn that we supposed the best, a dinner was set before us, which we could not eat. This was the first time, and except one, the last, that I found any reason to complain of a *Scottish* table; and such disappointments, I suppose, must be expected in every country where there is no great frequency of travellers.[47]

These passages are a fair sample of the *Western Islands*, though occasional phrases or sentences where the two modes blend are more striking or amusing. "Such capricious and temporary waters," says the Rambler, "cannot be expected to produce many fish." And again he antithesizes a species of geese. "They are so tame as to own a home, and so wild as sometimes to fly quite away." [48] A reflection on the character of the Highlanders which appears to me to be the longest stretch of abstraction in the whole book is about heavy enough to be a *Rambler*.[49]   .

Much the same is to be said of *Taxation No Tyranny*. Here argument of a general political character—on "fundamental principles, or common axioms, which being generally received are little doubted, and being little doubted have been rarely proved" [50]—is interspersed with more specific examination of the question at issue. "Suppose it true, that any such exemption is contained in the charter of *Maryland,* it can be pleaded only by the *Marylanders*." [51] The first fifteen hundred words of the essay, a passage among the most homogeneously Johnsonian, will be found about as heavy as a moral *Rambler*.[52]

The *Life of Pope* is an exception among the *Lives,* containing more elaborate discussion than any other; in choosing a passage from it for comparison with Addison and Hazlitt I have followed Professor Chandler, who used great discrimination in finding a passage so specially Johnsonian. But a like passage from the *Life of Dryden,* for example, is almost as difficult to find as one from the *Western Islands.* So common throughout the *Lives* are paragraphs like the following:

> Davenant was perhaps at this time his favourite author, though Gondibert never appears to have been popular; and from Davenant he learned to please his ear with the stanza of four lines alternately rhymed.[53]

One series of paragraphs, however, on such ductile topics as Dryden's genius, his learning, his prose style, his refinement of the language,[54] offers some good examples of Johnson's essay style as it survived in the *Lives* wherever it found sustenance.

> Yet it cannot be said that his genius is ever unprovided of matter, or that his fancy languishes in penury of ideas. His works abound with knowledge, and sparkle with illustrations. There is scarcely any science or faculty that does not supply him with occasional images and lucky similitudes; every page discovers a mind very widely acquainted both with art and nature, and in full possession of great stores of intellectual wealth. Of him that knows much, it is natural to suppose that he has read with diligence; yet I rather believe that the knowledge of Dryden was gleaned from accidental intelligence and various conversation, by a quick apprehension, a judicious selection, and a happy memory, a keen appetite of knowledge, and a powerful digestion; by vigilance that permitted nothing to pass without notice, and a habit of reflection that suffered nothing useful to be lost. A mind like Dryden's, always curious, always active, to which every understanding was proud to be associated, and of which every one solicited the regard, by an ambitious display of himself, had a more pleasant, perhaps a nearer way to knowledge than by the silent progress of solitary reading. I do not suppose that he despised books, or intentionally neglected them; but that he was carried out, by the impetuosity of his genius, to more vivid and speedy instructors; and that his studies were rather desultory and fortuitous than constant and systematical.

In the comparison of passages made in this chapter I have been thinking more of parallelism and antithesis than of diction. I have not much to say about the progress of Johnson's diction, to what degree at different times it was abstract, general, non-sensory, or philosophic—and this for the reason that these qualities of diction, being dependent on context, are not measurable or countable in words as such. Professor Taylor has proved beyond doubt, I think, that the average number of syllables in Johnson's words is as great in the *Lives of the Poets* as in the *Ramblers*.[55] This, however, need not persuade us to any further conclusion. There are long words and long words. It is conceivable that Johnson's words should have

continued of the same average length yet have become less philosophic. And this, I believe, is what did happen. Certainly, even
when they continue philosophic, they are less often exaggerated or
freakish.[56]

Another matter on which I have little to say is the decrease in
sentence length which took place between the *Rambler* and the
Lives of the Poets. Professor Taylor has already treated the matter
thoroughly. His painstaking statistics show that in the *Ramblers*
Johnson averaged 43.1 words per sentence, in the *Idlers,* 33.4, in
the *Lives,* 30.1[57] Perhaps this was an improvement in Johnson's
writing; perhaps he may be read the more easily for it. But it would
be difficult to say how far this is independent of the changes in
subject matter which we have discussed, and more difficult to say
whether anything peculiarly Johnsonian evaporated with the length
of the sentence.[58]

NOTES

1. "Samuel Johnson," *Encyclopaedia Britannica,* 11th ed., vol. xv (Cambridge, 1911), p. 470, col. 2. Cf. *Johnsonian Miscellanies* (Oxford,
   1897), II, 351–2, Tyers' *Sketch;* Leslie Stephen, *Samuel Johnson*
   (London, 1878), pp. 168, 186.
2. See below.
3. "Dr. Johnson's Style," *Macmillan's Magazine,* LVII (1888), 190–4.
   Cf. the opinion of Alexander Chalmers, below, and Allen T. Hazen,
   Samuel Johnson's Prefaces & Dedications (New Haven, 1937), p.
   xxii, n. 19.
4. *Macaulay's and Carlyle's Essays on Samuel Johnson,* ed. William
   Strunk, Jr. (New York, 1895), p. 60.
5. *Encyclopaedia,* p. 468, col. 2.
6. *Life* I, 440. The above is less than a third of the whole passage.
7. Mr. Geoffrey Scott, after a study of Boswell's Journals and "papers
   apart," came to the conclusion "that, whenever the *Life* contains a
   long and closely reasoned chain of discussion between a group of
   speakers, the source did not consist of a number of brief notes, subsequently enlarged at leisure, but in an immediate feat of memory
   where the entire argument was swiftly preserved in condensed language and remained in that form until Boswell came to write the
   Life," *Private Papers of Boswell* (Mount Vernon, N.Y., 1928–34),
   VI, 144.
8. This conversational device of Johnson's, by which he so often raises
   himself to a height from which to descend emphatically into his

sentence, is the mark of a man who must find other strong means of emphasis in his writing.

9. *Life* I, 410; II, 90, 234, 367; III, 332; IV, 4, 98. It will be seen that these are not confined to the middle part of Johnson's career.

10. *Doctor Johnson* (New York, 1935), p. 49.

11. We have already had occasion to quote perhaps the best example, Johnson's correction of himself in pronouncing judgment on *The Rehearsal*. "He seemed," says Boswell of this occasion, "to take a pleasure in speaking in his own style" (*Life* IV, 320). Sir Walter Raleigh explains that "Johnson's talk was free from self-consciousness; but Boswell, when he was in the room, was conscious of one person only, so that a kind of self-consciousness by proxy is the impression conveyed" (*Johnson on Shakespeare* [London, 1929], p. xxxi). It appears to me rather that Johnson's "complacency," his consciousness and amused acceptance of his own worth, included a certain study of himself and intention to be what he was. See, for example, *Life* I, 204, 443; II, 15, 66, 362; III, 7, 260; IV, 166, 179, 183–4; *Letters* (New York, 1892) II, 313–14, No. 860.

12. *Life* II, 249.

13. *Life* I, 204; IV, 183–4; cf. II, 323.

14. *Works*, edited by John Hawkins (London, 1787–8), I, 164.

15. Robert Anderson, *Life of Johnson* (1815), p. 322, quoted in *Miscellanies* II, 391.

16. *Letters of the 1st Earl of Malmesbury* (1870), I, 302, quoted in *Life* II, 520, App. B.

17. *Life* IV, 284. For further illustration see *Works* I, 385; *Life* V, 12; *Miscellanies* II, 237–48, Reynolds' imitation of Johnson's conversation.

18. C. B. Tinker, *Dr. Johnson & Fanny Burney* (New York, 1911), p. 71. Cf. Bowles's description of Johnson's conversation, *Life* IV, 236–7.

19. *Miscellanies* I, 348.

20. Hayward's *Piozzi*, I, 297, quoted in *Miscellanies* I, 347, n. 3.

21. *Macaulay's and Carlyle's Essays on Samuel Johnson*, ed. William Strunk, Jr. (New York, 1895), p. 61.

22. *Works* X, 371.

23. *Letters* I, 251, No. 326.

24. For example, Johnson wrote in the *Journey:* "To make this way, the rock has been hewn to a level with labour that might have broken the perseverance of a *Roman* Legion" (*Works* X, 353), while to Mrs. Thrale he had written, "These roads have all been made by hewing the rock away with pickaxes, or bursting it with gunpowder" (*Letters* I, 243, No. 323). Cf. Johnson's descriptions of the Buller of Buchan, *Letters* I, 237, No. 322 and *Works* X, 335. Cf. Boswell's different way of treating the subject with emphasis, *Life* V, 100.

25. Cf. the opinion of Dr. Hill, *Letters* I, xiii. Mr. Augustine Birrell says of the letters, "They are in every style, from the monumental to the utterly frivolous" ("The Transmission of Johnson's Personality," *Johnson Club Papers* [New York, 1899], p. 14). Cf. his *Obiter Dicta: Second Series* (London, 1887), "Dr. Johnson," pp. 143–4.

26. "Dr. Johnson's Style," *Macmillan's Magazine*, LVII (1888), 193.

27. *Letters* I, 47–8, No. 78.

28. *Letters* II, 350, No. 900.

29. *Letters* II, 351–2, No. 901.

30. *Letters* I, 118, No. 170.

31. *Life* I, 324.

32. *Life* II, 281.

33. *Letters* I, 142–7, No. 206.

34. In his frivolous style I find Johnson not at his happiest. His resources are too limited; he seems too much to descend as the great lexicographer to a few simple tricks of naiveté that would not be thought funny in another man. There is, for example, his way of harping on a word, an over-plain kind of repetitious bumptiousness. "I enquired of my barber after another barber; that barber, says he, is dead, and his son has left off, to turn maltster. Maltsters, I believe, do not get much money" (*Letters* I, 174). "Here is a rout and bustle; and a bustle and a rout" (*Letters* I, 366, No. 432). Cf. *Letters* I, 166, No. 237; I, 175, No. 254. Johnson's best frivolity is his gentle teasing of females; e.g., *Letters* II, 136–7. But on the whole the Rambler is out of place, elephantine among the fragilities of prattle and gossip. Also he has too charitable a nature. It is possible to admire his playful letters in that it is wonderful he could write them at all, as he himself thought of a woman who could preach, but it is impossible to call them fine and mean what we mean when we refer, let us say, to Madame de Sévigné's "lanternes" or to the dainty nastiness of Horace Walpole. See Walter B. C. Watkins, *Perilous Balance* (Princeton, 1939), pp. 38–9 for a comparison of the letters to Mrs. Thrale and the *Journal to Stella*.

35. The earliest available—unless one will study Johnson's Pembroke College Latin prose exercises, one of which has been printed by Dr. Hill (*Life* I, 60, n. 7). It seems to me that the germs are there. "Quaedam minus attentè spectata," begins the young Johnson, "absurda videntur, quae tamen penitus perspecta rationi sunt consentanea."

It might be illuminating to see some of the periodical essays which Johnson is said to have contributed to the *Birmingham Journal* in 1733. See *Life* I, 85 and *Courtney* p. 2.

For the opinion that Johnson's characteristic manner does not appear in his early works, see *Miscellanies* I, 466, Murphy's *Essay;*

Works I, 22; Robert Anderson, *Life of Johnson* (London, 1795), p. 229. For the opposite opinion, that which I am advancing, see, besides *Life* I, 87–9, Alexander Chalmers, *British Essayists* (London, 1817), xix, xliii; Edmund Gosse, *Leaves and Fruit* (New York, 1927), pp. 360–1.

It is perhaps true that after the *Rambler* Johnson showed less inclination to deviate from his characteristic style. There are, for example, in his early writing some excursions in irony that must surprise the reader who has known only the major works. In "a Compleat Vindication of the Licensers of the Stage," 1739, Johnson approaches the plain, bitter statement of Swift. "There are scattered over this kingdom several little seminaries, in which the lower ranks of people, and the younger sons of our nobility and gentry are taught from their earliest infancy the pernicious arts of spelling and reading, which they afterwards continue to practise, very much to the disturbance of their own quiet, and the interruption of ministerial measures. These seminaries may, by an act of parliament, be at once suppressed, and that our posterity be deprived of all means of reviving this corrupt method of education, it may be made felony to teach to read without a license from the Lord Chamberlain" (*Works* xiv, 57). Passages of the same "modest proposal" technique may be found in *Marmor Norfolciense*, 1739 (*Works* xiv, 25, 32), and in "A Project for the Employment of Authors," in the *Universal Visiter,* April 1756 (*Works* xiv, 206).

36. Cf. *Life,* I, 87.
37. The first 800 words (*Works* IX, 431–4 ". . . many agreeing in the same account"). The quotient for multiplications of two or more elements of implicit parallel is 1.75; for antithesis II of all types, 2.00. Cf. *ante* p. 30, n. 58; p. 44, n. 32. The last part of this Preface is matter of fact, explanatory of the writer's policy in translation.
38. *Work* IX, 432. Cf. *Life* I, 88–9. And Boswell points out Johnson's hand in the Dedication to Warren the bookseller.
39. *Life* I, 506, App. A.
40. A passage of 1,500 words from which this is taken (*Works* xii, 139, "Lord Carteret began . . ."–142, ". . . it cannot continue") has for implicit parallels of two or more elements a quotient of 1.47; for all types of antithesis II, 2.00.
41. The question whether Johnson's extensive revisions for the fourth edition of the *Rambler*, 1756, should be considered evidence of a reform in style is rather involved, and since I believe they should not, I have removed my discussion of the matter to Appendix C, *post* pp. 152–4.
42. "Dr. Johnson's Style," *Macmillan's Magazine,* lvii (1888), 190. He refers to the fact that Boswell found only one instance of "*Brown-*

ism" in the papers which Johnson wrote for the *Literary Magazine* in 1756. Cf. *Life* I, 308.

43. "If the 'Lives of the Poets' be thought an exception to Dr. JOHNSON'S general habit of writing, let it be remembered that he was for the most part confined to dates and facts, to illustrations and criticisms, and quotations; but when he indulged himself in moral reflections, to which he delighted to recur, we have again the rigour and loftiness of the RAMBLER, and only miss some of what have been termed his *hard words*" (Alexander Chalmers, *British Essayists* [London, 1817], XIX, xliii).

44. This *Rambler* of 1,000 words (*Works* VI, 103–9) has for implicit parallel of two or more elements a quotient of only .70; though for all types of anthithesis II a quotient of 1.30, much nearer to that of more abstract *Ramblers*.

45. Chapters XIII–XV, a passage of 1,600 words (*Works* XI, 41–7), have for implicit parallel of two or more elements a quotient of .56; for all types of antithesis II, 1.56. I include the second short paragraph of the quoted passage, with its doublet of two elements of implicit parallel, for the sake of showing how such elements occur even in the narrative of *Rasselas*.

46. Chapters XXVII–XXVIII, a passage of 1,400 words (*Works* XI, 74–80), have for implicit parallel of two or more elements a quotient of 2.14; for all types of antithesis II, 2.43.

47. *Works* X, 338–9.

48. *Works* X, 359, 380.

49. *Works* X, 428, "It may likewise . . ."–434, ". . . perceive the benefit," a passage of 1,500 words. For implicit parallels of two or more elements the quotient is 1.00; for all types of antithesis II, 2.47.

50. *Works* X, 93.

51. *Works* X, 118.

52. *Works* X, 93–9, ". . . conceive them free." For implicit parallel of two or more elements the quotient is 1.47; for all types of antithesis II, 2.13.

Mrs. Thrale wrote of *Falkland's Islands*, " 'Tis Johnson . . . that interests us, and your style is invariably the same" (*Piozzi Letters* I, 318, quoted, *Life* III, 19, n. 2).

53. *Works* II, 390–1.

54. *Works* II, 382, "His literature . . ."–388, ". . . reason wants not Horace to support it," a passage of 1,500 words. For implicit parallel of two or more elements the quotient is 1.67; for all type of antithesis II, 1.93.

55. Warner Taylor, *The Prose Style of Johnson* (Madison, 1918), p. 29. I present an ellipsis of his table of average word length.

Rambler	1st 10	1.54
	Last 10	1.59
Idler	1st 15	1.51
	Last 16	1.53
Lives of the Poets *		
	Narrative	1.53
	Exposition	1.59
Eminent Lives *		1.53

* Sections from the lives of Addison, Prior, Pope, Cowley, Milton, Waller, Butler, and Dryden.

** Sections from the lives of Savage [1744], Drake [1740], and Boerhaave [1739].

56. Boswell says, "So easy is his style in these Lives, that I do not recollect more than three uncommon or learned words; one, when giving an account of the approach of Waller's mortal disease, he says, 'he found his legs grow *tumid*' . . . . Another, when he mentions that Pope *emitted* proposals . . . and a third, when he calls Orrery and Dr. Delaney, writers both undoubtedly *veracious* . . . ." But Dr. Hill supplies eight more examples (*Life* IV, 39 and n. 1).

57. Taylor p. 35, Table II. These figures are for "indicated" (punctuated) sentence length. In another table Professor Taylor shows that both "indicated" and "real" (structural) sentence length decrease (p. 41, Table V).

58. Professor Taylor says of Johnson's later style, "All the old devices remained, even more pronouncedly often . . . but the sentences became shorter, the movement tense and energetic" (p. 33). Something like this may perhaps be conceded. Shorter sentences would seem to make shorter intervals between primary emphases and less distinction among emphases. Professor Sherman says, "Herein we see the essential difference between the condensed book-style and the condensed oral. The one . . . gains speed by leaving meaning to be implied within the sentence, the other outside of it." And he believes that the terseness of short sentences varies "according to the leap or omission of thought between. It is the length of the leap rather than the shortness of the periods that makes an author seem laconic" (L. A. Sherman, *Analytics of Literature* [Boston, 1893], pp. 301–2, 303, n. 1). I should say that between the short sentences of Johnson's later style there is a very short average leap, that they differ from the members of his earlier long sentences chiefly in the omission of connectives and change of punctuation.

It is interesting, however, to note that of all other English prose masters, only Dryden seems to have diminished his sentence in like degree as he grew older (Edwin H. Lewis, *The History of the English Paragraph* [Chicago, 1894], pp. 106–7, n. 2).

DONALD DAVIE

🖎

Syntax in Wordsworth's *Prelude*

"He told me of the attraction that an exhaustive study of the
English language was beginning to exert over him. I, for my
part, deplored the denseness of such a concrete language, the
excessive richness of its vocabulary and its pleasure in trying to
reincarnate the thing itself, as in ideographic writing; whereas
French, a more abstract language, which tries to signify rather
than represent the meaning, uses words only as fiduciary symbols like coins as values of monetary exchange. English for me
was still at the swapping stage.

There was some nodding and shaking of the head. That was
precisely, if he was to be believed, just what he most needed
. . .: to take on weight and mass in the language of
Newton."

St.-John Perse
André Gide: 1909 [1]

We have to understand that when St.-John Perse speaks of the Englishman as enamoured of "nature," he means the "nature" of Isaac
Newton. If the clue to Newton had not been given, we might have
gone astray. We might have thought first of Wordsworth. For it is

From *Articulate Energy* (Routledge & Kegan Paul, 1955), pp. 106–16. Reprinted by permission of the publisher and author.

Wordsworth who springs most readily to mind as the sort of English poet that the Frenchman finds alien, the poet "enamoured of nature" and "rediscovering his infinite in the cosmic abyss." But the abyss, we now realize, is not what evoked in Wordsworth "fleeting moods of shadowy exultation"; what the French poet means is "a world of atoms in motion, devoid of all secondary sense qualities, such as colour, scent, taste and sound, ordered by causal laws and explicable only in terms of mathematics" [2]—in short, the world of abstract "matter" in which the early experimenters seemed to find themselves, when they followed out the implications of their conscientiously "concrete" experiments.

Far from making against Wordsworth, Perse's view of poetic language, I shall suggest, is the one best fitted to account for some of Wordsworth's verse. Only in terms of words as "fiduciary symbols" can Wordsworth's blank-verse in *The Prelude* be properly appreciated. In those passages of *The Prelude* where Wordsworth is trying to convey most exactly the effect of the natural world upon himself, his words ("ties" and "bonds" and "influences" and "powers") will carry the reader only (as Valéry says) so long as he does not loiter, so long as they are taken, as coins are taken, "as values of monetary exchange." Wordsworth's words have meaning so long as we trust them. They have just such meaning, and just as much meaning, as Perse and Valéry suggest.

We can make a start by pointing out that Wordsworth's world is not pre-eminently a world of "things." His language has not, in St.-John Perse's sense, "weight and mass." It is not concrete. Because in the Preface to *Lyrical Ballads* Wordsworth castigated some earlier poets for giving no proof that they had ever truly *looked* at natural phenomena, it is often supposed that his own verse is full of such phenomena rendered in all their quiddity and concreteness. But this is a sort of optical illusion. What Wordsworth renders is not the natural world but (with masterly fidelity) the effect that world has upon him. He is at all points a very long way from "trying to reincarnate the thing itself, as in ideographic writing." As Lionel Trilling remarks:

> Wordsworth never did have the special and perhaps modern sensibility of his sister or of Coleridge, who were so aware of exquisite particularities. His finest passages are moral, emo-

tional, subjective; whatever visual intensity they have comes
from his response to the object, not from his close observation of it.[3]

On the contrary, I have heard more than one student complain of
Wordsworth's diction that it is too "abstract." I shall argue that the
diction of *The Prelude* is neither abstract nor concrete, but something between the two.

This gives me the chance to introduce a very weighty objection
to Ernest Fenollosa's theory of poetic language. According to him,
"At the base of the pyramid lie *things,* but stunned, as it were."
T. C. Pollock, however, sees in this view the fallacy of "Misplaced
Concreteness":

> If an abstract term is the sign of an abstraction from an indi-
> vidual experience (E) or a group of individual experiences
> (E), a non-abstract or a concrete term would be the sign of
> that from which the abstraction was drawn, the non-abstract
> individual experience (E) or the non-abstract individual ex-
> periences (E) in the group of experiences (E). The opposite
> of an abstract term would therefore be, not the name of a
> specific or "concrete" object, but the sign of a total or concrete
> *experience* (E). The error arises because of the assumption that
> the abstraction is from *objects,* instead of from *experiences*
> (E). (On the contrary, what we call "objects" are psycholog-
> ically abstractions from *experiences* (E).)

As Pollock goes on to show,[4] this statement is only the counterpart
in linguistic theory of a fact of linguistic history: the fact established
by Jespersen that words originally stood for whole *experiences,* which
were only subsequently broken down into "seen" things and "un-
seen" feelings about them, or significances in them. Fenollosa's
account of metaphor is at odds with Jespersen, as his account of abstraction is at odds with Pollock.

Now if Wordsworth was concerned to render his responses to the
natural world, he was concerned with experiences, and these were
"concretions" from which he did not care to abstract (as his sister
and Coleridge did) that part of them which we call "objects" or
"things." It follows that ideographic writing, in which words em-

body things, is *more abstract than* writing in which words are fiduciary symbols for elements of an experience.

This view of words as symbols is advanced by Coleridge in a famous passage from *Biographia Literaria:*

> The best part of human language, properly so called, is derived from reflection on the acts of the mind itself. It is formed by a voluntary appropriation of fixed symbols to internal acts, to processes and results of imagination, the greater part of which have no place in the consciousness of uneducated man; though in civilized society, by imitation and passive remembrance of what they hear from their religious instructors and other superiors, the most uneducated share in the harvest which they neither sowed nor reaped (ch. 17).

It will be recalled that this statement is made when Coleridge is objecting to Wordsworth's recommendation of rustic language, on the grounds that such language can provide only poor and meagre syntax:

> The rustic, from the more imperfect development of his faculties, and from the lower state of their cultivation, aims almost solely to convey insulated facts, either those of his scanty experience or his traditional belief; while the educated man chiefly seeks to discover and express those connections of things, or those relative bearings of fact to fact, from which some more or less general law is deducible. For facts are valuable to a wise man, chiefly as they lead to the discovery of the indwelling law, which is the true being of things, the sole solution of their modes of existence, and in the knowledge of which consists our dignity and our power.

Coleridge points out what Perse and Valéry have led us to expect, that if a language is deficient in "fixed symbols" for "internal acts," it will also be deficient in syntax. I shall proceed to show that Wordsworth, when he abandoned rustic diction and took to rendering "internal acts," "processes and results of imagination," used for the purpose an elaborate syntax, and that an important part of his vocabulary is neither abstract nor concrete, but made up of fixed fiduciary symbols.

In *The Prelude* the syntax is elaborately correct:

> I deem not profitless those fleeting moods
> Of shadowy exultation: not for this,
> That they are kindred to our purer mind
> And intellectual life; but that the soul,
> Remembering how she felt, but what she felt
> Remembering not, retains an obscure sense
> Of possible sublimity, to which
> With growing faculties she doth aspire,
> With faculties still growing, feeling still
> That whatsoever point they gain, they still
> Have something to pursue.   (II. 331–41)

Dr. Leavis comments on this passage:

> It would be difficult to suggest anything more elusive than
> this possibility which the soul glimpses in "visionary" moments
> and,
>> Remembering how she felt, but what she felt
>> Remembering not,
> retains an "obscure sense" of. Perhaps it will be agreed that,
> though Wordsworth no doubt was right in feeling that he had
> something to pursue, the critic here is in a different case. If
> these "moments" have any significance for the critic (whose
> business it is to define the significance of Wordsworth's poetry),
> it will be established, not by dwelling upon or in them, in the
> hope of exploring something that lies hidden in or behind their
> vagueness, but by holding firmly on to that sober verse in
> which they are presented.[5]

What is recommended here is what Perse and Valéry recommend: taking the verse at a run, not pausing on the nouns for fear they congeal
into the starting unfathomable eyes that appalled Hofmannsthal,
but attending rather to the syntactical weave. If this is what Dr.
Leavis means, the testimony is all the more valuable as coming from
a reader who in other cases (on Milton, for instance), is cautious
not to grant the poet all that he asks for. What Wordsworth asks
for here is for all his words to be considered only in their context.
Yet it is different from what Pound asks for in the *Cantos*. These

moods, exultations, senses, sublimities, and faculties will be no clearer at the end of *The Prelude* than they are here; and yet the poem will not be a botch, for what will be clear at the end is the relationship between them, the articulation. The nouns are not concrete; but the verbs are, and may be lingered over. In short, this is poetry where the syntax counts enormously, counts for nearly everything.

Earlier, however, in his chapter on Wordsworth, Dr. Leavis has remarked of this blank-verse:

> Wordsworth in such passages as are in question produces the mood, feeling or experience and at the same time appears to be giving an explanation of it. The expository effect sorts well with—blends into—the characteristic meditative gravity of the emotional presentment ("emotion recollected in tranquillity"), and in the key passages, where significance seems specially to reside, the convincing success of the poetry covers the argument: it is only by the most resolute and sustained effort (once it occurs to one that effort is needed) that one can pay to the argument, as such, the attention it appears to have invited and satisfied (p. 159).

And he directs us to William Empson to see how ill the argument stands up to scrutiny, once one gives attention to it.

On this showing, the syntax of *The Prelude* is not doing what it offers to do. It seems to be explaining, while in fact it is meditating, ruminating, at all events *experiencing* more fully than one does when one explains. But I am not sure that Wordsworth even pretends to explain. Elsewhere Dr. Leavis makes the point like this:

> Even if there were not so much poetry to hold the mind in a subtly incompatible mode of attention, it would still be difficult to continue attending to the philosophic argument, because of the way in which the verse, evenly meditative in tone and movement, goes on and on, without dialectical suspense and crisis or rise and fall. By an innocently insidious trick Wordsworth, in this calm ruminative progression, will appear to be pre-occupied with a scrupulous nicety of statement, with a judicial weighing of alternative possibilities, while actually making it more difficult to check the argument from which he will

emerge, as it were inevitably, with a far from inevitable conclusion (p. 162).

Here the expression "an innocently insidious trick" sends us back
to the idea of Wordsworth's syntax as somehow conjuror's patter.
On the other hand the "movement" that "goes on and on without
dialectical suspense and crisis or rise and fall" is, it seems, one of
the elements that work against argument. And this movement is
as much a movement of syntax, a movement of the mind, as it is
a movement in the ear. "Dialectical" admits as much. The syntax
therefore presents what is really going on: meditation, not argument; and it is therefore authentic, not a play of misleading forms.
This confirms me in my original explanation: that this is largely a
poetry of verbal symbols which must be taken on trust (almost but
not quite like notes or chords in music), for the sake of the articulations jointed between them.

It is wrong to think that this poetry aimed at even the effect of philosophic argument. That Wordsworth thought, at Coleridge's instigation, that he might be a philosophic poet is here beside the point; we
are speaking of what the poetry does, not of what the poet intended
it to do. And in any case, this is the prelude to a philosophic poem,
not the poem itself. When that poem appeared, the poetry was not
of this kind, as Dr. Leavis acknowledges—"the doctrinal passages of
The Excursion . . . are plain enough."
    The critics were misled, not by the syntax of *The Prelude*, but
by its vocabulary, which appears to be "abstract." It is certainly
more "abstract" than a great deal of English poetry, but it is not
abstract in any strict sense. Its verbs are concrete, and its nouns are
verbal symbols, neither concrete nor abstract. That it was the vocabulary that got in Dr. Leavis's way is proved, I think, by his
admission that, for him, the Hartleian poem of 1805–6 gives more
the effect of philosophic argument than the revised version of 1850.
Dr. Leavis presents what he calls "a representative improvement,"
by printing a passage in both the versions. At the risk of being
tedious, I shall present both passages, and consider his comments on
them. First, the version of 1805–6 (II. 238–266):

               Bless'd the infant Babe,
       (For with my best conjectures I would trace

The progress of our Being) blest the Babe,
Nurs'd in his Mother's arms, the Babe who sleeps
Upon his Mother's breast, who, when his soul
Claims manifest kindred with an earthly soul,
Doth gather passion from his Mother's eye!
Such feelings pass into his torpid life
Like an awakening breeze, and hence his mind
Even [in the first trial of its powers]
Is prompt and watchful, eager to combine
In one appearance, all the elements
And parts of the same object, else detach'd
And loth to coalesce. Thus, day by day,
Subjected to the discipline of love,
His organs and recipient faculties
Are quicken'd, are more vigorous, his mind spreads,
Tenacious of the forms which it receives.
In one beloved Presence, nay and more,
In that most apprehensive habitude
And those sensations which have been deriv'd
From this beloved Presence, there exists
A virtue which irradiates and exalts
All objects through all intercourse of sense.
No outcast he, bewilder'd and depress'd:
Along his infant veins are interfus'd
The gravitation and the filial bond
Of nature, that connect him with the world.
Emphatically such a Being lives,
An inmate of this *active* universe.

In 1850 this becomes (II. 233–254):

Blest the infant Babe,
(For with my best conjecture I would trace
Our Being's earthly progress) blest the Babe,
Nursed in his Mother's arms, who sinks to sleep
Rocked on his Mother's breast; who with his soul
Drinks in the feelings of his Mother's eye!
For him, in one dear Presence, there exists
A virtue which irradiates and exalts
Objects through widest intercourse of sense.

No outcast he, bewildered and depressed:
Along his infant veins are interfused
The gravitation and the filial bond
Of nature that connect him with the world.
Is there a flower, to which he points with hand
Too weak to gather it, already love
Drawn from love's purest earthly fount for him
Hath beautified that flower; already shades
Of pity cast from inward tenderness
Do fall around him upon aught that bears
Unsightly marks of violence or harm.
Emphatically such a Being lives
Frail creature as he is, helpless as frail,
An inmate of this active universe . . .

Dr. Leavis remarks, "No one is likely to dispute that the later version is decidedly the more satisfactory." However, I mean to dispute it.

I prefer the earlier version in the first place because it does more to deserve that "active" which in 1805 got the italics denied to it in 1850. Not only are there more active verbs in the first version, but they are more energetic. In 1805 the child *claims* kindred and *gathers* passion, where in 1850 he "drinks in" feeling. His mind *spreads,* is eager to combine, tenacious and *apprehensive.* (The Latinate pun delivers the muscular grasp of the policeman apprehending the lag.) The later version is mawkish, emphasizing the frailty of the child, his weakness. In the first version the Mother's love is an energy, comparable with the force of gravitation and the chemical force that stirs the torpid life. ("Torpid," of course, was a technical term of eighteenth-century science.) In the later version, the Mother's love is presented as tenderness, and even then as combined or confused with pity. The "gravitation," which survives into the later version, is out of place there, in a context of imagery that is predominantly and weakly visual ("*shades* of pity"), where at first it had been muscular and dynamic. The pseudo-syntax of the rhetorical question ("Is there a flower . . . ?") goes along with this pervasive slackening of tension, this retarded and unsteadied movement.

If I ask myself what grounds Dr. Leavis can have for preferring the later version, I can only suppose he is attracted by the relative concreteness (heaven knows it is phantasmal enough) of the flower and even the "Unsightly marks of violence or harm." I would sum up the difference between these two versions by saying that, in the earlier draft, Wordsworth is rendering the experience of being a child at the mother's breast. He is doing this in the only way possible, from inside the child's mind, by rendering in his verse the movements of the child's consciousness, stirring here, checked or sluggish there, drawn this way by powerful currents, dammed back somewhere else. In the later version the poet is sometimes inside the child's mind, sometimes inside the mother's, sometimes inside the spectator's; and by thus shifting his point of view, he denies himself the chance of rendering with fidelity the movements in the child's mind or the mother's or the spectator's. Undoubtedly the language of the earlier version appears more abstract, but it is not therefore ratiocinative. It seems to me that its strength is all in its energetic verbs, and the nouns that attend them ("powers," "elements," "parts," "forms," "sensations," "objects") are correspondingly thin and general. And of course this energy in representing movements of the mind fits in with the fact that Hartley, Wordsworth's master here, was the last of the mechanic psychologists, such as influenced Pope, who explained the movements of the mind in terms drawn ultimately from mechanics.

Mr. John Jones, in his very valuable book on Wordsworth, has lately insisted on the extent to which Wordsworth always thought in these eighteenth-century terms:

> There is . . . a conservatism in the context of Wordsworth's thought. He is not in revolt against the Great Machine, the master-image of eighteenth-century science and philosophy. Only the phrase is unwordsworthian (though there is enough of pure eighteenth-century poetic in him to allow a reference to his wife's spirit, in relation to her body, as "the very pulse of the machine"): he would prefer something more supple, like "this universal frame of things." His complaint is that nobody has as yet observed its component parts with sufficiently devoted care, or experienced fully the power and beauty of its movement.

In *The Prelude,* Wordsworth uses the word "things" with astonishing frequency. The Concordance reveals that the 1850 text alone accounts for about one-third of its occurrences in the entire bulk of his poetry. "I looked for universal things"; "I conversed with things that really are"; Wordsworth will make his verse "deal boldly with substantial things"—the word is clearly and consistently referred to the main theme of the poem. His search for universal things is on one side a search for particularity: in his insistence upon constancy, boundedness, irreducibility, he betrays the imaginative impression of a traditional English materialism. But he is more than a materialist, in that he enquires not only for the particular but for the powerful. Here his resources are heavily taxed. In order to express essential energy, he is too often led to personify spirit, motion, power itself, in a context of vague declamation. . . .[6]

But Wordsworth can do better than that. In passages such as the one just considered, of 1805, he conveys the power as well as the particularity, the different kinds of pulse in the natural machine, by the precisely discriminated energies of his verbs, which concretely act out the powers he is speaking of. In him perhaps one may applaud what Fenollosa applauded in Shakespeare, his "persistent, natural, and magnificent use of hundreds of transitive verbs."

NOTES

1. Tr. Mina Curtiss, *Sewanee Review*, LX (1952), p. 601.
2. R. L. Brett, *The Third Earl of Shaftesbury: a Study in Eighteenth-century Literary Theory* (London, 1951), p. 14.
3. Lionel Trilling, *The Liberal Imagination* (New York, 1950), p. 133.
4. Pollock, *The Nature of Literature* (Princeton, 1942), p. 62.
5. F. R. Leavis, *Revaluation* (London, 1936), pp. 173-4.
6. John Jones, *The Egotistical Sublime: a History of Wordsworth's Imagination* (London, 1954), pp. 34-5.

E. M. W. TILLYARD

Scott's Linguistic Vagaries

To set forth and account for Scott's varied use of language would need specialised erudition and the compass of a substantial book. I have neither the equipment nor the inclination to meet these two needs. All I seek to do is to note that the language of Scott's novels has been taken for granted with surprising coolness and to call attention to some of its strangeness. I shall illustrate mainly by *The Monastery,* linguistically far the strangest of the novels, and through such illustration I may comment incidentally on the progress or degeneration of Scott's fictional art.

The Waverley Novels succeeded so suddenly and overwhelmingly that they quickly became classics and models. Men took them as one of the great fictional norms and found them natural rather than strange. Natural they may have been compared with the run of Neo-Gothic fiction, but in some ways they are strange: strange in their play from the superficial to the profound, strange in the way their author caused them to yield to public opinion, strange in the disorder of their linguistic elements.

The linguistic pattern of Scott's first Scottish novels, that is of the series from *Waverley* to *A Legend of Montrose,* is indeed pretty clear. He used a contemporary English idiom, inherited from the eighteenth century, for description, narrative, and the speech of the more edu-

From *Essays Literary and Educational* (Chatto & Windus, 1962), pp. 99–107. Reprinted by permission of the publisher and Mr. Stephen Tillyard.

319

cated, and Lowland Scots for the speech of the humbler folk. In
his English he uses an occasional "Av" or " 'Tis" if he wishes to
stress an earlier date or feels melodramatically inclined, but he is
always near his natural inheritance. Behind him we find Johnson,
Horace Walpole (Gothic or ungothic), Hume, Mrs. Radcliffe, and
so on. Now he will remind of Goldsmith's limpidity, now of Clara
Reeve's sententiousness, but he does nothing to surprise us, except
in the wonderful use to which he puts the different parts of his
inheritance.

Scott's difficulties began with *Ivanhoe,* and he recognised them.
Having exchanged Scotland for England and the post-Restoration
period for the early Middle Ages, he could not continue as before.
What emerges from the Dedicatory Epistle is first an uneasy feeling
of conscience that he ought to archaise quite considerably; and second the conviction that if he did as he ought he would be unread-
able, like Chatterton. He defended an "unnatural" modernisation
on the plea that elements common to medieval English and the
English of his own day were far larger than was generally supposed:
actually nine-tenths of the whole. But though he acted on this defence
through much of *Ivanhoe,* his conscience insisted on a minimum of
archaism; and to satisfy it he made his characters talk fitfully a
language which has been described as "Wardour Street," "Tushery,"
or "Ye Olde." They are not consistent in its use, but they incline to
affect it when they are being highminded or in a situation near the
comic. And the tushery can vary in strength. It is not always as
strong as in the following passage:

> Nay, but fair sir, now I bethink me, my Malkin abideth not
> the spur—Better it were that you tarry for the mare of our
> manciple down at the Grange, which may be had in little more
> than an hour, and cannot but be tractable, in respect that she
> draweth much of our winter fire-wood, and eateth no corn.

Scott went to many places for his tushery. He got little precedent
from the novel. Clara Reeve, Mrs. Radcliffe, and M. G. Lewis use
eighteenth-century English, more or less formal. Only Walpole in
The Castle of Otranto gave him a lead. There we get such things as:

> "Villain! monster! sorcerer! 'tis thou hast done this! 'tis thou
> hast slain my son!"

and

> "Sir Knight, whoever thou art, I bid thee welcome. If thou
> art of mortal mould, thy valour shall meet its equal; and if thou
> art a true knight, thou wilt scorn to employ sorcery to carry thy
> point."

But the first passage is followed by one so little archaic as

> "Think no more of him; he was a sickly puny child; and
> Heaven has perhaps taken him away, that I might not trust
> the honours of my house on so frail a foundation."

Walpole in fact rarely pushes his archaism beyond what was usual
in the more solemn modes of eighteenth-century drama, in the historical plays, for instance, that Sheridan transfixed so neatly in *The
Critic*: in this from Murphy's *Grecian Daughter*,

> *Philotas.* By Heav'n thou wrong'st me: didst thou know, old
> man—
> *Melanthon.* Could not his rev'rend age, could not his virtue,
> His woes unnumber'd, soften thee to pity?

or this from Thomas Francklin's *Earl of Warwick*,

> Good Suffolk, lay aside
> The forms of dull respect, be brief, and tell me.
> Speak, hast thou seen her? Will she be my queen?
> Quick, tell me ev'ry circumstance, each word,
> Each look, each gesture: didst thou mark them, Suffolk?

or this from Richard Glover's *Boadicea*,

> Why didst thou leave the fair Italian fields,
> Thou silken slave of Venus? What could move
> Thee to explore these boist'rous northern climes,
> And change yon radiant sky for Britain's clouds?
> What dost thou here, effeminate? By Heav'n,
> Thou shouldst have loiter'd in Campania's villas,

And in thy garden nurs'd, with careful hands,
The gaudy-vested progeny of Flora.

If such mild archaising was behind *The Castle of Otranto,* it may
have been one of the miscellany of things behind *Ivanhoe* and much
of the later Scott.

In the main, Scott went farther afield for his tushery. He had
become acquainted at a very early age with archaic English through
Percy's *Reliques,* and because of his prodigious memory these must
have been a permanent part of his mind's furniture. He was soaked
in Shakespeare and he was well versed in other Elizabethans.
Berners's Froissart is another obvious source of the archaisms of
Ivanhoe. We are apt to underestimate the extent and the boldness
of Scott's archaising because we miss his originality in giving currency to many words or phrases that had dropped out. Ernest Week-
ley pointed this out in an article in *The Atlantic Monthly* for 1931
called *Walter Scott and the English Language.* Influenced by Percy
and Shakespeare, Scott revived, among others, "passage of arms,"
"red-handed," "henchman," "stalwart." Very few readers of Scott
are aware of such revivals: one of the reasons why they have taken
his use of language so coolly.

When Scott archaised he did so with riotous eclecticism. It is a
commonplace that his imitation of Euphuism through the mouth
of Sir Piercie Shafton in *The Monastery* is most inaccurate; and
naturally, for his exuberant mind was ill suited to the niggling
accuracy required for successful pastiche. F. A. Pottle in his most
interesting essay on the different types of memory in Boswell and
Scott in *Essays on the Eighteenth Century,* presented to D. Nichol
Smith, showed that Scott always added to what he remembered,
being unable to suppress his creative urge: a process analogous to,
or accounting for, his falsifying Lyly. It also argues a state of mind
that would draw on Chaucer, an old ballad, Froissart, and Shakespeare in the same paragraph as readily as Horace Walpole mixed
his styles in the Gothic of Strawberry Hill. Indeed these words of
Eastlake in his *History of the Gothic Revival* would apply *mutatis
mutandis* to Scott's archaisms:

> The interior of Strawberry Hill was just what one might ex-
> pect from a man who possessed a vague admiration for Gothic
> without the knowledge necessary for a proper adaptation of its

features. Ceilings, screens, niches etc. are all copied, or rather
parodied, from existing examples, but with utter disregard for
the original purpose of the design. To Walpole Gothic was
Gothic and that sufficed.

Add this tushery to the generally eighteenth-century ground of
the language of *Ivanhoe* and you have something quite fantastically
strange. It is Scott's triumph that he could be gloriously at ease in
this strangeness and end by deceiving men into thinking he was
doing something natural. Not that the triumph was not also a
tragedy. In his attempt to cope with the English Middle Ages after
coping with eighteenth-century Scotland, Scott chose an instrument
altogether coarser than the one he had discarded; and though he
showed a giant's strength in wielding it, nothing could alter the fact
of its inferiority.

Scott tells us in the 1830 introduction to *Ivanhoe* that he chose
an English subject for fear of cloying his readers with too much
Scotland. In his next book, *The Monastery,* he reverted to Scotland
but sought innovation by choosing a period intermediate between
the eighteenth century and the reign of Richard I. But it appears
from the turns and the inconsistencies of the language he used that
for about a third of the book he proceeded in uncertainty, hesi-
tating between the manners of the Scottish novels and of *Ivanhoe.*
In his first chapter, to be sure, describing the monastery of Ken-
naquhair and its setting at the time of religious unrest in sixteenth-
century Scotland he was sure of himself, because there is no dialogue
and he can write in the language that was most natural to him. His
troubles begin in the second chapter when after describing the tower
of Glendearg and its inhabitants he embarks on a conversation between these and the English troopers who have been overrunning
this part of the Lowlands. Elspeth Glendinning and her two sons
belonged to a decent class of Scottish yeomen, and we know how
Scott would have made them talk if he had followed his natural
inclinations. All he allows Elspeth in the way of Scottish speech is
a single *nae* for *no*; otherwise she talks English, as do her sons.
When the kindly English captain, Stawarth Bolton, departs, Elspeth
exclaims, "God be with you, gallant southern!," to which one boy
retorts, "I will not say amen to a prayer for a southern," and the
other, "Is it right to pray for a heretic?"; to which Elspeth replies:

The God to whom I pray only knows; but these two words, southern and heretic, have already cost Scotland ten thousand of her best and bravest, and me a husband, and you a father; and, whether blessing or banning, I never wish to hear them more.

What is so remarkable in these speeches is that they are neither in the Scots that such characters would have used in the Scottish novels nor in the tushery they would probably have used in *Ivanhoe*.

The scene now changes to the castle of Lady Avenel, widow of Walter Avenel, a Baron of ancient descent. Hearing that the tower of Glendearg has been spared by the English marauders, she decides to take refuge there to escape the dangers that threaten her castle. She is accompanied in her flight by her shepherd and his wife alone. When Martin and Tibb Tacket open their mouths, Scott, in spite of his treatment of the Glendinnings' speech, allows them to break into the Scots of which he was the supreme master. There follow the best things in this very unsatisfactory novel: the flight of Lady Avenel with her infant daughter and the two Tackets across the moor, their kind reception by Elspeth Glendinning, and the subsequent life of the combined households. These are in Scott's cleanest and most delicate domestic vein: the minute frictions set up by the different social positions of the two families and the compromises by which they are overcome are recounted or hinted at with the skill of a great master. And Elspeth Glendinning, oblivious of her previous speech, talks the Scots that she should of course have talked from the beginning.

"And what made you, ye misleard loons," said Dame Elspeth to her two boys, "come yon gate into the ha', roaring like bullsegs, to frighten the leddy, and her far frae strong? Could ye find nae night for daffin but Hallowe'en, and nae time but when the leddy was reading to us about the holy Saints? May ne'er be in my fingers, if I dinna sort ye baith for it!"

When the scene changes to the monastery, Scott has to decide what language his monks are to use; and, in spite of the success of what has just gone before, he makes these sixteenth-century Scottish monks talk much like their brethren in the late twelfth-century setting of *Ivanhoe*. Here is part of the first conversation; between the Abbot and his Sacristan.

> "The lady is unwell, holy father," answered the Sacristan, "and unable to bear the journey."
>
> "True —ay—yes— then must one of our brethren go to her— Knowest thou if she hath aught of a jointure from this Walter de Avenel?"
>
> "Very little, holy father," answered the Sacristan, "she hath resided at Glendearg since her husband's death, wellnigh on the charity of a poor widow, called Elspeth Glendinning."
>
> "Why, thou knowest all the widows in the countryside?" said the Abbot. "Ho! ho! ho!" and he shook his portly sides at his own jest.

Unsettled by his decision on the speech of the Scottish monks, Scott goes back on his other decision to make Elspeth Glendinning talk in the Scots that becomes her; for, when the Sacristan comes to Glendearg and talks with her about the sick lady, all the Scots she can attain to is an occasional *nae doubt,* and the pattern of her talk is this kind of thing:

> And yet is the Holy Scripture communicated for our common salvation. Good father, you must instruct mine ignorance better; but lack of wit cannot be a deadly sin, and truly, to my poor thinking, I should be glad to read the Holy Scriptures.

From now till near half way the queerest linguistic confusion reigns. For instance, in the eighth chapter Elspeth talks English for a long stretch, breaks into a bit of Scots, reverts to English, and then resumes her Scots for a moment. A humble character, Peter the Bridgeward, speaks tushery: "By my sooth, sir, you look sorely travelled and deadly pale." When Halbert Glendinning encounters the ghostly White Lady, both description and dialogue are in the pure idiom of the Neo-Gothic romance:

> "Speak!" he said, wildly tossing his arms, "speak yet again— be once more present, lovely vision!—thrice have I now seen thee, yet the idea of thy invisible presence around or beside

me, makes my heart beat faster than if the earth yawned and gave up a demon."

Not only Elspeth switches from English to Scots and back again, but so does the homely Hob Miller. Unlike Elspeth's, his English is mainly tushery ("And so I say, dame, an ye be so busied with your housewife-skep, or aught else . . .") while his Scots is perfunctory. Into the existing linguistic chaos breaks Sir Piercie Shatton with his pseudo-Euphuism. The final degradation is when Martin the shepherd, who had been the occasion of Scott's changing to the idiom proper to such characters, uses the colourless language of the inferior romantic novels of the late eighteenth century:

> God help me, there may be truth in what thou sayest—but walk slower, for my old limbs cannot keep pace with your young legs—walk slower, and I will tell you why age, though unlovely, is yet endurable.

After this lapse Scott begins to settle into what was to be the linguistic norm of most of his later novels. There are a few returns to Scots, but one hardly notices them; and when Halbert gets out into the wider world to seek his fortunes, the linguistic tone is the historico-heroic one, full, energetic, unsubtle, that began with *Ivanhoe* and that was to serve Scott's turn so usefully in his later popular successes. In the scenes in Avenel Castle with Julian Avenel, his timid mistress, Henry Warden the Protestant preacher, and Halbert Glendinning, we feel that Scott at last knows his own mind; his energies, though coarsened, are unimpeded. In *The Abbot* he maintained the temper he had reached in the course of *The Monastery*. There may be a dozen bits of Scots in the whole book, but for all its Scottish setting it is linguistically in full harmony with its successor, set in England, *Kenilworth*.

Thereafter Scott was occasionally tempted to return to his earliest manner, but a Scottish setting was not in itself sufficient to give the incentive. *The Fair Maid of Perth* maintains the historico-heroic norm, and we get in it a thing like, "Nay, God-a-mercy, wench, it were hard to deny thee time to busk thy body-clothes." It was only when Scott felt the paramount urge to work his remaining Jacobitism out of his system that he consented to resume his old linguistic habits in *Redgauntlet*. Twice he made a partial return: first, and in a more important way, in *The Pirate;* second in *The Fortunes of Nigel.* In *The Pirate* Scott returns for a little to his true domestic vein in describing the households of Jarlshof and Stourburgh, but in the end melodrama prevails. In *The Fortunes of Nigel* there are no complete circles where the Scottish idiom is used, and the tushery is especially strong:

> O! Saint Dunstan has caught his eye; pray God he swallow not the images. See how he stands astonished, as old Adam and Eve ply their Ding-dong! Come, Frank, thou art a scholar; construe me that same fellow, with his blue cap with a cock's feather in it, to show he's of gentle blood, God wot.

But while the hero, Nigel Olifaunt, speaks English, against all probability as fresh from Scotland, his servant, Richie Moniplies, speaks Scots consistently. The other character who speaks Scots is the king himself, Scott, I take, feeling unable to be quite false to James's written words. But it sounds queer when he talks thus, while one of his Scots nobles speaks an English of which the following is a sample:

> It is a lie, a false lie, forge it who list!—It is true I wore a dagger of service by my side, and not a bodkin like yours, to pick one's teeth withal—and for prompt service—Odds nouns! it should be prompt to be useful.

In neither novel are there the turns and contradictions that make *The Monastery* so strangely unstable for near half of its course.

Scott's linguistic vagaries are matched by his states of mind. Generalisations, like those of Bagehot's, about the way Scott always views his material from without are false. When in his early Scottish novels he felt free to use the speech that came most naturally to him he can be (I do not say always was) as close to his scenes and characters as Jane Austen. But in response to the public demand he abandoned the intimacy he had loved and turned his prodigious vitality to pageantry and stirring improbabilities. For these ends he created a strange linguistic amalgam, an amalgam that suited his readers so well that they overlooked its strangeness. *The Monastery* is uniquely interesting as showing the conflict between Scott's two modes in the very act of being resolved.

F. W. BATESON

The Language of the Victorians

If one compares, as one fairly may from the similarity of the matter, the diction of Thackeray's novels with Fielding's, or Dickens's with Sterne's, a fact of some interest emerges. Fielding and Sterne are quite as sentimental as Thackeray and Dickens, but the emotions that their novels communicate are one remove farther away. The emotions are released by the situations; they lie *behind* the words. The emotions of Dickens and Thackeray, on the other hand, are rawer and more exposed. They *adhere* to the words, which provide an emotional accompaniment to the situations.

The difference is the measure of the change which the English language had undergone in the century dividing the four novelists. In 1750 the tendency was for words to be purely denotative—to be restricted, that is, to their primary and "official" meanings. It was the tribute exacted from the language by the intellectualism of the age. But with the coming of the nineteenth century, with the coming not only of the romantic movement in poetry but of the hundred other movements in life and thought that went to make up the Victorian complex, the rigidity of the language relaxed. The emotions, no longer compelled to hide behind an intellectual structure, began to express themselves directly, and the connotations of words gradually came to seem as important as, and sometimes more im-

From *English Poetry and the English Language* (Clarendon Press, 1934), pp. 98-113. Reprinted by permission of the publisher and author.

portant than, their denotations. Precision of statement was less necessary; suggestiveness and "atmosphere" had taken its place.

The new models of style were the Elizabethan and Jacobean
writers. ("From the common opinion," said Coleridge, "that the
English style attained its greatest perfection in and about Queen
Anne's reign I altogether dissent.") [1] Byron, with his keen eye for
an affectation, ridiculed the change of fashion. He was "told that
the new school were to revive the language of Queen Elizabeth, the
true English: as every body in the reign of Queen Anne wrote no
better than French, by a species of literary treason." [2] And it is
true there was an element of artificiality in the revival. For the
language of the early nineteenth century is really quite different
from that of the early seventeenth century. Both periods may be
said to have sacrificed denotation to connotation, but it was to two
different kinds of connotation. In the metaphysical period the connotation of a word *grew* out of its denotation—the two are so entangled that it is impossible to know where one begins and the
other ends. But the connotation of a nineteenth-century word was
superimposed upon its denotation—the denotation it had possessed
in the eighteenth century—and the two meanings exist separately
and, as it were, side by side. It was possible, that is, given the appropriate context, to employ a word either for its denotation alone
or for its connotation alone. But the enhanced significance of
Jacobean diction, the resonance that gave it its prestige with the
Victorians, depends precisely upon the impossibility of separating
what a word denotes from what it connotes. (It is the grand secret
of the prose of the Authorized Version of the Bible.) Jacobean diction is both precise and profound. The best mid-Victorian diction,
on the other hand, though sometimes precise (Mill is precise, Bagehot is precise) and sometimes profound ("a network of tentacular
roots reaching down to the deepest terrors and desires"), rarely if
ever unites the two qualities either in its prose or its poetry. The
Victorians spoke two languages, reflecting the divided aims and
origins of their civilization: a language of the heart, and a language
of the head. It is not necessary to call this hypocrisy (they were the
victims of irresistible tendencies), but poetically the bifurcation was
a disaster.

A modern historian has noted as a peculiar characteristic of nineteenth-century political thought the "multiplicity of elements un-
absorbed into a common thing." [3] The lines of thought are parallel

and never meet. But Victorianism is more easily defined in terms
of its feelings than of its thoughts. A Victorian who thought at all
was bound apparently to think differently from everybody else. The
rival systems of Carlyle, Mill, Ruskin, Spencer, Newman, and
Arnold are such poles apart that they scarcely even contradict each
other. It is only in feeling that they are comparable. There, however,
their limitations and excesses are curiously the same. The emotional
centre of Victorianism, as I see it, is conveniently indicated in a remark attributed to Tennyson: "the evils he denounces are individual,
only to be cured by each man looking to his own heart." [4] The
evils the Victorians denounced were always individual, and the
"heart," the conscience, was always their cure. (The conscience is
the real hero not only of the novels of rationalists like George Eliot
but also of such a work as Newman's *Grammar of Assent*.) Dallas,
one of the best of the Victorian critics, commented on Tennyson's
line,

> The individual withers, and the world is more and more:

> But I am not sure whether the essence of this thought might
> not be expressed in the very opposite terms: the individual
> prospers, and the world is less and less. The great point to be
> seized is that there is gradually being wrought a change in the
> relation of the individual to the mass. Whether we regard that
> change as a growth or as a withering will depend very much
> on what we think of the individual. If the individual in whom
> we are most interested is what is generally understood by a
> hero, then certainly it must be confessed that he withers. The
> little men and the private men and all the incidents of privacy
> are coming into repute. We dwell far more than we used to do
> on the private side of human life. Now the private virtues are
> becoming public, and the private life is rising into public im-
> portance.[5]

But the acclamations and accusations of the private conscience, if
intense and profound, are necessarily vague. They elude words. A
feeling of moral rapture or remorse can only be translated into adequate words with the help of just such an organized religion or
philosophical system as the Victorians were unable to provide. And
since such feelings must be expressed at all costs it was the words

that suffered. The diction became as vague and diffuse as the emotions.

The pioneers of the English romantic movement—Wordsworth, Coleridge, and Southey—had been handicapped by the uncongeniality of the language they found in use. The second generation of romantic poets (Tennyson, Browning, Mrs. Browning, FitzGerald, and Arnold) were more fortunate in possessing a language that suited them. It was easier for them to write. Their poems do not suffer from the lapses and inconsistencies of style that disfigure the earlier poets. But, though it was easier for Tennyson and Arnold to write well, it was next to impossible for them to write supremely well. The language with which Wordsworth and Coleridge had wrestled and which they had sometimes succeeded in compelling to their purposes, was excellent of its kind, though it was not their kind—a tyrant, but a tyrant worthy of their daggers. The necessity under which they lay of resisting the linguistic tendencies of the previous century was itself a stimulus. But the language that Tennyson found to his hands was a flabby and submissive thing. He did what he could with it; he was a natural stylist, with an inborn interest and instinct for words.[6] And yet, with all his critical awareness, with all his charm and fluency, what a poor thing relatively Tennyson's style is! Slow, monotonous, overcoloured, overmusical, its essential diffuseness only emphasized by the niggling detail. "A poet," Coleridge has observed, "ought not to pick nature's pocket: let him borrow, and so borrow as to repay by the very act of borrowing. Examine nature accurately, but write from recollection; and trust more to your imagination than to your memory."[7] Tennyson trusted more to his memory than to his imagination, and more to his note-books than to his memory. But this fussy accuracy of his, distracting though it is, was in a way praiseworthy. It was Tennyson's protest against the vagueness, the emotional mist, in which the diction of Victorian poetry was wrapped. The style to which he naturally tended was, I believe, something cooler and more concentrated than the condition of the language ever permitted him to achieve:

> You'll have no scandal while you dine,
> But honest talk and wholesome wine,
>   And only hear the magpie gossip
> Garrulous under a roof of pine;

For groves of pine on either hand,
To break the blast of winter, stand;
And further on, the hoary Channel
Tumbles a billow on chalk and sand.

I seem to detect in these lines to F. D. Maurice, as at moments in "The Palace of Art" and "In Memoriam," a distant hint, a tantalizing premonition, of a poetry of the might-have-been in which a Horace collaborates with a Marvell.

But, with all the deductions made that must be made, Tennyson did obtain a minor success. The style that he elaborated was as economical and as precise as the language permitted. Its virtue is its consistency, and it was a consistent style because it was a conscious style. The peculiarities of Victorian English had been taken into account, its merits had been made the most of, its vicious propensities had been partially discounted. Tennyson did not try to write either in ignorance of or in indifference to the linguistic tendencies of his time. His poems are made out of the diction of the day—"the best words in the best order" that were then available; and his limited success serves to show up the failure of the other romantic poets of his generation. Tennyson was at least aware of the condition of the language he was compelled to use. His contemporaries, on the contrary, were *language-proof*. They bluntly refused to concern themselves with problems of diction and style. "The poet," they would have agreed with Newman, "is a compositor; words are his types; he must have them within reach, and in unlimited abundance." [8] And the consequence of this mechanical conception of composition was that, falling unconscious victims to the contradictory tendencies of the period, they cannot strictly be said to have a *style* at all. They have idiosyncrasies of expression; but that is another matter.

A theory of poetry that has no place for diction must offer something in its stead. The Victorians offered the subject. The romantic ideal of style was, as we have seen, "something which must derive its poetic validity entirely from the matter committed to it." [9] The earlier romantic poets had derived this matter from the subconscious mind. If they selected one subject rather than another, it was because some subjects will stimulate the subconscious mind more than others. They had not fallen into the mistake, into which the later poets fell, of considering some subjects essentially poetical. "A great artist," Byron once said, "will make a block of stone as sublime as a mountain, and a good poet can imbue a pack of cards with more poetry than inhabits the forests of America." [10] With this dictum we may contrast Matthew Arnold's war-cry: "All depends upon the subject; choose a fitting action, penetrate yourself with the feeling of its situations; this done, everything else will follow." [11] The subject was the red herring of Victorian criticism, and many of the errors of that criticism—its neglect of Donne, its half-heartedness to Blake, its disparagement of Shelley [12]—are directly traceable to its influence. But it would be incorrect to attribute all the deficiencies of the Victorian poets to the doctrine of the subject. The most that can be said is that it encouraged them in their habits of linguistic indifference. The real case against mid-Victorian poetry, other than Tennyson's, is not that it rests upon a mistaken basis of theory but that it is badly written.

The example of Matthew Arnold is especially instructive because Arnold was not naturally a poet but a man of letters. His place is with such writers as Addison and Goldsmith, and Mr. Aldous Huxley to-day—writers who, one feels, at whatever period they happen to be born, *must* express themselves through literature, though the particular literary form they may select is ultimately immaterial and dependent on the fashion of the moment. Poetry happened to possess more prestige than any other form in the mid-ninteenth century, and Arnold wrote poems. But I can find no trace in all his intelligent and readable verse of any specifically poetic originality. The sensibility reflected in it is not that of Arnold himself but of his age, and the style is an amalgam of the language that was then available for poetry. And what language it was!

> And Wordsworth! Ah, pale Ghosts, rejoice!
> For never has such soothing voice
> Been to your shadowy world convey'd,
> Since erst, at morn, some wandering shade
> Heard the clear song of Orpheus come
> Through Hades, and the mournful gloom.

Apart from the vicious exclamations—a pet trick of Arnold's, like the forcible-feeble use of italics, and both traceable to a desperate effort to impart an artificial emphasis to a naturally unemphatic diction—was it necessary to describe *Ghosts* as *pale*? If Hades is populated by wandering *shades* need we be told that it is *shadowy?* Is not *gloom* always *mournful?* And logical confusion is added to the redundancy. Wordsworth's *soothing* voice is compared to Orpheus's *clear* song. But why, especially in the gloom of Hades, should a clear song be soothing? One would have imagined that it would be more likely to be disturbing. What finally is the significance of *at morn?* Is not Hades always equally dark? Or, if there are gradations of light, are we to visualize the relative darkness or the relative brightness of morning?

The passage I have quoted is not in the least exceptional. Read hurriedly it is not unimpressive. But once it is subjected to a critical scrutiny the vagueness of its diction and the looseness of its thought are inescapable. The words are the ghosts of words. Two words have to be used to do the work of one. And the trickle of meaning is obscured in a fog of associations conjured up by the implied reference to parallel passages in the *Odyssey,* the *Georgics,* and the *Aeneid.* It would be unfair, however, to lay all the blame on Arnold, who merely accepted the style and the language current in his time. It is the limitations of that style and that language, especially in conjunction, that I wish to emphasize. Arnold's style is clear, his diction diffuse. There were therefore two alternatives that he evaded: he could either have clarified his diction, as Tennyson to some extent did; or, like the Pre-Raphaelites, he could have diffused his style.

"Poetry, in our day," Landor wrote in the laconic preface to the 1859 edition of *The Hellenics,* "is oftener prismatic than diaphanous: this is not so: they who look into it may see through." It was a concise definition of the central difference between Landor's own style (which approximates to that of such mid-eighteenth-century writers as Akenside) and that of the Victorian poets. Landor is transparent; the Victorians are opaque. But the definition, in 1859, was more relevant to the poetry of the immediate future than to that of the immediae past. Matthew Arnold, the bulk of whose verse was published between 1849 and 1857, certainly wrote in a style that it was impossible, for those who looked into it, to see through. But was it *prismatic?* The word describes far better, not Arnold's neutral tones, but the iridescent poetry of the Pre-Raphaelites. "The Blessed Damozel" *is* prismatic. And so are "Goblin Market," "The Life and Death of Jason," and "Atalanta in Calydon." But, with the exception of "The Blessed Damozel" (first published in *The Germ* in 1850), these poems date from the years 1862–7.

The distinction of the Pre-Raphaelites, Rossetti's and Swinburne's in particular, was to have brought back into Victorian poetry a love of words for their own sake. Rossetti "collected" words. "I have done but little in any way," he wrote to his brother in 1849, "having wasted several days at the Museum, where I have been reading up all manner of old romaunts, to pitch upon stunning words for poetry. I have found several." [13] The finds are scattered through his poems —"grame," "dole," "grout," "teen," &c. No one probably would claim now that Rossetti's "stunners" helped his poetry. They are symptomatic, indeed, of the irresponsibility that accompanied his enthusiasm. (A word was "stunning" often only because it was out-of-the-way.) But the mistake was a fault on the right side in 1849. Rossetti's verbal excesses were tonic just because they were verbal. To the pundits who thundered—Matthew Arnold among them—"Choose better subjects," Rossetti retorted "Choose better words." The two slogans may have been both unduly simplified, but Rossetti's was at least the more practical and the more heartening. The early Victorians had tried all sorts of subjects with very little success; they had not tried all sorts of words.

Tennyson is a partial exception to this generalization. But Tennyson, though decidedly a better poet than most of the Pre-Raphaelites, did not exert a comparable influence on the younger writers. His style—that is, the *direction* of his style—was opposed to the linguistic tendencies of the nineteenth century. The Rossettis and Swinburne, on the other hand, were in full sympathy with those tendencies. They encouraged and exploited them. The vagueness and diffuseness of Victorian English, only a nuisance to Tennyson, were admirably adapted to express the dreamlike quality of their vision:

> A little while a little love
> The hour yet bears for thee and me.
> > (*Rossetti.*)
> Not a lily on the land,
> Or lily on the water.
> > (*Christina Rossetti.*)
> I heard all night and all the hours of it.
> > (*Swinburne.*)

The diffuseness of such phrases is different from the diffuseness of "In Memoriam" or Arnold's poems. It is a paraded diffuseness, deliberate and ostentatious. The Pre-Raphaelites *tried* to be diffuse. The secret of their influence is that they fitted to the blurred meanings and dim associations of Victorian diction a mode of apprehension and a style that were equally blurred and dim. They wrote *with* the language, whereas Tennyson, Arnold, and the Brownings (in their several degrees of more or less) wrote *against* it, and their reward is the inevitability—"the carol, the creation"—that sets Swinburne at any rate in the same class as a Spenser, a Donne, and a Dryden. The "Atalanta" choruses, "The Triumph of Time," and the poem on Baudelaire ("Ave atque Vale"), to name no others, are perfect of their kind—though one may not like the kind. Tennyson's poetry, on the other hand, is never absolutely perfect (Keats would always have done it rather better), though as a kind it is natural to prefer it.

The diffuseness of Victorian English was ultimately derived from a loosening of the connexion between the connotations and the denotations of words. The two meanings, as we have seen, had come to exist almost independently, with a mutual loss of vividness and precision. A word had its normal meaning, its "dictionary" meaning, and, side by side with that, a secondary meaning created by the contexts in which it was used. The difficulty therefore for the hearer or reader on each occasion was to be certain which meaning was intended—or rather, how *much* of each meaning, the proportion of primary and secondary meaning being constantly variable. And it was just the indecision in which this condition tended to terminate —in other words, the feeling of *vagueness*—that the Pre-Raphaelites exploited. Swinburne's words are vague because he has included all their meanings, primary and secondary, impartially. It is impossible to know which aspect of a word, which centre of meaning, he wished to emphasize. But the impossibility is the point. The incongruousness that the reader experiences, the difficulty of connecting up the juxtaposed implications of the diction, leads to precisely that surrender of the logical faculty, with the consequent feeling of revelation, that the Pre-Raphaelite style requires.

> Before the beginning of years
> There came to the making of man

> Time with a gift of tears;
> Grief with a glass that ran.

"The chorus of Swinburne," Mr. T. S. Eliot remarks, "is almost a parody of the Athenian: it is sententious but it has not even the significance of a commonplace . . . it is effective because it appears to be a tremendous statement, like statements made in dreams; when we wake up we find that the 'glass that ran' would do better for time than for grief, and that the gift of tears would be as appropriately bestowed by grief as by time." [14] But the objection is irrelevant. The Pre-Raphaelites do not deal in revelations but in the *feeling* of revelation. There are no statements, in the ordinary sense, in their poems at all. What they communicate, with untiring artistry and superb *élan*, is a state of mind—the state of mind of a dreamer. The value of that state of mind is, of course, another question.

The detail that is an occasional characteristic of Pre-Raphaelite verse, and the air of an unnecessary precision that accompanies it, have the effect paradoxically of accentuating the prevalent vagueness. The numbers that Rossetti and Swinburne delight in are an example of this:

> She had three lilies in her hand,
> And the stars in her hair were seven.
> > (*Rossetti.*)
> There were four apples on the bough.
> > (*Swinburne.*)

Why *three* lilies, *seven* stars, *four* apples? The reader concludes that the numbers must be important because they are specified so carefully. But they are not important. What Swinburne and Rossetti were interested in was not the exact number of the lilies, stars, or apples, but the feeling of exactness those numbers convey. Rossetti has described the Pre-Raphaelite ideal as "the constant unison of wonder and familiarity so mysteriously allied in nature, the sense of fulness and abundance such as we feel in a field, not because we pry into it all, but because it is all there." [15] It is an excellent definition. Pre-Raphaelite poetry, like the world of dreams, is both strange and familiar. But the technical basis of this "constant unison of wonder and familiarity" is, on the one hand, an abuse of language, and, on the other hand, an abuse of detail.

NOTES

1. "On Style" (*Essays and Lectures*).
2. *Letters and Journals*, ed. R. E. Prothero, vol. iv. 1900, p. 490.
3. Crane Brinton, *English Political Thought in the Nineteenth Century*, 1933, p. 293.
4. *Tennyson. A Memoir. By his Son*, vol. i, 1897, p. 468.
5. *The Gay Science*, vol. ii, 1866, p. 280.
6. His casual comments prove it: "Wordsworth seemed to him *thick-ankled*"; "I can't read Ben Jonson, especially his comedies. To me he appears to move in a wide sea of glue" (*Tennyson. A Memoir. By his Son*, vol. ii, 1897, pp. 505, 205)—two judgments that could not be improved upon.
7. *Specimens of the Table-Talk*, vol. i, 1835, p. 208.
8. Op. cit., p. 251.
9. I have borrowed this excellent definition from Professor Lascelles Abercrombie's *Romanticism*, 1926, p. 25.
10. *Letters and Journals*, ed. R. E. Prothero, vol. v, 1901, p. 557.
11. "Preface" (*Poems*, 1853).
12. Palgrave's *Golden Treasury* omits Donne and Blake altogether. Arnold ("Byron" in *Essays in Criticism: Second Series*) detected in Shelley "the incurable want of a sound subject-matter"—an opinion shared by Patmore (*Principle in Art*, 1890, p. 114).
13. *Family Letters*, vol. ii, 1895, p. 51.
14. *The Sacred Wood*, 1920, p. 135.
15. *Collected Works*, vol. i, 1901, p. 444. Rossetti's abuse of numbers may have been encouraged by the "kisses four" of "La Belle Dame sans Merci" (one of his favourite poems). Keats deleted the phrase in the final draft of the poem.

W. A. WARD

✍

On Dickens

All Dickens's critics admit him to be "lively," but there is very little agreement about where the "liveliness" comes from, or what it is, or what its value is. George Henry Lewes, an intelligent and perceptive man, said this:

> For the reader of cultivated taste there is little in his works beyond the stirring of their emotions—but what a large exception! We do not turn over the pages in search of thought, delicate psychological observation, grace of style, charm of composition; but we enjoy them like children at a play, laughing and crying at the images which pass before us.[1]

The mistake Lewes makes, which is typical of much of the more recent criticism of Dickens, is in thinking with his mind's eye. But to understand Dickens you must think with the ear. The "delicate psychological observation" is achieved by an ear alive to the meaning of nuances of tone and alive to the human consequences of using habitual patterns of speech. The writer in English most like Dickens is Joyce. *Finnegans Wake* was much influenced by Dickens, and that is the book above all that insists on the deeper meaning of words heard over words seen. Critics who have never felt the con-

Revised from *Listener* (23 May 1963), pp. 870–71, 874. Reprinted by permission of the publisher and author.

sequences of an inexact ear have the habit of reading merely with
their eyes, and the mistake gives rise to this sort of remark:

> Apart from *David Copperfield* and *Great Expectations,* Dickens's
> psychology is most convincing when he is dramatising sensa-
> tions of guilt, fear, and panic.[2]

Yet if you listen for a moment to the way the words strike you in
reading Dickens, that is obviously not true. What Professor Hardy
means by "psychology" is what she can account for, or what Dickens
thought he could account for and explain: experience that he
thought that he had fully understood, at least enough to dominate
it and use it for a didactic purpose. The best bit of *Martin Chuzzlewit* becomes Jonas's guilt, in that view, and the best bit of *Oliver
Twist* Fagin in the condemned cell. An image of Dickens is constructed that leaves you unable to understand why so many of the
voices stick in the ear. A sense of the importance of people like
Jingle in Pickwick, or of Sam Weller, or of the Artful Dodger, is
left untouched. Gloom descends on Dickens. He becomes more
like Conrad than Fielding; his affinities are held to lie with Kafka
and Dostoievsky rather than with Cobbett and Surtees. Pickwick,
Pecksniff, Podsnap, Daniel Quilp, Mr. Bumble—all take second
place; the humour is stifled or shown to be the result of mere personal hysteria. The critic takes refuge in the blanket word "gusto,"
and that is the best he can do towards explaining the energy and
vitality of the prose. This is the position John Gross arrives at in a
recently published volume of essays, *Dickens and the Twentieth
Century* (1962). The "flat" characters are left to be accepted on the
valuation Strindberg made of Mr. Barkis—that his entire character
was limited to one word, "Willin'."

Perhaps it is because so many English critics labour under the
shadow of D. H. Lawrence that a fear of form in language has
grown up. To talk about the form of prose is to be accused of aesthet-
icism. But with Dickens you have to talk about prose. A large
part of the meaning of the novels is there in the prose, in the way
one manner of speaking cuts into another, contradicts it, or modifies
it. And the changes of pace and manner in the narrative are as important as the events which carry the plot forward. Indeed they
are the events which carry it forward. Attention to the forms of prose
means attention to the meaning of the way people talk to each

other, what they mean by what they say. This passage from *Pickwick Papers* illustrates what I mean:

> "Eh?" said Mr. Magnus; and then he repeated the sneer with increased effect. "But you shall answer it, sir."
>
> "Answer what?" said Mr. Pickwick.
>
> "Never mind, sir," replied Mr. Magnus, striding up and down the room. "Never mind."
>
> There must be something very comprehensive in this phrase of "Never mind," for we do not recollect to have ever witnessed a quarrel in the street, at a theatre, public room, or elsewhere, in which it has not been the standard reply to all belligerent inquiries. "Do you call yourself a gentleman, sir?" "Never mind, sir." "Did I offer to say anything to the young woman, sir?"—"Never mind, sir." "Do you want your head knocked up against that wall, sir?"—"Never mind, sir." It is observable, too, that there would appear to be some hidden taunt in this universal "Never mind," which rouses more indignation in the bosom of the individual addressed, than the most lavish abuse could possibly awaken" (ch. 24).

What the passage makes clear at once is that Dickens got his information by *listening*. And that he feels that what he hears has a representative significance.

Attention to "form" in Dickens means attention to what can be learnt by listening to the way people talk, to "forms" of speech. What the critic has to do is to come closer in to the speech and manner of the people so that he can *hear* how Dickens makes his enquiry. It is not enough to brush off all that delighted imitation with the word "gusto" or "responsiveness." Mr. Pecksniff's first appearance in *Martin Chuzzlewit* displays much of what I mean:

Mr. Pecksniff begins to speak of the new architectural pupil he has persuaded to come to his coaching school, which does not exist, at a high premium:

> "Yes," said Mr. Pecksniff, after a short pause, during which he had been silently smiling, and shaking his head at the fire: "I have again been fortunate in the attainment of my object. A new inmate will very shortly come among us."

"A youth, papa?" asked Charity.

"Ye-es, a youth," said Mr. Pecksniff. "He will avail himself of the eligible opportunity which now offers, for uniting the advantages of the best practical architectural education, with the comforts of a home, and the constant association with some who (however humble their sphere, and limited their capacity) are not unmindful of their moral responsibilities."

"Oh Pa!" cried Mercy, holding up her finger archly. "See advertisement!"

"Playful—playful warbler," said Mr. Pecksniff. It may be observed in connection with his calling his daughter "a warbler," that she was not at all vocal, but that Mr. Pecksniff was in the frequent habit of using any word that occurred to him as having a good sound, and rounding a sentence well, without much care for its meaning. And he did this so boldly, and in such an imposing manner, that he would sometimes stagger the wisest people with his eloquence, and make them gasp again.

His enemies asserted, by the way, that a strong trustfulness in sounds and forms, was the master-key to Mr. Pecksniff's character (ch. 2).

Such a trustfulness, is, in fact, the key to most of Dickens's characters. They are misled by language, or exploit it in order to mislead. Their views of reality are shaped by their command of grammar, syntax, and vocabulary; and a critique which seeks to account for the vitality of the prose and the inclusiveness of the vision would most profitably start by working out the extent of Dickens's virtuosity in representing such a complex variety of idioms. To name instances: at the beginning of the chapter Mr. Pecksniff is knocked down by the wind and brought with exaggerated solicitude into the parlour where his two daughters sit him down to tea: this, after his hat, brownpaper parcel, umbrella, gloves, and bump on the top of his head, the bits of pickled brown paper, brandy and water, and a smoking dish of ham and eggs have all been introduced with characteristic relish. Miss Pecksniff then sits down on a low stool at her father's feet:

It must not be inferred from this position of humility, that the youngest Miss Pecksniff was so young as to be, as one may say, forced to sit upon a stool, by reason of the shortness of her legs. Miss Pecksniff sat upon a stool, because of her simplicity and innocence, which were very great: very great. Miss Pecksniff sat upon a stool, because she was all girlishness, and playfulness, and wildness, and kittenish buoyancy. She was the most arch and at the same time the most artless creature, was the youngest Miss Pecksniff, that you can possibly imagine. It was her great charm. She was too fresh and guileless, and too full of childlike vivacity . . .

and so on.

It is true that the way we read the irony here is directed by our existing understanding of Miss Pecksniff—but the falsity of her attitudes is, more importantly, suggested to us by the control of the language, the delicacy of the emphasis which exposes the falsity. Dickens imitates a selection of the various falsities of ordinary speech, and in doing so refers outside this immediate fictional situation. The irony of the passage seems almost to be directed at the fact that there should be a fictional situation at all; the art is deliberately fantastic and theatrical, we are kept from taking it seriously, and attention is directed to the truth of the remarks rather than to any plausibility of the invented scene. We do not recognize the things said as true of Miss Pecksniff, but rather as true in that they define a common kind of falsity. Miss Pecksniff only serves as an occasion for the comment, exposing that particular falseness for what it is: communicating the precise feeling of what it is to encounter the language of such a person, aligning us with him in jovial irritation. All this exhibits a poise and versatility giving access to a psychological observation of extreme delicacy.

Again, in his description of Mr. Pecksniff's naming of his daughters, Dickens is summoning us to recognize the exactness of his references to the false language adopted on such occasions:

Mr. Pecksniff was a moral man: a grave man, a man of noble sentiments, and speech: and he had had her christened Mercy. Mercy! Oh, what a charming name for such a pure-souled being as the youngest Miss Pecksniff! Her sister's name was Charity. There was a good thing! Mercy and Charity! And Charity, with her fine strong sense, and her mild, yet not reproachful gravity, was so well named, and did so well set off and illustrate her sister!

We are referred here to a tone of voice which takes the naming of the characters as indeed representing the attitudes of playful seriousness Mr. Pecksniff wishes to have accepted. "There was a good thing! Mercy and Charity," refers to a particular kind of obfuscating joviality which we recognize at once. The vitality of the passage comes from the playful references which are packed into it, to the falsities of language which the pedlars of these attitudes avail themselves of. The spectacle is one of the artist's assuming the mask of each pose in turn and then, laughingly, dropping it, so that we are made aware of what that attitude means.

Mr. Pecksniff, in fact, is not a character in any real sense. He is a device that enables Dickens to exhibit his ability to imitate the speaking voice and to catch thereby the precise tone of a wealth of attitudes. He draws on the prodigious resources of his ear. Pecksniff suddenly stops while he is eating, and says:

> "Even the worldly goods of which we have just disposed," said Mr. Pecksniff, glancing round the table when he had finished, "even cream, sugar, tea, toast, ham—"
> "And eggs," suggested Charity in a low voice.
> "And eggs," said Mr. Pecksniff . . .

Here the emptiness of the cliché "worldly goods" is remarked on. But, more brilliantly, we are made aware of the cliché of the pattern. The attentive serious pupil, suggesting to the master a helpful remark, which is neither taken nor offered as serious or helpful, but serves to keep the ball in the air, bolsters the speaker, gives him support in accepting him on his own valuation, serves to ingratiate the pupil, and presents an attitude of seriousness without its content. The subtlety of the reference is beyond description. The words work with a speed and richness that give a sense of the copiousness and abundance that exist in real life. What matters is that the portentous solemnity Mr. Pecksniff displays is danced out in the form of the language and rendered absurd in being yoked to such trivial subject-matter—and this wealth of information is released through a musical organization of the prose and the careful control of tone.

But when we consider the events and "characters" in this chapter, it is at once clear that the narrative is organized in a rudimentary way. And this seems to be typical of the way Dickens arranges his plots; though in some of the later novels he develops them in a more complicated way so that they add to the significance of the whole. The young Martin Chuzzlewit, for instance, sits in front of the fire and leaves Tom Pinch out in the cold, demonstrating a selfishness which it is part of the declared intention of the book to expose. But the action Dickens invents to illustrate his egotism and the change which later occurs in young Martin is inadequate. It is machinery and conveys no impression of vitality. This is often so in Dickens's plots. If we think of his attempts at organizing and contrasting different areas of experience through a richly endowed series of events, or of enquiring into the nature of people through their experience of each other, Dickens again suffers in the most elementary comparison with writers like James or Conrad. Tom Pinch cannot carry the burden of moral approval he is called upon to bear: John Westlock is a mechanical stock character. It is not there that the liveliness is to be found.

But the events serve to bring Dickens's ear into play, and they provide him with a convenient means by which he can draw on the resources of a very complete experience of the English language. The insights in this chapter of *Martin Chuzzlewit* make themselves felt in discriminations between authentic and inauthentic tones of voice. John Westlock's "Both hands, Tom," when they are about to part, conveys more moral feeling than one would have expected from such a character. One is convinced by the tone of voice alone. Anybody could have said "Both hands, Tom": it gains its effect from its structural manner, the quietness and simplicity and finality of the voice, not from its being spoken by John Westlock and having the authority of his character to back it up and make it significant. We recognize the truth of what is said because Dickens imitates a manifold variety of idioms and forms exactly. And it is the language we all use. We know what it means. Reading the work is like being thrown into the deep end of the English language and tossed about among its forms and patterns. Dickens makes us aware that he is throwing us in by performing for us. He involves half his characters in the play with language. He presents himself as playing. We are meant to admire his virtuosity. But admiring it makes one aware of the differences of meaning implicit in manners of speaking and tones of voice.

Lewes's suggestion that there is no serious thought in the whole twenty volumes seems obtuse; though it is true that such thought as is presented in a form Lewes might have understood (that is to say, abstractly or in a formulated way) is often banal. But so what? Our experience of the fog which surrounds the Court of Chancery in *Bleak House* or of the prisons in *Little Dorrit* is not limited to what we are told about them. So far as they are formulated as ideas they are unconvincing. Looking for "intelligence" about society in *Bleak House* you find only the false rhetoric of Tom-All-Alone's connection with the *beau-monde*; and so on. But there is a landscape of language as well as of fictional device in the book. A complex variety of modes of speaking or of approaching reality is arranged and explored by the writer; the different modes of speaking are played off against each other; each character has his own idiom. An experience of *Bleak House*, like the experience of the language of *Martin Chuzzlewit*, and an impression of the inclusiveness of the social vision, come from encountering so various a selection of styles.

Dickens most frequently displays the limitations of his characters' ways of viewing life in their verbal idiosyncracies; and so far as the language they speak is an authentic imitation of the colloquial idiom, the characterization is immediately true. "Barkis is willin' " is, after all, typical in its finality and restrictiveness of linguistic form. Barkis could have said something else and, by repeating some other form of words, have meant the same thing. His character is as adequately represented by that remark as it would have been by any of a dozen others he might have made. Repetition is characteristic of his idiom; and to catch some one's idiom is to penetrate his mode of viewing life, the structure of his own reality, how much he knows and how much he can know. That Dickens's presentation of the idiom is so inclusive is, indeed, the real testimony to the depth and range of his awareness. It tells or shows how much he knew about life. His awareness derives from a sensitive and exact ear. He wrote his books for the speaking voice; and they should be read aloud.

NOTES

1. G. H. Lewes, "Dickens in Relation to Criticism," in *The Dickens Critics*, ed. George H. Ford and L. Lane (Ithaca, 1961), p. 73.
2. Barbara Hardy, *"Martin Chuzzlewit,"* in *Dickens and the Twentieth Century*, ed. J. Gross and G. Pearson (London, 1962), p. 117.

PATRICIA INGHAM

Dialect in the Novels of Hardy
and George Eliot

When Norman Nicholson speaks of men

> Euclidizing one and one and one
> To nowt but a nowt —[1]

the reader is not likely to overlook the dialect word and is virtually
obliged to wonder about the conscious avoidance of the more usual
one. Poetry constantly forces us to ask why this word is here. The
novel does not. This is particularly true of the use of dialect in
novels; it is not usually regarded as a significant element in the
novelist's technique, even when he uses a great deal of it. The
common assumption is that dialect is a rather inferior form of local
colour, and too technical to be the concern of anyone except the
linguist. But when a major novelist like Hardy uses it, we need
to ask those basic questions that we automatically ask about its use
in poetry: why and how? The answers to these questions can be
illuminating in a general way, whether the novelist concerned is
Hardy, George Eliot, Emily Brontë, D. H. Lawrence, or any other
of whom it would be rash to assume that something which figures
largely in his work is an irrelevancy. Dialect as a sporadic and often

347

effective element in poetic diction has a long history. It goes back to the sixteenth century and survives today. Its use as an important device in the English novel has been by comparison of short duration. Probably its antecedents are the many representations of low or vulgar speech in eighteenth-century novels, but it first begins distinctly with Scott. It ceases to be important about a hundred years later, one of its last effective users being Lawrence. Since the presence of dialect in the nineteenth-century novel is now often a hindrance to the reader, a critical evaluation of two outstanding uses may prove helpful.

Hardy, who in his lifetime was compared unfavourably with George Eliot in his use of dialect, is particularly worth close consideration, because misapprehensions here can distort his work to the point of caricature. This has been so from the start: twice in the nineteenth century the dialect in his novels was attacked, on grounds that were directly opposed to each other. The first attack, provoked by *The Return of the Native,* charged him with inaccuracy in the language of "his peasants" who, it said, "talk . . . as no people ever talk now." [2] The second attack, on the other hand, which arose through the comparison with George Eliot, accused him of being led by a "thorough knowledge of the dialectical peculiarities of certain districts" into writing "whole conversations which are, to the ordinary reader, nothing but a series of linguistic puzzles." [3] Shot at from both sides Hardy himself retaliated by pointing out that these charges arise from a misunderstanding of his aims.

But Hardy's own statements have been largely ignored, though there have been two rather indirect attempts at vindication. An account of the linguistic accuracy of the dialect,[4] however, is hardly an adequate answer to the first charge: the dialect in Hardy's novels lacks not only self-consistency, but also such strikingly characteristic features of the Dorset speech of his day as the particular pronunciation of *r*. There is not much meat for the linguist here, especially as a good deal of the effect is created by fairly general colloquialisms like *'em*.[5] That the dialect is roughly accurate no one would nowadays deny. Alternatively, the simple reiteration that the dialect gives local colour, which was gradually increased by Hardy during revisions as the idea of Wessex evolved,[6] does less than justice both to facts and literary effects; it is only half the truth that he added further touches of dialect as he revised.

With dialect in poetry nothing comes between the reader and the word to prevent him from registering its impact. Many things can intervene in a novel. Where dialect is used, as in Hardy, in dialogue only, the author's views on realism in the novel in general and on realism in dialect in particular become important. We need to know, if possible, what the author at least thought he was doing. Hardy spoke out on both these subjects. Consideration of what he said, taken with *all* the changes that he made in the use of dialect during his revisions of the major novels between their first publication and the definitive edition of 1912, and the total picture presented by that edition, can bring us to a sound assessment of literary aims and effects. It can also suggest ways of looking at the use of dialect by other novelists. It can suggest the questions that it is pertinent to ask, though not all of them will be equally pertinent to each novelist.

Hardy's general views on realism are clearly stated when he is discussing the fact that most writers of fiction, including such unlikely examples as Dumas père and Mrs. Radcliffe, would "cheerfully accept" the dictum of a very different kind of novelist, Zola, that "the novel should keep as close to reality *as it can*." [7] The explanation of their surprising agreement is that all novelists exercise "selection and cunning manipulation" to some extent, and Zola's "*as it can*" will be interpreted by each according to the degree of realism he aims at. Hardy himself is inclined to belittle novels which show exceptional fidelity to realistic detail and in which

> you are fully persuaded that the personages are clothed precisely as you see them clothed in the street, in the drawing room, at the assembly,

and where even

> the trifling accidents of their costume are rendered . . . They use the phrases of the season, present or past, with absolute accuracy as to idiom, expletive, slang. They lift their tea cups or fan themselves to date.
>
> But what of it? he asks, after our first sense of its photographic curiousness is past? [8]

He saw little merit in description as a form of photograph and would presumably, from his remarks on dialogue, have seen equally little merit in the latter as a form of tape-recorded speech. He is talking mainly about plot and descriptive detail, but his attitude to these is of a piece with his attitude to dialect.

What he says about the latter in his answer to *The Athenaeum* attack can be seen as a particular illustration of his general point of view, for he writes of the language of the rustics in *The Return of the Native* as

> intended to show mainly the character of the speakers, and only to give a general idea of their linguistic peculiarities.[9]

By contrast, George Eliot intended in general to include more realistic detail in her picture of the world. As she says in *Adam Bede* (1859), she prizes the "precious quality of truthfulness" that she finds in Dutch painting, and her own "strongest effort" is "to give a faithful account of men and things as they have mirrored themselves in my mind." She felt

> as much bound to tell you as precisely as I can what that reflection is, as if I were in the witness box narrating my experience on oath (ch. 17).[10]

As with Hardy's, these general views apply, evidently, to the particular instance of dialect in this novel where her "inclination to be as close as I could to the rendering of the dialect, both in words and spelling" was checked only by "the artistic duty of being generally intelligible." But for the latter she would have "given a stronger colour to the dialogue in 'Adam Bede'," which is modelled (and here she is precise) "on the talk of N. Staffordshire and the neighbouring part of Derbyshire." [11] So, ironically, it emerges that any detailed approach to Hardy's dialect should assume an intended impressionism and to George Eliot's an intended accuracy.

Moreover, Hardy tells us exactly how in his use of dialect he saw himself exercising "selection and cunning manipulation." He selects "the idiom, compass, and characteristic expressions" of "intelligent peasant talk." And he manipulates, in one way at least, by avoiding too accurate a representation of how dialect sounds because in the printing of standard speech

> hardly any phonetic principle at all is observed; and if a writer

attempts to exhibit on paper the precise accents of a rustic speaker he disturbs the proper balance of a true representation.[12]

Practice supports theory here, for it is evidently with considerations of this sort in mind that Hardy removed from later versions of the novels many spellings like *clane* "clean," *mane* "mean," *rale* "real," and *nate* "neat," which indicate fairly well an authentic Dorset pronunciation of M.E. *ẹ̄*. In other words, at times he deliberately makes the dialect less exact. At other times, of course, he makes alterations which improve it. Such are: the removal of what he must have come to recognize as "eye-dialect" forms, which like *woz* for *was,* are merely roughly phonetic representations of standard forms (*pore* "poor," *foke* "folk," *wimmen* "women," *grate* "great," *trew* "true"); and a consistent substitution of *'ee* for earlier *ye* (apparently, from its distribution, simply because he thought the former more authentically characteristic of the dialect). The selectiveness of this needs no stressing. It contrasts with George Eliot getting G. H. Lewes, who is "innocent of dialects," to "tone down" dialect speech in the proofs of *Adam Bede* only in the interests of intelligibility; and Charlotte Brontë, incidentally, doing the same for Emily.

Both the principles at work in Hardy's revisions and his minute care are obscured by the simplified account of the changes made in dialect during revisions of *The Mayor of Casterbridge* (1886) and *Tess of the D'Urbervilles* (1891). The statement that Hardy merely increases the dialect words and forms as a means of "heightening the Wessex atmosphere" [13] cannot stand unqualified even for, indeed particularly for, these two novels.

To begin with, it is necessary, as an examination of changes in the other major novels shows, to distinguish the minor rustic characters from major ones like Henchard and Tess. It is then seen to be true that with the minor figures alterations show, on the whole, a slight increase in dialectal and colloquial forms and uses. This appears in the speech of Christopher Coney, Solomon Longways, and the frequenters of Peter's Finger in *The Mayor of Casterbridge,* and in the Durbeyfields and the Crick household in *Tess of the D'Urbervilles.* It is also found in the alterations to the minor rustics in the other novels grouped with these two under the heading of *Novels of Character and Environment* in the 1912 edition: Reuben Dewy and the choir in *Under the Greenwood Tree* (1872); Bathsheba's employees in *Far from the Madding Crowd* (1874); Timothy Fairway and his cronies in *The Return of the Native* (1878); Mr. Melbury and his workmen, Grammer Oliver and Creedle in *The Woodlanders* (1887); Little Father Time and Arabella in *Jude the Obscure* (1895). It is noticeable, for instance, that in the later revised versions Hardy incorporated a scattering of initial *v-* for *f-* and initial *z-* for *s-*. Such forms are not frequent but they are familiar to standard speakers as typically South Western, and have an effect disproportionate to the number of their occurrences.

But alongside this spasmodic pointing up of dialect in the speech of even these minor characters go alterations actually involving a decrease of the dialectal and colloquial element. Examples in *The Mayor of Casterbridge* are: later *knew* for earlier *knowed* (furmity-seller); *serves* for *sarves* (stay-lace vendor); *your* for *yer* (Coney); *her face* for *'a, window* for *winder, they are* for *they be* (Mother Cuxsom); *were* for *wer* (Whittle); *worse* for *wuss* (Nance Mockridge); *swore* for *sweared, somebody* for *feller, haven't* for *ha'nt* (Charl). Similarly in *Tess of the D'Urbervilles* we find later *has she* for earlier *have she* (Mr. Durbeyfield); *might* for *mid* (Mrs. Rolliver); *hinders* for *do hinder* (Izz and Marian); *are you* for *are ye* (Groby). Clearly the process of retouching quite often suggests to Hardy that he has overdone his effects and he decides to lessen them in a fairly haphazard way. Not even a desire to be more intelligible would account for changes like these.

As the final picture presented by the 1912 versions shows, Hardy in no instance tried to make the language of even his most minor and most rustic character self-consistent. Nor is there any attempt as in William Barnes's dialect poems to make every instance or even most instances of a word conform to a dialectal norm. The dialect is deliberately and carefully impressionistic. The unrealism of such dialogue in Hardy's novels is as conscious as the unrealism of plots made up of "a selected chain of action best suited for their exhibition" of the author's "views of life" [14] and is defensible artistically on the same grounds. The language of these rustics is distorted by a selection of "Dorset effects" in just the same way as it is distorted by an evident attempt to imitate the language and attitudes of some of Shakespeare's comic characters. If the speech of Hardy's minor rustics is to be justified, it must be in terms of how effectively they function in the novel. And we can only decide about that by being clear as to how they are meant to function.

They contrast with George Eliot's minor figures, who exist as people in their own right, who are part of the social hierarchy and butts for the same kind of ironic comment as their betters. Hardy's minor figures are not characters observed but part of the novel's machinery. Either they are there for comic effect only, like the choir in *Under the Greenwood Tree,* or they push along the plot like Grammer Oliver in *The Woodlanders* or Crick in *Tess of the D'Urbervilles,* or they perform a whole range of choric functions from the purely comic, as in some of Creedle's remarks, to the ironic, as in the comments on Lucetta's marriage to Farfrae, or to the purely pathetic as in Whittle's surprisingly articulate account of Henchard's last journey:

> "And I followed en over Grey's Bridge, and he turned and zeed me, and said, 'You go back!' But I followed, and he turned again, and said, 'Do you hear, sir? Go back!' But I zeed that he was low, and I followed on still. Then 'a said, 'Whittle, what do ye follow me for when I've told ye to go back all these times?' And I said, 'Because, sir, I see things be bad with 'ee, and ye wer kind-like to mother if ye were rough to me, and I would fain be kind-like to you.' Then he walked on, and I followed; and he never complained at me no more" (ch. 45).[15]

The lack of realism in the speech of these minor rustics is intended and effective.

One cannot, however, make the same kind of simple statement about major characters in Hardy's novels who use dialect: Henchard, Tess, Gabriel Oak, Dick Dewy, and Marty South. Caution suggests that with any novelist it would be well to look carefully at major as opposed to minor characters who use dialect. They are likely to be involved with other major characters who use standard speech, and in the more "realistic" novelist to vary accordingly in their usage. For it is to be expected that, as in real life, such characters as are high enough up the social or educational scale to vary will modify their speech to suit their hearer, and use less dialect to a standard speaker, more to those who use dialect constantly. This simple principle is illustrated by Adam Bede: he uses very little dialect to Arthur Donnithorne and Mr. Irwine, but

whenever he wished to be especially kind to his mother . . .

fell into his strongest native accent and dialect, with which at
other times his speech was less deeply tinged (ch. 4).

Something of this is also observed in Mrs. Morel in *Sons and
Lovers*. But again examination of the material showing Hardy at
work suggests a different treatment on his part: it seems often to be
the broader requirements of the particular novel in question that
control the variations in a single speaker.

It is true that among minor increases in dialect in *The Mayor
of Casterbridge* are some that are put into the mouth of Henchard
himself, but they are more than counterbalanced not only by a
slightly larger number of decreases, but also by the removal from
chapter five of a heavily dialectal speech made by Henchard as
mayor at the banquet. The reason seems to be that Hardy's conception of the character shifted somewhat, and wishing to build up
Henchard's stature in order to make him more of a tragic figure,
he felt the need to stress his provincialism less, particularly when
showing him at the height of his success. In the same way the
demands of realism are to some extent cast aside with Gabriel Oak.
It is not true, although it has been alleged and one might expect
it, that in his conversations with the standard-speaking Bathsheba
we are reminded of his farming background "only by an occasional
'ee." [16] On the contrary the non-standard elements in his language
are increased precisely when he is talking to Bathsheba, particularly
when he is warning her against Troy. In this passage alone Hardy
changes *ruck of* to *ruck o'*, *downward* to *down'ard*, *talk to you* to
talk to 'ee, *towards him* to *towards en*, *pretend to you* to *pretend
to 'ee*, *beg you* to *beg of 'ee*, *use of it* to *use o't*, *wish you* to *wish 'ee*,
and *Are you not* to *Are ye not* (ch. 29). Several more changes in
the same direction are also made in some of Oak's other conversations with Bathsheba, and make it clear that Hardy wishes at these
points in the story to underline more emphatically that rusticity
and lack of surface refinement which cause her to compare this man
unfavourably with the smooth-speaking and dashing Troy. Presumably it is also to bring out a contrast and differentiate between
Bathsheba's two farmer-suitors that Hardy makes Oak use a number
of dialect forms (including the later addition of the strikingly obvious *'ill* for *will*) to Boldwood later in the book (ch. 52). All this
is not how such a dialect speaker would probably vary in fact, but
in terms of the desired contrasts, it works. The same aim seems to

lie behind Hardy's handling of Dick Dewy's usage in *Under the Greenwood Tree*: one of the passages in which Hardy noticeably increases Dick's use of dialect is in the scene between him and the vicar, where the latter, given the last touch of irresistible charm by his elegant silk umbrella, has just become Fancy Day's second and contrastingly genteel fiancé. Here Dick uses in the later versions *branch o'* for earlier *branch of*, *a' extra* for *an extra*, *prented* for *printed*, and the two rare and very noticeable forms *'ill* for *will* and *kip* for *keep* (IV. 7). The deliberate contrast in this scene is further emphasized by Fancy's particular concern with refinement of speech when, at the wedding,

> the propriety of everyone was intense, by reason of the influence of Fancy, who, as an additional precaution in this direction had strictly charged her father and the tranter to carefully avoid saying "thee" and "thou" in their conversation, on the plea that those ancient words sounded so very humiliating to persons of newer taste (V. 2).

Thus it is significant that it is in Dick's conversations with this very Fancy, who so carefully avoids dialect herself, that Hardy during his revisions actually changes *with you* to *with 'ee*, *help you* to *help 'ee*, *will you* to *will ye*, *you may* to *you mid*, *may as well* to *mid as well* and *you are* to *you be*.

Underlying the contrast between Oak and Troy, Dewy and the vicar, is the idea of language as a social index: dialect seen as something which places a man lower on the social and/or educational scale than one who uses standard speech. This brings us to a basic question to ask about novelists who use dialect or provincial speech: how do they regard its use as a social indicator, or in George Eliot's case, how do they regard those who so regard it? It is by exploring the answers to these questions that one unfolds the subtlety of George Eliot's use. To some extent she makes use of the framework that standard and non-standard speech provide to place Adam Bede in relation to Arthur Donnithorne, or Fred Vincy in relation to the Plymdales. But a more varying approach is also evident when one looks at the novels with an eye to what attitude she takes up. This seems sometimes to be quite straightforward: the Reverend Amos Barton has a tendency *for to do* a thing and wears a maize coloured dressing gown because he has "a knack of hitting on the

wrong thing in garb as well as in grammar" (ch. 2). Here she
seems to accept the idea of provincialism in language as a social
indicator in order to use it for direct comic effect. But she is ironic,
though cheerfully so, when she makes Mr. Casson the innkeeper
in *Adam Bede* speak scornfully of the local speakers of "the dileck"
because he himself was

> "brought hup among the gentry . . . an' got the turn o' their
> tongue when I was a bye" (ch. 2);

or when the Misses Gunn in *Silas Marner* (1861) are horrified by
Nancy Lammeter's pronunciation of *mate* for *meat, 'appen* for *perhaps* and *'oss* for *horse*

> which, to young ladies living in good Lytherly society, who
> habitually said 'orse, even in domestic privacy, and only said
> 'appen on the right occasions, was necessarily shocking (ch.
> 11).

The irony is double and less cheerful in *Middlemarch* (1871-2)
when Rosamond Vincy expresses irritation at her mother's use of
the pick of instead of *the best of*: the author is not totally in sympathy with the Mrs. Vincy who ultimately wants to substitute *the
most superior* for her original phrase (ch. 11). Sometimes it is impossible to say where George Eliot does stand in this matter. How,
for instance, are we to take the remark that Mr. Gambit (ch. 45)
"made none the worse accoucheur for calling the breathing apparatus
'longs'?" Are his talents as a speaker and as an accoucheur equally
deficient or merely irrelevant to each other?

All these examples are mere touches in a canvas rich in irony of
many kinds; but in one character at least, that of Esther Lyon in
Felix Holt (1866), someone accepts too wholeheartedly the view that
non-standard speech is not only an indication of social standing but
also of moral worth. In this, as in other things, Esther begins by
substituting an aesthetic for a moral viewpoint, and it is part of
the book's theme to show how under Felix Holt's influence she
changes. It is because she is so largely the novelist of social aspirations that the attitude which George Eliot takes to dialect as the
badge of the outsider, and the attitudes that she shows others taking, are so important. This is the most pertinent aspect of her use

of dialect to consider. It is surprisingly relevant also to Emily Brontë's use in *Wuthering Heights* (1847), where the only real dialect speakers are the servant Joseph and the despised Hareton; and Hareton seems gradually to be educated out of his Yorkshire speech by Catherine.

The question of Hardy's attitude is forced upon the reader by his treatment of those who, like Fancy Day, accept as an indication of general worth the purely social indications of dialect. He is critical of Fancy for preferring surface refinement to real worth, but sometimes he himself seems to accept passively the view that dialect is merely to be treated as a means of indicating the socially inferior and standard speech the socially superior. This is confirmed by the absence of non-standard elements from the language of originally lower class but admired figures such as Jude as an adult, Stephen Smith in *A Pair of Blue Eyes* (1873) and Swithin St. Cleeve in *Two on a Tower* (1882). On the other hand, in addition to Hardy's scorn of Fancy, there is some irony in his remark that Mrs. Garland, the artist's widow in *The Trumpet Major* (1880) (who is, after all, prepared to marry the prosperous miller) is sorry to find

> with what readiness Anne caught up some dialect-word or accent from the miller and his friends (ch. 1).

The irony becomes biting to the point of violence in his description of Henchard's disapproval of Elizabeth Jane's use of dialect words when he is angry with her from quite other causes. In the serial version of *The Mayor of Casterbridge* the description ran:

> One grievous failing [of Elizabeth's] was her occasional use of dialect words—those terrible marks of the beast to the truly genteel (ch. 20);

this was sharpened from the first edition onwards to "her occasional *pretty and picturesque* use."

This dislike of dialect does not really reflect on Henchard's social aspirations; it is more by way of being an irrational outlet for the fury he feels at discovering too late that he is not really the girl's father. The scathing irony is here Hardy's own, and seems directed with a particularly heartfelt bitterness not against Henchard so much as against those who feel that dialect is not genteel. Henchard himself can hardly be intended by "the truly genteel" even ironically meant. But the phrase is worth considering for the implication it has that alongside Hardy's acceptance of dialect speech as an indication of a certain inferiority exists a conflicting tendency to see it in a more idealized light.

Outside the novels, clear evidence of such an attitude is found in some of the things Hardy writes concerning the work of the Dorset dialect poet William Barnes, whom he admired so much. There is "no grotesqueness" in Barnes's use of dialect, since to a native "its sounds are as consonant with moods of sorrow as with moods of mirth"; he eulogizes

> the full significance the original words bear to those who read them without translation, and know their delicate ability to express the doings, joys and jests, troubles, sorrows, needs and sicknesses of life in the rural world as elsewhere; [17]

and he describes the impact made by readings of Barnes's poems on an audience "well acquainted with the nuances of the dialect." [18]

These remarks are meant, and they could never have been made by George Eliot, who is ultimately a little patronizing even towards Adam Bede.[19] Hardy's attitude to dialect in his novels was double: at times he will see it as a badge of inferiority, and at other times as language possessing "a delicate ability" to express the deepest feelings, the kind of language wrung out of a man, like extreme colloquialism, when he is particularly moved. This is actually seen to happen to Phillotson, Sue's schoolmaster husband in *Jude the Obscure,* at what for him is the most agonizing moment in the story as he tries to decide whether he is morally obliged to take the superficially immoral course and help his wife to leave him. At this point he goes to talk to a boyhood friend and fellow schoolmaster, Gillingham. Astonishingly, in the context of the correct English that Phillotson always uses in the rest of the book, the two lapse into dialect. In the earlier versions Phillotson uses the familiar *'ee* and even in the final version speaks bitterly of how he *toled* or "enticed" Sue out for walks when she was his pupil (IV. 4). Gillingham bluntly tells him that he is *rafted* ("disturbed") and urges him to the conventional course. The amount of dialect used in the scene is slight, and is accounted for by the explanation that they are lapsing into the language of their boyhood, but it has a disproportionate impact through its very unexpectedness. It verges on the poetic use of dialect and is akin to the agonized Macbeth's reference to *"blood-boltered* Banquo" or Lear's piercing question to the blinded Gloucester:

Dost thou *squiny* at me? [20]

Only an acceptance of dialect as an alternative form of speech to standard English would allow it. Hardy and Lawrence may do this: George Eliot never.

This particularly powerful use of dialect was probably part of Hardy's original intention in *Tess of the D'Urbervilles.* He evidently meant Tess herself to use it in this way, a way particularly appropriate to a character at once rustic and grand, sensitive and uneducated. In the serial and first and second editions he writes:

Mrs. Durbeyfield still habitually spoke the dialect; her daughter . . . used it only when excited by joy, surprise, or grief (ch. 3).

Possible illustrations of such a use which survive even in the 1912 edition are when Tess, pressed by Clare to marry him, wonders in agonized soliloquy "Why *don't* somebody tell him all about me?" (ch. 28); and when in her letter to Angel she urges him to say only that he will come soon and then she will *bide on* (ch. 48).

But in the fifth edition (1892) Hardy explicitly abandons his intended "poetic" use by changing the passage quoted above to read as it still did in 1912:

her daughter . . . spoke two languages; the dialect at home, more or less; ordinary English abroad and to persons of quality.

This changed intention is borne out by the decrease in some thirty or so examples of Tess's use of dialect in the 1912 edition, mainly in her conversations with Alec d'Urberville or with Angel.[21] Hardy reverts to the simpler use: an uncritical acceptance of dialect as a social indicator. This, to some extent, had been present in the novel from the start; witness Alec's question to Tess, found even in the first edition:

How is it that you speak so fluently now? Who has taught
you such good English? (ch. 45).

It is not difficult to guess why he abandoned his original intention
for Tess: it was too difficult to fulfil alongside the frequent use
in the novel of lavish dialect by characters like the Durbeyfields,
the Cricks, and the other dairymaids. In particular it was necessary
to distinguish Tess strongly from her feckless parents and from the
other worthy but inferior milkmaids, and Hardy fell back on the
method he had used with Stephen Smith and Swithin St. Cleeve.

He made a more successful attempt at this ambitious use of dialect
in *The Woodlanders,* his own favourite amongst his novels. This
work illustrates clearly the same manipulation of dialect for special
and precise effects that we have seen in *Far from the Madding
Crowd* and *Under the Greenwood Tree,* and also the idealized
concept of dialect as a language powerful in its own right hinted
at in *Jude the Obscure* and the early versions of *Tess of the D'Urbervilles.* The hero and heroine of this novel, in the sense of the two
figures ultimately most admired, are Giles Winterbourne and Marty
South, of whom it is specifically said that she

> alone, of all the women in Hintock and the world, had approx-
> imated to Winterbourne's level of intelligent intercourse with
> nature (ch. 44).

It is to be expected that such a character as Marty, poor and ill-edu-
cated, would constantly use dialect, or at least be very clearly marked
out by her speech as one low on the social and educational scale.
But this is not so: an examination of the 1912 version shows that
she, like Giles, uses for the most part a speech almost unmarked by
rustic peculiarities. The result is that when she occasionally uses
a dialect word the effect is all the more striking. An example is her
remark to the coachman when she has been given a lift on the outside of Mrs. Charmond's coach and overhears the occupant yawning:

> "Why should she yawn?" she asks,
> "Oh, because she's been used to such wonderful good life,
> and finds it dull here. She'll soon be off again on account of it."
> "So rich and so powerful, and yet to yawn . . . then things
> don't *fay with her any more than with we!*" (ch. 5).

It is striking, too, that in this particular novel Hardy made remarkably few alterations in the dialect when he revised. The handful of dialect forms in Marty's speech are decreased: earlier *with she* becomes later *with her, a tempting* becomes *tempting* and *on'y* becomes *only*. Yet in the most important speech that Marty makes, she speaks in obvious dialect, and the lines are all the more poignantly effective through her freedom from dialect elsewhere. This most moving use comes in the final and crucial passage of the book spoken over Giles's grave which gives Hardy's own perspective on the events and characters. Hitherto the reunited Grace Melbury and Fitzpiers have dominated the scene. But they are now displaced by the dead Giles and Marty herself:

> "Now, my own, own love . . . you are mine, and only mine; for she has forgot 'ee at last, although for her you died! But I—whenever I get up I'll think of 'ee, and whenever I lie down I'll think of 'ee again. Whenever I plant the young larches I'll think that none can plant as you planted; and whenever I split a gad, and whenever I turn the cider wring, I'll say none could do it like you. If ever I forget your name let me forget home and heaven! . . . But no, no, my love, I never can forget 'ee; for you was a good man, and did good things" (ch. 48).

Hardy cheats by using one concept of dialect for the Creedles of this world and another for the Martys, but the skill of his manipulation brings it off. This is probably the most powerful use that dialect in the novel is capable of, and it is correspondingly rare, depending as it does on dialect seen as a form of speech which goes to the heart of the matter and not as a mere deviation from a norm. The finest use that Lawrence makes of dialect is of this kind, when in *Sons and Lovers* (1913) he allows both Paul and his mother to turn to dialect in moments of intimacy. Sometimes the use is a half mocking attempt to gloss over emotion; at other times, with Paul and Clara, it is heartfelt. The difference between Lawrence and Hardy here lies in the characters' consciousness of what they are doing. But it is based on the same attitude to dialect.

An analysis of the use of dialect in novels is best made with a clear picture of the novelists' aims and strengths in mind. The effectiveness of George Eliot's use depends on grasping its relation to her concern with human aspirations and self-deceit. With Hardy one needs to remember that in the more tragic novels there is an uncertainty of attitude to events: a shift from seeing them as an inevitable outcome of individual character to seeing them as blows of Fate. Tess's life is an illustration, and Hardy's very ambivalence towards it is an enrichment. And in the shifting of his attitude to dialect, two basically irreconcilable views produce some of his most powerful effects.

Probably not even Hardy and George Eliot have exhausted all the possible uses to be made of dialect in the novel. But their contrasting achievements have not been surpassed. The shift of interest among novelists away from dialect now makes it unlikely that they ever will be.

NOTES

1. *The Pot Geranium* (London, 1954), p. 59.
2. *Athenaeum*, 23 November 1878, p. 654.
3. *Spectator*, 8 October 1881, p. 1278.
4. Sabra D. Gilcreast, *The Dorset Dialect in the Wessex Novels of Thomas Hardy* (Columbia University unpublished thesis). Microfilm in Dorset County Library.
5. No attempt has been made in what follows to distinguish such uses from dialectal ones. The evidence shows that both are used together for similar effects.
6. Mary Ellen Chase, *Thomas Hardy from Serial to Novel* (Minneapolis, 1927), pp. 56 and 100.
7. "The Science of Fiction," *New Review*, April 1891, pp. 315–19.
8. "The Profitable Reading of Fiction," *Forum* (New York), March 1888, pp. 57–70.
9. *Athenaeum*, 30 November 1878, p. 688.
10. All George Eliot references are to the Cabinet edition of 1878–80.
11. Letter to W. W. Skeat, quoted in the English Dialect Society's *Bibliographical List* 1 (1877), p. viii.
12. *Athenaeum*, 30 November 1878, p. 688.
13. Chase, p. 56.
14. "Candour in English Fiction," *New Review*, January 1890, pp. 15–21.
15. All references to Hardy's novels, unless otherwise indicated, are to the 1912 edition.
16. Gilcreast, p. 13.

17. Preface to *Select Poems of William Barnes* (London, 1908,) pp. vii–viii.
18. Obituary of Barnes, *Athenaeum*, 16 October 1886, p. 502.
19. *Adam Bede*, ch. 19.
20. *Macbeth*, IV.1.123; *King Lear*, IV.6.136.
21. I have made grateful use of Miss Juliet Grindle's collation of the editions of *Tess of the D'Urbervilles*.

IAN WATT

↙

The First Paragraph of James's *Ambassadors*

When I was asked if I would do a piece of explication at this conference, I was deep in Henry James, and beginning *The Ambassadors:* so the passage chose itself; but just what was explication, and how did one do it to prose? I take it that whereas explanation, from *explanare,* suggests a mere making plain by spreading out, explication, from *explicare,* implies a progressive unfolding of a series of literary implications, and thus partakes of our modern preference for multiplicity in method and meaning: explanation assumes an ultimate simplicity, explication assumes complexity.

Historically, the most systematic tradition of explication is presumably that which developed out of medieval textual exegesis and became the chief method of literary instruction in French secondary and higher education in the late nineteenth century. *Explication de texte* in France reflects the rationalism of nineteenth-century Positivist scholarship. At its worst the routine application of the method resembles a sort of bayonet drill in which the exposed body of literature is riddled with etymologies and dates before being despatched in a harrowingly insensitive *résumé.* At its best, however,

From Henry James, *The Ambassadors,* edited by S. P. Rosenbaum (W. W. Norton & Co., 1964), pp. 465–84. First published in *Essays in Criticism,* X (1960), pp. 250–74. Reprinted by permission of the publishers and author.

explication de texte can be solidly illuminating, and it then serves to remind us that a piece of literature is not necessarily violated if we give systematic attention to such matters as its author, its historical setting, and the formal properties of its language.

Practical Criticism, on the other hand, as it was developed at Cambridge by I. A. Richards, continues the tradition of the British Empiricists. Inductive rather than deductive, it makes a point of excluding linguistic and historical considerations, so as to derive—in appearance at least—all the literary values of a work empirically from the words on the page. In the last thirty years the emphasis of Practical Criticism on the autonomy of the text has revolutionised the approach to literary studies, and has proved itself a technique of supreme value for teaching and examining students; I myself certainly believe that its use should be expanded rather than curtailed. Yet, at least in the form in which I picked it up as a student and have later attempted to pass it on as a teacher, both its pedagogical effects and its basic methodological assumptions seem to me to be open to serious question. For many reasons. Its air of objectivity confers a spurious authority on a process that is often only a rationalisation of an unexamined judgment, and that must always be to some extent subjective; its exclusion of historical factors seems to authorise a more general anti-historicism; and—though this objection is perhaps less generally accepted—it contains an inherent critical bias in the assumption that the part is a complete enough reflection of the literary whole to be profitably appreciated and discussed in isolation from its context. How far this is true, or how far it can be made to appear so by a well-primed practitioner, is a matter of opinion; but it is surely demonstrable that Practical Criticism tends to find the most merit in the kind of writing which has virtues that are in some way separable from their larger context; it favours kinds of writing that are richly concrete in themselves, stylistically brilliant, or composed in relatively small units. It is therefore better suited to verse than to prose; and better suited to certain kinds of either than to others where different and less concentrated merits are appropriate, as in the novel.

As for its pedagogical effects—and here again I have mainly my own past experience in mind—Practical Criticism surely tends to sensitise us towards objects only within a certain range of magnitude: below that threshold it becomes subjective and impressionist, paying very little attention to the humble facts of the grammar and syntax of the words on the page; while, at the other extreme, it often ignores the larger meaning, and the literary and historical contexts of that meaning.

As a practical matter these restrictions may all be necessary for the pupil and salutary for the teacher; and I mention them mainly to justify my present attempt to develop the empirical and inductive methods of Practical Criticism in such a way as to deal with those elements in a literary text whose vibrations are so high or so low that we Ricardian dogs have not yet been trained to bark at them.

It is mainly in these penumbral areas, of course, that the French *explication de texte* habitually operates; but its analysis of grammar and of the literary and historical background are usually a disconnected series of discrete demonstrations which stop short of the unifying critical synthesis that one hopes for. Until fairly recently the same could have been said, and perhaps with greater emphasis, about the German tradition of literary scholarship, with its almost entirely independent pursuit of philology and philosophy. More recent trends in *Stilforschung* however—of which Wolfgang Clemen's *The Development of Shakespeare's Imagery* (Bonn, 1936), was an early example—come closer to, and indeed partly reflect, the more empirical Anglo-American models of literary criticism; while, even more promising perhaps for the study of prose, though seemingly quite independent of the influence of Practical Criticism, is the development, mainly from Romance philology, of what has come to be called "stylistics."

For my purposes, however, it remains not so much a method as a small group of isolated, though spectacular, individual triumphs. I yield to no one in my admiration for Leo Spitzer's *Linguistics and Literary History* (Baltimore, 1948), or for the continual excitement and illumination offered in Erich Auerbach's *Mimesis* (1946: trans. Willard Trask, Princeton, N.J., 1953); their achievements, however, strike me mainly as tributes to the historical imagination and philosophical understanding of the German mind at its best; I find their brilliant commentaries on words or phrases or passages essentially subjective; and if I am tempted to emulate the *bravura* with which they take off from the word on the page to leap into the farthest empyreans of *Kulturgeschichte,* I soon discover that the Cambridge east winds have condemned me to less giddy modes of critical transport.

Yet what other models are there to help one to analyse a paragraph of Jamesian prose? Some of the historical studies of prose style could, conceivably, be applied; but I am fearful of ending up with the proposition that James was a Ciceronian—with Senecan elements, of course, like everyone else. As for the new linguistics, the promises as regards literary analysis seem greater than the present rewards: the most practical consequence of my exposure to Charles Fries's *The Structure of English: an Introduction to the Construction of English Sentences* (New York, 1952), for example, was to deprive me of the innocent pleasure that comes from imagining you know the names of things. Structural linguistics in general is mainly (and rightly) concerned with problems of definition and description at a considerably more basic level of linguistic usage than the analysis of the literary effect of Henry James's grammatical particularities seems to require.

Perhaps the most promising signs of the gaps being filled have come from what are—in that particular area—amateurs: from Francis Berry's *Poets' Grammar* (London, 1958), or Donald Davie's *Articulate Energy* (London, 1955). But they don't help much with prose, of course, and they aren't basically concerned with grammatical structure in the ordinary sense; although Davie's notion that the principle of continuity in poetry is, after all, primarily grammatical and rational, at least lessens the separation between the stylistic domains of poetry and prose, and suggests some ways of studying how syntax channels expressive force.

Virtually helpless,[1] then, I must face the James passage alone as far as any fully developed and acceptable technique for explicating prose is concerned; but there seem to be good reasons why practical criticism should be supplemented by some of the approaches of French and German scholarship, and by whatever else will lead one from the words on the page to matters as low as syntax and as high as ideas, or the total literary structure.

I

Strether's first question, when he reached the hotel, was about his friend; yet on his learning that Waymarsh was apparently not to arrive till evening he was not wholly disconcerted. A telegram from him bespeaking a room "only
5   if not noisy", reply paid, was produced for the inquirer at

the office, so that the understanding they should meet at
Chester rather than at Liverpool remained to that extent
sound. The same secret principle, however, that had
prompted Strether not absolutely to desire Waymarsh's
10   presence at the dock, that had led him thus to postpone
for a few hours his enjoyment of it, now operated to make
him feel he could still wait without disappointment. They
would dine together at the worst, and, with all respect to
dear old Waymarsh—if not even, for that matter, to him-
15   self—there was little fear that in the sequel they shouldn't
see enough of each other. The principle I have just mentioned as operating had been, with the most newly disembarked of the two men, wholly instinctive—the fruit
of a sharp sense that, delightful as it would be to find him-
20   self looking, after so much separation, into his comrade's
face, his business would be a trifle bungled should he
simply arrange for this countenance to present itself to the
nearing steamer as the first "note" of Europe. Mixed with
everything was the apprehension, already, on Strether's
25   part, that it would, at best, throughout, prove the note of
Europe in quite a sufficient degree.[2]

It seems a fairly ordinary sort of prose, but for its faint air of
elaborate portent; and on second reading its general quality reminds
one of what Strether is later to observe—approvingly—in Maria
Gostrey: an effect of "expensive, subdued suitability." There's certainly nothing particularly striking in the diction or syntax; none
of the immediate drama or rich description that we often get at the
beginning of novels; and certainly none of the sensuous concreteness
that, until recently, was regarded as a chief criterion of good prose
in our long post-imagistic phase: if anything, the passage is conspicuously un-sensuous and un-concrete, a little dull perhaps, and
certainly not easy reading.

The difficulty isn't one of particularly long or complicated sentences: actually they're of fairly usual length: I make it an average
of 41 words; a little, but not very much, longer than James's average
of 35 (in Book 2, ch. 2. of *The Ambassadors*, according to R. W.
Short's count, in his very useful article "The Sentence Structure
of Henry James," *American Literature*, XVIII [March 1946],
71–88).[3] The main cause of difficulty seems rather to come from

what may be called the delayed specification of referents: "Strether" and "the hotel" and "his friend" are mentioned before we are told who or where they are. But this difficulty is so intimately connected with James's general narrative technique that it may be better to begin with purely verbal idiosyncrasies, which are more easily isolated. The most distinctive ones in the passage seem to be these: a preference for non-transitive verbs; many abstract nouns; much use of "that"; a certain amount of elegant variation to avoid piling up personal pronouns and adjectives such as "he," "his," and "him"; and the presence of a great many negatives and near-negatives.

By the preference for non-transitive verbs I mean three related habits: a great reliance on copulatives—"Strether's first question *was* about his friend"; "*was* apparently not to arrive": a frequent use of the passive voice—"*was* not wholly *disconcerted*"; "a telegram . . . *was produced*"; "his business *would be* a trifle *bungled*": and the employment of many intransitive verbs—"the understanding . . . remained . . . sound"; "the . . . principle . . . operated to." My count of all the verbs in the indicative would give a total of 14 passive, copulative or intransitive uses as opposed to only 6 transitive ones: and there are in addition frequent infinitive, participial, or gerundial uses of transitive verbs, in all of which the active nature of the subject-verb-and-object sequence is considerably abated—"on his learning"; "bespeaking a room"; "not absolutely to desire"; "led him thus to postpone."

This relative infrequency of transitive verbal usages in the passage is associated with the even more pronounced tendency towards using abstract nouns as subjects of main or subordinate clauses: "question"; "understanding"; "the same secret principle"; "the principle"; "his business." If one takes only the main clauses, there are four such abstract nouns as subjects, while only three main clauses have concrete and particular subjects ("he," or "they").[4]

I detail these features only to establish that in this passage, at least, there is a clear quantitative basis for the common enough view that James's late prose style is characteristically abstract; more explicitly, that the main grammatical subjects are very often nouns for mental ideas, "question," "principle," etc.; and that the verbs —because they are mainly used either non-transitively, or in infinitive, participial and gerundial forms,—tend to express states of being rather than particular finite actions affecting objects.

The main use of abstractions is to deal at the same time with many objects or events rather than single and particular ones: and we use verbs that denote states of being rather than actions for exactly the same reason—their much more general applicability. But in this passage, of course, James isn't in the ordinary sense making abstract or general statements; it's narrative, not expository prose; what need exploring, therefore, are the particular literary imperatives which impose on his style so many of the verbal and syntactical qualities of abstract and general discourse; of expository rather than narrative prose.

Consider the first sentence. The obvious narrative way of making things particular and concrete would presumably be "When Strether reached the hotel, he first asked 'Has Mr. Waymarsh arrived yet?' " Why does James say it the way he does? One effect is surely that, instead of a sheer stated event, we get a very special view of it; the mere fact that actuality has been digested into reported speech—the question "was about his friend"—involves a narrator to do the job, to interpret the action, and also a presumed audience that he does it for: and by implication, the heat of the action itself must have cooled off somewhat for the translation and analysis of the events into this form of statement to have had time to occur. Lastly, making the subject of the sentence "question" rather than "he," has the effect of subordinating the particular actor, and therefore the particular act, to a much more general perspective: mental rather than physical, and subjective rather than objective; "question" is a word which involves analysis of a physical event into terms of meaning and intention: it involves, in fact, both Strether's mind and the narrator's. The narrator's, because he interprets Strether's act: if James had sought the most concrete method of taking us into Strether's mind—" 'Has Mr. Waymarsh come yet?' I at once asked"—he would have obviated the need for the implied external categoriser of Strether's action. But James disliked the "mere platitude of statement" involved in first-person narrative; partly, presumably, because it would merge Strether's consciousness into the narrative, and not isolate it for the reader's inspection. For such isolation, a more expository method is needed: no confusion of subject and object, as in first-person narration, but a narrator forcing the reader to pay attention to James's primary objective—Strether's mental and subjective state.

The "multidimensional" quality of the narrative, with its continual implication of a community of three minds—Strether's,

James's, and the reader's—isn't signalled very obviously until the fourth sentence—"The principle I have just mentioned as operating . . ."; but it's already been established tacitly in every detail of diction and structure, and it remains pervasive. One reason for the special demand James's fictional prose makes on our attention is surely that there are always at least three levels of development —all of them subjective: the characters' awareness of events; the narrator's seeing of them; and our own trailing perception of the relation between these two.

The primary location of the narrative in a mental rather than a physical continuum gives the narrative a great freedom from the restrictions of particular time and place. Materially, we are, of course, in Chester, at the hotel—characteristically "the hotel" because a fully particularised specification—"The Pied Bull Inn" say—would be an irrelevant brute fact which would distract attention from the mental train of thought we are invited to partake in. But actually we don't have any pressing sense of time and place: we feel ourselves to be spectators, rather specifically, of Strether's thought processes, which easily and imperceptibly range forwards and backwards both in time and space. Sentence three, for example, begins in the past, at the Liverpool dock; sentence four looks forward to the reunion later that day, and to its many sequels: such transitions of time and place are much easier to effect when the main subjects of the sentences are abstract: a "principle" exists independently of its context.

The multiplicity of relations—between narrator and object, and between the ideas in Strether's mind—held in even suspension throughout the narrative, is presumably the main explanation for the number of "thats" in the passage, as well as of the several examples of elegant variation. There are 9 "that's"—only two of them demonstrative and the rest relative pronouns (or conjunctions or particles if you prefer those terms); actually there were no less than three more of them in the first edition, which James removed from the somewhat more colloquial and informal New York edition; while there are several other "thats" implied—in "the principle [that] I have just mentioned," for instance.

The number of "thats" follows from two habits already noted in the passage. "That" characteristically introduces relative clauses dealing not with persons but with objects, including abstractions; and it is also used to introduce reported speech—"on his learning that Waymarsh"—not "Mr. Waymarsh isn't here." Both functions are combined in the third sentence where we get a triple definition of a timeless idea based on the report of three chronologically separate events: "the same secret principle, however, that had prompted Strether not absolutely to desire Waymarsh's presence at the dock, that had led him thus to postpone for a few hours his enjoyment of it, now operated to make him feel that he could still wait without disappointment."

Reported rather than direct speech also increases the pressure towards elegant variation: the use, for example, in sentence 1 of "his friend," where in direct speech it would be "Mr. Waymarsh" (and the reply—"*He* hasn't come yet"). In the second sentence— "a telegram . . . was produced for the inquirer"—"inquirer" is needed because "him" has already been used for Waymarsh just above; of course, "the inquirer" is logical enough after the subject of the first sentence has been an abstract noun—"question", and the epithet also gives James an opportunity for underlining the ironic distance and detachment with which we are invited to view his dedicated "inquirer," Strether. Later, when Strether is "the most newly disembarked of the two men," we see how both elegant variation and the grammatical subordination of physical events are related to the general Jamesian tendency to present characters and action on a plane of abstract categorisation; the mere statement, "Mr. Waymarsh had already been in England for [so many] months," would itself go far to destroy the primarily mental continuum in which the paragraph as a whole exists.

The last general stylistic feature of the passage to be listed above was the use of negative forms. There are 6 "noes" or "nots" in the first 4 sentences; four implied negatives—"postpone"; "without disappointment"; "at the worst"; "there was little fear": and two qualifications that modify positiveness of affirmation—"not wholly," and "to that extent." This abundance of negatives has no doubt several functions: it enacts Strether's tendency to hesitation and qualification; it puts the reader into the right judicial frame of mind; and it has the further effect of subordinating concrete events to their mental reflection; "Waymarsh was not to arrive," for example, is not a concrete statement of a physical event: it is subjective—because it implies an expectation in Strether's mind (which was not fulfilled); and it has an abstract quality—because while Waymarsh's arriving would be particular and physical, his *not* arriving is an idea, a non-action. More generally, James's great use of negatives or near-negatives may also, perhaps, be regarded as part of his subjective and abstractive tendency: there are no negatives in nature but only in the human consciousness.

II

The most obvious grammatical features of what Richard Chase has called Henry James's "infinitely syntactical language" (*The American Novel and its Tradition*, New York, 1957), can, then, be shown to reflect the essential imperatives of his narrative point of view; and they could therefore lead into a discussion of the philosophical qualities of his mind, as they are discussed, for example, by Dorothea Krook in her notable article "The Method of the Later Works of Henry James" (*London Magazine*, I [1954], 55–70); our passage surely exemplifies James's power "to generalise to the furthest limit the particulars of experience," and with it the characteristic way in which both his "perceptions of the world itself and his perceptions of the logic of his perceptions of the world . . . happen simultaneously, are the parts of a single comprehensive experience." Another aspect of the connection between James's metaphysic and his method as a novelist has inspired a stimulating stylistic study—Carlo Izzo's "Henry James, Scrittore Sintattico" (*Studi Americani*, II [1956], 127–142). The connection between thought and style finds its historical perspective in John Henry Raleigh's illuminating study "Henry James: The Poetics of Empiricism" (*PMLA*, LXVI [1951], 107–123), which establishes connections between Lockean epistemology and James's extreme, almost anarchic, individualism; while this epistemological preoccupation, which is central to Quentin Anderson's view of how James worked out his father's cosmology in fictional terms (*The American Henry James*, New Brunswick, 1957), also leads towards another large general question, the concern with "point of view," which became a crucial problem in the history and criticism of fiction under the influence of the sceptical relativism of the late nineteenth-century.

In James's case, the problem is fairly complicated. He may be classed as an "Impressionist," concerned, that is, to show not so much the events themselves, but the impressions which they make on the characters. But James's continual need to generalise and place and order, combined with his absolute demand for a point of view that would be plastic enough to allow him freedom for the formal "architectonics" of the novelist's craft, eventually involved him in a very idiosyncratic kind of multiple Impressionism: idiosyncratic because the dual presence of Strether's consciousness and of that of the narrator, who translates what he sees there into more general terms, makes the narrative point of view both intensely individual and yet ultimately social.

Another possible direction of investigation would be to show that the abstractness and indirection of James's style are essentially the result of this characteristic multiplicity of his vision. There is, for example, the story reported by Edith Wharton that after his first stroke James told Lady Prothero that "in the very act of falling . . . he heard in the room a voice which was distinctly, it seemed, not his own, saying: 'So here it is at last, the distinguished thing.'" James, apparently, could not but see even his own most fateful personal experience, except as evoked by some other observer's voice in terms of the long historical and literary tradition of death. Carlo Izzo regards this tendency as typical of the Alexandrian style, where there is a marked disparity between the rich inheritance of the means of literary expression, and the meaner creative world which it is used to express; but the defence of the Jamesian habit of mind must surely be that what the human vision shares with that of animals is presumably the perception of concrete images, not the power to conceive universals: such was Aristotle's notion of man's distinguishing capacity. The universals in the present context are presumably the awareness that behind every petty individual circumstance there ramifies an endless network of general moral, social, and historical relations. Henry James's style can therefore be seen as a supremely civilised effort to relate every event and every moment of life to the full complexity of its circumambient conditions.

Obviously James's multiple awareness can go too far; and in the later novels it often poses the special problem that we do not quite know whether the awareness implied in a given passage is the narrator's or that of his character. Most simply, a pronoun referring to the subject of a preceding clause is always liable to give trouble if one hasn't been very much aware of what the grammatical subject of that preceding clause was; in the last sentence of the paragraph, for example, "the apprehension, already, on Strether's part that . . . it would, at best, . . . prove the 'note' of Europe," "it" refers to Waymarsh's countenance: but this isn't at first obvious; which is no doubt why, in his revision of the periodical version for the English edition James replaced "it" by "he"—simpler, grammatically, but losing some of the ironic visual precision of the original. More seriously, because the narrator's consciousness and Strether's are both present, we often don't know whose mental operations and evaluative judgments are involved in particular cases. We pass, for instance, from the objective analysis of sentence 3 where the analytic terminology of "the same secret principle" must be the responsibility of the narrator, to what must be a verbatim quotation of Strether's mind in sentence 4: "with all respect to dear old Waymarsh" is obviously Strether's licensed familiarity.

But although the various difficulties of tense, voice, and reference require a vigilance of attention in the reader which some have found too much to give, they are not in themselves very considerable: and what perhaps is much more in need of attention is how the difficulties arising from the multiplicity of points of view don't by any means prevent James from ordering all the elements of his narrative style into an amazingly precise means of expression: and it is this positive, and in the present case, as it seems to me, triumphant, mastery of the difficulties which I want next to consider.

Our passage is not, I think, James either at his most memorable or at his most idiosyncratic: *The Ambassadors* is written with considerable sobriety and has, for example, little of the vivid and direct style of the early part of *The Wings of the Dove,* or of the happy symbolic complexities of *The Golden Bowl.* Still, the passage is fairly typical of the later James; and I think it can be proved that all or at least nearly all the idiosyncrasies of diction or syntax in the present passage are fully justified by the particular emphasis they create.

The most flagrant eccentricity of diction is presumably that where James writes "the most newly disembarked of the two men" (lines 16–17). "Most" may very well be a mere slip; and it must certainly seem indefensible to any one who takes it as an absolute rule that the comparative must always be used when only two items are involved.[5] But a defence is at least possible. "Most newly disembarked" means something rather different from "more newly disembarked." James, it may be surmised, did not want to compare the recency of the two men's arrival, but to inform us that Strether's arrival was "very" or as we might say, "most" recent; the use of the superlative also had the advantage of suggesting the long and fateful tradition of transatlantic disembarcations in general.

The reasons for the other main syntactical idiosyncrasies in the passage are much clearer. In the first part of the opening sentence, for example, the separation of subject—"question"—from verb—"was"—by the longish temporal clause "when he reached the hotel," is no doubt a dislocation of normal sentence structure; but, of course, "Strether" must be the first word of the novel: while, even more important, the delayed placing of the temporal clause, forces a pause after "question" and thus gives it a very significant resonance. Similarly with the last sentence; it has several peculiarities, of which the placing of "throughout" seems the most obvious. The sentence has three parts: the first and last are comparatively straightforward, but the middle is a massed block of portentous qualifications: "Mixed with everything was the apprehension—already, on Strether's part, that he would, at best, throughout,—prove the note of Europe in quite a sufficient degree." The echoing doom started by the connotation of "apprehension"—reverberates through "already" ("much more to come later") "on Strether's part" ("even he knows") and "at best" ("the worst has been envisaged, too"); but it is the final collapse of the terse rhythm of the parenthesis that isolates the rather awkwardly placed "throughout," and thus enables James to sound the fine full fatal note; there is no limit to the poignant eloquence of "throughout." It was this effect, of course, which dictated the preceding inversion which places "apprehension" not at the start of the sentence, but in the middle where, largely freed from its syntactical nexus, it may be directly exposed to its salvos of qualification.

The mockingly fateful emphasis on "throughout" tells us, if nothing had before, that James's tone is in the last analysis ironic, comic, or better, as I shall try to suggest, humorous. The general reasons for this have already been suggested. To use Maynard Mack's distinction (in his Preface to *Joseph Andrews*, Rinehart Editions, New York, 1948), "the comic artist subordinates the presentation of life as experience, where the relationship between ourselves and the characters experiencing it is a primary one, to the presentation of life as a spectacle, where the primary relation is between himself and us as onlookers." In the James passage, the primacy of the relation between the narrator and the reader has already been noted, as has its connection with the abstraction of the diction, which brings home the distance between the narrator and Strether. Of course, the application of abstract diction to particular persons always tends towards irony,[6] because it imposes a dual way of looking at them:

few of us can survive being presented as general representatives of humanity.

The paragraph, of course, is based on one of the classic contradictions in psychological comedy—Strether's reluctance to admit to himself that he has very mixed feelings about his friend: and James develops this with the narrative equivalent of *commedia dell'arte* technique: virtuoso feats of ironic balance, comic exaggeration, and deceptive hesitation conduct us on a complicated progress towards the foreordained illumination.

In structure, to begin with, the six sentences form three groups of two: each pair of them gives one aspect of Strether's delay; and they are arranged in an ascending order of complication so that the fifth sentence—72 words—is almost twice as long as any other, and is succeeded by the final sentence, the punch line, which is noticeably the shortest—26 words. The development of the ideas is as controlled as the sentence structure. Strether is obviously a man with an enormous sense of responsibility about personal relationships; so his first question is about his friend. That loyal *empressement,* however, is immediately checked by the balanced twin negatives that follow: "on his learning that Waymarsh *was not* to arrive till evening, he *was not* wholly disconcerted": one of the diagnostic elements of irony, surely, is hyperbole qualified with mock-scrupulousness, such as we get in "not wholly disconcerted." Why there are limits to Lambert Strether's consternation is to transpire in the next sentence; Waymarsh's telegram bespeaking a room "only if not noisy" is a laconic suggestion of that inarticulate worthy's habitually gloomy expectations—from his past experiences of the indignities of European hotel noise we adumbrate the notion that the cost of their friendly *rencontre* may be his sleeping in the street. In the second part of the sentence we have another similar, though more muted, hint: "the understanding that they should meet in Chester rather than at Liverpool remained to that extent sound"; "to that extent," no doubt, but to *any other?*—echo seems to answer "No."

In the second group of sentences we are getting into Strether's mind, and we have been prepared to relish the irony of its ambivalences. The negatived hyperbole of "not absolutely to desire," turns out to mean "postpone"; and, of course, a voluntarily postponed "enjoyment" itself denotes a very modified rapture, although Strether's own consciousness of the problem is apparently no further advanced than that "he could still wait without disappointment."

Comically loyal to what he would like to feel, therefore, we have him putting in the consoling reflection that "they would dine together at the worst"; and the ambiguity of "at the worst" is followed by the equally dubious thought: "there was little fear that in the sequel they shouldn't see enough of each other." That they should, in fact, see too much of each other; but social decorum and Strether's own loyalties demand that the outrage of the open statement be veiled in the obscurity of formal negation.

By the time we arrive at the climactic pair of sentences, we have been told enough for more ambitious effects to be possible. The twice-mentioned "secret principle," it appears, is actually wholly "instinctive" (line 17); but in other ways Strether is almost ludicrously self-conscious. The qualified hyperbole of "his business would be a trifle bungled," underlined as it is by the alliteration, prepares us for a half-realised image which amusingly defines Strether's sense of his role: he sees himself, it appears, as the stage-manager of an enterprise in which his solemn obligations as an implicated friend are counterbalanced by his equally ceremonious sense that due decorums must also be attended to when he comes face to face with another friend of long ago—no less a person than Europe. It is, of course, silly of him, as James makes him acknowledge in the characteristic italicising of "the 'note' of Europe",[7] but still, he does have a comically ponderous sense of protocol which leads him to feel that "his business would be a trifle bungled" should he simply arrange for this countenance to present itself to the nearing steamer as the first "note" of Europe. The steamer, one imagines, would not have turned hard astern at the proximity of Waymarsh's sacred rage; but Strether's fitness for ambassadorial functions is defined by his thinking in terms of "arranging" for a certain countenance at the docks to give just the right symbolic greeting.

Strether's notion of what Europe demands also shows us the force of his aesthetic sense. But in the last sentence the metaphor, though it remains equally self-conscious, changes its mode of operation from the dramatic, aesthetic, and diplomatic, to something more scientific: for, although ten years ago I should not have failed to point out, and my readers would not, I suppose, have failed to applaud, the ambiguity of "prove," it now seems to me that we must choose between its two possible meanings. James may be using "prove" to mean that Waymarsh's face will "turn out to be" the "note of Europe" for Strether. But "prove" in this sense is intransitive, and "to be" would have to be supplied; it therefore seems more likely that James is using "prove" in the older sense of "to test": Waymarsh is indeed suited to the role of being the sourly acid test of the siren songs of Europe "in quite a sufficient degree," as Strether puts it with solemn but arch understatement.

The basic development structure of the passage, then, is one of progressive and yet artfully delayed clarification; and this pattern is also typical of James's general novelistic method. The reasons for this are suggested in the Preface to *The Princess Casamassima,* where James deals with the problem of maintaining a balance between the intelligence a character must have to be interesting, and the bewilderment which is nevertheless an essential condition of the novel's having surprise, development, and tension: "It seems probable that if we were never bewildered there would never be a story to tell about us."

In the first paragraph of *The Ambassadors* James apprises us both of his hero's supreme qualities and of his associated limitations. Strether's delicate critical intelligence is often blinkered by a highly vulnerable mixture of moral generosity towards others combined with an obsessive sense of personal inadequacy; we see the tension in relation to Waymarsh, as later we are to see it in relation to all his other friends; and we understand, long before Strether, how deeply it bewilders him; most poignantly about the true nature of Chad, Madame de Vionnet—and himself.

This counterpoint of intelligence and bewilderment is, of course, another reason for the split narrative point of view we've already noted: we and the narrator are inside Strether's mind, and yet we are also outside it, knowing more about Strether than he knows about himself. This is the classic posture of irony. Yet I think that to insist too exclusively on the ironic function of James's narrative point of view would be mistaken.

Irony has lately been enshrined as the supreme deity in the critical pantheon: but, I wonder, is there really anything so wonderful about being distant and objective? Who wants to see life only or mainly in intellectual terms? In art as in life we no doubt can have need of intellectual distance as well as of emotional commitment; but the uninvolvement of the artist surely doesn't go very far without the total involvement of the person; or, at least, without a deeper human involvement than irony customarily establishes. One could, I suppose, call the aesthetically perfect balance between distance and involvement, open or positive irony: but I'm not sure that humour isn't a better word, especially when the final balance is tipped in favour of involvement, of ultimate commitment to the characters; and I hope that our next critical movement will be the New Gelastics.

At all events, although the first paragraph alone doesn't allow the point to be established fully here, it seems to me that James's attitude to Strether is better described as humorous than ironical; we must learn like Maria Gostrey, to see him "at last all comically, all tragically." James's later novels in general are his most intellectual; but they are also, surely, his most compassionate: and in this particular paragraph Strether's dilemma is developed in such a way that we feel for him even more than we smile at him. This balance of intention, I think, probably explains why James keeps his irony so quiet in tone: we must be aware of Strether's "secret" ambivalence towards Waymarsh, but not to the point that his unawareness of it would verge on fatuity; and our controlling sympathy for the causes of Strether's ambivalence turns what might have been irony into something closer to what Constance Rourke characterises as James's typical "low-keyed humor of defeat" (*American Humor*, 1931).

That James's final attitude is humorous rather than ironic is further suggested by the likeness of the basic structural technique of the paragraph to that of the funny story—the incremental involvement in an endemic human perplexity which can only be resolved by laughter's final acceptance of contradiction and absurdity. We don't, in the end, see Strether's probing hesitations mainly as an ironic indication by James of mankind's general muddlement; we find it, increasingly, a touching example of how, despite all their inevitable incongruities and shortcomings, human ties remain only, but still, human.

Here it is perhaps James's very slowness and deliberation throughout the narrative which gives us our best supporting evidence: greater love hath no man than hearing his friend out patiently.

III

The function of an introductory paragraph in a novel is presumably to introduce: and this paragraph surely has the distinction of being a supremely complex and inclusive introduction to a novel. It introduces the hero, of course, and one of his companions; also the time;

the place; something of what's gone before. But James has carefully avoided giving up the usual retrospective beginning, that pile of details which he scornfully termed a "mere seated mass of information." All the details are scrupulously presented as reflections from the novel's essential centre—the narrator's patterning of the ideas going forwards and backwards in Strether's mind. Of course, this initially makes the novel more difficult, because what we probably think of as primary—event and its setting—is subordinated to what James thinks is—the mental drama of the hero's consciousness, which, of course, is not told but shown: scenically dramatised. At the same time, by selecting thoughts and events which are representative of the book as a whole, and narrating them with an abstractness which suggests their larger import, James introduces the most general themes of the novel.

James, we saw, carefully arranged to make "Strether's first question," the first three words; and, of course, throughout the novel, Strether is to go on asking questions—and getting increasingly dusty answers. This, it may be added, is stressed by the apparent aposiopesis: for a "first" question when no second is mentioned, is surely an intimation that more are—in a way unknown to us or to Strether —yet to come. The later dislocations of normal word-order already noted above emphasise other major themes; the "secret principle" in Strether's mind, and the antithesis Waymarsh-Europe, for instance.

The extent to which these processes were conscious on James's part cannot, of course, be resolved; but it is significant that the meeting with Maria Gostrey was interposed before the meeting with Waymarsh, which James had originally planned as his beginning in the long (20,000) word scenario of the plot which he prepared for *Harper's*. The unexpected meeting had many advantages; not least that James could repeat the first paragraph's pattern of delayed clarification in the structure of the first chapter as a whole. On Strether's mind we get a momentously clear judgment at the end of the second paragraph: "there was detachment in his zeal, and curiosity in his indifference;" but then the meeting with Maria Gostrey, and its gay opportunities for a much fuller presentation of Strether's mind, intervene before Waymarsh himself finally appears at the end of the chapter; only then is the joke behind Strether's uneasy hesitations in the first paragraph brought to its hilariously blunt climax: "It was already upon him even at that distance—Mr. Waymarsh was for *his* part joyless."

One way of evaluating James's achievement in this paragraph, I suppose, would be to compare the opening of James's other novels, and with those of previous writers: but it would take too long to do more than sketch the possibilities of this approach. James's early openings certainly have some of the banality of the "mere seated mass of information": in *Roderick Hudson* (1876), for example: "Rowland Mallet had made his arrangements to sail for Europe on the 5th of September, and having in the interval a fortnight to spare, he determined to spend it with his cousin Cecilia, the widow of a nephew of his father. . . ." Later, James showed a much more comprehensive notion of what the introductory paragraph should attempt: even in the relatively simple and concrete opening of *The Wings of the Dove* (1902): "She waited, Kate Croy, for her father to come in, but he kept her unconscionably, and there were moments at which she showed herself, in the glass over the mantle, a face positively pale with irritation that had brought her to the point of going away without sight of him. . . ." "She waited, Kate Croy"—an odd parenthetic apposition artfully contrived to prefigure her role throughout the novel—to wait.

One could, I suppose, find this sort of symbolic prefiguring in the work of earlier novelists; but never, I imagine, in association with all the other levels of introductory function that James manages to combine in a single paragraph. Jane Austen has her famous thematic irony in the opening of *Pride and Prejudice* (1813): "It is a truth universally acknowledged, that a single man in possession of a good fortune must be in want of a wife;" but pride and prejudice must come later. Dickens can hurl us overpoweringly into *Bleak House* (1852–3), into its time and place and general theme; but characters and opening action have to wait:

> London. Michaelmas Term lately over, and the Lord Chancellor sitting in Lincoln's Inn Hall. Implacable November weather. As much mud in the streets, as if the waters had but newly retired from the face of the earth, and it would not be wonderful to meet a Megalosaurus, forty feet long or so, waddling like an elephantine lizard up Holborn-Hill. Smoke lowering down from chimneypots. . . .

In Dickens, characteristically, we get a loud note that sets the tone, rather than a polyphonic series of chords that contain all the later melodic developments, as in James. And either the Dickens method, or the "mere seated mass of information," seem to be commonest kinds of opening in nineteenth-century novels. For openings that suggest something of James's ambitious attempt to achieve a prologue that is a synchronic introduction of all the main aspects of the narrative, I think that Conrad is his closest rival. But Conrad, whether in expository or dramatic vein, tends to an arresting initial vigour that has dangers which James's more muted tones avoid. In *An Outcast of the Islands* (1896), for example:

> When he stepped off the straight and narrow path of his peculiar honesty, it was with an inward assertion of unflinching resolve to fall back again into the monotonous but safe stride of virtue as soon as his little excursion into the wayside quagmires had produced the desired effect. It was going to be a short episode—a sentence in brackets, so to speak, in the flowing tale of his life. . . .

Conrad's sardonic force has enormous immediate impact; but it surely gives too much away: the character, Willems, has been dissected so vigorously that it takes great effort for Conrad—and the reader—to revivify him later. The danger lurks even in the masterly combination of physical notation and symbolic evaluation at the beginning of *Lord Jim* (1900): "He was an inch, perhaps two, under six feet . . .": the heroic proportion is for ever missed, by an inch, perhaps two; which is perhaps too much, to begin with.

It is not for me to assess how far I have succeeded in carrying out the general intentions with which I began, or how far similar methods of analysis would be applicable to other kinds of prose. As regards the explication of the passage itself, the main argument must by now be sufficiently clear, although a full demonstration would require a much wider sampling both of other novels and of other passages in *The Ambassadors*.[8] The most obvious and demonstrable features of James's prose style, its vocabulary and syntax, are direct reflections of his attitude to life and his conception of the novel; and these features, like the relation of the paragraph to the rest of the novel, and to other novels, make clear that the notorious idiosyncrasies of Jamesian prose are directly related to the imperatives which led him to develop a narrative texture as richly complicated and as highly organised as that of poetry.

No wonder James scorned translation and rejoiced, as he so engagingly confessed to his French translator, Auguste Monod, that his later works were "locked fast in the golden cage of the *intraduisible.*" Translation could hardly do justice to a paragraph in which so many levels of meaning and implication are kept in continuous operation; in which the usual introductory exposition of time, place, character, and previous action, are rendered through an immediate immersion in the processes of the hero's mind as he's involved in perplexities which are characteristic of the novel as a whole and which are articulated in a mode of comic development which is essentially that, not only of the following chapter, but of the total structure. To have done all that is to have gone far towards demonstrating the contention which James announced at the end of the Preface to *The Ambassadors,* that "the Novel remains still, under the right persuasion, the most independent, most elastic, most prodigious of literary forms"; and the variety and complexity of the functions carried out in the book's quite short first paragraph also suggest that, contrary to some notions, the demonstration is, as James claimed, made with "a splendid particular economy."

NOTES

1. This was before the appearance of the English Institute's symposium *Style in Prose Fiction* (New York, 1959), which offers, besides two general surveys and a valuable bibliography of the field, stylistic studies of six novelists, including one by Charles R. Crow, of "The Style of Henry James: *The Wings of the Dove.*"
2. Henry James, *The Ambassadors* (Revised Collected Edition, Macmillan: London, 1923). Since there are a few variants that have a bearing on the argument, it seems desirable to give a collation of the main editions; P is the periodical publication (*The North American Review,* clxxvi, 1903); 1A the first American edition (Harper and Brothers, New York, 1903); 1E the first English edition (Methuen and Co., London, 1903); N.Y., the "New York Edition," New York and London, 1907–9 (the London Macmillan edition used the sheets of the American edition); CR the "Collected Revised Edition," London and New York, 1921–31 (which uses the text of the New York Edition). It should perhaps be explained that the most widely used editions in England and America make misleading claims to use the text "of the revised Collected Edition," but actually follows the first English edition in the last variant; while the "Anchor" edition, claiming to be "a faithful copy of the text of the

Methuen first edition," actually follows the first American edition, including the famous misplaced chapters.

1.5.   reply paid NY, CR; with the answer paid P, 1A, 1E.

1.5.   inquirer P, 1A, 1E, CR; enquirer NY.

1.6.   understanding they NY, CR; understanding that they P, 1A, 1E.

1.12.   feel he NY, CR; feel that he P, 1A, 1E.

1.15.   shouldn't CR; shouldn't NY; should not P, 1A, 1E.

1.17–8. newly disembarked, all eds. except P: newly-disembarked.

1.22.   arrange for this countenance to present NY, CR; arrange that this countenance should present P, 1A, 1E.

1.23.   "note" of Europe CR; "note", for him, of Europe, P, 1A, 1E; "note", of Europe, NY.

1.25.   that it would P, 1A, NY, CR; that he would, 1E.

3. I am also indebted to the same author's "Henry James's World of Images," PMLA LXVIII (Dec., 1953), 943–960.

4. Sentences one and four are compound or multiple, but in my count I haven't included the second clause in the latter—"there was little fear": though if we can talk of the clause having a subject it's an abstract one—"fear."

5. Though consider Rasselas, ch. xxviii: "Both conditions may be bad, but they cannot both be worst."

6. As I have argued in "The Ironic Tradition in Augustan Prose from Swift to Johnson," Restoration and Augustan Prose (Los Angeles, 1957).

7. See George Knox, "James's Rhetoric of Quotes," College English, XVII (1956), 293–297.

8. A similar analysis of eight other paragraphs selected at fifty page intervals revealed that, as would be expected, there is much variation: the tendency to use non-transitive verbs, and abstract nouns as subjects, for instance, seems to be strong throughout the novel, though especially so in analytic rather than narrative passages; but the frequent use of "that" and of negative forms of statement does not recur significantly.

↙

The Holy Language of Modernism

I

One of D. H. Lawrence's finest stories is "Odour of Chrysanthemums." One of John Crowe Ransom's finest poems is "Prelude to an Evening." In both, action is eloquence; eloquence is the truth of the action. In both, again, words alone are not "certain good."

"Odour of Chrysanthemums" begins with a coal-train coming from Selston and a woman walking toward Underwood. The woman, standing aside, is "insignificantly trapped" between the train and the hedge, thus prefiguring the greater trap later on, the "mouse-trap" in the coal-pit where Walter Bates is smothered to death. This first scene is dusk, a transitional time, the birds are scared off by the noise of the train and when the train passes the scene is all abandonment, stagnation. The miners coming from the pit are "shadows," diminished. There is a cottage "three steps down from the cinder-track"; in the little garden there are flowers, apple-trees, and pink chrysanthemums like clothes hung on bushes—a seemingly innocent image to be tested later when the chrysanthemums are linked to alien experience; but for the moment, the flowers are handsome in our minds. At this point the scene is dominated by Elizabeth Bates, Walter's wife: five months pregnant, "imperious," "set," mistress of silence, disillusionment, and pertinacity. We are to think of her, in a preliminary image, as part of the imperious, possessive world of daylight; separated from the dark, intimate world of the pits. Her life is an ode to Duty; she protects her children and possesses herself. When her little boy John tears at the chrysanthemums and drops the petals on the ground, she rebukes him; then breaks off a twig of the flower and puts it in her apron-band, it is her possession, her trimming, it adorns her. Her father, an engine-driver, stops his engine when it reaches the cottage; Elizabeth gives him tea, bread, and butter, and enough conversation to rebuke him for his intention of marrying again. There is talk of Walter, who has "another bout on," hitting the bottle. When Elizabeth goes back into the cottage she begins the long, angry wait for Walter: darkness settles down, "uncertain." Elizabeth's daughter Annie comes home from school, and they have their tea in gloom, anger, and fear. Annie sees the flowers: "Don't they smell beautiful!" But her mother rejects them now: "No," she says, "not to me. It was chrysanthemums when I married him, and chrysanthemums when you were born, and the first time they ever brought him home, drunk, he'd got brown chrysanthemums in his button-hole." Marriage, birth, drunkenness, sorrow, and later on, death itself: the chrysanthemums are life itself, their smell the odour of life; Annie rushes to receive it, Walter wears it, but Elizabeth will have it only if it embellishes her. In the kitchen, they wait; the children try to escape into their "play-world," Elizabeth has no escape except in recrimination. "He'll come home when they carry him"; and he does. "He can lie on the floor", as he will. "I know he'll not go to work to-morrow after that": true. The children are sent to bed; Elizabeth goes to look for Walter, but tentatively and with the delicacy of her station. Walter's mother comes to keep her forlorn company. The news is out: Walter has been hurt, "a lot o' stuff come down atop 'n 'im." In fact, he is dead. The colliers bring his body into the cottage. "There was a cold, deathly smell of chrysanthemums in the room." He is stripped, laid out, washed. Elizabeth looks at him:

> In her womb was ice of fear, because of this separate stranger with whom she had been living as one flesh. Was this what it all meant—utter, intact, separateness, obscured by heat of living? In dread she turned her face away. The fact was too deadly. There had been nothing between them, and yet they had come together, exchanging their nakedness repeatedly. Each time he had taken her, they had been two isolated beings,

far apart as now. He was no more responsible than she. . . .
And her soul died in her for fear: she knew that she had never
seen him, he had never seen her, they had met in the dark, and
had fought in the dark, not knowing whom they met nor whom
they fought. And now she saw, and turned silent in seeing. For
she had been wrong. She had said he was something he was
not; she had felt familiar with him. Whereas he was apart all
the while, living as she never lived, feeling as she never felt.[1]

This is not the end of the story, but we may pause here to make a
few comments.

The roots of the story are given, by implication, in Lawrence's
essay "Nottingham and the Mining Country." There Lawrence
describes his origin, the life, the coal-mines. The pit, he says, "did
not mechanize men." In fact, the men working underground achieved
a strange intimacy, "a contact almost as close as touch, very real and
very powerful." This persisted even above ground, where the men
lived "instinctively and intuitively," caring little about duty and
competition, continuing their fellowship in the pub. This way of
life set the colliers apart from their wives, daylight people concerned
with hard facts, the home, the children. The rift was exemplified,
Lawrence says, in their attitude to flowers: the miner loved his
garden, his flowers, with something of the artist's love, appreciative,
not possessive. But the women loved flowers only as possessions: "If
they see a flower that arrests their attention, they must at once pick
it, pluck it. Possession! A possession! Something added on to *me*!" [2]
This perception, rooted in Lawrence's early life, is the source of the
present story: the conflict figured in such terms as male and female,
darkness and light, appreciation and possession, intuition and reason.
But Lawrence exemplifies this conflict so completely, imagines it
with such density, that it stands out as an independent image. The
essay deploys an argument, an idea; in the story, Lawrence's imagination is engaged with an image of life; it is understood that argument and idea must now look after themselves. Idea and argument
are admitted only if they are compatible with the greater thing, the
human image.

"Odour of Chrysanthemums" ends:

At last it was finished. They covered him with a sheet and left
him lying, with his face bound. And she fastened the door of

the little parlour, lest the children should see what was lying there. Then, with peace sunk heavy on her heart, she went about making tidy the kitchen. She knew she submitted to life, which was her immediate master. But from death, her ulti-mate master, she winced with fear and shame.

The note is balance: poise between two recognitions, not a slick antithesis. Yet there is no constriction. Life will prevail until death prevails. Hence the tone of the prose is subdued, modest, and firm; as if to summarize the kind of experience which teaches, from which one learns. The diction is bare, because on the one side there is pri-vation which must now be turned to worthy account, and on the other there is Elizabeth's former sensibility, now recalled with shame as a bogus possession. Hence there are no metaphors, no similes, no analogies: if Elizabeth is to move out into "life" she must do so honestly and with proper caution; there is no question here of a sudden plunge into the life-stream. Most of the effect of this pas-sage depends, therefore, upon the syntax, which must be strong enough to move Elizabeth into life and yet not boisterous, since the achievement of that life must be earned. The syntax must figure a sense of loss consistent with the possibility of new life. So the phrase, "lest the children should see what was lying there," does not put a distance between Elizabeth and her husband; rather, it gives, with proper apprehension, the distance already between them from the beginning and now, in the nature of the case, irrevocable. The con-version, the turning toward life now against the pressure of failure and loss, is featured in the bare idiom of action; fastening the door, tidying the kitchen. These are the tokens of a new life, and they define its quality: ordinary, indeed, but right and true. They cor-respond to the old gestures; the denial of the chrysanthemums, Elizabeth's rebuke administered to her father, and so on. The new gestures are the perennial things, but they share in a new spirit. They are merely what they are, but that is enough. Like the corpse itself, in Elizabeth's new eyes: "After all, it was itself." So when we speak of the bareness of Lawrence's writing in this last passage, we mark its propriety; that is, how the bareness registers the delicate balance between what is irrevocable and what is possible. Richard Blackmur said that the business of rhythm is "to move perception into meaning, and so to move meaning into words." Reading Lawrence's passage, we think of rhythm and syntax as part of the narrator's business: his perception is greater than Elizabeth's because it contains Elizabeth's, but that perception recognizes, too, a natural rhythm in the woman's new life. If we speak of it as syntax, that is merely to say that the new life is given in the strain between the new and the old feelings; a strain taken, in the detail of the sentences, by the syntax. But there is no need to separate the strain of syntax from the movement, the moving force, of the rhythm: in the writing, they are one.

Ransom's poem exists in two versions: the original poem, written in 1934, and the revised version, notably altered in 1962.[3]

The first version is a poem of eight quatrains. A man who has been out in the world is returning to his wife and children. It is bound to be a difficult homecoming, because he is of a demanding turn of mind and he is about to lay claim to his wife's soul: she must share his experience, his vision, however dreadful. On his way home he rehearses a speech for the hard occasion. It goes somewhat as follows. "Do not force me to give myself over to you, to the home, the children, the warmth. I have been away, I am tired, perhaps ill, but the illness cannot be cured by the domestic arts, it is too deep. The images I bring are monstrous to you, but you must adopt them, if for no other reason than that they are mine. So: even if the fancy is extreme, imagine a confusion of dream and reality, night and day. And think, then, that the images which have terrified you in your sleep are irrelevant, phantoms which die when you awake. Imagine now that you are giving out the oranges, the children are there, and yet you feel, with me, in the sunny room an invisible evil, preparing to strike. You are afraid: fear is part of the apparition. So you attend to your daily chores, but you are holding yourself apart from them, listening for the noise of evil and fear. Now it is evening: you are like a waning moon, I am Orestes, accusing the Eumenides which are now neither mine nor yours, but ours. You and I are confronting the Furies; so that even if the children are hungry you will merely smooth their heads, absent with me in my experience. We meet there in the body of our fear, our evil." (The paraphrase is rough, but it will suffice.) There the poem ended, and it remained in that form for many years; the poet was busy with other interests. But gradually he came to dislike his Prelude. The poem became, he says, "disagreeable" to his ears, not because he tired of its rhythm, its diction, its syntax, or even because

he thought he might now manage these matters better: but because
he came to think of it as a "vindictive" poem and of its hero as a
villain. At the same time he wanted somehow to redeem his hero, he
was reluctant to kill him off, there was clearly something in him
worth maintaining. So Ransom took up the privilege of tinkering
with the poem, until it became clear that he must somehow change
the entire story. He would redeem his hero by allowing him to
change; the story would continue until the man's speech came to a
more equable accommodation, a finer justice. So Ransom added four
stanzas, as if the man, recanting, were to say: "I would have my
return a splendid occasion, like Ulysses to Penelope. Our intimacy
would not dissolve my fear, rather capitalize upon it. But as I approach the house I hear 'No!'; and I prefer to think that it marks
my own refusal rather than yours. I will have no stratagems of
fancy. Indeed, I have been a prodigal husband, a prodigal father. I
went away to escape from the knowledge of good and evil. Now I
am disfigured. But every step I took has sent me back. Now that
I am here, I will observe the scruple of silence, because words
incited my treason. I will creep back into the fold, making no demands upon anyone but myself. Now in the room you 'shine' upon
our children and this, like the children, is 'good'."

To moralize this a little: we are to think of husband and wife, one
flesh as *Genesis* says, but retaining two distinct affiliations. The wife's
role is perennial, her identity and her role are one and the same;
her allegiance is fundamental, tribal, varying little from one generation to another. The husband is a man of his time, a modern man
with the distinctly modern experience of evil. We think of him
when Henry James invokes the imagination of catastrophe, when
Gide speaks of the *acte gratuit,* when Stevens speaks of the con-
noisseur of chaos, when Picasso describes a modern painting as a
horde of destructions. He is a David compelled to invent Goliaths
because he must, because the image of evil must be of the nature
of its creator. What he brings with him, back from the world, is
evil and a sense of evil's lineaments: it is a contamination, he is
"the tired wolf/Dragging his infected wound." His first thought is
to make his wife share in this condition, and for that he is a villain,
as Ransom says. But we may go somewhat further. The husband
does not want to be enclosed by the domestic order; he wants to
replace that order by something closer to his nature, perhaps by a
great disorder. The new disorder will enforce itself because it is

strong enough to do so; it is not a modern condition for nothing. At this point the husband is proposing an Existentialist ethic: the great disorder must be daring, personal, authentic, as we say. It cannot work by rote or routine: children learn by rote the Kings of France, and this is innocent, but a man puts away childish things, at whatever cost.

It is worth mentioning that Ransom redeems his hero by making him something of an artist and allowing him to make evil his poetic material. The villain was always a modern man; now he becomes a poet, perhaps, and the evil becomes his *donnée*. Jamesian readers concede to the artist his *donnée*. Ransom mentions that two texts were implicated in the circumstances which prompted him to change his poem; Charles Coffin's study in the theology of *Paradise Lost* and Kenneth Burke's *The Rhetoric of Religion*. I am almost led to think that another book has been forgotten, Edmund Wilson's *The Wound and the Bow*, which presents the myth of Philoctetes as the idea of art and neurosis, neurosis the content of art, form the cure. In the revised Prelude the husband is not forced to disown his vision; it is enough that he contains it. The husband will not impose it now upon his wife: as Ransom says in prose, "he will not ask of her the impossible." The artist carries his wound; the wife has her own allegiance, and her tribal right to it. As a fruitful woman she has her own *donnée*; in the creation of the children the husband has collaborated, but this makes a domestic world in the wife's keeping. This is just. An artist will bear with his evil as well as he can, but he must not demand that the infection be caught by his wife: one of the offices of art is to assimilate the evil and, then, to let the poor artist live.

The first lines in the new section of Ransom's poem read:

> I would have us magnificent at my coming;
> Two souls tight-clasped; and a swamp of horrors.
> O you shall be handsome and brave at fearing.

The rhythm makes it clear that the magnificence is theatrical as well as erotic: this husband wants the swamp of horrors as keenly as the embrace; hence the two phrases, poised against each other for an effect at once vibrant and pretentious. The man is indeed disfigured. The applause in the third line is a little vulgar. But three stanzas later the artist's will has been contained, the tragic *décor* is waved aside, and the scene is now, willingly, domestic:

> I am here; and to balk my ruffian I bite
> The tongue devising all that treason;
> Then creep in my wounds to the sovereign flare
> Of the room where you shine on the good children.

And Ransom says, in a gloss: "There will be many interims yet when he will be out in the free world again, busied in his own way professionally. But every time he takes his leave he will have said to them and himself: I shall return."

If we place Ransom's revised poem beside Lawrence's story, we say, to begin with, that both are concerned with familiar and familial situations. Both assume that human relationships are real and, for the poetic question, inescapable; as in a conversion the wife, in the story, turns toward her dead husband and then toward life itself; and in Ransom's poem the husband turns toward his living wife and toward life itself. The conversion, the turning, makes the action, the soul of the drama. If we ask why Ransom changed a poem already well received and established, the answer is easy: he sought Reality and Justice, in Yeats's terms, "Reality and Justice in a single thought." The first version of the poem had at least enough reality to mark its presence in the landscape of modern poetry, but the poet was not satisfied as to its justice, its responsiveness to the possibility of things.

The strictly verbal part in these decisions is small. That is: Ransom and Lawrence are writers, highly conscious artists, and they labour joyfully with words, but they grant that there is a vital world before and after the words. True, without the words, there would be no story and no poem; but we are encouraged to believe that, for other great benefits, Ransom and Lawrence would be prepared to give up their claim upon words. If man's life on earth were satisfactory in other respects, these writers would not demand that, in addition, it be superlatively endowed with words. Ransom and Lawrence are entirely free from that gross superstition of the Word which has threatened to dominate modern literature. Erich Heller, discussing Hegel, speaks of "the ambition of the human mind to dominate reality to the point of usurping its place." And he argues

that in the tradition of poetry that leads from Romanticism through
Baudelaire, Mallarmé, Rimbaud, and Valéry to Rilke's *Duino Elegies*
and the *Sonnets to Orpheus* "external reality has no claims any more
to being real":

> The only real world is the world of human inwardness. The
> concrete form of this reality is the poem in its pure absolute-
> ness. *Gesang ist Dasein.* Song is existence. . . . Imagination is
> reality.[4]

The question is incorrigible. In the first chapter of the *Enquiry
concerning Human Understanding* Hume distinguishes between
two kinds of moral philosophy: the first "considers man chiefly as
born for action"; the second considers him "in the light of a reasonable rather than an active being." But the distinction has been put to
odd use in literature. From Schopenhauer to Eliot, Valéry, and
Beckett, much of modern literature has yielded up the idiom of action, committing itself to the idiom of consciousness. Many writers
take as their chief labour the transformation of experience into consciousness. Admittedly, the idiom of action, in the political sense,
has had a cruel passage in the twentieth century, but to replace it
by the idiom of consciousness is a desperate stratagem. Consciousness
becomes the object of life, experience merely its attendant means,
grist to the mill. In Ransom and Lawrence language is proposed
as a wonderfully delicate instrument of perception, a great means to
a greater end. The end itself may be conceived as silence: well and
good, these writers would accept that condition. In their poems and
fiction, language defines and qualifies the writer's sense of life, but
it does not preempt experience. Words intervene, but always on the
understanding that nearly everything else in life is more important
than words. Nothing in Lawrence's story is as important as men in
a coal-mine. In Ransom's poem, words are used to enable the poet
to make a juster image of life; but it is understood that "life," in that
sentence, is not necessarily or primarily an affair of words. The
words claim an instrumental role, nothing more. It seems proper.[5]

II

For better or worse, however, the high poetry of this century has
proceeded along different lines. Call them Symbolist lines; the

poetry we call modern, thinking for an example of *Prufrock and Other Observations.* The Symbolist deals with experience by treating it as a plane surface upon which selected images are placed in silent relation. Visual metaphors, visual analogies: the crucial moment is deemed to be the moment of vision, when all the images are held in focus by the poet's imagination. Indeed, it is characteristic of Symbolism that it identifies Imagination with Vision. The Symbolist poet assumes that meaning takes the form of a visual pattern. This perhaps accounts for our sluggishness in coming to terms with poets who live by a different allegiance; as Whitman's sense of life is a sense of human contact. In poetry, Whitman moves by touch, not by sight. Marshall McLuhan has argued that the invention of the printing press and the change from an oral to a typographic culture have specialized our ways of knowledge: our minds work by seeing meaning as we see black marks on a white page without hearing the sounds for which they stand. The evidence is not entirely convincing: there are difficulties, especially where the reception of manuscripts is concerned. But the general argument is hard to refute and I do not know that it has yet been refuted. In the present context it links silent reading, spatial analogies, the promotion of sight over its four sensory colleagues, the idea of a book as a solid object rather than a transcript of speech, the poem as a well-wrought urn. There is clearly a relation between this aspect of Symbolism and the force of the "closed system" as the modern figure of knowledge.

A further word on this point. The traditional poets invariably assume that the grammatical structure which we call a sentence is an excellent instrument for the representation of reality. Composing a sentence is an act of faith: you believe that the mind can deal with experience in that way by directing a flow of energy through a subject, a verb, and an object. If this seems too rigid, you qualify the report by bringing one sentence to bear upon another. The Symbolist, by and large, rejects this belief. Valéry is a case in point. He argues, in all his writings on literature, that a bourgeois demon resides in conventional grammar and syntax and must be defeated. Syntax and grammar are always on the side of the common man; they serve his common purposes. The poet must use all his sceptical intelligence to thwart this demon, twisting language into configurations from which there is no "practical" escape. Valéry also argues that the daily manners of language try to impose themselves upon the poet by insinuating the attitudes they imply: the true poet defeats the attitudes by evading the grammatical forms. There are several possibilities, given a poet sufficiently determined. He can pretend to take the attitudes seriously while using them for his surreptitious purpose. He can withhold immediate commitment from the common words by locating expressiveness in the "presence," the poetic form as such. He can exalt the uselessness of art. He can push the poem toward the equivocal condition of music, thereby defeating the aims of a common world. The ideal poetic language, in Valéry's theory, is a systematic deviation from the common forms: its intent is subversive. The poet may resort to parody, if all else fails. The result is that when we are reading a Symbolist poem in a Symbolist spirit, we are the music while the music lasts; it is wilful to read in any other way or to ask local questions.

We need an authoritative example; from Section III of *The Waste Land,* "The Fire Sermon," lines 187 to 206:

> A rat crept softly through the vegetation   187
> Dragging its slimy belly on the bank
> While I was fishing in the dull canal
> On a winter evening round behind the gashouse   190
> Musing upon the king my brother's wreck
> And on the king my father's death before him.
> White bodies naked on the low damp ground
> And bones cast in a little low dry garret,
> Rattled by the rat's foot only, year to year.
> But at my back from time to time I hear
> The sound of horns and motors, which shall bring
> Sweeney to Mrs. Porter in the spring.
> O the moon shone bright on Mrs. Porter
> And on her daughter   200
> They wash their feet in soda water
> *Et O ces voix d'enfants, chantant dans la coupole!*
>
> Twit twit twit
> Jug jug jug jug jug jug
> So rudely forc'd.
> Tereu [6]

It is obviously useless to ask, with that passage in our minds, any of the following questions: who is speaking? what is the point of his story? whose white bodies lay naked on the ground? These questions assume that there is a world-without-words to which Eliot's words pay tribute; as, in common usage, the word "box" acknowledges the existence of a certain object which does not depend upon a word for its existence. A reader determined to answer our questions might say, to the first, "Tiresias; but he somehow includes the Buddha, Ferdinand Prince of Naples, Ovid, and Verlaine": and to the second, "Well, the story is merely ostensible: the words in that order make a kind of inner landscape, Marshall McLuhan calls it psychological landscape, which is at once subject and object; it has to do with Eliot's theory of the objective correlative or Santayana's theory of the correlative object"; and to the third, "Frankly I don't know, it could be any bodies, animal or human." Questions more obviously in accord with the nature of the passage would include the following: what is going on, when "rat's foot" is preceded by the punning rhyme, "rattled"? What is going on when the speaker, whoever he is, quotes or recalls diverse fragments from Ovid, Verlaine, the Grail Legend, Australian popular song, Marvell, *The Tempest,* John Day, and Middleton? Why does the passage suddenly change in tone at that first insistent rhyme, "year" with "hear"? Why are we given "wreck" instead of "wrack" in the bit from *The Tempest?* These questions are not likely to set a reader's heart astir, but they are more relevant than the first list, because they do not call a wordless world in judgment upon Eliot's words. The second list of questions would be relevant even if—the fancy may be allowed for a moment —there were nothing in the universe but words. Indeed, this fancy is not too grotesque, in the present circumstances. Symbolist poetry yearns for a world in which the governing laws and conditions would be those of Pure Poetry; purely internal laws, marking internal re-lations between one word and another. In such a world, time would be replaced by prosody. In the passage from "The Fire Sermon" no effect is allowed to escape from the words, to leave the medium of language. The images and figures do not leave the poem; do not allow themselves to be withdrawn from the poem, even if the inno-cent reader's intention is to restore them again to their poetic home when he has tested them in the impure world. It is characteristic of these words that they refuse to leave a setting which is assertively verbal. It is not possible, for example, to attach the words to a speaker who may be conceived as, in some respect, independent of the words. Indeed, it is destructive to the nature of the words to assume that a speaker, a character replete with history and personality, has spoken them. The words are not completed by our conceiving for their speaker a personal identity. It is more useful to conceive a possible state of mind, or a state of feeling, which is secreted in these words. Hence the best way to read the lines is not to ask what each phrase means; but rather, what quality, in each sequence, the phrases share. That quality may then be found to attach itself to a state of feeling which cannot be given in any other terms.

It is customary to say that the explanation for this strange and fascinating way of using language is to be found in the works of F. H. Bradley and now in T. S. Eliot's Harvard thesis of 1916, *Knowledge and Experience in the Philosophy of F. H. Bradley.* I quote a few sentences in which Eliot summarizes Bradley's argument: kinship between Eliot's prose style and Bradley's has been noted. "It is only in immediate experience that knowledge and its object are one." "We have no right, except in the most provisional way, to speak of *my* experience, since the I is a construction out of experience, an abstraction from it; and the *thats,* the browns and hards and flats, are equally ideal constructions from experience, as ideal as atoms." "The only independent reality is immediate experience or feeling." " 'My' feeling is certainly in a sense mine. But this is because and in so far as I *am* the feeling." "Experience is nonrelational." [7] These sentences are related to Bradley's general philosophical position, but more particularly to certain passages in his *Essays on Truth and Reality,* including this one:

> Now consciousness, to my mind, is not original. What comes first in each of us is rather feeling, a state as yet without either an object or subject. . . . Feeling is immediate experience without distinction or relation in itself. It is a unity, complex but without relations. And there is here no difference between the state and its content, since, in a word, the experienced and the experience are one. [8]

In Eliot's thesis, "feeling is more than either object or subject, since in a way it includes both." Finally:

> In describing immediate experience we must use terms which offer a surreptitious suggestion of subject or object. If we say presentation, we think of a subject to which the pres-

entation is present as an object. And if we say feeling, we think
of it as the feeling of a subject about an object. . . . It may
accordingly be said that the real situation is an experience
which can never be wholly defined as an object nor wholly enjoyed as a feeling, but in which any of the observed constituents
may take on the one or the other aspect.[9]

Perhaps this is enough: what we need is something of the context
in which Eliot refers to "the continuous transition by which feeling
becomes object and object becomes feeling."

We shall make another detour before returning to "The Fire Sermon." There is a passage in *Le Degré Zéro de l'Écriture* where
Barthes discusses the distortion to which Victor Hugo tried to subject
the alexandrine; and he goes on to argue that modern poetry
"destroys the spontaneously functional nature of language, and
leaves standing only its lexical basis." "The Word shines forth above
a line of relationships emptied of their content, grammar is bereft
of its purpose, it becomes prosody and is no longer anything but an
inflexion which lasts only to present the Word." Connections, he
says, "are not properly speaking abolished, they are merely reserved
areas, a parody of themselves, and this void is necessary for the
density of the Word to rise out of a magic vacuum, like a sound
and a sign devoid of background, like 'fury and mystery'." [10] The
poet's words are not necessarily obscure: rather, they are sibylline,
oracular, incantatory, possessing everything for lucidity except
official relations. The meaning of a phrase, a line, a word, in the
passage from "The Fire Sermon" is every impression that attaches
itself to those sounds; an assertion which reminds readers of Bradley
that the famous Chapter XIV of *Essays on Truth and Reality* is
called: "What is the real Julius Caesar?" *The Waste Land*, the real
Waste Land, is the sequence of those impressions, so far as they may
be said to constitute a sequence by attending upon the sequence of
the words: the impressions are of course different for each reader.

But the eloquence of "The Fire Sermon" is not wild or uncontrolled. Clearly, the man who put those words in that order is a
craftsman: it would not be enough merely to be a pupil of F. H.
Bradley. In "Sur la Technique Littéraire" Valéry speaks of a totally
new and modern conception of the poet. "Ce n'est plus le délirant
échevelé, celui qui écrit tout un poème dans une nuit de fièvre,
c'est un froid savant, presque un algébriste, au service d'un rêveur
affiné." The figure will answer. The poet of "The Fire Sermon" is

an algebraist; a dreamer; a philosophical idealist; and much besides.
But we have still to explain why all the dreams cross in the words;
and why it is possible to say, without tautology, as Hugh Kenner
said without tautology, that Eliot is the most verbal poet in the language. Some reasons are clear enough: it cannot be easy to find words
for "an experience which can never be wholly defined as an object
nor wholly enjoyed as a feeling"; where feeling becomes object and
object becomes feeling. There is also the distinctively Symbolist problem, which Valéry treats in "Analecta, Tel Quel II": "the self flees
all created things, it withdraws from negation to negation: one might
give the name 'Universe' to everything in which the self refuses to
recognize itself." The self refuses to recognize itself in any part of
the universe until the entire universe is transformed into subjective
terms, every apprehended object becoming subject. This is orthodox
Idealism: it is also orthodox Symbolism; not two things, but rather
one feeling. But "The Fire Sermon," although understandable perhaps in these terms, goes beyond them in that direction. Thinking of
Eliot's poem, one might give the name "Saint LANGAGE" to that
alone in which the self recognizes itself. Recognition is willing or
desperate: willing if we emphasize the sheer luxury of the words,
the gypsy phrases and cadences, the impression that a man who can
pass his entire life among such words is the happiest of men:
desperate, if we emphasize the allusions, and Eliot's need of them,
fragments against his ruin. Presumably the function of the allusions
is to give the sensibility other grounds than itself, grounds in
history, literature, religion, revelation, the grounds of our beseeching;
but a sensibility is outraged if it cannot find grounds in its present
place. If every combination is possible, we practise freedom while
aching for necessity. In a chapter on Solipsism in *Knowledge and
Experience* Eliot writes:

> The point of view (or finite centre) has for its object one con-
> sistent world, and accordingly no finite centre can be self-
> sufficient, for the life of a soul does not consist in the con-
> templation of one consistent world but in the painful task of
> unifying (to a greater or less extent) jarring and incompatible
> ones, and passing, when possible, from two or more discordant
> viewpoints to a higher which shall somehow include and trans-
> mute them.[11]

In *The Waste Land* Eliot calls this higher perspective Tiresias, adumbrating a quasi-divine vision: "we are led to the conception of an all-inclusive experience outside of which nothing shall fall," he says in *Knowledge and Experience*. In his review of *Ulysses*, he distinguished between "narrative method" and "the mythical method," a distinction which requires the idea of greater and lesser perspectives to make it intelligible; by developing the mythical method, Joyce had taken an important step "toward making the modern world possible for art." (Eliot's review appeared in the *Dial* in November 1923, a year after *The Waste Land*.)

I am suggesting that much in *The Waste Land* may be explained by reference to Eliot's distinction between narrative method and the mythical method. Narrative method is based upon the commonly accepted separation of subject and object: each is itself, intact. The personal equivalent is the notion of a literary character, easily recognised, identifiable by his name. The chosen medium is words, but most of them are common and they are placed in commonly accepted arrangements. Books which are based upon these easy assumptions are called novels: so the novel as a form came to an end, according to Eliot, with Flaubert and James. The mythical method, on the other hand, is based upon immediate experience, the primacy of feeling, the conception of an all-inclusive experience outside of which nothing shall fall, the idea of subject and object as utterly transcended in a quasi-divine perspective (Tiresias in *The Waste Land*, Homeric parallels in *Ulysses*). Instead of common words in common places there is, I suggest, Language itself; conceived now as an infinitely rich storehouse of images and figures and, increasingly in Eliot, identified with the infinite Word of God.

This may sound fanciful, so I invoke Valéry again; in this passage at the end of "La Pythie":

> Honneur des Hommes, Saint LANGAGE,
> Discours prophétique et paré,
> Belles chaînes en qui s'engage
> Le dieu dans la chair égaré,
> Illumination, largesse!
> Voici parler une Sagesse
> Et sonner cette auguste Voix
> Qui se connaît quand elle sonne

N'être plus la voix de personne
Tant que des ondes et des bois! [12]

Such a Voice is mythical in Eliot's sense, since it includes and transmutes the lesser voices of waters, woods, persons, characters, and so forth. We are clearly thinking in such terms when we advert to language as magic, or when we speak of language as a racial possession, or when, reviewing *Ulysses* in 1923, we mention *The Golden Bough.* Using language in this way, it seems natural to have Ferdinand Prince of Naples, the Phoenician Sailor, the one-eyed seller of currants, and all the women in the world becoming Tiresias. For Eliot, for Bradley, there can be no question of a Wordsworthian liaison between man and Nature; no question, either, of men sharing their experiences and communicating by doing so. The only part of Bradley's *Appearance and Reality* (1893) which Eliot chose to quote in his notes to *The Waste Land* disengages itself from such a hope. In Chapter XXIII Bradley says that "we behave as if our internal worlds were the same." We err. Continuing the argument, Bradley writes:

> Our inner worlds, I may be told, are divided from each other, but the outer world of experience is common to all; and it is by standing on this basis that we are able to communicate. Such a statement would be incorrect. My external sensations are no less private to myself than are my thoughts or my feelings. In either case my experience falls within my own circle, a circle closed on the outside; and, with all its elements alike, every sphere is opaque to the others which surround it. . . . In brief, regarded as an existence which appears in a soul, the whole world for each is peculiar and private to that soul.[13]

It is like Leibniz without God.

Perhaps our first impression here is wonder that such a view of the mind's situation could ever have secreted, in Bradley's pupil, a great poem: in the idealist circumstances it hardly seems worthwhile speaking at all. But the second impression is better; that for such an extreme idealist, Language is the only place, the only possible home: either Language or that metaLanguage which we think of as Silence. The liaison of man and Nature is surreptitious, probably bogus, certainly futile; only the mind's dialogue with itself remains.

Perhaps this is to go too far in the declared way, taking the poet as literally as the philosopher. Just as Bradley cleared himself of an imputed Solipsism, so Eliot clears himself of a charge of Philosophy: he is a poet, after all. Against the persuasion of his official idealism, there are the deeper persuasions of poetry, Dante, Shakespeare, Virgil, Milton; and the final persuasion of Christian belief in which time is redeemed and the higher dream is made flesh. Perhaps these are the right qualifications to make, while returning to the poem. Without the qualifications, we are in danger of reducing the poem to a set of more or less interesting ideas; forgetting that to Eliot, as to Bradley, "a mere idea is but a ruinous abstraction"; forgetting, too, that it was Eliot who praised Henry James for possessing a mind so fine that no idea could violate it. With the passage from "The Fire Sermon" in front of us again, we see that what came first was not an idea but feeling, "a state as yet without either an object or subject." The nearest expressive equivalent, at a guess, is rhythm, especially if we think of it as defining itself, at that stage, without words at all. In "The Music of Poetry" Eliot reported that in his own experience "a poem, or a passage from a poem, may tend to realize itself first as a particular rhythm before it reaches expression in words, and that this rhythm may bring to birth the idea and the image . . ." [14] Certainly, an account of our passage would be a limited and misleading affair if it did not register, as a chief moment, the change of rhythm at line 196; and the swifter transitions, line by line, from that until the line from Verlaine. To speak of these qualities as constituting "the music of poetry," is to mean only this: that the words give an impression of serving and fulfilling a rhythmic pattern. Eliot remains true to the original feeling by remaining true to its first rhythm. The words, when they are found, maintain a double allegiance: they are required to define the rhythm of feeling, so they must be at once subjective and objective. Beyond that requirement and because of the larger organization of the entire poem, the words must also imply a superhuman consciousness soon to be called Tiresias.

The first consequence is that, to a reader hostile to idealist assumptions, many of these lines appear wilfully arch and secretive: they go through the motions of grammar and syntax without committing themselves to these agencies. They are neither one thing nor another, neither wholly subject nor wholly object: without proposing themselves as paradoxes, they are paradoxical. I assume that the reasons

for this character are now agreed. What follows is that, in verse of
Eliot's kind, incidents drawn from whatever sources cannot have the
same status which they would have in, say, a novel, or in a different
kind of poem. In the *Metamorphoses* Ovid tells the story of the
rape of Philomela by King Tereus of Thrace: Eliot recalls it in "A
Game of Chess," line 99. Trico's song in Lyly's *Alexander and
Campaspe* includes the lines:

> Oh, 'tis the ravished nightingale.
> *Jug, jug, jug, jug, tereu!* she cries.

Matthew Arnold's "Philomela" is one thing, John Crowe Ransom's
"Philomela" another: the story is diversely recited. How it appears
in the mind of God, there is no knowing: what is the real Philomela,
is a delicate question. In *The Waste Land* it is neatly relevant to
"The Fire Sermon," a homily preached by the Buddha against the
diverse fires of lust and other passions. How it appears in the superhuman mind called Tiresias is given in lines 203–206; the nightin-
gale's twit, the Elizabethan word of fornication, then a fine phrase of
justice from Middleton's *A Game at Chess,* and lastly the simple
vocative, Tereu. Ovid's story is given, indeed, but only its gist: the
story in so far as it survives transposition in the "inclusive consciousness," Tiresias. In that strange place, one image melts into another:
hence Eliot's idiom of melting, transition, becoming, deliquescence,
and so forth.

To resume a long argument: it is easy to think of Eliot as Eliot
thought of Swinburne: "only a man of genius could dwell so exclusively and consistently among words . . ." But it is better to
qualify that report by adding another, from "The Music of Poetry,"
where Eliot speaks of the poet as occupied with "frontiers of consciousness beyond which words fail, though meanings still exist."
The phrases remind us of the plays, especially of *The Cocktail Party;*
remind us, too, that in the plays the work once performed in the early
poems by "Saint Langage" is now done by human saints, from
Becket to Celia. The sibylline element is now miracle, "the way of
illumination," the mystery of holiness, martyrdom. Tiresias is the Un-
identified Guest, until he too is transcended by Celia. The effort of
the plays is to allow people, now, to live and act by a Holy Language.
Language, the ancient place of wisdom, is guaranteed by conscience
and consciousness, as in *Four Quartets.* This is why "the poetry does

not matter." Value has ceased to be, in any narrow sense, a verbal matter; except that verbal matters persist as accurate signs of conditions now themselves verbal. The procedures of *The Waste Land* are not disowned, but they are transposed into the terms of human action and suffering: transitions and perspectives now take other forms, visible in acts, relationships, chances, sufferings. Bradley is not disowned, but he is required to accommodate himself to the later Shakespeare: that is one way of putting it.

III

I have considered two "ways" of writing. In the first, words are deemed to be instrumental; in Eliot's way, words are used as if they constituted the only "certain good," everything else in the world being categorically imperfect. The description is blunt, but it will serve as a general account. The two ways are based upon rival senses of life, rival interpretations of human feeling. In reading Lawrence or Ransom, it would make a great difference if the reader were to feel, however bluntly: "the thing is incredible; I simply do not believe it." But in reading the lines from "The Fire Sermon," the reader finds that the question of believing or not simply does not arise: if it arises, he is a recalcitrant reader, wilfully going against the grain of the language.

It may be said that too much has been made of the differences. It would be possible to reduce the gap between the two ways by showing the degree to which objects in each are transposed into subjective terms, and feeling is transposed into objective terms. Neither Lawrence nor Ransom is a camera: Eliot is not a Solipsist. This is true. But it would be a false solution to imply that, at some point, the two ways meet: the differences cannot finally be resolved. Eliot writes a literature of process, Lawrence and Ransom a literature of product. Lawrence and Ransom assume that every relevant feeling may be expressed in terms of human gesture, human action: Eliot believes that such expression may be bogus, that there are states and processes of feeling which cannot be expressed in such terms; these require, for valid expression, more surreptitious forms in language and music. And so forth: the differences may be given in various idioms.

It must be conceded, of course, that a poem as authoritative as *The Waste Land* certifies whatever procedures it uses; new poems break old laws. But Eliot's early way, as a matter of artistic principle, is open to certain difficulties. It could be maintained, for instance, that words are not the best medium for expressing life as process: musical comparisons enforce the point. There is a sense in which the most remarkable achievements of Joyce, Virginia Woolf, and Eliot in this way are primitive by comparison with certain achievements of Debussy. The inescapable gap between one word and the next is a limitation: composers have the advantage there. But a more serious limitation is the arbitrariness of the Symbolist language: there is nothing in Nature by which it may be judged. No Symbolist ever recognises the court of Nature: he always demands that he be tried in a court of his peers; that is, in the court of Language. Every detail in *The Waste Land* may be glossed; subject to the qualification that the gloss is irrelevant. It then becomes a question for the reader to decide whether he wants an irrelevant gloss or not: in many cases my own answer is "yes, I do." When Eliot writes:

> A woman drew her long black hair out tight
> And fiddled whisper music on those strings. . . .

it is foolish to ascribe even a notional existence to this woman or to conclude from the use of the past tense that she might have been encountered thus engaged in London or Vienna. If we take her as a domesticated version of the maenad in Shelley's "Ode to the West Wind," or one of the mermaids in "Prufrock," or a figure in a painting by Hieronymus Bosch, this is as far as we should presume. Official glosses tell us of the Grail, the Chapel Perilous, and the Knight's monstrous visions. But we share Blackmur's sense that these matters are beside the point. Quoting these and the following lines, Blackmur waves the exegetes aside and exclaims: "For myself, I muse and merge and ache and find myself feeling with the very senses of my thought greetings and cries from all the senses there are." That is: the lines are wonderful because of what their "sensual metaphysics" does to a responsive reader. There is nothing more to be said, except that it would be just as relevant to ascribe the effect of the lines to a sensual prosody as to a sensual metaphysics; more relevant, perhaps, since it would restore the words to their source within. If a reader is struck by "the Sublime," he can only report the event, and declare that in his particular mind the sublime poem has grown to great constancy. The best in this Symbolist kind are great shadows, unverifiable but unanswerable.

NOTES

1. *English Review,* VIII (June 1911), p. 433: collected in *The Prussian Officer and Other Stories* (London, 1914).
2. *New Adelphi,* III (June–August 1930), pp. 255–63, 276–85, 286–97: collected in *Phoenix,* ed. Edward D. McDonald (New York, 1936).
3. The first version is given in *Selected Poems* (London, 1947), p. 62. The second appeared in *Kenyon Review,* XXV, no. I (Winter 1963), pp. 70–71; followed by Ransom's commentary, pp. 72–80. Poem and commentary are now collected in the enlarged *Selected Poems* (New York: Alfred A. Knopf, Inc., London: Eyre & Spottiswoode, Ltd., 1964), pp. 99–111. Reprinted by permission of the publisher.
4. "The Realistic Fallacy": *Listener,* 53 (19 May 1955), pp. 888–89; revised version in George J. Becker (ed.), *Documents of Modern Literary Realism* (Princeton, 1963), pp. 591–98.
5. This part of the essay is a revised version of my *The Ordinary Universe* (London, 1968), pp. 169–79.
6. T. S. Eliot, *Collected Poems 1909–1962* (New York: Harcourt, Brace & World, Inc., London: Faber and Faber, Ltd., 1963), pp. 70–71. Copyright 1936, by Harcourt, Brace & World, Inc., copyright © 1963, 1964, by T. S. Eliot. Reprinted by permission of the publishers.
7. T. S. Eliot, *Knowledge and Experience in the Philosophy of F. H. Bradley* (London, 1964), pp. 19, 30, 31, 27.
8. F. H. Bradley, *Essays on Truth and Reality* (Oxford, 1914), p. 194.
9. *Knowledge and Experience,* pp. 22, 25.
10. Roland Barthes, *Writing Degree Zero,* trans. Annette Lavers and Colin Smith (London, 1967), pp. 52–53.
11. *Knowledge and Experience,* pp. 147–48.
12. Valéry, *Oeuvres* (Paris: Gallimard, 1959), vol. I, p. 136. Reprinted by permission of the publisher. This passage is also quoted in Elizabeth Sewell, *Paul Valéry: the Mind in the Mirror* (Cambridge, 1952), p. 33.
13. F. H. Bradley, *Appearance and Reality* (London, 1902), p. 346.
14. T. S. Eliot, *On Poetry and Poets* (London, 1957), p. 38.